Roosevelt and Batista

Roosevelt and Batista

Good Neighbor Diplomacy in Cuba, 1933-1945

Irwin F. Gellman

UNIVERSITY OF NEW MEXICO PRESS

Albuquerque

For my wife Barbara

Acknowledgments

Those who assisted in completing this study deserve thanks which I cannot repay; I hope that by acknowledging their help to me I can, to some extent, express my profound professional and personal sense of gratitude. First, I would like to thank the staffs at the various libraries and archives where I did my research. The Library of Congress, the Columbus Memorial Library, the Franklin D. Roosevelt Library, the University of Delaware Library, the Houghton Library, and the National Archives all contributed to making this a thorough study.

A special note of thanks goes to Patricia Dowling and Kathie Nicastro who made certain that I looked at and received the necessary documents at the National Archives. Pat Dowling's knowledge and her suggestions led me to files which provided the greatest possible breadth and depth in the diplomatic records. Paul White of the Audio-Visual Division also helped in finding photographs which best illustrated some of the occurrences of the era. James George, Jr., presently at California State College at Bakersfield, directed me to important Department of Agriculture files on sugar negotiations. Without his assistance, I would never have found them.

Second, I would like to express my appreciation to Carolyn Sung and Charles Cooney of the Manuscript Divison at the Library of Congress. Chuck especially led me to various collections where I found essential material. Georgette Dorn of the Latin American, Portuguese, and Spanish Division also assisted in finding me secondary sources and in making it a pleasure to do research in her division.

While the above individuals principally assisted in gathering information, Paul Glad and Paul Conkin, then at the University of Maryland, assisted in developing my research and writing skills. Although my debt to these two men is great, without the direction of Donald W. Giffin and the kindnesses he has shown me, I am certain that I would not have completed my studies.

I would like to thank various individuals at Indiana University for assistance. Robert Quirk, David Burks, and Phyllis Petersen read the manuscript, and their suggestions helped to add greater clarity. I especially appreciate the time and effort that Martin Ridge gave me in the art of reading and writing critically. Yet if my professional debt to the above mentioned individuals is great, my debt to David M. Pletcher stands alone. His guidance, forebearance, and understanding can be seen throughout my work. If anyone can truly be labeled scholar and gentleman, these terms apply to him.

I would also like to thank the people I interviewed for their time and consideration: Willard Beaulac, Adolf Berle, Philip Bonsal, Spruille Braden, Ellis Briggs, Arturo Mañas, H. Freeman Matthews, and Herminio Portell Vilá. Many hours were spent discussing my views with the Rafael Porro Fuentes family, and Dr. Porro's insights and suggestions gave a perspective which stimulated my thinking on Cuban views.

Finishing the manuscript only begins the next problem of publishing. I would like to express my gratitude to Frank Freidel for reading my study and encouraging publication. The staff at the University of New Mexico Press ably assisted me. At Morgan State College Frances St. Clair and Janice Davis typed parts of the manuscript.

Lastly, I must thank my family and friends, especially my aunt, Lenora Seigelmann, whose kindnesses and confidence in my ability allowed me to complete my graduate training. Of all the people who had to endure the trials of researching and writing this manuscript, my wife suffered with the greatest understanding and provided encouragement. All of the above are reflected in the benefits which the reader can derive from this study. They all gave their best efforts in assisting me. However, they are not responsible for errors of fact or interpretation. If there are any, I alone am responsible for them.

Contents

Illustrations

1

Continuity and Change:

The Development of Good

Neighbor Diplomacy in Cuba

Since Fidel Castro's accession to power, there has been a veritable flood of literature concerning the changes that have taken place in Cuba. Some critics who are not busily taking part in that debate are discussing the role of the United States in the Cuban Revolution of 1959. In dealing with that controversial subject, authors have had a tremendous amount of material readily available to support their various positions, yet a void still exists. Although many have lightly scanned the causes of the revolution, the events that took place from about 1934 to 1959 still need careful scrutiny, for in that quarter century, the revolutionary forces matured.

This study covers the period from 1933 to 1945, and therefore, does not try to answer all questions about the causes of the 1959 revolutionary struggle; in fact, I have made a conscious effort not to allow current interpretations to influence my account of an earlier era. Because of the inaccessibility of Cuban diplomatic records, this book carefully explores the United States' position. I am confident that the Cubans will eventually give their own account of this crucial era.

The rise of Fulgencio Batista and the long presidency of Franklin D. Roosevelt marked the beginning of new movements in both countries, although many ongoing traditions continued during this period. By the time Batista relinquished his political control over the island in late 1944 and Roosevelt died in early 1945, the politics that they helped to shape formed the basic ingredients for relations between the two countries that endured until Castro's assumption

of power. What happened in the twelve years of Good Neighbor
diplomacy is the fascinating, largely untold story of the relations
between a superpower and an island seeking its identity. The
successes and failures of the interactions of the two nations clearly
demonstrated the extent to which seemingly unrelated events
affected both countries in their bilateral relations. If the old
bromide "damned if you do, damned if you don't" was ever valid, it
surely applies to the case of United States-Cuban relations from
1933 to 1945.

In 1933 Cuba was in the midst of a prolonged economic
depression. The people were also expressing increasing hostility to
the brutal oppression of the dictator Gerardo Machado. The
struggle to remove the tyrant intensified, but little could be done to
alleviate the economic plight of the nation. Finally in August,
Machado was forced to flee the island, and a provisional government led by the traditional politicians replaced the dictatorship.
After a brief interlude of rejoicing and of vengeance upon survivors
of the old regime, the interim government began to face mounting
criticism for its failure to act vigorously for reform. Since this
regime could not respond to all the complex problems on an island
torn by economic and political strife, it quickly met the same fate
that had befallen Machado's government.

On September 4, 1933, a group of dissatisfied sergeants revolted
against their superiors and took control of the military forces. To
assure the success of their rebellion, they looked for allies in the
civilian sector. Almost immediately after the revolt, the students
and other groups that had staunchly opposed Machado and the
provisional government offered to form a coalition with the new
military establishment, thus driving the traditional politicians from
authority. Led by Sergeant Fulgencio Batista and a well-known
physician and university professor, Ramón Grau San Martín, the
new regime claimed to have carried out more than just another
coup d'etat. Announcing that their program reflected the nationalistic aspirations of the Cuban people, the students and sergeants
initiated a new period in the island's history. For a brief span of
four months, these groups—indeed the generation of 1930 that they
represented—took authority away from the veterans of the Spanish-American War and placed it in the hands of the younger
generation. Their rule attempted to reform past inequities, and as a
result of their efforts, the Revolution of 1933 became an integral

part of the island's nationalistic heritage, although its importance is often overlooked.

Many have forgotten or neglected the changes that occurred during Grau's presidency. Some have claimed that this was a frustrated revolution or a pseudorevolution; others have argued that there never really was a revolution. The critics who made these charges could not explain the positive achievements of the Grau regime. Thus they not only ignored the concrete reforms in social and economic legislation achieved under Grau, but they also minimized the most significant development of the revolutionary struggle. A new feeling of nationalism swept across the island, and it had only begun to gain momentum. By the end of Batista's presidency in 1944, the reforms of the 1933 revolution had been institutionalized. Grau's programs, including better schools for rural inhabitants, improved working conditions for laborers, and assistance to domestic industry, were all incorporated into the island's drive toward modernization. The capstone of these efforts was the Constitution of 1940, one of the most advanced documents of its kind in Latin America. Even though critics claim correctly that not all of these reforms were completely implemented, they should not assert that the Revolution of 1933 was either frustrated or forgotten. Its fires grew and spread during Batista's first era, and from its live coals burst the flames of the Revolution of 1959.

Unfortunately for the Cuban nation, the beneficial consequences of the Revolution of 1933 did not extend to the country's political system. The rise of Batista was more than just the ascendency of a new personality in Cuban politics; the military establishment for which he spoke had taken on a new role. While Machado ruled, the civilian government directed the military's operations, but after Batista assumed command of the military, this relationship was slowly reversed. After the sergeants' revolt, Grau and Batista temporarily shared authority while the deposed politicians searched for a way to regain power. Finally the old politicians allied themselves with the new military leadership to force Grau's resignation, but in so doing, they demonstrated their inability to act independently of Batista. Batista quickly recognized the politicians' ineptness and gradually extended his authority. No one seriously questioned his absolute control until he finally finished his presidential term.

While the military dominated the government's functions, the opposition formed under Grau's leadership. Feeling himself betrayed by Batista's desertion to the ranks of the traditional politicians, Grau refused to cooperate with Batista's governments. Instead, two coalitions emerged. The politicians who defended Batista had a conservative label attached to them; those in the opposition were radical. Neither side would cooperate with the other, and as a result, a certain rigidity developed in the political system. Before Machado's exodus political cooperation was difficult but feasible; during Batista's first era it was almost impossible.

Batista used the fragmentation of the political parties to his advantage. He learned how to control his own coalition, and he also kept his opponents disorganized. But he also realized the popularity of reform movements. To assure his authority and sap the strength of the opposition, he identified with nationalistic aspirations. Many criticisms were leveled at Batista during his first reign, but there was no foundation to accusations that he was an absolute ruler and the agent of the status quo. In reality he tried to play to conservative and reformist audiences at the same time, but he received applause only from the conservative bloc.

By the closing months of World War II, Cuba had made major alterations in its internal structure. Somehow revolutionary change and military authoritarianism commingled. A measure of political stability had been restored and the economy was experiencing a spectacular boom. Despite these positive accomplishments of Batista's reign, the net effect of his rule had been to disillusion the Cuban people. Tragically, his successors to the presidency could not eradicate that bitter heritage before Batista once again assumed absolute control in 1952 with his second coup d'etat. This time, however, he followed the course that Machado had charted—even to fleeing the island by plane when his time had come. Another generation, using slogans that Batista had forgotten, forced his hasty departure.

The rise of Batista practically coincided with the New Deal in the United States. Not only was Franklin Roosevelt responsible for initiating new domestic legislation, but he also popularized the term "Good Neighbor" for the United States' hemispheric policy. By the end of his administration, he had received widespread acclaim for instituting a new type of diplomacy toward Latin America, but most of his admirers failed to understand that the evolution toward the commitments of nonintervention and noninterference had started before Roosevelt entered the White House.

There was a change in diplomacy under Roosevelt, but it was in mood only. The tactics were altered, not the strategy; the fundamental objectives of the United States in the Western Hemisphere remained constant. While the Good Neighbor Policy put a stop to use of United States troops to maintain order in the hemisphere, the United States continued to work for stability within Latin American states in order to protect American investments.

An examination of Good Neighbor diplomacy in Cuba reveals that the policy combined change with continuity. In the summer of 1933 Roosevelt dispatched Sumner Welles to prevent anarchy in Cuba, but the ambassador failed in his mission. Realizing his failure, he even called for military intervention, and when that request was rejected, he asked for and received permission to withold recognition from Grau's revolutionary government. No American troops landed on Cuban soil to assure domestic tranquility during those hectic days, but the slow and painful policy of nonrecognition increased tension and ultimately assured Grau's resignation.

Jefferson Caffery succeeded Welles as ambassador to Cuba. If Welles's activities had started controversy, Caffery's aroused even more. While Caffery reiterated the commitment to nonintervention, he allied himself with Batista to force Grau from the presidency, hoping for a coalition that the United States could recognize. As a result of the manipulations of Caffery and Batista, Grau resigned. Stability was eventually restored, but in the process, many Cubans blamed the United States for stopping the revolution before it had run its course.

Ironically, the Roosevelt administration used Cuba as a model of Good Neighbor diplomacy in spite of these events. The United States claimed truthfully that it had not landed troops on Cuban soil, and in early 1934, to strengthen its nonintervention declaration, the Roosevelt administration even abrogated the Platt Amendment, which the United States had originally forced the Cubans to write into their Constitution of 1901, legalizing American military intervention on the island for the sake of stability. The abrogation of the Platt Amendment defined what the Roosevelt administration meant by nonintervention in Cuba: the United States would not use its troops to maintain stability. After Caffery finished his tour of duty, the meaning of nonintervention was extended. The remaining ambassadorial appointees in the Good

Neighbor period were instructed to abstain from any interference in the island's local politics. The United States realized that policies of interference embittered bilateral relations more than any others, so subtler programs were substituted for them. Nonintervention and noninterference meant nothing more than this change in tactics.

While the United States interpreted nonintervention as an end to the overt use of troops and to the ambassador's active, public participation in local politics, the implications of the new policy were not extended to economic relations. In fact, as overt political intervention decreased, economic influence rose. In 1903 the two nations had negotiated a commercial treaty that lowered the tariff levied on Cuban sugar by the United States; in turn, the island granted concessions on a wide variety of American agricultural and industrial goods. Cuban governments also borrowed heavily from American financiers for public works projects, with the State Department scrutinizing all loans.

These policies remained in effect until the New Deal, but under Roosevelt, new programs replaced the outdated ones without altering the basic relationship. The reciprocal trade agreement of 1934 superseded the outdated commercial treaty, and although the new agreement helped to stimulate the depressed Cuban economy, it also bound the island closer to the domestic policies of the mainland. New Deal legislation provided quotas for tobacco and sugar, and when the United States unilaterally changed its agricultural programs, Cuba felt the effects of policies which it could neither control nor offset. Besides launching a new foreign trade program, the United States government replaced private financing as the source of loans to Cuban regimes. Thus by the end of World War II, the island looked to the United States for the survival of its agricultural exports and for aid that included diversification programs and public works projects. Overt intervention had stopped because it no longer served the best interest of the United States. Economic domination was less objectionable in the conduct of foreign relations—and just as effective, for by 1945 the United States exercised even greater control over the Cuban economy than it had before 1933.

Throughout the Good Neighbor era, the American embassy had no difficulty in constructing policies with which to carry out these subtler kinds of control. American representatives continually stated that the United States would not intervene either militarily or politically, but these assurances did not change the overwhelming power of the American ambassador to influence political decisions through economic actions. Whether through economic or political pressure, he retained his privileged position. While he and his staff contrived to separate their various economic and political programs into convenient compartments, Cuban politicians were not able to comprehend the subtle distinctions, which never were clearly defined. The embassy could not understand why the island's leadership was unable to adjust to this new relationship. Instead of trying to fathom the Cuban mentality, American policy-makers should have directed their attention to the inconsistencies of their own policies. As long as the basic objectives of the United States' strategy toward Cuba remained unaltered, why should Cuban politicians change their guiding assumptions?

These trends in the relations between Cuba and the United States, as well as the internal events in both countries, shaped policy formulation in both nations throughout the Good Neighbor period. The rise of Batista and his responses to internal pressures guaranteed political stability in Cuba, and this stability was reinforced by the American embassy's efforts to preserve internal peace for the protection of its nationals. Batista's governments also sought to continue their power by increasing sugar exports, and the United States in turn instituted the sugar quota, which assured a gradual commercial revival in Cuba. The interweaving of these economic and political programs was successful as far as it went. When changes became necessary, they were gradual and fragmentary rather than radical.

The traditional relationship, evolving over four decades, probably could not have been expected to lead to anything else, but one thing was certain. By the end of World War II, many Cubans were blaming the United States for the inadequacies of their internal structure. Castro subsequently used this latent hostility to unite his forces, but before he was even born, other nationalists had similar ideas. In many ways the Revolution of 1933 foreshadowed the Revolution of 1959. Only by exploring the earlier movement can one place the later upheaval in its proper perspective.

2

The Overthrow of Machado

In the midst of the Great Depression, American voters selected Franklin Roosevelt as their president. He had promised them economic recovery and the hope of a New Deal. The political situation in Cuba showed no signs of improvement, for Gerardo Machado y Morales governed the island as its virtual dictator. Not only did voters in the United States express concern for their own domestic difficulties, but Cubans also paid close attention to events on the mainland.

This close relationship had emerged long before the 1932 presidential election. Even before the Spanish-American War, the two nations had firm connections and after the war, their ties grew still stronger. The Reciprocity Treaty of 1903 provided a reduced tariff for Cuban sugar entering the mainland, and in return, the United States received tariff preferences on a wide variety of its exports to the island. In the Permanent Treaty of the same year, the United States guaranteed Cuba's political stability by assuming responsibility for the maintenance of the island's internal tranquility. Long aware of Cuba's strategic importance, the United States also gained the right to erect naval stations on the island.[1]

These early treaties established economic leverage for the United States. Cuba had evolved into a sugar monoculture that relied on the United States for its economic survival. Even before the depression struck the United States, Cuba felt the effects of economic insecurity. From 1924 through 1929, the average price received by Cuba for sugar exported to the United States slipped from 4.25 cents per pound to 2.41 cents per pound. By the time Hoover left office four years later, the Cuban sugar producers only received .88 cents per pound. During the same period commercial activity between the countries also declined. In that five-year period, Cuban exports to the United States decreased from

$362,265,000 to $208,754,000. When Roosevelt entered the White House, Cuban exports to the United States dropped to $57,112,000. United States exports to Cuba plunged even more drastically from $171,571,000 in 1924 to $127,051,000 in 1929. Four years later, they stood at $22,674,000. The correlation between the price that the Cubans received for sugar and their ability to purchase American goods followed a direct proportion. When Cuba could not sell her principal export on the mainland, United States exporters to the island could be assured of a business loss.[2]

When the depression destroyed the prevailing economic order in Cuba, the political order was also affected. The Cuban people quickly forgot Machado's good qualities, and political adversaries began to emerge. As more and more Cubans faced economic privation, the opposition grew bolder. Some of Machado's enemies attempted a coup d'etat in August 1931, but the army easily quelled that revolt. After its failure, some opposition leaders fled the island and added to the growing list of exile communities. Prominent Cuban politicians now led concerted forces in the United States, establishing their headquarters in Miami and New York City, determined to oust Machado.[3]

While these exiles exerted pressure from outside, other groups carried on the struggle from within. Machado's method of eliminating his antagonists involved intimidation, deportation, and finally assassination. Machado, for example, had stopped the expansion of organized labor. Since the Cuban Communist Party gained a great deal of its strength and prestige from labor unions, this group, too, felt the president's wrath. As a result, these two groups formed underground movements dedicated to their oppressor's downfall. Student and faculty sectors quickly became disenchanted with the increasingly dictatorial rule, and they also began to speak out against the dictatorship. The administration retaliated by closing schools, but this did not decrease student friction. When the students found that they could not use educational facilities to express their discontent, they formed secret organizations such as the Student Directorate, whose sole purpose was to overturn the existing government. Young professional people, a highly nationalistic segment of the population, were affected by the depressed conditions and also moved into the opposing camp. These middle-class opponents formed a secret society known as the A.B.C.; after its inception in December 1931, this group had carried out an active assassination campaign against government officials and sympathizers. As Machado's repressive measures grew more pronounced after 1931, opposition to his regime increased, with both sides becoming adept in the use of a number of terroristic tactics.[4]

While Cuba confronted its crisis, indications of a shift in the United States' attitude toward the island republic became more pronounced. Although the Hoover administration maintained its neutral stance, other segments of the American public demonstrated their disapproval of Cuba. In addition to the attacks of the exile groups in the United States and the hostile newspaper and magazine accounts of Machado's brutality, business circles in the United States demanded political stability. United States congressmen like Representative Hamilton Fish of New York and Senator William Borah of Idaho openly berated Machado for his oppressive tactics. These voices grew louder and emphatically more critical as the depression deepened.[5]

Faced with economic disaster at home, neither Roosevelt nor Hoover mentioned the Cuban predicament in their campaigns, although both had wide knowledge of hemispheric affairs. Roosevelt had traveled to several Central and South American nations in his earlier years and had learned to read Spanish. After his election he refrained from making any statement on Cuba, and in his inaugural address he mentioned his foreign policy objectives only briefly, alluding to some vague and undefined concept of the Good Neighbor Policy, but giving no inkling of how this program would be implemented.[6]

Even though the new president's motives remained hidden, newspapers in the United States expressed the hope that the Roosevelt administration would be able to resolve the island's turmoil without recourse to armed intervention. Cubans too were generally optimistic about the results of the American election. Some felt that the United States would now grant the republic economic assistance in the form of a lower sugar tariff and a new reciprocity treaty. In the political realm, the opposition hoped that the United States would offer moral encouragement but no military intervention. Machado naturally believed that Roosevelt would continue the existing relations. Although each segment of Cuban society viewed the election of the new president from the perspective of its own needs, all groups were agreed on one point: they wanted prompt action by the American government.[7]

Roosevelt directed his attention to hemispheric affairs in a speech before the governing board of the Pan-American Union on April 12, 1933. At his first Pan-American Day address, the president alluded to his inaugural speech, assuring his listeners that his Latin American policy would emphasize the idea of the Good Neighbor. Roosevelt wished to build a system of cooperation, and he also hoped to lower the high trade barriers.[8]

This did not mean that Roosevelt was unaware of Cuban problems. Although he issued no public statement on the vexing question of American intervention, he was privately seeking a solution. His primary belief was that the United States would not intervene. Instead, he provided a rather simplistic answer. He hoped to negotiate a commercial treaty with the Cuban government which, he thought, would alleviate the island's economic and political unrest. Roosevelt failed to take into consideration the hostility of the Cuban populace to the Machado dictatorship.[9]

Roosevelt had given the Good Neighbor Policy its impetus, but the Department of State would have to formulate a feasible program. The new secretary of state, Cordell Hull, had served in Congress for a quarter of a century, and had gained recognition as a staunch Democrat, an avid Wilsonian in world affairs, and a fervent believer in lowering international trade barriers. His only significant contact with Latin America had occurred during the Spanish-American War. Hull formed a volunteer regiment, which arrived in Cuba after the fighting had stopped, but he himself remained on garrison duty for five months, until May 1, 1899, helping to establish a local government, exploring some of the interior, and learning a little Spanish. Thirty-four years later Hull's attention focused once more on Cuba. Three days after Roosevelt's Pan-American Day address, the secretary held a press conference, at which he commented on the Cuban situation for the first time, stating that the United States had not given any consideration to military intervention and would handle its relationship with Cuba like any other contact between two sovereign states.[10]

Roosevelt and Hull did not have enough time to devote any more of their attention to the Cuban crisis. Hull was soon sent to the London Economic Conference, which completely occupied him from the beginning of June to the first week of August, and Roosevelt faced the frantic days of early New Deal legislation. Both could speak in generalities, but a new ambassador had to be charged with the practical supervision of Cuban relations.[11]

Hoover had appointed Harry F. Guggenheim, heir to a family copper fortune in South America, to the ambassadorial post at Havana. While prosperity prevailed, there was no need to question the wisdom of the appointment. But when Cuba began to be confronted by complete chaos, neither the ambassador nor the State Department wanted to assume any responsibility for the island's dismal situation. Under these circumstances, Guggenheim faced a thankless task. No action would be taken until the Democratic administration assumed office, and as a result, the ambassador merely reported the increasingly anarchic conditions.[12] Privately, he wrote of his anxieties and confided, "I am patiently waiting for my release from Washington. I have asked some of my friends to try to have me relieved as promptly as possible. As you can well imagine, under the present circumstances my work is difficult and I am unable to do anything really constructive."[13]

The beleaguered ambassador's hopes were soon answered. Roosevelt relieved Guggenheim of his post and announced that Assistant Secretary of State Sumner Welles would replace him. This selection was made for a variety of reasons. First, Welles was widely regarded as one of the foremost experts in the United States on Latin American affairs and expecially on the Caribbean. Besides this crucial expertise, the new ambassador had the confidence of the president. Both men had been educated at Groton and Harvard. While Welles served as chief of the Latin American Affairs Division for the Department of State in Washington, Roosevelt was completing his career as assistant secretary of the navy. They became acquainted and ultimately formed an intimate friendship. Shortly after Roosevelt assumed the presidency, he appointed Welles as the fourth assistant secretary of state, dealing with Latin American affairs. With Welles's appointment, Franklin Roosevelt demonstrated his acute concern for the island's problems and the priority that he attached to his new ambassador's mission.[14]

Sumner Welles brought a long and distinguished record of diplomatic service to his new assignment. He was born in New York City on October 14, 1892. Upon completion of his college training in 1914, he decided on a career in the diplomatic corps. At the age of twenty-two, the young college graduate entered the foreign service on July 15, 1915, as a secretary assigned to the Tokyo embassy. At the end of his two-year tour of duty, Welles requested a transfer to a Latin American post, feeling that this area of the world was crucial to the interests of the United States and hoping to specialize in the affairs of the Western Hemisphere. The Department of State approved his request and assigned him to Buenos Aires in late November 1917. He proved to be an effective officer in his new post, and after completing his tour of duty, he became assistant chief of the Division of Latin America in 1920. After only one year of service, Welles assumed the post of acting chief of the division at the age of twenty-eight. During his tenure Welles dealt mainly with problems in Cuba, Haiti, the Dominican Republic, and Central America.[15]

Welles was forced to resign from the foreign service in 1925. He had spent eight of the ten years of his career contemplating and resolving Latin American issues. During six of these years, the Caribbean area received most of his attention. After he resigned, Welles undertook a series of missions at the request of the president in Honduras, Santo Domingo, and Nicaragua. In each case, Welles had far greater mobility than an ambassador and relied heavily on this unusual freedom of action. He became the initiator of preventive policies to resolve potentially explosive situations that might lead to American intervention. He was a pragmatic diplomatic agent, making good use of his intimate knowledge of Latin American institutions and acting with the self-confidence that ultimately led to the successful completion of his mission.[16]

He had accepted the special roles assigned to him by Republican presidents, but after 1928, he frequently communicated with Franklin Roosevelt on subjects concerning the role of the United States in Latin America. By 1933 Welles had two principal goals for the Western Hemisphere. He wanted to remove the factors that contributed to anarchy and revolution, and he hoped to eliminate the specific causes of friction between the United States and Latin America. Now he had the opportunity to realize these wishes.[17]

Even before the election, Roosevelt had requested Welles to prepare his ideas on a Latin American program, and Welles responded. Turning briefly to economic relations, Welles wrote that the United States should find some way to lower the existing

tariff barriers in order to stimulate the flow of trade in the Western
Hemisphere. In the political realm, he argued, the United States
must abandon its traditional emphasis on unilateral action in favor
of a multilateral approach involving cooperation with Latin
American governments. Welles also advanced two policies for
dealing with revolutionary conditions throughout Latin America.
First, he staunchly supported nonrecognition of revolutionary
governments until national elections had been held so that the
people would have a chance to make their voices heard; second, he
advocated nonintervention by United States armed forces unless
American lives were in peril or some other dire emergency arose.
Through these policies, Welles held, the United States would be
breaking with the mistakes of previous administrations and following a course of action that would lead to greater understanding and
friendship within the hemisphere.[18]

Four days after his selection as ambassador on April 24, Welles
issued a press release telling reporters that he supported
Roosevelt's Good Neighbor Policy. He then turned to his Cuban
assignment and pledged to respect Cuban sovereignty and to
negotiate a new reciprocal trade agreement. With these pledges,
Welles declared that his primary mission was to seek an economic
solution for Cuban instability and not to interfere in domestic
politics.[19]

Welles made no public mention of the political crisis in Cuba,
but privately he wrote to Samuel G. Inman, "I fully agree, in
principle, with you that any policy tending towards intervention is
to be avoided. I fully concur in your belief that Cuban responsibilities must be undertaken by the Cuban people themselves so long
as their method of assuming them keeps within constitutional lines.
Finally, I also agree that it is impossible to undertake this work in
Cuba with any definite program cut and dried before me."[20]

Welles, the seasoned diplomat, Hull, the experienced Democratic congressman, and Roosevelt, the pragmatic politician, had
given their individual views of how the Good Neighbor Policy
should be initiated. Now they worked together to draft the
instructions that would decide the course of action in the first
application of the program. The directive that Welles carried to
Cuba represented the efforts of all three men, and it was completed
on May 1. After discussing the generally deteriorating conditions on
the island and the growing brutality of the Machado regime, the

document gave Welles the delicate assignment of correcting the situation without appearing to intervene in the island's domestic politics. He was to point out to Machado that the government's terrorism and repression must stop. If the Cuban government wished, the United States would offer its help in resolving the political impasse. Besides taking these political measures, Welles was also to negotiate a new reciprocal trade agreement. While the instructions gave a wide degree of latitude to the ambassador, they ended on a cautious note. Welles must always bear in mind that Cuba was to be treated as a sovereign nation, and he should not make any decision that would increase the likelihood of the United States invoking the Platt Amendment.[21]

Late in the afternoon of May 7, Welles ended his three-day voyage aboard the United Fruit liner *Peten*. An immigration launch came to meet him, and soon he reached the docks, where Cuban officials and people from the American embassy greeted him. The Cubans finally had their first glimpse of the tall, lean, erect ambassador, who dressed elegantly and appeared youthful. Upon his arrival, Welles told his audience that his first mission would be to renew the disrupted flow of commerce between the two nations in order to restore the prosperous conditions that had existed before the depression.[22]

Overnight the ambassador became a political celebrity. To many Cubans he embodied the prospect for peace and personified a hope that temporarily allayed their frustrations. On the day of the ambassador's arrival, Machado freed some one hundred political prisoners, and on the following day, he transferred the role of censorship from the military authorities to the ministry of the interior.[23]

While some felt relief, others were skeptical. The announcement of Welles's interest in negotiating a commercial agreement led some of the leaders of the anti-Machado factions to believe that the United States had abandoned their cause. If Machado's antagonists saw few signs of encouragement, government authorities could not rejoice either, for few Cuban officials knew Welles, and his record gave little idea of his views on the political crisis. The Cuban leadership had heard rumors of statements by Welles to his friends that he would force Machado from office, and those whispers were encouraging to the enemies of the regime. Every faction was anxious about Welles's position, for all wanted and needed his support—Machado to save his regime, the opposition to overthrow it, and the people to relieve their distress. How could Welles satisfy everyone at once?[24]

On the morning of May 11 Welles presented his credentials and called for the start of reciprocal trade negotiations to revise the treaty of 1903. Even after these began, many Cubans still speculated on the ambassador's role in solving the political dilemma. The instructions that Welles carried concerning this problem were imprecise, but before his first private interview with Machado on May 13, his plan had been carefully formulated. He told the Cuban president that the United States wanted to assist the Cuban people in resolving the political crisis, emphasizing that no economic improvement could be achieved without political tranquillity. He then outlined a plan that called for national elections in the autumn of 1934, even though Machado's term did not expire until May 20, 1935. Welles also wanted the Cuban government to restore constitutional guarantees and end acts of repression by its agents. When political conditions were stabilized, he thought, the regime should also abolish censorship and end the state of martial law.[25]

Machado replied that he was then attempting to restore normal constitutional rule, and he welcomed American assistance in establishing a political truce in preparation for elections. Not only did Machado appreciate the ambassador's suggestions, but he emphatically declared that he would not be a candidate for reelection under any circumstances. If necessary he would resign at an appropriate moment before the voting so that his administration would not be accused of controlling the electoral machinery.[26]

Even though the situation was tense, Welles did not anticipate any necessity for Machado's resignation. The Cuban president still held the loyalty of the armed forces. If he left power prematurely, chaos would result, since the opposition had no constructive program beyond the dictator's removal. Without an orderly government to control the population, Welles predicted, the possibility of United States intervention would increase immeasurably.[27]

Another crucial ingredient for a satisfactory completion of Welles's mission was the reciprocal trade agreement. Its negotiation would divert attention from political agitation to constructive bargaining. Welles predicted that these economic negotiations would raise the spirits of the Cubans by offering the hope of increased prosperity. Not only would the public support negotiations, but the administration would also be forced to cooperate, for its very survival depended on the friendship of the United States. The ambassador continually stressed that his government could not make any definite proposals under the existing political situation, making clear to the Cuban officials that these discussions were purely exploratory. In the final analysis, Welles's program entailed the use of economic bargaining as a lever to initiate the desired constitutional and electoral reform for the national elections.[28]

Five days after his talk with Machado, Welles gave Roosevelt his assessment of the island's problems, admitting that the situation was "both more precarious and more difficult than I had anticipated."[29] According to Welles, during his first administration Machado had probably given the island the best government it had ever had, but the depression had instilled in the people a detestation of Machado without precedent in the island's history. The envoy explained his program and its goals, assuring Roosevelt that mediation was the only conceivable answer. Welles stressed that Cuba had become the experimental laboratory for the Good Neighbor Policy; therefore, Roosevelt could not afford to intervene in Cuban affairs either militarily or through overt diplomatic action. Such manuevers would jeopardize the entire policy because Latin Americans would lose confidence in the administration's hemispheric objectives.[30]

Welles then entered into talks with the opposition forces in Cuba to gain their cooperation for his mediation. Shortly after these probings started, reports began circulating that the opposition would call a halt to its terroristic activity. These rumors had concrete foundation, for Welles had begun speaking with Dr. Cosme de la Torriente, a former ambassador to the United States and president of the assembly of the League of Nations who held a position in the *Unión Nacionalista*, the political party that opposed the dictator. During a discussion on May 25, Welles stood firm against any program outside the constitutional framework, asserting that the Cuban Congress would have to pass any new electoral legislation. Cosme de la Torriente agreed. Since he objected to both revolution and American intervention, the only possible

alternative was mediation. At the conclusion of their talk, the
Cuban opposition leader promised that he would contact other
factions to obtain their cooperation in reaching a solution.[31]

While the opposition sectors discussed the idea of mediation, the
Cuban government quickly responded to Welles's proposal in an
interview which Machado granted on May 27 to *Diario de la
Marina,* a conservative newspaper representing the views of the
Spanish community. He declared that his government favored
political conciliation and that he saw no reason why the various
factions could not meet and reach some accord. In addition to this
public pronouncement, Secretary of State Orestes Ferrara assured
Welles that Machado desired his mediation.[32]

Both sides had now demonstrated their willingness to come to
the conference table, but Welles thought that a settlement might
be generally delayed by the political instability. Even though
Machado was cooperating by gradually relaxing police control and
censorship regulations and the chief opposition forces were halting
their terroristic campaign, Welles realized that the opposition was
only an amorphous conglomeration of various factions. How could
the participating groups stop dissidents from renewing the violence? The ambassador also saw indications of further disagreement
with the opposition. With the talk of future national elections, the
various groups had begun to jockey for positions in the upcoming
campaign by making extravagant claims about stopping any form
of American diplomatic intervention.[33]

At the beginning of June the antagonistic groups were still
demanding Machado's immediate resignation and the appointment
of an impartial secretary of state to conduct elections. The
ambassador rejected such a move because it would create a
vacuum that the opposition could not fill. Political parties simply
would not have adequate time to organize, and any election under
such circumstances would be farcical.[34]

To placate the opposition and work within the existing order, on
June 2 Welles proposed to Machado his plan for a settlement,
urging immediate reform of the electoral code so that the various
factions could form political parties. Under such a proposal, the
Cuban people would be assured the opportunity of choosing an
acceptable executive. Welles thought that a preliminary step for
national elections would be the restoration of the office of
vice-president and the selection of a man to fill it who would have

the support of all groups and would supervise the elections. Welles also favored shortening the terms of the future president and the incumbent congressmen. The ambassador told Machado that all these steps could be implemented within six months under present conditions, and Machado assured him that he would cooperate in carrying out these proposals.[35]

Welles had justified his proposals to the Cubans, but he also felt that the State Department should understand his rationale. He reported that under his plan the United States could not be accused of intervention. Not only would Cuba be saved from the precedent of a provisional or unconstitutional regime, but the actions that he proposed would also lead to enduring reforms in the Cuban electoral code and constitution. To proceed satisfactorily, Welles stressed, stability was essential, and Machado and he agreed that the president would insist upon the completion of his term until a definite agreement had been reached. Even this accord left a certain degree of ambiguity that still had to be resolved. Machado told American newspapermen on June 3 that he had every intention of completing his term. Welles saw him three days after this statement and urged him to refrain from making such provocative public statements, arguing that these declarations only increased agitation and stimulated the opposition.[36]

While Welles moved through the political maze in Cuba, Undersecretary of State William Phillips directed the department's policies. The undersecretary had a long and distinguished record in the department and was also a personal friend of Roosevelt. During Hull's absence at the London Economic Conference, Phillips became involved in Cuba's growing conflict. His principal function was to deal with the Cuban ambassador to the United States, Oscar B. Cintas, and to impress upon him that Welles had the full support of the administration. As early as June 7, Welles had reported that Havana newspapers were carrying stories that he would shortly be recalled because Roosevelt no longer supported his efforts. Phillips phoned Cintas and told him that such accounts were unfounded; later in the day, he issued a press release to that effect. This declaration was only the first of a long series of department press releases assuring the public that the president and the department had complete confidence in their representative. Machado constantly attempted to bypass Welles's authority by trying to go directly to the White House, and although such efforts failed,

Phillips had the job of squelching the rumors that Welles did not have Roosevelt's support and listening to Cintas's harangues about the American ambassador's anti-Machado activities.[37]

While the Machado administration was testing Welles's strength in Washington, Machado moved closer to mediation talks, announcing to the press on June 7 that he favored constitutional reforms and proposing the appointment of a vice-president who could not be a presidential candidate in the 1934 elections. While the vice-president was being selected, political parties would be reorganized, and general elections would be held on November 1, 1934. Machado, furthermore, announced that Howard Lee McBain, dean of the graduate faculties at Columbia University, would aid in electoral reform. Three days after the president's declaration, Cosme de la Torriente accepted the mediation. Although he abhorred Machado's rule, he argued even more strenuously against any possible use of the Platt Amendment, stating that although the United States had not yet invoked it, intervention might become a reality if the situation deteriorated.[38]

Once Cosme de la Torriente accepted mediation, the tempo quickened. More and more opposition leaders began to speak favorably of talks, and on June 16 the highly influential A.B.C. announced its participation. Some violence still continued, but the mediation appeared to be working.[39] Hubert Herring, a well-known Latin Americanist, assessed the situation after the A.B.C. made its decision to join the discussions. He hoped for a political solution, but also added a separate note on the ambassador's role, giving some indication of Welles's predicament. "Mr. Welles will be generously damned, no matter what he does or does not do: I submit, however, that the damning should be withheld and that he should be given a fair chance."[40]

Because of the cooperation shown by Machado and the opposition, Phillips reported to Roosevelt on June 20 that Welles was ready to start the actual proceedings. Not only were the political forces anxious to discuss the situation, but the ambassador also felt that the Cuban people were desirous of a settlement. Welles's instructions, vague at the outset of his mission, had now taken definite form. Through his mediation efforts, he would work for political reorganization ultimately ending in a new Cuban government. With this political settlement, stability would return.[41]

In such a climate, the ambassador could proceed toward his next objective—economic revival. As early as June 2 Welles reported to Assistant Secretary of State Jefferson Caffery that his entire effort in Cuba was "predicated upon his having authority to undertake negotiations for a new reciprocity treaty at a very early date."[42] Welles had the impression that Roosevelt would ask Congress for authority to negotiate executive reciprocal trade agreements. When the ambassador learned that this legislation would not be presented, he expressed disappointment. Welles felt that he had to proceed with the negotiations in order to ensure beneficial economic and political efforts in Cuba and to aid American exporters. Phillips replied to Welles's request on June 8, giving him permission to continue bargaining on a treaty that would be submitted to the Senate for ratification in the next session.[43]

Besides negotiating the commercial treaty, Welles hoped to aid the Cuban economy by revising the island's foreign debt payments. Like most other Latin American nations, Cuba was having difficulty balancing its budget. While the government tried to meet its own payroll, American bankers applied pressure for payment on their loans. Welles hoped that some agreement between the Cubans and the American bankers could be negotiated to satisfy both parties, and he began his efforts to find a solution. The program had been completed: economic stabilization would complement political peace.[44]

With the completion of the preliminary negotiations, Welles attempted to clarify his position in the conflict, assuring the Cubans that he was not intervening in their domestic affairs but only offering to mediate in order to avoid such an action. He also told the Cubans that this mediation effort involved no contractual obligation on the part of the United States or Cuba, but, Welles informed the State Department, the Cubans did not understand the distinction.[45]

Even though the ambassador's position was vague, he had managed to convince the Cubans to discuss their grievances. On June 22 Machado extended an invitation to the political exiles to return to Cuba with full protection guaranteed by his government, and on the same day he confided to Welles that his government was ready to come to the conference table. Welles's persuasiveness had its effect. The Machado-controlled daily, *Heraldo de Cuba*, reviewed Welles's action and editorialized that he was not intervening but acting as a friend of the Cuban people. On June 24 Roosevelt also lauded the ambassador, saying that he was greatly pleased with Welles's conduct.[46] Even the hostile *New Republic* wrote in late June that for "the first time in years there is a ray of hope in regard for Cuba."[47]

From their various points of view, the Cubans who joined the bargaining felt that they had something to gain. Machado probably gave his assent because he could not afford a direct confrontation with Welles. The Cuban president also seemed to believe that no matter what happened, the United States would not alter its policy of supporting the constitutional regime. Lastly, the dictator hoped to gain needed time to see if he could resolve his country's financial and political crisis. The opposition also had its reasons for engaging in the talks. They had nothing to lose as long as Machado controlled the governmental apparatus and had the loyalty of the armed forces. Certainly, Welles's prestige and support would enhance their bargaining position. In the final outcome, they would be able to claim credit for the political compromise which would never have been achieved without their consent.[48]

Although the Cubans were the negotiators, Welles held the key to the talks. He had been the dominant influence in persuading the Cubans to accept mediation, working on the premise that the only way to avoid American intervention was to have Machado and the opposition reach an agreement. For two months Welles had advocated that the Cubans solve their own internal problems, and in his opinion most of the factions felt that mediation was the best method for reaching a settlement. When the mediation began, the two opposing forces met to resolve the island's political struggle, but the proposal had been formulated and initiated in the American embassy.[49]

Powerful forces were working for political compromise, but how many people did this effort represent? The government officials, the old politicians, the A.B.C., and other segments of society, lent their support. What of those sectors who rejected the mediation formula? How much of the populace did they represent? How strong was the movement against mediation before it had even begun?

These questions cannot be answered with exact numbers, but the antagonists to the proposed talks were many and vocal. When

Machado initiated a campaign against labor and the Communist Party early in his administration, these groups retaliated by forming the initial opposition to his regime. By 1931 an undeclared war also raged between the students and the government. Another group that participated in the assault against Machado was the exile community. Some exiles who had originally supported the dictator were now disenchanted with his rule. General Mario García Menocal, former president of the republic, led such a group from Miami, insisting on revolution as the only solution. Welles saw Menocal as a particular threat and repeatedly requested that American authorities in Miami carefully watch his group's activities so that they could not interfere. Lastly, even within the groups that decided to participate, some members refused to abide by the leadership's decision. Their refusal to join the discussions further weakened the mediation. These factions would not rest until they had driven the tyrant from power, and they saw mediation only as a form of appeasement.[50]

The intransigence of the militant opposition did not stop the bargaining. Cuban negotiators met on July 1, and on this auspicious occasion, Welles read a message from Roosevelt congratulating the Cubans for initiating discussions that would lead toward a peaceful solution to the island's conflict.[51] Roosevelt echoed the ambassador's sentiments when he emphasized "that the restoration of political peace is a necessary and essential preliminary step on the way to Cuba's economic recovery."[52] After conveying Roosevelt's message, Welles read one of his own, stressing that he was offering his services as an impartial party operating in a private capacity. Whenever he thought that his services were no longer desired, he would end his involvement. Once these opening remarks had been recorded, Welles met separately with each group, and negotiations began in earnest.[53]

The United States had demonstrated its desire to aid the Cubans in their hour of crisis, and the Cuban press responded favorably. *Diario de la Marina* set the tone on July 3, declaring that Roosevelt and Welles had shown the Cuban public and all of Latin America that the United States was implementing the idea of the Good Neighbor. The paper now called for a concerted effort by the negotiators, because the "United States had placed in our hands a thread of the initial fate of a new policy, of an American 'New

Deal' which affects, in a more or less direct way, all the Powers of the earth."[54] The question that remained unanswered was how the Cubans would respond to this challenge.

During the month of July, Welles saw indications that the negotiations would reach a successful conclusion. The government granted personal guarantees of safety to the opposition leaders and freed even more political prisoners, announcing that these people would not be molested by the authorities. The ambassador also reported that martial law would soon be removed and constitutional guarantees would shortly be reestablished in Havana. Along with these positive signs, Welles thought that the general political atmosphere was improving, for he observed a significant decrease in terroristic activity. According to him the only actively antagonistic sectors were the Menocalistas, the students, and the Communists. Welles assured the State Department that his political and economic objectives were about to be realized: Machado would resign his post in favor of a compromise candidate by May 1934, and the negotiations on the reciprocal trade agreement would be completed by the end of the month. The ambassador wrote on July 21 that the bargaining had reached the stage for presenting definite proposals. Earlier in the month he had even set late September as the target date for his mission's termination, so that he could return to Washington to prepare for the Montevideo Conference.[55]

Although the general conditions appeared to be satisfactory, Welles indicated some obstacles. He noted that the political factions had divided into warring camps, each advocating its own political solution. The ambassador also reported that conditions warranted the immediate restoration of constitutional guarantees in Havana and he pressed Machado for such a decree.[56]

Toward the end of July, the Cuban government showed increasing hostility toward Welles and his mediation. On July 25 Cintas relayed to the State Department Machado's growing disdain for Welles's conduct. He complained to Phillips that Welles had threatened some government officials with armed intervention unless Machado restored constitutional guarantees. The Cuban ambassador added that rumors were circulating in Havana that Welles was even trying to remove Machado from the presidency. Cintas adamantly condemned the ambassador's behavior and stated that his efforts were "doomed to complete failure."[57]

While Cintas was trying to put pressure on the American

government, Machado took action by restoring constitutional guarantees and passing a general amnesty. This act pardoned the opposition, the police, and the *porra*, Machado's secret police, for crimes committed since 1927. Although the law appeared to be a conciliatory gesture, the opposition reacted violently against what they considered a reprieve for the perpetrators of the government's brutality. The tension increased even more when Machado made unexpected appearances before the Cuban Senate and Chamber of Representatives on July 26, declaring that Welles was acting solely in an individual capacity as a friend of the Cuban people and not as an agent of the United States government. Machado called for congressional support in order to complete his term and issued a plea for Cuban nationalism to counteract United States intervention.[58]

Machado was trying desperately to preserve his power, but Welles had anticipated the possibility of hostility on the part of the dictator. He had already reported that he feared the constant changes in Machado's temperament, noting the president's instability. Welles refused to allow the dictator's conduct to interfere with the progress of the mediation, and on July 27, the ambassador greeted the mixed commission that had been selected to draft new electoral laws. For the first time in two years, opposition and government members met in one body to discuss ways of ending hostilities, and Welles used this opportunity to reply to Machado's speech, asserting that while he was happy to be regarded as a friend of the Cuban people, his first duty was as representative of the United States and its president. With this statement, Welles emphasized not only that he was working as the agent of his government, but also that he had Roosevelt's confidence. He had now removed any doubt that he was acting as an impartial observer, and he used the occasion to the fullest advantage. He urged the commission to find a prompt solution, warning the negotiators that until their deliberations were completed, the island could not expect any economic improvement.[59]

While the delegates were searching for an acceptable answer, Howard McBain was submitting his recommendations on electoral reform to Welles. The ambassador thought that they were excellent suggestions and began efforts to have them enacted into law. Although Welles held optimistic hopes for McBain's reforms and for the efforts of the mixed commission, their work ended in futility. Machado was not destined to leave the presidency as the result of the mediation.[60]

Welles devoted his energies to the growing political complications, and he paid little attention to local events in Havana. José Izquierdo, the mayor of Havana, demanded on July 25 that every omnibus driver buy gasoline from the Sinclair Oil Company's garages, where he collected a tax. Several of the bus drivers' unions decided to strike against these grafting exactions, and by the first of August, clashes between workers and soldiers had been reported. The following day a wave of sympathy strikes encompassing the entire transportation industry spread across the island. In less than a week, an apparently spontaneous movement with no organized leadership had paralyzed the island's movements. The reaction of the people and the government was just as startling; the public did not riot, and the government made no attempt to force the laborers back to work. Everything simply came to a halt.[61]

The strike had started with limited economic goals and little if any leadership, but it became "a powerful political offensive directed against the dictatorship."[62] On August 5 Machado threatened that he would declare martial law and a state of war, but this announcement had no noticeable effect on the strikers.[63] Ruby Hart Phillips, wife of the *New York Times* correspondent in Cuba, commented on August 6, "This strike is a marvelous thing—an entire nation folds its arms and quits work, passively sitting still. I don't know exactly what they can accomplish and apparently the people are more or less vague. They either intend to starve themselves to death or force the United States to take pity on them and step in. Anyway, from the laborer in the street to the wealthy, or once wealthy, business men they are determined to see this through, no matter what happens."[64]

Welles did not mention the labor dispute until August 3 because he was concentrating on the mediation efforts. Even then, he felt that the talks were proceeding satisfactorily and added that he and the opposition leaders were trying to end any danger of a general strike. When Welles learned that Machado had acted to have his Liberal Party members withdraw from the mediation until the strike was settled, he hurried to see Machado the next day to press for continuation of the mediation. The ambassador was against any delaying tactics, especially since the commission had almost solved all the problems of reforms, and McBain's recommendations would shortly be introduced to the Cuban Congress for consideration. By August 5 Welles realized that the strike might have a devastating effect on his work, and he tried to prod the commission members to move with greater haste.[65]

The race between the mediation and the strike increased speculation on the possibility of Machado's resignation. Reports were circulating on Sunday, August 6, that the president would shortly leave office. The strike had stopped everything, and a strange quiet gripped the capital. Welles reported on this condition, but he knew that the calm would not last, so he presented Machado with a plan recommending the appointment of an impartial secretary of state to take temporary command of the government. The president would ask Congress for a leave of absence, and Congress would then pass the reform legislation recommended by the mixed commission, shortening the congressional terms. After these steps had been completed, a vice-president would be selected to govern until national elections could be held.[66]

Welles hoped that Machado would resign to prevent further bloodshed and chaos. The ambassador also reminded Machado that the United States could invoke the Platt Amendment under these tense conditions, although it did not want to take such drastic action. The president replied that he would resign only after a vice-president had been inaugurated, for he feared that his departure would cause a greater catastrophe than his continued presence. Welles disagreed, but he was unable to shake the dictator's determination. Since this approach had failed, the emissary decided on a new strategy. He would try to erode Machado's influence with the political parties in the Congress.[67]

Before Welles had an opportunity to try his new tactic, an unexpected event occurred that changed the entire political complexion of the nation. The day after Welles's fruitless discussion with the president on August 7, an unidentified radio station purposely broadcast the story that Machado had resigned and that the people should rejoice. Multitudes flooded into the streets and began to celebrate, but the exultation ended abruptly when government troops opened fire on the joyous mob. By evening about twenty people had died, and over one hundred were injured. Violence replaced quiet, troops patrolled the city, and the intensity of the struggle increased. At the end of the day's tragic events,

Congress went into special session and suspended constitutional guarantees.[68]

When Roosevelt learned of the events, he still maintained that conditions did not warrant armed intervention, telling reporters that as long as Cuba had a semblance of stability and American lives were not in danger, the United States would not invoke the Platt Amendment. The morning after the riot, Welles conferred with Machado, informing him that Roosevelt had approved his plan for Machado's resignation, but the dictator refused to consider such a proposal. Welles was in a quandary, for as long as Machado continued to rule, he saw no hope of successful mediation. The United States had one remaining alternative short of intervention—it could withdraw its recognition if Machado did not agree to resign in a reasonable period. Welles thought that some disorder would result, but the United States could take precautionary measures by sending two warships to Havana harbor.[69]

Machado realized that he could not depend on the American ambassador for support, and he began to rely on his instinct of self-preservation. He called Cintas on August 8, telling him to inform Phillips that as ruler of Cuba, Machado would not accept any ultimatum for his resignation and claiming that he would shortly restore tranquillity. To carry out this pledge, on August 9 the dictator declared a state of war. He also had a resolution introduced before the Chamber of Representatives condemning Welles for violating Cuban sovereignty by threatening intervention.[70]

When Welles heard of the presidential message, he parried by asking Hull to inform the Cuban ambassador that he was acting with full "approval and authorization."[71] He reviewed the current situation, stressing that the Cuban officials had come to believe that the United States would not interfere under any circumstances. While Welles did not desire United States intervention, he did want the Cubans to fear the threat of such an action.[72]

The struggle between Welles and Machado reached its peak in the United States when Roosevelt granted an interview with Ambassador Cintas on the afternoon of August 9 at his residence at Hyde Park. Cintas hoped that Roosevelt would support Machado's regime, but this was not the reason for the invitation. Roosevelt reminded the ambassador that the world was watching the Cuban turmoil and emphasized that Welles had his full confidence. The only feasible solution to the crisis, he said, was for Machado to leave office. Cintas replied that Machado could not resign because his honor was at stake. Roosevelt, in turn, suggested that Machado did not have to resign just because of the political conflict; since the Cuban people were starving, he could attribute his action to the economic crisis. Roosevelt felt that Machado's resignation would thus seem a noble gesture.[73] At the conclusion of their talk, the two issued a joint statement announcing that "the problems of starvation and of depression are of such immediate importance that every political problem should be met in the most patriotic spirit in order to improve conditions at the earliest possible moment."[74]

Roosevelt's simplistic solution, giving Machado an alternative reason for leaving office, had little appreciable effect on existing conditions. With its empty streets, idle workers, and scarcity of foodstuffs, Havana appeared to be in the grip of an epidemic. Ruby Hart Phillips wrote that the "atmosphere is tense, no longer cheerful. Peoples' faces are getting grim and drawn. It is now merely a question of who can hold out the longest without their nerve breaking."[75] Even though the military still controlled Havana, the strike continued unabated. Machado fought to hold his power by appealing to the nationalistic spirit that had originally swept him into office: he declared that he was trying to save Cuba from American intervention.[76]

Besides appealing to patriotism, the president, with the aid of Ferrara, had the Liberal Party reject Welles's mediation. Machado put pressure on the other parties to do the same, but the politicians wavered, not knowing where to place their trust. Ferrara tried to convince Welles that Machado should remain in power until conditions improved, but Welles, buoyed by Roosevelt's statement of support, replied that Machado would have to leave.

While Ferrara sparred with Welles in Havana, Cintas maneuvered in Washington, asking Hull to recall the ambassador for consultation, in order to allow Machado time to restore order. This request was quickly dismissed; Roosevelt told Cintas that Welles would remain at his station. Even though Hull would not withdraw Welles, he did want Welles to clarify his position, to assure both the American and the Cuban public that the United States was not coercing anyone on the island. There was no such thing, according to Hull, as the "Welles plan"—only the Cuban plan.[77]

During this critical period of stalemate, a public consensus appeared to be forming in the United States. Roosevelt had not announced any action that could be interpreted as a movement toward armed intervention. Other officials in Washington showed deep concern over the island's plight, but they favored the president's course. An argument against involvement came from the United States ambassador to Mexico, Josephus Daniels. He reported that in the Mexicans' opinion all of Latin America opposed unilateral armed intervention, and he suggested that the United States should consult the ABC powers (Argentina, Brazil, and Chile) and Mexico in order to arrive at some solution. Daniels also reminded Hull that the United States had to be especially careful of Latin American sensitivities because of the upcoming conference at Montevideo. The United States news media also argued against the enforcement of the Platt Amendment.[78] The *Baltimore Sun* probably summed up the feeling best when it stated that this "absence of jingoism is as it should be."[79] It held that the United States should continue its watchful waiting.

On the evening of August 10 Welles conferred with various political leaders in order to gain their approval for his scheme of having Machado ask for a leave of absence. Welles had already spoken with General Alberto Herrera, who had consented to form a cabinet composed of all political factions. The general had been chief of staff of the Cuban army under Machado, and shortly after Welles's arrival, Machado had appointed him secretary of the army and navy. He was later selected as a member of the government's mediation team, where Welles grew to trust him and decided that he would be capable of heading the government until a vice-president was elected in 1934.[80]

Welles confided to the State Department that in his opinion Machado would accept this plan for several reasons. First, Machado would save face by appointing a member of his own cabinet; also his safety would be assured, and the Liberal Party would not have to fear reprisals by a hostile regime. The army would support its commander, and the opposition had approved the plan. Lastly, Welles assured the department, the United States could not be charged with intervention. The Cubans would make their own decisions.[81] Welles declared that the plan was "essentially a Cuban solution of the Cuban problem."[82]

Before Welles had a chance to confront Machado, the army

decided to take independent action. On the afternoon of August 11 a group of officers demanded the president's removal. When Machado learned of the revolt, he hurried to the army headquarters at Camp Columbia, where he found that the officers were adamant in their ultimatum that he resign within twenty-four hours. Later in the day Ferrara informed Welles that Machado was preparing to resign and place Herrera in command. By late evening rumors were already circulating that the dictator was going to resign.[83]

Why did the army revolt? Although Welles has been accused of fomenting the rebellion with threats of intervention, the evidence does not bear out such allegations. Welles consistently worked within the political process and seemed to deal with Herrera solely because he was a member of the government's delegation. Until the officers' revolt, Welles's program did not involve the military. The best and most logical answer lies in the rationale that the military men gave for the revolt. They wanted to protect the island from possible intervention, because they feared that any such move would place their careers in jeopardy. The armed forces could be disbanded or reorganized if American troops landed. With such alternatives facing them, they decided to act in their own interest.[84]

Early in the morning of Saturday, August 12, a radio broadcast announced that Machado had resigned. At first, the people were skeptical, but once confirmation came, the city began to rejoice. By midmorning, the people were celebrating throughout the capital, and at 10:00 A.M., the guns of Cabañas Fortress boomed to let people know that Machado had been deposed. Late in the afternoon, Machado rushed from his country estate to the airport, leaving Cuba forever. The more fortunate followers of the dictator fled the island by plane or ship. Those who remained would soon feel the vengeance of the Cuban people.[85]

Once Machado departed, his cabinet resigned, except for Herrera. According to a constitutional amendment of 1928, he automatically became provisional president. Although the military men and the political opposition had originally supported him, now they suddenly decided that the general was too closely associated with the previous administration. A new man would have to be selected. Herrera remained in office only long enough to appoint Dr. Carlos Manuel de Céspedes secretary of state; then he resigned, following the rest of Machado's retinue into exile. Less than twenty-four hours after the dictator left the island, Céspedes became president ad interim. Since he succeeded to the presidency through Cuba's constitutional process, the United States automatically extended recognition to him.[86]

During this three-month episode, Welles had developed three themes in his conception of the Good Neighbor Policy as it applied to Cuban relations. First, he steadfastly held that the Platt Amendment should not be invoked, even though he did advocate the threat of intervention and even the policy of nonrecognition when Machado refused to capitulate. Second, the ambassador continually stressed that any replacement for Machado had to be chosen in a constitutionally prescribed manner. Last, Welles recognized that any political settlement would also have to entail economic aid to ensure stability. While Cubans celebrated Machado's departure, Welles could also rejoice because he had achieved his first two goals. He now had to plan for the implementation of his program for economic improvement.

The struggle between the dictator and the ambassador had ended. Welles had arrived in Havana to stabilize the unsettled conditions by an economic agreement, but he quickly perceived the priority of a political settlement. From the middle of May to the first week of August, Welles used all the tools of his profession to solve the crisis by mediation. When mediation seemed to be working, Machado balked, refused to relinquish his power, and fought for survival with all his cunning. The dictator pleaded for national unity, condemned the ambassador, requested Roosevelt's aid, and declared a state of war. While Machado tried to retain his power, Welles summoned all his diplomatic skills to replace the president. He stopped calling himself an impartial mediator and used his official role as ambassador to apply pressure. Even in the period of greatest uncertainty, Welles looked to the politicians for Cuba's salvation and never attempted to erode the tyrant's strength in the armed forces. Before Welles had a chance to mobilize the politicians against their leader, the military acted and the dictator fell.

Although Welles was congratulated by American and Cuban commentators for aiding in the removal of Machado without involving American troops, he could not claim credit for his mediation efforts. The direct cause of the victory was in the action of the military. Ironically, one of the dictator's staunchest allies was responsible for his demise. The military had succeeded where the politicians had faltered. While the Cubans celebrated their new freedom, few took time to examine the momentous implications of the armed forces' decision. But this was not the time for reflection and contemplation, for the old regime had fallen. August 12, 1933 was a time for rejoicing; the time would come for remembering and hunting those that had inflicted misery.[87]

3

The Failure of Constitutional Government

Cuba's national vendetta began with a manhunt for Machado's supporters. The rejoicing at the dictator's departure had subsided, and the memories of governmental atrocities returned vividly, sparking an irresistible impulse for vengeance. In the early evening of August 12, a sudden torrential downpour interrupted the searching of an excited mob, but by the following day, at least fifty *porristas,* members of Machado's secret police, had been captured, wounded, or killed.[1] Ruby Hart Phillips recorded the "terrible things which happened that day! Civilization stripped away in one stroke, leaving savages thirsting for blood."[2] The sacking of homes and the ricocheting of rifle bullets could be seen and heard throughout the capital. When the dictator's last Havana chief of police, A. B. Ainciart, was cornered on August 20, he committed suicide rather than surrender. Later in the day, thousands cheered while some of the crowd hoisted his mutilated corpse to a crossarm of an electric light pole. When the rope snapped, the body fell to the ground, where someone saturated it with gasoline and applied a match. As the flames rose, the mob shouted its approval.[3]

While the Cubans sought vengeance, the United States watched and commented. At first, the American press described the murders as justified responses to Machado's brutality and expressed the hope that Cuba would shortly return to order. Toward the end of the month, however, the papers began to plead for an end to the bloodshed and for the process of rebuilding to begin, for Cuba needed stability more than retribution.[4] Machado had gone, but, the *Miami Herald* incisively commented, "Revolution, like war, does not end in victory."[5]

After Hull and Roosevelt conferred about the chaos that had

resulted from Machado's departure, the president released to the press on August 13 a statement ordering naval vessels to the island. He emphasized that he had no intention of intervening in Cuban affairs and that he took this action only as a precautionary measure to protect American lives that might be placed in jeopardy by the internal disorder. Roosevelt was perfectly satisfied with the constitutionality of the new regime, and he declared that as soon as the Cuban government restored normal conditions, the ships would be withdrawn.[6]

In the early morning of August 14, two destroyers entered Havana harbor. Welles assured the commanding officer that there was no need to land troops, for the Cuban army was quickly reestablishing order. Even though Welles saw no necessity for any display of force, he thought that the mere presence of the ships had a quieting effect on the unsettled conditions. After the ships had spent one day in the harbor, Hull phoned to ascertain whether any Cubans had construed this action as intervention. Welles replied that the Cubans did not think anything of the sort; in fact, they felt that the move had beneficial consequences in the maintenance of order. Later in the day, Welles reported that conditions had improved sufficiently to warrant the removal of one ship. The ambassador was now confident that Céspedes could handle the situation.[7]

The collapse of the old regime quickly signaled an end to the strike in the capital, but unrest continued in the countryside. Workers on the sugar plantations struck for higher wages, better living conditions, and recognition for their unions. On August 21 laborers seized a sugar mill at Punta Alegre in Camagüey Province, and within a month an estimated total of thirty-six mills had been captured. Communist agitators appeared to influence some of this movement, but even the Communist leaders failed to grasp the magnitude of the people's disenchantment with existing conditions. When thirty of the most prominent American businessmen in Cuba went to see Welles on August 29 to complain of Communist penetration into the work force, the ambassador agreed that some foreign agitators were in Cuba, but he did not think that they represented a significant threat. He dismissed the idea of Communist infiltration, reasoning that the dissatisfaction of labor stemmed from the economic structure imposed by a tyrannical regime. Only a restoration of constitutional government would improve the situation, and the ambassador felt that the island was returning to normal much sooner than he had expected.[8]

Even though Welles anticipated the restoration of stability, he feared that the exiles' return would quickly complicate a delicate situation. Menocal flew to Havana on August 20, and Carlos Mendieta and Roberto Méndez Peñate arrived by sea two days later. Mendieta was especially popular for his leadership in the Unión Nacionalista, which Machado had outlawed. More significantly, he was the only prominent political leader who had refused to condone Machado's tactics or attend his second inaugural ceremony, arguing that the entire procedure was illegal. Thousands cheered his arrival, and he gained additional popularity when he went immediately to the presidential palace and embraced Céspedes while the cheering throngs watched.[9]

Although the Cubans appeared elated over the arrival of the political exiles, Welles remained apprehensive. Fearing that these groups would pose a threat to the existing constitutional regime, he tried to convince Menocal that the continuation of the Céspedes government was imperative for Cuba's future stability. The envoy noted that none of the returning leaders had spoken out in favor of Céspedes, and he planned to confer with them to gain the needed support for the new government.[10]

As soon as Dr. Carlos Manuel de Céspedes y Quesada was inaugurated on the morning of August 13, Welles asked for and received American recognition of the new regime. The new president had been born in New York on August 12, 1871; he was the son of the Cuban patriot who had called for Cuban independence on October 10, 1868. During his exile, the younger Céspedes was educated in the United States and later studied in Germany and France. He became a lawyer, but when the War for Independence broke out on the island, Céspedes returned and gained the rank of colonel. When Cuba finally won its independence, he continued to work in the service of the new republic as a legislator, diplomat, and cabinet officer. From 1914 to 1922 Céspedes was the minister to the United States. Upon the completion of this assignment, he returned to Cuba, where he was appointed secretary of state in 1922. The election of Machado did not affect Céspedes's career; the new president appointed him minister to France and later ambassador to Mexico.[11]

While he had a creditable reputation for personal integrity and ability, Céspedes lacked certain qualities that Cuban nationalism of 1933 demanded in a leader. He was the first president not born on the island, and as a result of his service in the diplomatic corps, he had spent much time abroad. Since he had held diplomatic posts under the Machado regime, he had the additional handicap of not having played even a minor role in the dictator's overthrow. Lastly, writers also noted that Céspedes was indecisive, and in a time of stress this character trait would inhibit his effectiveness.[12]

Perhaps the Céspedes government could have survived in spite of the new president's personal deficiencies, had he not also been confronted by another more serious charge from the Cuban nationalists: that he was the creation of the American ambassador. There was considerable truth in this accusation. Welles and Céspedes had become friends when they both held diplomatic positions in Washington. During the Cuban presidential election crisis of 1920–21, Welles thought enough of Céspedes's talents to recommend him as a compromise candidate for president in order to resolve the political impasse. Welles arrived in Havana on February 23, 1921 to discuss the possibility of having both presidential contenders withdraw in order to select a third compromise candidate, a procedure which Welles favored.[13]

Neither Boaz Long, the American minister to Cuba, nor General Enoch Crowder, special representative of President Woodrow Wilson, had considered Céspedes, but Welles argued forcibly:

> The advantage of Dr. Céspedes' presidency would be—first, his thorough acquaintance with the desires of this Government; second, the prestige which his name gives him in Cuba; third, his complete disassociation from active politics during a long term of years; four, his personal integrity; five, his sincere desire to better conditions in Cuba and the freedom from any desire to benefit himself financially as the result of his presidency, because of his personal fortune; six, his amenability to suggestions or advice which might be made to him by the American Legation.[14]

Consciously or unconsciously, Welles began and ended his argument in Céspedes's behalf with the assumption that he would favor United States interests.

While Welles served in Cuba, he suffered enormously because of charges that he put Céspedes in the presidential palace. He had tried to do so in 1921, but in the midst of his troubles, he denied this allegation. In a letter to Samuel Inman he declared: "I had no more to do with the selection of Doctor Céspedes as Provisional President of Cuba than you did. From the very commencement of the Mediation negotiations, the political leaders and public opinion in general were casting about for the name of some honest, high minded, non-political Cuban who could serve as Vice President of the Republic after amendment of the Constitution, and to whom the Government could be turned over by General Machado." Céspedes had not been involved in Cuban politics for many years, and this absence from the political turmoil was also beneficial. Welles asserted that Céspedes's name had been mentioned in early June and that the candidate had gained the necessary support when members of Unión Nacionalista formally presented his name in late July. After very little discussion, the other revolutionary segments involved in the mediation supported the nomination. When Machado fled, the same credentials were needed for the man who would serve as secretary of state. Welles reiterated: "The Department of State and myself had absolutely no connection whatever with the selection of Doctor Céspedes, directly or indirectly, and I feel that, in justice to our policy in Cuba, in justice to the parties responsible for the selection of Doctor Céspedes, and in justice to the Secretary of State and myself, that misapprehension should be most decidedly corrected."[15]

In spite of such denials, the ambassador gave Céspedes his warm support; he also had confidence in the new cabinet selections. With the exception of the A.B.C., the cabinet was drawn not from the revolutionary sectors but from the old school of politicians.[16] Welles ignored the radicals, believing that the traditional leadership represented a "new deal for Cuba."[17] Other commentators echoed Welles's assessment of the cabinet for its honesty and personal integrity, but added that the leadership was as yet untested and had few forceful members. Machado had left the island, but the political system that he had constructed remained intact.[18]

With the successful transfer of political power, Welles turned his attention to economic recovery. On the day Céspedes was sworn into office, the ambassador proposed that the new government should receive financial aid from the United States. The ambassador hoped that the Roosevelt administration could grant a small loan to Cuba in order to pay the salary arrears of government workers. If this measure could not be taken, Welles wanted permission to negotiate with American bankers to accept a limited moratorium on the payment of the foreign debt. Not only the ambassador but others as well recognized the importance of economic aid and suggested solutions for these problems ranging from reductions in the United States' sugar tariff to an outright loan or bond issue.[19]

By August 20 the ambassador had formulated a definite program. As he pointed out, the Cuban treasury was empty; some government employees had not been paid for months; industry was "practically at a standstill. Poverty and destitution exist throughout the Republic."[20] If the United States did not act to rectify this situation, Welles felt that the Cuban government would have no alternative but to declare a moratorium on its foreign debt. He thought that the floating debt of Cuba, which amounted to about $45 million of which $10–15 million represented salary arrears, should be submitted to a claims commission for verification, and the United States should grant the Céspedes government an immediate loan to pay the legitimate salary arrears. The ambassador also suggested that the United States send a commission of technical experts to examine Cuban finances. This action would have a beneficial effect in that it would show that the United States was actively promoting economic improvement. Lastly, Welles wanted a new commercial treaty centering on a sugar quota to help revive the depressed industry.[21]

Welles's ambitious program was doomed to failure. The Treasury Department announced that it could not grant a loan, and treasury officials doubted that the Reconstruction Finance Corporation could either. When the American financial commission issued a preliminary report, it could not formulate any constructive financial program either.[22] By the beginning of September Welles had demonstrated his desire to grant economic assistance to the Céspedes regime, but the urgency of his requests failed to stimulate his superiors to action.

While Welles struggled with Cuban economic problems, he was dismayed to recognize the beginning of political fragmentation. The unifying force that had held the political factions together vanished when Machado fled. While still calling for the complete liquidation of the dictator's regime, each group simultaneously

turned to its own objectives. The lack of army discipline, agitation
created by returning exiles, and the hostility of the students made
for additional confusion. The ambassador hoped that the old
Congress would remain in session, but since the congressmen feared
vengeance, they went into hiding. Welles's insistence on the
preservation of constitutional rule limited the force of the
government's emergency proposals: how could the government act
without any Congress? Welles reported sadly on August 24 that
Céspedes would not be able to complete Machado's term, for
stability and order could be assured only by holding early
elections.[23]

Despite Welles's pessimism, the Cuban government started to
show signs of vitality. The arrival of American destroyers had a
quieting effect, and the general strike showed signs of weakening.
The looting and rioting were ebbing, for a military edict had
banned parades and other demonstrations that could result in
outbreaks of violence. On August 24 Céspedes moved boldly,
repealing the constitutional changes that had been enacted under
Machado in 1928. The decree restored the Constitution of 1901,
which strongly reflected American influences, particularly in
calling for individual rights and separation of powers. The constitution provided for a president, elected to a four-year term and
limited to two terms, and for a vice-president and a two-chamber
congress. Besides restoring the old constitution, Céspedes removed
congressmen and supreme court justices who had taken office after
May 20, 1929. He also announced that free and impartial general
elections would be held on February 24, 1934, and that the new
officials would be inaugurated on May 20. While these preparations
were being carried out, Céspedes would rule as dictator for nine
months with the aid of a consultative commission. Activity now
shifted to the formation of political parties and speculation over
who would emerge as the next president. Welles commented
optimistically that Céspedes had made an excellent decision which
would insure continued stability.[24]

Since Welles believed that conditions were improving, he
recommended his own recall. As early as August 19, the *Miami
Herald* reported that the ambassador would return to Washington
and the Jefferson Caffery would be his successor. On the same day,
Welles recommended just such an action to the State Department.
He did not foresee any political crisis, for the Cuban government

had the confidence of the people. Céspedes had accepted a new electoral code based on McBain's reforms, which meant that Cuba would have a new constitutional regime sometime in 1934. Welles also felt that his position was becoming the subject of political controversy.[25] Since he had developed close friendships with the Cuban president and his cabinet, Welles reported that he was "now daily being requested for decisions on all matters affecting the Government of Cuba."[26] He saw the possible implications of this dependence and did not want the growing opposition to unite against the American embassy for its alleged intervention. Welles stressed that the new ambassador should carefully avoid political involvement unless some emergency arose. Otherwise, Caffery should operate behind the scenes and concentrate on economic recovery.[27]

Before returning, Welles wanted to initiate negotiations for a new reciprocity treaty which Caffery would consummate. After Welles started the bargaining for the treaty, there would be nothing to keep him in Cuba unless some unexpected trouble broke out. If this happened, he felt that he could deal with the situation more easily than a new emissary, for he had already established the necessary contacts. Barring any such contingency, however, he wished to leave the island by September 1 in order to prepare for the Montevideo Conference. Roosevelt approved his plan but recommended that he remain until September 15; meanwhile the department would announce the termination of his mission.[28]

Welles was preparing for his departure when the first unexpected event occurred. On September 2 a hurricane struck the island, doing its worst damage in Camagüey Province. The next day, reports indicated that a hundred were dead, thousands were injured, and at least 100,000 were homeless. Government agencies sought to care for the people affected by the disaster, and Céspedes left the capital to inspect the devastated area in the east.[29]

Political storms were brewing as well. When Céspedes assumed power, the ambassador felt that political conflict had been resolved. Some disorder continued, but Welles believed that conditions would return to normal. He overlooked the pent-up antagonisms toward Machado's followers that the Cuban people had released. For him the revolution had ended, but many Cubans felt that only a continuing revolutionary government would institute a new justice that would redress their grievances. Unfortunately for Céspedes, his government did not appear radical enough to gain popular support. The president not only lacked personal magnetism, but he was also faced with mounting unrest. The national economy lay prostrate, labor agitation grew, the recently freed Cuban press abused its newly acquired independence with inflammatory articles against the government, and no one knew how the political parties would organize. The students represented another cause for concern, for instead of returning to classes, they started to denounce the new government. Could these students finally reconcile themselves to the new regime, or would they move back into the opposition?[30]

Céspedes was also confronted by another possible source of friction: the military. Until the removal of Machado, the army had played a secondary role in political affairs, depending on the United States to prevent instability. They were satisfied with the lavish privileges that the dictator had bestowed upon them, such as high salaries, good uniforms, comfortable homes, and servants. When the officers decided to oust the tyrant, they also, unknowingly, ended their tradition of political neutrality.[31] Ruby Hart Phillips pointed out three days after the dictator fled, "Now for the first time the people realize how easy it is for the army to force a change in government."[32]

Although some people may have realized the consequences of the army's decision, the officers did not know how to cope with their new status. Instead of accepting the responsibility for Machado's demise and playing a dominant role in determining the nation's destiny, they tried to return to their original position. They succeeded only in creating a power vacuum. Mob violence flared, and discipline within the ranks corroded when soldiers joined in the frenzied search for the *porristas*.[33]

The officiers tried to reestablish discipline at the end of August, but their laxity enabled oppostion to surface from within the ranks. The common soldier had been treated reasonably well under the old regime, but he resented the caste system that allowed the officers to live in the cities while he was confined to the less comfortable barracks. In many cases noncommissioned officers conducted the affairs of the armed forces while the officers attended to their private pursuits. After the officers left the post at night to go home, it would be relatively easy to start an enlisted men's revolt. As early as August 15 rumors began to circulate about such a revolt.[34] When the *New York Times* correspondent, James Phillips, warned Welles on August 20 of an impending insurrection, the ambassador dismissed the idea as idle gossip. Phillip's wife could not believe that the embassy staff had not been informed of this possibility; she wrote despairingly, "Welles simply cannot imagine there can be any trouble brewing when apparently everything is so quiet."[35]

Even if the ambassador rejected the idea of unrest within the ranks, the dissatisfied sergeants did not share his opinion. On August 26 the so-called Junto de los Ocho formed by dissident noncommissioned officers began meeting at the enlisted men's club at the army headquarters, Camp Columbia, to organize the lower ranks in order to obtain better conditions and opportunities for advancement. Sergeant Fulgencio Batista, the Junta's secretary, was to play a key role in the subsequent events and was eventually to emerge as the rebel leader. The movement reached its climax on the evening of September 4, when the sergeants at army headquarters staged their revolt. The insurrection quickly spread to all parts of the island, and before the officers could act in their own behalf, the noncommissioned officers announced that they were assuming control. The officers were simply informed that they no longer had command of the armed forces. Overnight a new echelon of the military had been created, but there were also major complications. The sergeants had ousted the old leadership, but they had not provided for a new chain of command. How would the officers retaliate?[36]

The radical groups outside the government had planned their own coup d'etat at the same time that the sergeants revolted. Circumstances would now force an alliance among these groups, which had acted independently of one another until September. Members of the Student Directorate rushed to Camp Columbia and convinced the sergeants to expand their movement into a new revolutionary struggle to depose the Céspedes regime. This expansion meant that the noncommissioned officers and their student allies would have to form a new government. The leadership of both groups accepted this challenge and decided to write a program. What emerged was a highly nationalistic formula calling for the reorganization of the economic and political systems by means of a constituent assembly. The new leaders also intended to carry out a program in which tribunals would punish the guilty in both the military and civilian sectors for previous crimes. At the same time they demonstrated their willingness to form a responsible government by rejecting Communist influence and by honoring past debts, both foreign and domestic.[37]

These unexpected events shocked Welles. His cable early in the morning of September 5 announcing the revolt revealed his initial hostility to the new regime. The insurrection, he said, had "been fomented by the extreme radical elements", and he labeled the three university professors in the new junta as Communist sympathizers.[38] Welles predicted that in such an atmosphere disorders would shortly erupt, either in the form of another general strike or as a counterrevolution within the army. Quiet still gripped Havana, but Welles requested the dispatch of warships as a precautionary measure.[39]

Céspedes was still out of the capital inspecting hurricane damage when the sergeants and students overthrew his regime. Before he returned, his cabinet met, but the members refrained from taking any decisive steps. Céspedes learned of his removal only when he arrived in Havana on September 5. That afternoon he met with the cabinet to seek some means of staying in power, but in view of the close bond between the revolutionaries and the new military leadership, the members decided to tender their resignations. Céspedes then met with the insurrectionists and pleaded with them, claiming that he was as revolutionary as they were, but his arguments were useless. The revolutionary junta demanded his retirement. After Céspedes's initial emotionalism, he shook hands with the leaders of the junta and went home.[40]

Welles reported these events to the State Department, stressing that he would try to prevent armed intervention, but pointing out that such a move might become necessary. The ambassador wanted the Latin American representatives to be informed of the precarious situation to prepare them for the possibility of intervention. Welles could not see any way for the new government to survive, for the leading political factions that had participated in the Céspedes government were adamantly opposed to the new leadership.[41]

In the midst of this chaotic activity, Batista went to see Welles at the embassy to discuss the recognition question, but the ambassador refused to discuss the subject. He wanted to know what steps had been taken to ensure stability, and he was not impressed with the sergeant's reply. According to Welles's report, he did not make any mention of intervention, but Batista's recollection was quite different, for he later wrote that the ambassador requested permission to land marines so that they could protect American lives, homes, hotels, and companies. Batista refused to sanction any such violation of Cuban sovereignty, and the meeting ended with neither man achieving his goals. In any case, this first contact between Welles and a representative of the junta indicated the ambassador's antagonistic attitude toward the new government. Welles cherished the concept of constitutionality, and the new regime violated the very principle on which he based his mission.[42]

The sergeants' revolt not only altered the government's composition, but also marked the emergence of this new political personality, Fulgencio Batista y Zaldívar. Born on January 16, 1901 in the town of Banes in Oriente Province, Batista represented the Cuban mestizo with his dark complexion, broad nose, and high cheek bones. His parents were *guajiros*, peasants of the countryside, where he lived until 1915, when his mother died. From that date Batista wandered from one job to another until April 1921 when he joined the army as a private; this decision was the turning point in his life. After two years in the service he determined to advance by learning typing and stenography. His study was rewarded, for in August 1928, Batista, now a corporal, passed an examination for army sergeants and became a stenographer. By 1931 he had risen to full sergeant attached to the general headquarters at Camp Columbia, where he held the confidence of many officers in the Machado regime. In this ·position of trust, he had access to confidential documents, and as a member of the A.B.C., he provided information to the opposition. Once Machado had fled, Batista took an active role in organizing the noncommissioned officers. Although he did not act alone in the revolutionary plot, his persuasive oratory and pleasing personality placed him in charge of the new military establishment. Batista quickly compensated for what he lacked in formal education and refinement by using his political acumen, which made him the most important personality in Cuban politics for the next eleven years.[43]

The alliance between the sergeants and the Student Directorate necessitated the formation of a new government. After the actual revolt, nineteen leaders met to determine an acceptable form of government while preparations for the election were being made. The conference resulted in the selection of a five-man revolutionary junta whose members had not served in the previous administration. Ranging in age from thirty-nine to forty-eight, the members of the pentarchy had not participated in the struggle for independence in 1898. Dr. Ramón Grau San Martín, a physician and popular professor at the University of Havana, was selected to head the ministry of public instruction and fine arts, and health and welfare; Sergio Carbó, one of Cuba's leading journalists and publishers, was appointed to the ministry of interior, war, navy, and communications; José Irizarri, a well-known financial expert and professor at the university, became minister of public works, agriculture, and commerce; another professor and distinguished lawyer, Guillermo Portela, was selected to direct the ministry of state and justice; lastly Porfirio Franca, an economist and a leading figure in the business community, was appointed minister of the treasury. Although Batista did not become a cabinet member, he was chosen to lead the armed forces as its provisional commander in chief. Welles exaggerated when he said that the members of the new junta were radicals; actually, they represented a highly nationalistic segment of Cuban society whose main "fault" was to oppose and later overthrow the government that Welles had molded.[44]

In the late afternoon of September 5, Welles met with the political leaders of the deposed government. They felt that the only way to avoid prolonged intervention was to form a coalition government, but that to counteract the influence of the sergeants, the United States would have to land troops in Havana, Santiago de Cuba, and possibly two other posts. At the end of this conference, the ambassador spoke with Hull and asked for permission to land marines in order to protect American lives and property. After conferring with Roosevelt, Hull told Welles that the president refused to sanction the use of troops unless the embassy were in physical danger. The secretary also argued against intervention because landing the small number of available marines might provoke even greater turmoil, rather than leading to stability. Hull wanted Welles to make it clear to the new Cuban leaders that they would have to protect foreigners and the American embassy. Welles replied that the junta could not undertake such a commitment because no one in Cuba really knew who had power to make even the simplest decisions.[45]

The following morning Welles and Hull continued their discussion of the situation. The ambassador admitted that Havana remained quiet, but his information from the interior showed serious disturbances. Hull reiterated that the ambassador must maintain a neutral position in the ensuing power struggle. The secretary believed that the Cuban problem centered on the army's loyalty. Welles agreed and then brought up the question of recognition because the junta was demanding it. He recommended that the United States should not consider such a request, and Hull agreed to follow Welles's plan until the junta had demonstrated its ability to maintain order. Once this condition had been fulfilled, recognition would again be considered.[46]

In the midst of this hectic activity, Welles momentarily gained the hopeful impression that the revolutionaries and the traditional leadership would form a coalition government. He had spoken with Grau early in the morning and believed that the pentarchy would construct a new cabinet composed of all factions. As a result of this conference, the ambassador held a meeting with the Céspedes coalition and told the members that the United States would not intervene and that they should solve their own internal problems. Under these circumstances, the leading political factions agreed to support the junta in its program of conducting a constitutent assembly and holding national elections. Welles saw some possibility of success in this movement, but he cautiously advised the State Department that the United States' policy should be one of watchful waiting without any recognition until further developments. For the time being, the Cubans were to determine their own fate.[47]

By evening Welles had dramatically altered his position. When Céspedes's secretary of war, Horacio Ferrer, came to see him, he told Welles of his plan to seize one of Havana's fortresses and start a revolt against the pentarchy in order to restore Céspedes. Ferrer hoped that the United States would actively support this counter-revolution by landing marines until the ousted president could unite the nation behind his regime. Welles thanked Ferrer for advising him of the plot, but stated that the United States could not be a party to any such conspiracy.[48]

Although Welles discouraged the insurrectionist's hopes, he asked Hull and Roosevelt to support the plan because Céspedes had been overthrown by a mutiny. Without mentioning the Platt Amendment specifically, the ambassador argued that the United States had an obligation to help maintain constitutional government. Welles believed that the United States' best interests would be preserved if the nation supported limited intervention.[49] Since other Latin American nations had been informed of the United States' position, "the landing of such assistance would most decidedly be construed as well within the limits of the policy of the 'good neighbor' which we have done our utmost to demonstrate in our relations with the Cuban people during the past 5 months."[50] Welles felt that any action to restore the constitutional regime would thus be consistent with his concept of the Good Neighbor Policy.

The ambassador defended his position by pointing out that Cuba was tottering on the brink of disaster. Encouraged by the political ineptitude of the pentarchy, the Communist groups were increasing their hostile activity. He also reported that various members of the Céspedes government were being hunted by the radical groups, but had fled to safety. In the midst of the anarchy, the ambassador still hoped that Céspedes could regain his lost presidency. Welles told the department that all the political factions were meeting at the palace to discuss such a possiblity, but the meeting ended in failure. The junta refused to surrender its control, and again Welles prophesied doom. The present government lacked both popular support and the ability to maintain order.[51] Welles predicted that if Céspedes were not restored, a "soldier-workman" government would appear and rule until a general revolution overthrew it.[52]

In spite of Welles's gloomy description, Roosevelt and Hull refused to consider intervention. As Hull stated, they felt "very strongly that any promise, implied or otherwise, relating to what the United States will do under any circumstances is impossible; that it would be regarded as a breach of neutrality, as favoring one faction out of many, as attempting to set up a government which would be regarded by the whole world, and especially throughout Latin America, as a creation and creature of the American Government."[53] Although Welles was disappointed, he followed orders and stated, "I shall not under any conditions request the landing of a single man unless I fell that American lives are in actual immediate danger."[54] Despite this pledge, he continued to relay pessimistic accounts of the situation.[55]

Welles had been firmly rebuffed, but he doggedly pushed for the use of troops, arguing that the president and the secretary of state had misinterpreted the existing state of affairs. The ambassador agreed that the United States should not take any action that could be interpreted as installing a Cuban government with United States military power, but he felt that an irresponsible group had deposed the legitimate government.[56] If Céspedes were reinstated with the support of all the important political factions and of the United States, Roosevelt could not be charged with supporting any one faction; he would be "lending friendly assistance at the request of the Cuban Government presided over by an impartial President and supported by every element of importance in the Republic."[57] Welles stressed that the United States would intervene only temporarily and that this action would be preferable to letting the island slide into anarchy and then having to intervene.[58]

While threats of intervention pervaded the political atmosphere, the pentarchy struggled desperately to avert such a disaster. Speaking for the junta, Grau stated that the "Platt Amendment gives the United States the right to intervene only when any form of Cuban government proves unable to maintain peace and order, but it does not give the right to dictate what kind of government Cuba shall have."[59] He hoped that Roosevelt would adhere to his interpretation. Other members of the junta also promised to maintain order and blamed alarmists for trying to provoke United States intervention. Even some Cuban who had originally supported Welles's mediation felt that intervention was unnecessary. They held that the ambassador had submitted exaggerated reports resulting in the presence of a large number of United States warships surrounding the island and making intervention possible. Four Americans returning from Cuba on September 7 admitted that they had seen no danger to American lives during their visit.[60]

The Cuban historian Herminio Portell Vilá returned to Havana in the midst of the hurricane. Writing to James A. Robertson on September 10, 1933, Portell Vilá assessed the chaotic events from his vantage point. He felt that "Mr Welles' pride was very much hurt because his chosen government was overthrown, but the truth is that that government might have been the bridge for a permanent one, but not the permanent one itself." As far as the pentarchy went, the membership had its strengths and weaknesses, but the Cuban historian asserted, "I know them not to be communists."[61]

While the junta was establishing control on the island, the Cuban ambassador to the United States, Manuel Márquez Sterling, was presenting the pentarchy's position in Washington and assuring Caffery that the junta was not Communist oriented or supported. Not only were Communists denied admittance into government circles, but the junta was also actively trying to suppress disturbances caused by the Communist Party. The government hoped that it could establish a new administration out of all the factions that had opposed Machado. In the interim, the junta was preserving order and also had the loyalty of the armed forces. Márquez Sterling asked Caffery what the United States wanted in return for recognition, but the assistant secretary refrained from setting any conditions, asserting only that stability and order had to be maintained.[62]

As the diplomatic manuevering in Washington and Havana intensified, the United States appeared to be on the verge of landing troops. Within three days of Welles's initial call for ships on September 5, a protective squadron had encircled the island, consisting of thirty warships which ranged from a battleship to coast guard cutters. In addtion to this naval cordon, a detachment of some one thousand marines was being assembled at Quantico, Viginia, for possible overseas duty. The military situation was further complicated when it was announced that Secretary of the Navy Claude Swanson was going to visit Welles. Although the secretary's trip had been planned before the revolt, Swanson's announcement of a casual social call did not seem plausible. He arrived in Havana harbor on September 9, talked with Welles aboard ship,[63] and left two hours later while crowds lined the docks and radicals yelled, "Don't welcome the American ships! They are coming to kill Cubans!"[64] These remarks contrasted strongly with the cheers that had greet American ships when Machado was ousted.[65]

Roosevelt began to exercise his own brand of diplomacy in the midst of the new crisis. On September 6 he called in the Latin

American representatives from the ABC countries and Mexico. He told them that he had sent ships to Cuba solely to protect American lives and had not contemplated intervention, hoping that the Cubans could solve their own domestic problems. A the end of the conference the president promised to keep the four Latin American countries informed of any change in policy. While Roosevelt held his meeting, the chief of the Division of Latin American Affairs, Edwin Wilson, spoke with representatives of ten other Latin American nations. Hull tried to explain the American position with the statement that although the United States did not wish to intervene, it had a responsibility under the Platt Amendment.[66]

These responsibilities were just what Latin Americans feared. Foreign Minister Puig and Ambassador Daniels agreed that any intervention would damage inter-American relations and impair any constructive results that might be accomplished at Montevideo. Daniels suggested to Roosevelt and Hull that if conditions grew worse, the ABC nations, Mexico, and Peru should be asked to cooperate in finding a solution for Cuban instability. Puig was working for such an accord, but Argentina refused to condone any kind of intervention. Seeing the staunch position of Argentina, other Latin American states would not participate in any settlement, because they too might be accused of intervention.[67] Hull spoke to Daniels by phone on September 9, declaring that the United States was doing "everything possible to prevent intervention. The last thing on earth we want to do is intervene."[68]

Hull was expressing not only his own view, but also the consensus of the administration as set forth at a cabinet meeting the previous day. Before the meeting Roosevelt spoke with Secretary of the Interior Harold Ickes about ordering all ships lying off Cuba not to land marines for the sole purpose of protecting private property.[69] Roosevelt had already taken the precaution of issuing a directive that troops would be landed only to protect lives and then the "use of guns or small arms is to be avoided except as last resort and only if you are definitely fired upon first."[70] The issue was then brought up at the cabinet meeting where the discussion was long and "tense." Ickes reported that the intervention question was debated and that everyone "was against intervention unless it was actually forced upon us."[71]

Cabinet sentiment seemed to reflect American public opinion. While newspaper editorials stressed different aspects of the new revolt, they were unanimous in their reluctance to support United States military involvement.[72] Four influential magazines also praised Roosevelt and Hull for their hands-off policy but demanded an economic settlement and an end to the Platt Amendment, intervention, and business domination of the island. The *Nation* went so far as to urge the recognition of the new regime.[73] Probably the *St. Louis Post-Dispatch* best described the American desire to avoid intervention:

> Whatever the result, whether the new overturn means peace or war in Cuba, it is to be hoped that this country's policy of avoiding intervention will be maintained. The dispatch of American warships as a safeguard for our citizens in Cuba is sufficient. If Cuba cannot remain united after expelling the tyrant, violence may be renewed there, but violence, perhaps to greater degree, would follow our landing of troops. If she can attain unity under wise leadership, Cuba has an opportunity to walk alone, and it cannot be improved by foreign intervention.[74]

Welles still maintained his contrary stance in spite of the widespread opposition, in both United States and Latin American opinion, to armed intervention. Both his ideas and his diplomatic skill had been subjected to great strains since his arrival in Cuba. The ambassador had originally been sent to the island to halt its growing political anarchy and at the same time to avoid any possibility of intervention. Machado's flight signaled the successful completion of Welles's initial assignment. The ambassador then started to construct a political and economic base for permanent stability and order. First he played a dominant role in the selection of the provisional government; then he actively encouraged the United States to lend economic assistance. During the short span of the Céspedes regime, Welles not only saved the United States from military intervention but also preserved his most cherished principle of constitutionality.

Welles worked diligently for the permanence of the new regime, but he ignored the social discontent caused by the political and economic stagnation of the Machado era. Although he noted many of the disruptive forces that existed within the nation, he never recognized the magnitude of the people's grievances against the political system. While the ambassador endeavored to preserve order, the malcontents demanded a genuine social revolution based on their desire to promote Cuban nationalism. In spite of the forces working to oust the traditional establishment, Welles remained undaunted in his belief that the political structure was fundamentally sound. To assure the government's success, he requested immediate economic assistance in the form of loans or grants followed by a reduction of the United States' sugar tariff and by a new commercial treaty. Even though administration officials never acted favorably on any of his requests, Welles believed that conditions on the island had stabilized enough to warrant his return to Washington unless some unforeseen event occurred.

The unexpected happened when the hurricane wreaked havoc on the eastern end of the island. Céspedes immediately went to inspect the stricken area, and while he was away from the capital, the second unpredictable event occurred—the sergeants removed most of their officers, and the students rushed to ally themselves with the military rebellion. Both of these sudden actions destroyed the ambassador's plans. During the confusion of the sergeants' revolt, Welles pressed for the restoration of the Céspedes regime with United States military intervention. As vehemently as Welles argued for force, Hull counseled against it, feeling that the United States must end its interference in the internal affairs of the Latin American states. Since the two men differed fundamentally in their evaluation of the Good Neighbor Policy, Roosevelt not only had to decide which policy would be followed, but also had to find a way to placate both men, one of them his secretary of state and the other a close friend and his ambassador.

How could the president face both ways at once? Only a masterful politician could resolve the dilemma and hold the allegiance of both men. To Hull, Roosevelt extended his assurance that there would be no intervention except as a last resort; to Welles, he announced his complete faith in the ambassador's ability, sent warships to surround the island, and followed the ambassador's advice to withhold recognition of the junta. Roosevelt walked the narrow path between outright intervention and strict neutrality. While neither Hull or Welles approved of the entire position, both men seemed satisfied; at the same time, their feelings were not hurt and their loyalty had been preserved.

The conflict over policy and the ensuing results had far wider ramifications. Roosevelt was not only responding to the wishes of Hull and Welles, but also listening to the plea of his longtime friend, Ambassador to Mexico Josephus Daniels, to Latin Americans opposed to intervention, and to public opinion in the United States, which was hostile to any foreign involvement. During the struggle over intervention, Roosevelt had evolved the most famous tenet of the Good Neighbor Policy to which he would adhere throughout his administration: the United States would not intervene militarily in the affairs of Latin American states.

4

Grau and Welles:
The Tragedy of Defeat

While the Roosevelt administration searched for a consistent Cuban policy, the revolutionary junta faced its own internal dilemma. Since the regime was a heterogeneous alliance drawn together by the unexpected events of the sergeants' revolt, the pentarchy never really functioned or even formalized a program. Porfirio Franca did not take office nor attend any cabinet meetings, and José Irizarri and Guillermo Portela participated reluctantly, ready to resign at a moment's notice. Only the Student Directorate, which sought a nationalistic program, and the sergeants, who groped for a means to maintain power, remained steadfast in their allegiance.[1]

For other reasons besides political uncertainty, September was an inauspicious month to take command of the government. The *zafra*, the sugar-cutting season, began in January and usually went on until May, but the 1933 harvest lasted less than three months. In addition workers who had been paid two or three dollars a day for their toil in prosperous times now received only forty to fifty cents. As a result of the depressed conditions, laborers demonstrated their restiveness by threatening and even seizing some sugar mills in the interior, and Communist-led strikes and the aggressive tendencies of the labor unions in the cities aroused even greater apprehension of further conflict.[2]

After only three days in power, the junta decided to establish a presidential form of government with the participation of the opposition. At first the Student Directorate acceded to this plan, specifying only that the new president could not represent the old political establishment, but the students quickly reversed their decision and chose Grau San Martín for provisional president. On September 10 representatives from all factions were summoned to the presidential palace and informed of the *fait accompli*. The opposition leaders were astounded and angry because they had been led to believe that the new president would be chosen by mutual agreement. Frustrated and humiliated, the opposition leadership announced that it would not join the newly formed government.[3]

On the afternoon of September 10, Ramón Grau San Martín became provisional president of Cuba. Born on September 13, 1887, in La Palma in Pinar de Río Province, he was the son of a wealthy Spanish merchant who had immigrated from Catalonia. He was educated by private tutors until he took his medical degree from the University of Havana in 1908. He continued his studies abroad, and upon his return he built one of the largest and most lucrative practices on the island, specializing in diseases of the digestive tract. Recognition of his medical competency came in 1921 when he was made professor of physiology in the medical school of the University of Havana.[4]

Grau was slightly over six feet tall, thin, and anemic looking. A bachelor, he devoted most of time to his practice and his students. Although he never participated in politics, his close association with the students precipitated his arrest in 1930 for conspiring against the Machado regime. While in prison, he continued to conduct classes, and upon his release in 1932 he went into exile in New York and Miami, returning to Cuba after the dictator's ouster. When he received his appointment to the pentarchy and later to the presidency, there was no doubt that the students had selected him. A cheering crowd assembled for the inauguration, but no diplomatic representatives attended the ceremony; all were waiting to see how the United States would respond.[5]

Portell Vilá watched the inauguration and reported that Grau assumed the presidency so that he could form a cabinet acceptable to the United States, but this political move did not meet with a positive response. In fact, while praising the new regime, the Cuban historian attacked Welles's activity within his country and the American warships surrounding the island:

> The attitude of the State Department, the threatening presence of scores of American battleships, entering and leaving Cuban ports without saluting and deliberately ignoring that they were in foreign ports, have added fuel and it is almost

impossible to talk friendly relations with the United States now, everybody bitterly denouncing 'American imperialism' and a naval demonstration whose justification nobody can understand. Whoever advised the latter, he did a most unfortunate thing. The lynching and rioting so common under the Céspedes regime have been absolutely suppressed by the new government, but the overthrow of Céspedes was brought about by a typical 'cuartelazo' fo sergeants, corporals and privates of the Army and Navy in which, it is also true, there was no bloodshed. Students, intellectuals, professors and so forth joined that movement.[6]

Under this cloud of uncertainity, Grau assumed office and tried to restore a semblance of stability. The new president was fortunate in his first cabinet selections. José Barquin, a public accountant noted for his honesty, became secretary of the treasury; Carlos Finlay, son of the famous Cuban physician who assisted in finding the cause of yellow fever, was appointed secretary of sanitation; Eduardo Chibás, father of the student leader, was chosen secretary of public works; and Antonio Guiteras was appointed secretary of government.[7]

While five men still held supreme authority in the government, Grau and Guiteras emerged as the dominant personalities. Raised in a middle-class Cuban family, Antonio Guiteras Holmes was born in 1906 to a Cuban father and an American mother. He was a tall man, excessively thin and somewhat stooped; and his reddish-brown hair and freckles were decidedly unusual for a Cuban. He studied pharmacy at the university until 1928, when he was expelled for his activities in the Student Directorate. He then traveled throughout the island as a sales agent for medical products, but his job did not satisfy his hatred for the dictator. In 1932 he led an attack on the military barracks in San Luis, Oriente Province; the attack failed, and Guiteras was sentenced to prison. When Machado proclaimed the amnesty in 1933, Guiteras was freed. After the September revolt, he rushed from the interior to the capital, where he became involved in the ensuing power struggle.[8]

At the age of twenty-seven, Guiteras became the most radical and powerful cabinet member, drawing his support from leftist sympathizers. He spoke infrequently, but he was decisive where

Grau hesitated. He was fervently nationalistic and thought that economic imperialism was the cause of Cuba's problems. With such a viewpoint, he was a continual source of anxiety to foreigners, especially Americans, and opponents called him everything from a Communist to a dope fiend.[9]

After the inauguration Welles commented on the government's chances of success, stating that the presidential form of government had replaced the pentarchy because of the antipathy toward the junta and the expectation that centralized control would bring United States recognition. The envoy felt that this decision signaled a return toward normal conditions and also commented that he did not see any counterrevolutionary movement threatening the new regime. He believed that within a few days he would know better the government's chances for survival. This prompt assessment was crucial, for as the ambassador pointed out, no Cuban government could survive for a protracted period without foreign recognition. If the regime could attract public support, maintain order, collect taxes, and appoint responsible officials, he suggested that the State Department consult with the Latin American nations about recognition.[10]

Nevertheless, a pessimistic note crept into Welles's analysis. He thought that the students and other radical groups still dominated the government and pointed out that the new regime had done little to quell the anarchical conditions in the interior. In addition to these unfavorable signs, the government had placed restrictions on the press as severe as those that had been in effect under Machado, but it had not stopped agitators from attacking the American embassy for its refusal to grant immediate recognition. Besides these internal weaknesses, the ambassador also saw signs of external hostility. When Batista was promoted on September 8 to the rank of colonel and permanent army chief of staff, the ex-officers lashed out against the appointment of a noncommissioned officer to the commanding role. Another source of friction was the political opposition. Although the Céspedes coalition had not refused to support the Grau regime, Welles did not belief that its leadership would accept the new government. Under these conditions, the ambassador did not see how Grau could fulfill the requirements for recognition.[11]

The day after the inauguration, the Roosevelt administration announced that it would recognize any government that showed the ability to maintain order and stability and had the support of the Cuban people. The opposition quickly illustrated how difficult these requirements would be to satisfy when it refused to support the existing regime.[12] As a result of this refusal and because of the inability of the new regime to govern effectively, Welles recommended that recognition be withheld because "conclusive evidence has now been presented to my satisfaction that the existing regime represents only the students, a few radical agitators and a small number of insignificant radical groups which have no political importance or following whatever."[13] The ambassador not only recommended this action but also thought that the United States should refrain from publishing a favorable sugar quota because any such move might be interpreted as support for the regime. Welles thought that only one course of action was available: to continue watching Cuban developments and to allow him to remain on the island past his scheduled departure on September 15. Recognizing his experience and contacts, Hull announced that Welles would remain indefinitely at his post.[14]

Even though the United States reaffirmed its nonrecognition policy, the Roosevelt cabinet disapproved the use of American troops, and in a radio broadcast on September 16, Caffery also stressed that the State Department opposed armed intervention.[15] This official sentiment against the application of force did not materially aid the Cuban government's prospects for the coveted recognition. On September 17 when Grau requested recognition, Welles replied that the United States could not recognize his regime because it did not have the majority's support.[16] After Grau left, Welles remarked that Grau was an "impractical and visionary" leader. The envoy saw "little hope of success . . . from a government controlled by him and by the students."[17]

Welles now proposed a coalition government as the only conceivable way out of the political impasse. He no longer mentioned any possibility of intervention or of Céspedes's return to the presidency.[18] Writing on September 18, Welles warned the opposition that the United States would not impose any solution. He now vigorously argued against armed involvement even if United States property were damaged:

> By intervention we not only would seriously jeopardize our continental interests but we also would once more give the

Cuban people and particularly the Cuban leaders to understand that they do not have to assume the responsibility for
their lack of patriotism or lack of vision, and that the United
States Government stands always ready to repair the damage
which they themselves cause their own country. It is my
sincere belief that Cuba can never become a self-governing
republic so long as this feeling persists.[19]

Welles was not only expressing his opinion, he was also echoing
the administration's stance. Hull confided to Norman Davis that "I
am sitting up with the Cuban situation almost day and night in an
effort to keep out. I have some hope that we may succeed."[20] A few
days later, Roosevelt's trusted secretary, Louis Howe, wrote to a
well-known Latin American expert in the United States, John
Barrett, telling him, "you may be assured that intervention is not
contemplated; the Administration desires only that there be a
stable Cuban Government, capable of maintaining peace, law and
order throughout the Republic."[21]

After the Roosevelt administration announced its policy, the
Cuban political factions responded. On September 11 the most
prominent political parties declared their repugnance toward the
new regime and openly called for a coalition government. During
the remainder of the month, all factions supported the idea of
compromise, but none could present an acceptable plan, for each
demanded supremacy over the others. The fundamental and
historical distrust among the opposing political parties inhibited
every proposal that was suggested.[22]

While the delicate negotiations were being conducted, the island
seemed to be governed by sheer inertia. People refused to pay their
taxes, so no money came into the treasury. Laborers were still
seizing sugar mills; Communists were demonstrating; serious
rioting had broken out in Santiago de Cuba; and the government's
military forces squelched two armed revolts. Anchored in the
harbors and lying just over the horizon, United States warships
witnessed the havoc silently, while Grau's adherents used the
presence of these ships to excite nationalism and anti-Yanqui
feeling.[23]

In spite of all the internal and external dissension, Grau decided
to act. First, he declared the Constitution of 1901 inoperative and
announced that he would govern by decree. Then he decided that

elections for delegates to a new constitutional convention would be held in April 1934. Along with his political actions, Grau moved to ameliorate the plight of the workers, declaring that all laborers in industrial and commercial establishments would work no longer than eight hours a day. This reform met with general approval, but the president later initiated another law which aroused the objections of regional medical societies because it compelled their members to join one national federation.[24]

In the midst of apparent chaos, life went on as usual for most people. Tourist travel continued and even seemed to be stimulated by the unstable conditions. On September 22 two New Yorkers reported that Havana appeared gay, and some Californians commented that after hearing all the talk of revolution, they found the city tranquil. The *Miami Herald* commented, "If you wish to visit Cuba, go ahead. You may not see an uprising, but you should have a good time and be just as safe as when motoring or crossing a street in the United States."[25]

While inquisitive tourists looked for excitement in Havana, Grau's internal troubles increased immeasurably. On September 8 approximately five hundred disgruntled officers who had been driven from their positions by the sergeants' revolt moved into the exclusive, modern, American-owned Hotel Nacional. Welles, who had taken a suite there after the lease on his house had expired, predicted hopefully that the soldiers would probably not attack. The same evening, however, Batista ordered the premises searched for weapons. Since many civilians were living in the hotel, Welles acted to avoid a conflict. He talked with the commanding noncommissioned officer, Sergeant Díaz, about delaying the search, suggesting that he use his discretion and ask that the order be rescinded. Since the sergeant did not understand the term "discretion," Welles patiently explained its meaning. While the noncommissioned officer returned to headquarters for new orders, Welles and Adolf Berle sat in the middle of the hotel lobby. The officers were on one side and the soldiers on the other, both prepared for combat. The sergeant came back in a few hours, and the troops withdrew to positions surrounding the hotel.[26]

After the revolutionary army had encircled the hotel, Horacio Ferrer, speaking in behalf of the officers, again asked Wells to land American troops in order to restore the legitimate president, but this time the ambassador refused to consider any such scheme.

Even though Welles refused to support them, on September 12 the officers stubbornly announced their hope that Céspedes would declare himself the legitimate ruler.[27] Céspedes also declined to cooperate, however, stating that he would not be a "puppet in a comic opera revolution which would result in music played by machine guns."[28] Despite his refusal, the officers still agitated for Grau's removal on the grounds that his regime was illegal and communistic.[29]

During the remainder of September the two warring factions stood their ground, each charging the other with disloyalty. The rhetorical contest between the two antagonistic forces ended abruptly just before dawn on the morning of October 2 when someone fired a shot. Unfortunately for the bystanders, no advance warning had been given, and civilians were trapped in the line of fire. The battle raged for eleven hours, while the diplomatic corps worked to stop the needless bloodshed. Even though the diplomats' pleas went unheeded, the officers finally surrendered, hopelessly outnumbered. They had killed over a hundred soldiers and wounded an additional two hundred, while losing fourteen dead and seventeen injured. One other casualty complicated the death toll. Robert G. Lotpeich, a United States citizen and manager for Swift and Company in Cuba, was killed by a stray bullet while watching the battle from the top of a building.[30]

Following the battle on October 3, Hull announced that the United States would not alter its hands-off policy, regardless of the American's accidental death. After the secretary made his statement, the *Miami Herald* and the *Baltimore Sun* commended the State Department for its restraint.[31] Josephus Daniels also wrote Hull complimenting not only the department but also the Cuban government for its patience. He thought that the spectacle of the officers occupying an impregnable fortress and making demands on the government was intolerable: "It seems to me that the Grau San Martín government has shown remarkable patience in dealing with the situation. It is to be hoped that now the festering sore is opened, the same result may follow as when a surgeon lances a throbbing boil. Hungry mobs are dangerous and need to be suppressed—and fed—but swaggering militarists are most dangerous."[32]

When the actual fighting ceased, the accusations began. Students and other radicals charged Welles with complicity in the affair.

Some people, including Ruby Hart Phillips, accused the ambassador's military attaché of prodding the officers to continue their resistance. Welles countered these charges by denying any responsibility, and the State Department issued an unequivocal statement on his behalf. Later, the officers also admitted that Welles did not have any connection with the revolt. In spite of all these supporting statements, the rumor that Welles had allied himself with the officers became commonly accepted as a fact.[33] Possibly Hubert Herring analyzed the relationship between the ambassador and the officers best when he wrote, "It was not Mr. Welles's conspiracy; it was his bad luck."[34]

In the first serious threat to the government, Grau's coalition emerged victorious—or did it? The events leading up to the battle clearly illustrated the need to consolidate the government's forces. Even though the sergeants and the students joined the regime for different reasons, both groups realized that they had to support each other to maintain the government's viability. After the hotel battle, this unstable alliance disintegrated. Instead of joining in a united effort, each side looked suspiciously at the other and tried to gain a political advantage. Both soldiers and students saw the triumph as a clear indication of the govermment's durability, and the latent antagonism over ideology and program now emerged in a contest for power which caused an irreparable break.

Signs of the division appeared almost immediately when Welles spoke with Batista on the morning of October 4. During the month of September, the ambassador had watched the sergeant's power growing at the expense of the civilian government. Although neither man had confidence in the other, Welles now used Batista's strength to undermine the Grau regime. Batista, he said, was the only person in Cuba who had any authority and could protect American lives and property. Welles told Batista that Grau could not receive recognition because his regime did not have the support of the Cuban people. Suggesting that only the student radicals stood in the way of a settlement, he urged Batista to find a solution to Cuba's problems. The colonel agreed that a compromise was needed, but he felt that any agreement would take time to formulate. At the conclusion of their talk, Welles cautioned that another coup d'etat would have an adverse effect on Cuban stability.[35]

While the ambassador altered his tactics, the Roosevelt administration was considering changing the entire strategy. After the government's success at the hotel, the question of recognition presented itself again. On October 5 Hull and Roosevelt had spoken about the results of the battle and observed that the United States newspapers saw the victory as a consolidation of the Grau government. Even though Hull admitted that disorder existed, he was still contemplating the possibility of recognition.[36]

Welles adamantly opposed such a move, explaining that the administration had misinterpreted the events. The battle did not solidify the government's forces, but only demonstrated that as "Batista becomes more influential the power of the students and Grau San Martín diminishes."[37] The ambassador admitted that recognition would help preserve the regime, but he declared that Grau's removal was inevitable. If the United States granted recognition, it would do so against the wishes of the Cuban business interests, the Céspedes coalition, and the vast majority of the Cuban people. Since no Cuban government could survive without the support of the major political groups and the confidence of commercial and business circles, Welles recommended that the United States continue its watchful waiting.[38]

Batista's status was greatly increased by the hotel victory and his discussion with Welles. These events had not gone unnoticed by the students, who believed that they and not the army had been the victors. The Student Directorate began to realize that Batista might form a military dictatorship, so they tried to wrest power from the army. While the students initiated their campaign against Batista, Grau satisfied one of their longstanding demands when he issued a decree on October 6 making the university an autonomous institution. He declared that the secretary of education would no longer have any authority over the university's affairs, and he assured the maintenance of the institution by providing 2 percent of the ordinary Cuban budget for its support. Grau hoped that this action would placate the students and that the young radicals who had been engaged in political agitation for so long would shortly return to classes.[39]

The decree did not satisfy the demands of the student radicals; they now sought to squelch Batista's growing authority. The first open clash came on October 18, when the students attempted to replace Batista's appointee for the position of chief of police in Havana with one of their own supporters. Batista balked at such a usurpation of his authority, and in the first direct confrontation between the military and the students, the ex-sergeant emerged victorious. Five days after this reversal, the Student Directorate passed a resolution demanding that Grau determine in twenty-four hours whether he would remain subservient to Batista. On October 30 the body sought additional support at a meeting of the University Student Assembly where between 1,000 and 1,500 students gathered to discuss their political future. The meeting resulted in disorder, however, as the Student Directorate could not persuade the rest of the students to follow its program. When the radicals realized that their plans were being thwarted, about one hundred who supported Grau left angrily, while those who remained declared their opposition to Grau and the Student Directorate. By the first week of November, the student groups showed further signs of fragmentation. Some wanted to return to classes, while others doggedly advocated participation in the government. Whichever course the students chose, they could no longer be considered the same unified faction that had originally supported Grau on September 10.[40]

While the students argued among themselves, Batista moved closer to the conviction that Grau had to be replaced. On October 7 Batista finally reached the conclusion that the government was "a complete failure" and told Welles that he had scheduled talks with the opposition.[41] While these discussions were being arranged, the army leader informed the ambassador that he was trying to force the students to return to classes and was also dealing with the agitators in the countryside while protecting American sugar plantations.[42]

Welles had some hope for the success of these talks until Carlos Finlay returned from a trip to Washington on October 9. The secretary had gone to the United States to seek recognition and had discussed the question with Caffery on September 28. Somehow Finlay gained the impression that if the regime incorporated three opposition members in the cabinet, the United States would grant the desired recognition. Although Caffery denied any such commitment, Finlay's announcement inhibited the movement toward compromise. Only when the State Department issued a press release on October 11, denying that it was about to recognize the Cuban regime, did talks begin again.[43]

After discussions had resumed, Welles reported on October 19 that Grau sincerely wished to compromise: he would limit presidential powers, incorporate the opposition into his cabinet, and place legislative authority there. Even though Welles optimistcally thought that Batista and the political opposition would accept such a plan, on October 26 the students flatly rejected any idea of compromise. The effort to keep Grau in the presidency with a coalition cabinet had failed.[44]

Welles once again failed in his efforts to reach a compromise, and at the end of October, he presented his position on the Cuban crisis to Samuel Inman:

> There is just as much graft going on at the present moment as there was during Machado's Government. With a few exceptions, the members of the Student Directorate themselves are profiting at the expense of the public purse and are likewise profiting from concessions which their recent position of influence has made it possible for them to get in on. The chief activity of most of the students has been confined to ousting civil employees and replacing them with their own relatives or friends, and the result of this pastime is that, at the moment, there is no department of the Government that is able even to attempt to function.

Welles believed that there were honest and patriotic Cubans, but he thought that except for three cabinet members in Grau's government, the present regime was "composed either of self-seeking, small caliber politicians, or of fuzzy-minded theorists who have neither the training, the experience, nor the capacity to govern."

This harsh assessment of the regime's honesty and ability complemented the ambassador's reason for maintaining a nonrecognition policy, which was

> based on my firm belief that so long as the Permanent Treaty between the United States and Cuba exists, just so long and probably long afterwards, recognition by the United States of any Cuban Government gives that government a tremendous moral and financial support; and that, should that support be given by us to a government which has been patently a government of a scant minority, we would be making it difficult, if not impossible, for the Cuban people to determine

freely the government by which they desire to be governed. The present regime has never been supported by any political party, by any of the recognized revolutionary sectors, or by the neutral mass of the people, let alone the merchant and business classes. It has never been supported by a majority of the University professors, and it is not supported today by more than an infinitely small minority of the University students. If we had recognized it, the concession seekers, and among them many Americans, who were flocking around it would have at once made available money on a considerable scale, and the attempt of the Cuban people to shake off this administration would have long been postponed, although inevitable—and in the meantime economic ruin and actual starvation would have been the result. . . . I believe that we owe it to the Cuban people not to assist in saddling upon them for an indefinite period a government which every responsible element in the country violently opposed, and which is opposed today by the laboring classes and by the farmers, as well as by the political parties and by the business interests.

Welles hoped that he was following the correct policy, which was

based on justice, on a real appreciation of democracy, and should, in the long run, promote understanding and sympathy between the two peoples. It may not prove successful; a collapse of all government may occur; but I feel that that possibility would have been infinitely more likely to materialize had we accorded recognition and assisted the minority to dictate to the majority, as the United States Government did in the days of General Machado.[45]

Welles displayed his personal contempt for the leadership of the Cuban government, and he also made clear the extent to which his bias led him to advocate nonrecognition. The Grau regime destroyed what Welles considered his attempt to continue constitutional rule on the island. Instead of searching for the causes that had brought Grau to power and kept him there, Welles preferred simply to see a corrupt, inefficient government that had few supporters. He, therefore, recommended nonrecognition because he believed that recognition would give Grau undeserved prestige and support. The ambassador was certain the student-soldier regime would not survive, and he felt that the United States should not assist a minority government. Yet Welles had no way of comparing the Grau and Machado administrations; he did not have enough information to judge the integrity of the present office-holders; he certainly underestimated Grau's civilian support and failed to mention his military backing. Although he used rational diplomatic jargon, Welles was really giving his self-righteous assessment of a government that he personally abhorred. His disapproval of the Grau regime distorted the purpose of his mission, which was to restore peaceful conditions. Instead he adhered steadfastly to the policy of nonrecognition, which promoted continued anarchy and ultimately led to what Welles realized had to occur: another revolt.

While Welles belittled the Grau regime, Batista held his own political discussions with Carlos Mendieta as another possible replacement for Grau. Batista indicated that the students' intransigence had forced his action. On the same day that the students rejected Grau's proposal, the opposition offered to support Mendieta for the presidency. Even with the support of the antagonistic forces, Mendieta vacillated because of Batista's growing power and the Student Directorate's hostility. He also knew that he would only be provisional president, and his party wanted him to run for the full presidential term in the general elections. His indecision created a paradox for the opposition: although it vigorously objected to the existing regime, its chosen replacement refused to assume the burdens of the presidency.[46]

Increasing turmoil complicated the political negotiations. The A.B.C. Radical, a splinter faction of the original A.B.C., withdrew from the government on October 24, announcing that its membership could no longer support the existing government, and demanded Grau's resignation. Along with this political reversal, the government faced mounting violence in the interior caused by a railway strike, and terrorism had spread in the cities. Again a general strike appeared imminent, but it never gained mass support. The populace simply did not know where to place its confidence. Once more the regime seemed on the verge of collapse and Grau about to resign.[47]

On November 3 an internal crisis temporarily halted the efforts for a political compromise. The president summoned Batista to the palace, but the army leader refused to come, insisting that he and the original civilian junta meet with Grau at Sergio Carbó's home. At this meeting, Grau lost no time in attacking Batista, whom he angrily accused of conspiring to overthrow his regime in secret talks with the opposition. He reminded Batista that as leader of the republic he could remove him from his position as commander in chief. Grau went on to say that he had no intention of ruling under these adverse circumstances and was prepared to submit his resignation. Batista answered the charges and agreed that Grau could not remain president. The angry outburst gave satisfaction to no one, but it made on point abundantly clear: Batista and Grau were no longer allies.[48]

Welles was deeply involved with these crucial events when William Phillips called on November 6, asking if he wished to attend the Montevideo Conference. The ambassador declined because he did not want to leave until a settlement had been attained. Phillips, who was to be acting secretary of state in Hull's absence, suddenly realized that if Caffery departed for Montevideo as scheduled, he would be left with almost no expert advice on Latin American affairs.[49] The undersecretary grumbled in his diary: "Welles is doing no good in Havana; he has become so involved with the various political parties and is being so violently attack[ed] in the local press and otherwise that his presence there has no longer any 'healing' effect. However, he is determined to stick it out and the President certainly has no intention of recalling him. I very much fear that the Cuban situation will boil over during the next two months while I am in charge of the Department and I am not looking forward to any such problem."[50] To his relief, Phillips persuaded Hull to leave Caffery in Washington for consultation.

Phillips did not have long to wait for his foreboding to come true. Late in the evening of November 7, the A.B.C. revolted, along with discordant elements of the armed forces and several other splinter groups. Commanding some of the insurgents was Colonel Juan Blas Hernández, a celebrated and picturesque anti-Machado guerrilla leader who had staged a brief rebellion against Grau in September. Early the following morning, the insurgents attacked the avaiation hangars at Camp Columbia, but loyal troops repelled them. In the course of the day, the fighting intensified in the city, and by evening Grau proclaimed a state of war. By the second day of fighting, the rebels had been confined to Atares Fortress. Here

Blas Hernández was killed, and at 4:00 P.M. on November 9, the defeated rebels raised the white flag, thus ending the last organized resistance in Havana. At Atares alone over 150 had been killed and 250 wounded; all told, the two-day struggle was the most costly rebellion in the republic's history.[51]

The revolt temporarily disrupted any movement for political compromise. Batista took charge of the military and, along with most of the armed forces, remained loyal to the incumbent regime. This was not the time to debate Grau's merits; it was the moment to preserve the power of the new military. Even though the army had squelched the Havana uprising, anarchy continued to spread in the countryside. With the new outbreaks of violence, American newspapers no longer wrote of national consolidation. They now described the instability and called for all sides to reach some peaceful agreement.[52]

In the midst of this most serious challenge to the government, Grau issued his most-far-reaching labor decrees. On November 7 he declared that all labor had the right to organize, except for government employees, the army, and the police. Unions were to register in the ministry of labor under penalty of dissolution. They were to admit delegates from the ministery into their meetings, and their officials had to be Cuban citizens. Lastly, unions could not strike without first submitting their demands to a governmental system of arbitral boards whose decisions would be binding. The very next day, when the fighting was fiercest, Grau proclaimed the most significant labor decree of his administration, the Law of Cubanization of Labor or simply the "50% law." This law required that at least 50 percent of the employees of any enterprise be native Cubans. When a position was vacated, especially one held by a foreigner, it had to be filled by a native Cuban. Grau's decree provoked a violent response from the Spanish community, which resented the discrimination against foreign-born residents.[53]

Four days after the abortive revolt Welles asked to see Roosevelt. Since he was then being violently attacked by the students for alleged participation in the November revolt, the ambassador suggested that, in order to allay any suspicion that he was being recalled, an announcement would be made that he was returning at his own request. Next day Phillips spoke with the president, who hesitated momentarily for fear that Welles's return would be interpreted as his removal, but he agreed to a meeting at his retreat in Warm Springs, Georgia. The acting secretary issued a press release on November 15, stating that Welles had requested a conference with the president.[54]

With the meeting arranged, Welles left Havana on November 17 and saw Roosevelt two days later. During the interview, with Welles at his side, the president phoned Phillips in the capital. Roosevelt suggested that the acting secretary meet with the Latin American representatives there, as he himself had done when Céspedes was ousted, and show them a statement that Welles would draft. The president also told Phillips confidentially that Welles would shortly be replaced.[55]

Welles arrived in Washington on November 20 and discussed his ideas with Caffery and Phillips. His plan was to prepare the statement for Roosevelt and return briefly to Havana before assuming his duties as assistant secretary. While Welles argued for the declaration, the other two men were skeptical.[56] Phillips thought that Welles was adamant because of the utter confusion in Cuba, "the lack of any knowledge of the position of the United States and the necessity for clarifying the atmosphere by a public declaration."[57] Even on these grounds, Phillips objected because such an assertion could only be interpreted by the Cuban government as continued rejection. On November 22 Phillips and Welles finished drafting the statement and sent it to the president. Roosevelt phoned Phillips and told him that the proclamation was completely satisfactory and that he would give it to the press. Phillips cautioned Roosevelt that the Cuban regime would disapprove, but the president did not seem disturbed.[58] If the situation degenerated, he said, he would "withdraw the Embassy from Havana and all Americans from the Island."[59]

Roosevelt released the statement the following day, announcing that the United States had not recognized Grau because he did not represent the Cuban majority. Although the United States wished to extend the benefits of the Good Neighbor Policy to Cuba, no action could be taken until the island had a provisional government that had the support of the people and demonstrated stability. The president emphasized that the United States was not supporting any special political faction in Cuba but would recognize any government that met the stated prerequisites. He added that Welles would return to Havana but that Caffery would shortly replace him as the president's special representative.[60]

During Welles's twelve-day absence, the Cubans speculated about his meeting with Roosevelt. When the president announced that Welles would definitely leave, the students were jubilant, feeling that they had forced Welles's departure. The opposition expressed its shock at Welles's recall, but the Céspedes coalition was elated Roosevelt's decision not to recognize Grau. While both sides claimed his trip as a victory, Welles left for Havana by plane on November 27 and resumed his post two days later.[61]

Minor disturbances broke out on the island while Welles was in the United States, but revolutionary activity seemed to be subsiding. During this quiet period, the Uruguayan minister to Cuba, Benjamín Fernández de Medina, initiated another movement for compromise. Since Welles's departure he had been acting as a self-appointed mediator with Grau's consent. Two days before the American envoy returned, Fernández de Medina optimistically announced that he had a conciliatory program that he felt most of the opposition would support. The general plan was similar to that presented in September, keeping Grau in the presidency with cabinet participation by the opposition and security for the new military organization.[62]

While the Uruguayan minister was conducting his mediation, Welles went to see Grau at his urgent request. The feud between the two men had come into the open. Grau was bitter over Welles's refusal to recognize his regime, and Welles was disgusted by Grau's inability to reach a political compromise and his attempts to have Welles replaced as ambassador. The two antagonists discussed the situation, but the widening gulf between them made the meeting futile.[63] After the meeting, Welles reported that Grau was under the influence of the worst elements in his government and would not accept any compromise unless it was imposed upon him. The ambassador then expressed his frustration and his resentment for the man and the regime which had denied him a triumphant return to Washington: "Between the individuals in the government who are seeking to create a frankly communistic government in Cuba and those who are solely in the government for the profits they can obtain, both of which elements have the upper hand and are working together, Grau remains the figurehead he has been from the beginning."[64]

Once more a crisis arose to interrupt the delicate political maneuvering. About eight hundred employees of the American-owned Compañía Cubana de Electricidad had formed a union in August 1933 and asked for recognition. When their request was repeatedly ignored, the workers decided to strike unless forty-two demands were immediately granted. Besides the strike threat, the company had other problems because of its past relations with Machado. Before his election he had helped to develop and extend the company's holdings, and under his regime the company had gained a virtual monopoly on the island's electricity. Consumers had agitated for lower rates, but the dictator refused to listen to their protestations that the company's rates were approximately twice what was then being charged in American cities. After Machado's removal, the company was naturally a target for reprisals and reform. To counteract both the workers' strike and the consumers' hostility, the company asked for government mediation to help resolve the impending strike; it also offered to make a 20 percent reduction in its residential and commercial rates.[65]

On December 6 Grau answered the company's proposition by demanding a reduction of approximately 45 percent in all rates, plus other service compensations.[66] The company protested, and Phillips feared that the Cubans intended to nationalize it. He commented wearily that the "Cuban situation has begun to boil over again. In fact, it has never ceased boiling."[67] Only Batista's intercession on December 8 prevented a direct confrontation. He ordered the company, the union, and the government to study the demands for a week before taking any further action. Although the immediate threat to the company had been averted, no solution had been found.[68]

Welles made a last desperate effort to seek a political compromise that might restore stability. He was reluctant to make any definite plans for his return, believing that the political impasse would be settled by December 12. If there were no settlement by then, he would return immediately to the United States; if some solution were found, he wanted to remain until just before Caffery's arrival. Phillips spoke with Roosevelt about the ambassador's request, and they decided that he should leave Havana by December 13 to avoid the appearance that Caffery was hurrying to Cuba immediately after his predecessor's departure.[69] Even though Welles had been given a deadline, Phillips understood his predicament, for he wrote in his diary, "Sumner feels that his prestige would be increased 100% if he could return to the Department after he had accomplished his own desire, which is to rid Cuba of Grau San Martin; otherwise he will return to the Department without the prestige of having accomplished anything."[70]

On December 9 Welles predicted optimistically that he would return to the State Department having successfully completed his assignment. Two days later, he reported that within either twenty-four or forty-eight hours, Grau would agree to resign and Mendieta would become provisional president. Suddenly Welles's enthusiasm turned to dejection. The negotiations collapsed on the afternoon of December 11, when Grau reversed his earlier decision and refused to resign.[71]

Welles's ordeal was finally over. He had gone to Cuba with instructions to prevent any situation that could cause American intervention, and he had succeeded, but not in the way he wanted to. He was to leave the island without the prestige of having maintained his cherished principle of constitutionality. He left Havana on December 13 amidst the students' rejoicing and the opposition's laments. He returned to Washington two days later and was sworn in as assistant secretary of state concerned with Latin American affairs, replacing Caffery. Phillips commented that he was "thankful to get him out of the Cuban mess for he was certainly making no helpful contribution."[72] Actually Welles was not completely "out of the Cuban mess," for he would now direct the United States' policy toward the island from the State Department.[73]

Even before Welles left Cuba, American policy-makers had shifted their attention from the island's problems to the question of inter-American affairs. As the Seventh Conference of Inter-American States, at Montevideo, Uruguay, approached, the ABC nations and Mexico began to press the United States for a policy change with regard to Cuba.[74] While Hull was en route to the conference, the Uruguayan government announced that Cuba would be permitted to attend the meeting as an equal participant, since the Uruguayans had extended formal recognition to the Grau regime.[75] Hull sent Phillips a telegram from Rio de Janeiro stating that a number of Latin American nations including Argentina and Chile were joining in a movement to recognize Grau. Reading between the lines, the acting secretary sensed that Hull feared that the Cuban issue might disrupt the conference and hoped that "something could be done towards recognition before the Conference meets."[76] Phillips sympathized with his superior and wished for "some way to get out of our present difficulties with Cuba; if only Grau San Martin would make some move acceptable to the opposition parties, we might be able to recognize him."[77]

On November 27, after Hull arrived at Montevideo, he again pressed Phillips for reasons why the United States should not recognize Grau, but Welles insisted that Grau did not have the support of the population and that he maintained order only by dictatorial methods. The feeling persisted at Montevideo that the United States was on the verge of recognizing Grau's government. When two Uruguayan newspapers reported on November 29 that Hull favored recognition, he promptly denied it. This activity had its effect on Roosevelt. Responding to the increasing Latin American pressure, the president told Phillips that if the Latin Americans wished to recognize Grau, the United States should not stand in their way. Even if the Latin Americans recognized Grau, the United States would stand on the Warm Springs statement, but Roosevelt would be ready to consider any new Cuban developments.[78]

When the preliminaries were completed, the conference opened on December 3 with a remarkable degree of cordiality. The Latin American press gave it full coverage, while some United States newspapers showed an interest, especially those of the commercially-oriented eastern seaboard. Hull led the United States delegation. He hoped to build a strong bond of inter-American cooperation by the means of reciprocal trade agreements, but first he had to contend with the Cuban delegation. Dr. Angel Alberto Giraudy headed the delegation; other members were Dr. Herminio Portell Vilá and Alfred E. Nogeira. Besides the official membership, two leaders of the Student Directorate, Carlos Prío Socarrás and Juan Antonio Rubio Padilla, also attended.[79]

Although the Cubans received a warm greeting from the other delegates, they had not prepared a formal argument against the United States' intrusion. The representatives were fervent admirers of Grau and his nationalistic program, but none had ever attended an inter-American conference or knew anything about international procedure. The Cubans seemed convinced that if they could persuade Roosevelt to abrogate the Platt Amendment, the island could resolve its own dilemma. They paid no attention to their nation's depression or to the failure of the United States to extend economic assistance. One writer present at the conference sadly commented that all "they know is that the Platt Amendment must be ended. Once that is achieved, apparently, everyone will become good, true, beautiful and happy. The Cuban delegates here are young, heroic and faithful followers of Don Quixote."[80]

Alberto Giraudy fired the first round on December 13, attacking the United States for its failure to recognize Grau and cynically charging, "If Ambassador Welles' propagating the revolution . . . is not intervention . . . , if upholding a minority group against the wishes of the people is not intervention, if surrounding the island with warships is not intervention—then the United States has never intervened in Cuba!"[81] After this outburst, Hull tried to prevent any further display on the part of the Cubans by inviting Portell Vilá to visit him at his hotel suite on the afternoon of December 18 for a discussion of the Cuban predicament. While Portell Vilá condemned Welles for inhibiting Grau's program, Hull advocated moderation, trying to convince his guest that the United States was about to change its policy toward Cuba. In spite of Hull's argument that the Cubans would be making a mistake by continuing to attack the United States, the Cuban visitor was not dissuaded.[82]

The next afternoon, the intervention question came up for debate, and Portel Vilá rose to present the Cuban argument against intervention, announcing that "Cuba was born with the congenital vice of intervention."[83] He accused the United States of forcing the new republic to accept both the Permanent Treaty and the Platt Amendment. Concluding his speech, he told his audience that the United States was still intervening through its ambassador and proclaimed, "Cuba is and shall continue to be against intervention."[84]

While the Cubans were attacking the United States' interventionist policy at Montevideo and Hull was waging a counterattack to convince other Latin Americans that the Roosevelt administration was correcting past inequities, the American embassy in Havana was receiving new personnel. H. Freeman Matthews, a career diplomat who assisted Caffery during his tenure as assistant secretary, went to the Cuban capital on December 5, 1933.[85] Seven days later Ellis O. Briggs assumed his post as second secretary.[86] Briggs later reflected on his arrival at his first Cuban assignment, writing that "the Pearl of the Antilles, torn by revolution, resembled a madhouse."[87]

Jefferson Caffery directed the embassy's affairs. Born on December 1, 1886, in Lafayette, Louisiana, he attended Tulane University and was admitted to the Louisiana bar in 1909. He gave up the legal profession after two years and joined the foreign service in 1911. The new representative was a bachelor, tall, slender, dark complexioned, soft-spoken, and smartly dressed, and he appeared ideally suited for his new assignment. After twenty-three years of experience, Caffery had developed a cosmopolitan outlook and had the additional advantage of speaking fluent Spanish. As a career diplomat, he had an almost uncanny ability of gravitating to people who held power.

On May 6, 1933, Hull offered to appoint him to the Cuban ambassadorship after Welles had completed his mission, and Caffery gladly accepted. Since Machado's overthrow prolonged Welles's stay, Caffery temporarily returned to the State Department as assistant secretary. He arrived in Havana on December 18, although not as ambassador. He had ambassadorial powers, but Roosevelt had designated him special representative of the president until the nonrecognition issue was resolved.[88]

When Caffery and his staff began to work, they found conditions as chaotic as ever, but the events at Montevideo, the change in embassy personnel, and the Christmas season had brought a temporary lull. This short interlude enabled Caffery to formulate his program; he reaffirmed the nonrecognition policy and expressed his concern over communist tendencies in Cuba and the hastiness of Grau's radical decrees. Once Caffery had made it clear that the United States would not grant recognition, political activity increased. Grau again considered resignation, Guiteras demanded further movements to the left, and the rift between Batista and the regime became more pronounced.[89]

While the Cubans and the new emissary searched for the elusive political solution, Roosevelt was in the midst of rejecting the interventionist policy. At the Woodrow Wilson banquet on December 28, the president spoke about the prospect for world peace. Roosevelt was reacting to the national sentiment against international confrontation and entanglement.[90] He alluded to the achievements of Hull and the Latin Americans at Montevideo, but he went further in his plea for peace, stating that the "definite policy of the United States from now on is one opposed to armed intervention."[91] He went on to point out that the United States was not alone in its obligation to maintain constitutional governments, for this was the duty of every sovereign state. Looking back on 1933, Charles Beard concluded that "the year ended with foreign policy of non-entanglement, neutrality, and peace for the United States reaffirmed and reinforced."[92]

The new year brought no such stability to Cuba, as Caffery indicated on January 10 in his assessment of the Grau regime. The envoy agreed with his predecessor's conclusions that "all the better classes" of Cuban society regarded Grau's government as inefficient, inept, and unpopular. Caffery also believed that the regime was "supported only by the army and ignorant masses who have been misled by utopian promises."[93] In spite of this negative assessment, the emissary did not think that Grau could be overthrown unless either he willingly resigned or the United Sttaes intervened militarily. Grau had the support of the army. As far as the political opposition was concerned, Caffery found "little tendency to compromise and an insistence that the only way to clear up this situation is for us to intervene. They refuse to believe our insistent declarations against intervention."[94] For since none of the "better classes" supported his regime, Grau relied more and more on radical advisers like Guiteras. Even this radical movement did not help the opposition to unify, for, according to Caffery, each group mistrusted the other's motives. In order to end the political turmoil, Grau called for elections, but this did not appear to be the solution, for the opposition would not participate.[95]

Caffery met with Grau and Batista on the evening of January 10 to discuss the political situation. The president thought that he could hold fair elections, but he declared that if the opposition did not accept his offer, he would resign. After that meeting, Caffery was doubtful that such a proposal would be accepted. He did not think that the students and the cabinet would allow Grau to quit or that the opposition would approve Grau's election scheme.[96]

Since a solution could not be found through the various political factions, Caffery began to look to Batista to impose order. Unlike Welles, Caffery immediately won the army leader's friendship. On January 13 Batista bluntly asked Caffery what conditions the United States wanted met before it would recognize the government, and the envoy repeated Roosevelt's demand for a government supported by the Cuban majority. Batista had ignored this proposal when Welles was ambassador, but now he realized that Grau would have to leave the presidency before the United States would grant recognition.[97]

During the next two frantic days, Caffery worked energetically to persuade Mendieta to accept the presidency. Mendieta still vacillated, however, and Caffery feared that Cuba would be plunged into greater anarchy. Caffery nervously watched the power of Guiteras increase after the Student Directorate deserted Grau on January 6. He saw the government tacitly encourage the seizure of sugar companies. On January 10 all the land owned by Machado supporters was expropriated, and the government made preparations to distribute it among the workers. Finally, Caffery witnessed the seizure of the Cuban Electric Company after a strike on January 13 that left Havana without electricity for three hours. The next day Grau appointed an interventor to manage the company's plants in the employees' interests, and the strikers returned to work, literally controlling the operation. These radical actions increased the growing antagonism between Batista and Guiteras, and the schism between their supporters grew even wider. The situation seemed headed for anarchy again, but in the early hours of January 15 Grau announced his resignation. He retired to his home as a private citizen late that afternoon.[98]

Grau had ruled for 127 chaotic days, facing enormous resistance. In spite of this adversity, the revolutionary government had made itself the champion of frustrated Cuban aspirations by enacting more social and economic reforms than had ever been passed in the republic's history. The eight-hour day, the 50% law, a minimum wage for sugar cutters, the creation of the ministry of labor, recognition for the unions, and university autonomy were only a few of the measures that exhibited the government's desire to correct the injustices of past administrations. In addition, some of Grau's other decrees had highly nationalistic overtones. The seizure of the electric company and of two sugar mills owned by the Cuban-American Sugar Company demonstrated the government's willingness to act in behalf of its nationals against United States concerns. The suspension of the Chase National Bank's loan payments, negotiated by Machado, received the nation's approval, and the removal of Chadbourne as head of the Sugar Export

Corporation proved conclusively that the Cubans did not want a United States citizen directing the sales of its principal export and thereby controlling the vitality of the national economy.[99]

Despite this strong nationalistic and patriotic appeal, the government failed to consolidate the various revolutionary factions for the Grau regime represented not only a change in government, but also a revolution between generations, with the students constantly reminding the older establishment that it was responsible for Cuba's plight. While the radicals charged the traditional leadership with failure, they could not form a homogeneous program or party capable of maintaining a viable regime. Partly because Grau lacked a coherent economic policy, could not win opposition participation, and followed a tortuous course in internal politics, he had to rely increasingly on Batista's armed forces for support.[100]

With all these factors working against it, how did Grau's regime last as long as it did? Possibly Hubert Herring explained the reasons best when he wrote, "His was a Cuban movement; it sprang from the island itself; it was neither made nor blessed by the United States. Many who would normally have turned upon him were restrained by this fact."[101] In the midst of the chaos and confusion, a government had emerged that expressed and promoted the peoples' growing wishes for reform and renovation.[102]

This popular following did not have the strength to unify the diverse segments of the nation. The basic inconsistencies of the Grau administration gave the opposition, no matter how disorganized, ample grounds for attack from both the right and the left. The Communists bitterly assailed Grau because he was not a true revolutionary but merely another middle-class bureaucrat who had no intention of altering the fundamental fabric of Cuban society. To demonstrate its hostility, the Communist Party increased its insurrectionary activities in the cities and helped establish soviets in the sugar mills across the countryside. Opposition from the right complemented the enmity from the left. As Grau's decrees became more and more radical, the island's various business interests became increasingly vociferous in their antipathy to his regime. The major political factions that had been turned out of office also demonstrated their antagonism, but they did not lead the assault to topple the government. The old officer corps initiated the first serious revolt in October, and in November, some disenchanted soldiers and the A.B.C. moved against Grau. These attacks weakened the government, but Grau miraculously continued to hold power.[103]

Only when Batista actively joined the opposition was Grau's final ouster assured. The previous government had collapsed because once the army had withdrawn its support from Machado, the sergeants had refused to support Céspedes. The people, who were suffering most from the depression, were virtually ignored except when they echoed the ruling cliques in their demand for Machado's removal. Grau's demise followed the same pattern. When Batista saw a movement far more radical than he could support, when he realized the student's hostility might threaten his life, and when Caffery refused to alter the nonrecognition policy, Batista swung toward the prevailing sentiment for replacing the Grau regime.[104]

Welles stood squarely in the middle of the conflict because of his efforts of his mediation upon Machado, his role in establishing the Céspedes regime, and his staunch opposition against Grau. The ambassador justified his recommendation against recognition on the grounds that Grau lacked the necessary support for a popular and enduring government. This rationale accounted only for part of the ambassador's aversion; his reasons for recommending nonrecognition went much deeper. Welles subscribed to a rigid belief in constitutionalism and the orderly processes of change in government through elections. The Grau regime directly contradicted the ambassador's belief in peaceful change. Furthermore, Welles had aided in the formation of the Céspedes coalition and refused to negotiate with the radical elements in Cuba, as they objected to any dealings with him. Finally—and probably most damning—Welles simply failed to grasp the nature of the events that brought a man like Grau to power. Welles's pessimistic dispatches clearly indicated that he did not perceive the frustrations of the Cuban people and their crying need for social, economic, and political reform.[105]

Welles's importance was due to more than his personal resentment of Grau. The ambassador's refusal to grant recognition served as a catalytic agent that worked to the advantage of both sides in the domestic turmoil. As long as Welles effectively opposed the regime, the antagonistic sectors felt that Grau would fall. At the same time, Grau and his adherents could blame the United States for its problems and attack Welles personally for his alleged complicity in the conspiracies against the regime. Since the government was floundering without any consistent program, it needed this patriotic appeal against the encroachment of the American ambassador to help preserve its base of support. Welles became not only the man enforcing the policy, but also a tool for the warring factions to use as they wished.[106]

While the various factions tried to attain power and Welles conducted the embassy's affairs, Roosevelt sought to create a consistent policy toward the island. Despite his strong stance against armed involvement, Roosevelt adhered to Welles's policy of nonrecognition. Even after the battle at the hotel and the proddings of Hull, Phillips, and Daniels in favor of granting recognition, the president supported his ambassador. If he had done otherwise, he would have had to repudiate his representative and personal friend, and he was not prepared to consider such an action. He showed his support of Welles by allowing him to draft the Warm Springs declaration. Even in the midst of this reaffirmation of the nonrecognition policy, Roosevelt was moving slowly away from an interventionist policy. The Montevideo success, the continuing chaos on the island, and the isolationist sentiment at home forced Roosevelt to reassess the Cuban policy, and by the end of the year, the president had firmly committed the United States to nonintervention.[107]

In spite of these subtle movements toward a policy change, the various charges and countercharges against Welles and Grau clouded the fundamental issues. Not only were both men individuals, but they also personified the existing United States policy and the Cuban revolutionary struggle. The two individuals based the conduct of their affairs on entirely different philosophical and practical assumptions. The United States through its ambassador strove hopelessly for stability and order. Grau represented the nationalistic forces within the island that were crying for the justice so long denied them by an oppressive regime and for the livelihoods lost in a cruel and impersonal economic depression. To implement a program of massive renovation required a Herculean effort of all Cubans; such a program, however, was hopelessly bogged down in the traditional antagonism and bitter squabbles of the different political factions that were vying for supremacy.

The resignation of a president and the dismal failure of an ambassador's mission resulted from these conflicting issues. Grau might have survived had he compromised, but his adherents refused to give the opposition a voice in the government and at the same time demanded more and more radical reforms. Welles might have brought about recognition had the Céspedes coalition announced its support for Grau, but again the antagonistic forces would not consider such a proposal. As the result of the rigidity of all parties, Grau stumbled along from day to day, never certain that he would be president the following morning. When he finally resigned, he placed the blame squarely on the United States, declaring angrily on January 17, 1934, "I fell because Washington willed it."[108]

Many commentators have made equally harsh judgments,[109] but what of the inflexibility of the Cubans? Certainly Welles and his successor would not have persisted in their position without concrete evidence to support their views. During the four short months of the Grau regime, although Welles and Grau helped to shape the succession of events, they did not dictate the outcome. Both were part of larger struggles occurring simultaneously in their respective countries. The Roosevelt administration was attempting to alter a relationship with Cuba that gave the United States virtual control over the island's economic and political life, while the Cubans were seeking to establish their own identity and determine their own destiny. Both nations were trying desperately to liquidate the past, but one was moving too slowly, the other too fast. The tragedy of defeat—the tragedy of Welles and Grau—was that they were unable to cope with all the complexities of an extraordinarily complicated situation.

5

The Mendieta Regime:
The Triumph of Disorder

Grau's sudden resignation on January 15 shocked the Cuban political factions. They had become accustomed to constant rumors of an impending resignation, but once it came, no one had a clear mandate to assume the presidency. Batista and Caffery preferred Mendieta, while Guiteras and the students, supported by the navy and the police, backed Grau's secretary of agriculture, Carlos Hevia. Only when Mendieta publicly pledged his support for Hevia was the momentary deadlock resolved. The radicals had propelled a relatively unknown member of Grau's cabinet into the presidency, but they faced the hopeless task of finding a coalition powerful enough to support their choice.[1] As for Hevia, he expressed bewilderment: "I don't know what I am going to do now. Wait until tomorrow."[2]

The following afternoon, with only a few close friends present, Hevia took the oath of office. The new president reflected the dichotomy between the Cuban political generations. Only thirty-three years old, he associated himself closely with the radical students. Despite these affiliations, he had attended high school in New York and boasted about having received his college degree from the United States Naval Academy in 1919. After returning to Cuba, he had achieved a reputation as a competent engineer, and he had close business connections in the island's sugar industry for the next thirteen years; at the same time he grew to oppose Machado's regime, and in 1931 he led an abortive military revolt. Soon after Grau became president, Hevia joined his cabinet. With this background, he now confronted the impossible task of forming a viable government, for despite Mendieta's public declaration of support, other opponents, including some members of his own party, denounced the new administration. Hevia had been pushed into office as a test of strength, and he would lose his position in the same way. Unfortunately for the new president, his downfall had actually started before he had a chance to assume his duties.[3]

While Hevia searched for cabinet ministers, Batista and Guiteras fought for political supremacy. The military leader quickly realized that Hevia could not win the confidence of either the commercial circles or the Céspedes coalition, but this lack of support was not enough to drive Grau's followers from power. Batista had to gain the navy's acquiescence, and once this political maneuver was successfully arranged on January 17, Hevia's removal was assured. To forestall it, Guiteras tried to foment a general strike, but Batista thwarted his scheme. Early in the morning of January 18 the struggle for power between the two political contenders was resolved, and Hevia left office, sending his letter of resignation to the man directly responsible—Batista. A new record for brevity of office had been established for Cuban presidents: Hevia lasted only thirty-nine hours.[4] The *Miami Herald* sarcastically remarked, "The method of changing a president in Cuba has been solved. You sneak up behind him and cry 'Boo.' "[5]

With Hevia's removal, Secretary of State, Manuel Márquez Sterling, temporarily assumed the presidency and announced that the political factions would meet in the morning to choose a successor. The outcome was a foregone conclusion; after only one hour's debate, Carlos Mendieta y Montefur, colonel in the Spanish-American War and political leader of the Unión Nacionalista, became president.[6] After the politicians expressed their approval, Ruby Hart Phillips reported, "that island went crazy with excitement and relief. The public crowded around the Palace for blocks; they cheered until they were hoarse. They cheered President Roosevelt, Ambassador Caffery and Assistant Secretary of State Welles. In fact, Cuba has again recognized the United States."[7] For a brief moment, the prospect of peace replaced political turmoil.

The sixty-one-year-old Mendieta had been involved in Cuban politics for a quarter of a century. His reputation for honesty and courage was well known, but these credentials did not assure the island's domestic tranquillity. Radicals immediately tagged him as a conservative because of his close association with the old politicians and with the American embassy. His greatest weakness, however, came from his own personality. The new president suffered from an inability to make firm decisions, compounded by an almost obsessive desire to win sympathy from every segment of the divided Cuban society. Unwilling or unable to take bold actions against his adversaries, Mendieta gave the impression that the government was about to collapse, and his vacillation stimulated the opposition in its efforts to topple the regime.[8]

Caffery did not concern himself with the new president's personal deficiencies. Instead of opposing the new regime, the envoy reversed the United States' policy of the preceding four months by recommending recognition on the day Mendieta took office. To hasten the recognition procedure, Hull, who was returning from the Montevideo Conference, arranged to stop at Key West, Florida, in order to meet with Caffery. Although Hull refused to give reporters an official statement after the conference, he left the definite impression that recognition was imminent.[9]

While Hull continued on his way to Washington, Caffery sent additional dispatches to the State Department, asserting that Mendieta's accession was having a stabilizing effect on the island. The people were celebrating, Mendieta was maintaining order, and he had won the allegiance of every major faction on the island except for the extreme left and the old Machado advocates. Grau's unexpected departure for Mexico improved the situation even more, for with their most charismatic leader out of the country, the opposition forces had to cast about for new guidance.[10]

The optimism expressed by the old politicians, the opposition's confusion, the American embassy's support, and the strong pleas from the United States news media quickly determined Roosevelt's course of action. He recognized the Cuban government on January 23. When Caffery extended formal recognition on the following afternoon, most Cubans rejoiced over the dramatic turn of events.[11] Others, like Josephus Daniels, also congratulated Roosevelt; even the Grau admirers in Mexico, said Daniels, admitted "that you have taken a step that will not only help Cuba but strengthen sound Pan Americanism."[12] In the midst of this widespread approval, the news media in the United States urged further action. The *Baltimore Sun* welcomed Roosevelt's decision, but strongly recommended the negotiation of a new commercial treaty. Other newspapers and magazines echoed this opinion and also advocated abrogation of the Platt Amendment and other changes in the political treaty. Clearly, recognition was only the beginning of a program for the island's revival.[13]

United States recognition greatly strengthened Mendieta's chances for success, but he confronted a multitude of problems within his administration. Both Cuban and American commentators viewed the establishment of his government as a personal triumph for Batista over Guiteras, and Caffery reported that many of Batista's former enemies were now praising his work.[14] After interviewing the colonel at his headquarters, Damon Runyon told his readers in the *Miami Herald* that everyone in Cuba "admits that Fulgencio Batista is the boss, though not everybody in Cuba is altogether happy about it."[15]

Besides worrying about Batista's growing prestige, Mendieta had to placate his political allies. When the A.B.C. leader Martínez Saenz returned to the island, he and the president embraced, while a cheering crowd roared its approval. Martínez Saenz pledged his party's allegiance and as a result was appointed secretary of the treasury. In spite of the A.B.C. loyalty pledge, however, the new president frequently had to contend with the party's threats of withdrawing from the coalition because it opposed some government programs; the military's growing authority was also a problem. Thus, while the military and the A.B.C. strove for political advantage within the regime, Mendieta's personal power gradually corroded.[16]

In spite of internal bickering, Mendieta acted on February 3 to revoke the Constitution of 1901, and Machado's subsequent amendments to it, in favor of his own provisional statutes until a constituent assembly met. The new laws closely resembled the old constitution, but there were a few significant innovations. The constitutional rights of individuals were strongly reaffirmed; political offenders no longer faced a possible death sentence; the *ley de fuga*, which allowed a guard to shoot a prisoner who was supposedly trying to escape, was abolished; women over twenty-one received the right to vote; a council of state with from fifty to eighty members was established to function as a legislative body; and the executive's prerogatives were curtailed. Three days after this proclamation the government added Decree No. 3 to thwart future labor unrest. This decree empowered the administration to prohibit workers from striking until after a compulsory waiting period and also placed limitations on sympathy strikes. Any labor union that violated this law would be dissolved. Finally, in order to appease political offenders, on February 9 Mendieta declared an amnesty for all the participants in the upheavals of 1933, with the exception of Machado's supporters.[17]

These actions sustained the impression that Mendieta's assumption of power was having a stabilizing effect on the nation, but grumbling malcontents quickly appeared. Like Grau's, Mendieta's regime was soon attacked by an amorphous group of antagonistic forces. Labor soon responded negatively to what it considered a reactionary government. A small but vocal chorus of left-wing students and other young radical intellectuals openly opposed the regime. Since these groups no longer had a voice in the government, they turned to terrorism as a political weapon.[18]

Once the violence intensified, Guiteras became the government's chief source of anxiety. He was already something of a legend for his escapes from the various traps that Batista's soldiers set for him. Finally the police arrested him on August 8 for plotting the overthrow of the government. After protests by his supporters, a special court called then *Tribunales de Urgencia,* established to prosecute terrorists, quickly absolved him of the conspiracy charge, but the police still held him in custody for unlawful possession of firearms. Then without any explanation this charge was dropped, and on August 16 a group of enthusiastic supporters triumphantly escorted their hero home. Undaunted by the arrest, Guiteras continued his daring defiance of government authority, and on September 18 Caffery expressed his grave concern about the radical's future plans: "I believe it to be true that Guiteras will endeavor to find means to assassinate Batista and other chiefs of the military forces particularly disliked by the Autenticos."[20] This possibility haunted government officials throughout 1934 and during the early months of 1935.

But Guiteras's intrigues against the government were not Mendieta's immediate concern. As soon as labor was convinced that Mendieta would be the next president , a general strike was called, and shortly after his inauguration, government employees and electrical workers quit work. Later the National Railway Brotherhood defied a presidential decree prohibiting strikes for ninety days and walked off their jobs on January 28. At first Mendieta did not know how to respond to these violations of his labor decrees, and throughout the early part of February a veritable flood of workers joined in the movement to discredit the government. But their efforts failed; on February 9 the government announced a special emergency law authorizing the state to end strikes, and the movement began at once to subside. Thanks to the new legislation and to Batista's personal antagonism toward the work stoppages, the armed forces moved with precision to end the labor disruptions.[21] Still, economic disorders prevailed throughout the island, and Ruby Hart Phillips wrote dejectedly, "Really, nothing has been done. Strike after strike has been called, conference after conference to settle this or that without the slightest result. Mendieta is apparently trying to please everybody and the result may bear out the fable of the man who tried to please everybody and only succeeded in drowning his donkey. I hope Mendieta doesn't drown the island."[22] Phillips had correctly analyzed part of the dismal picture, but she overlooked one significant fact. Labor could disrupt the administration's effort to restore stability, but by themselves the unions could not muster the necessary forces to topple the regime.

While the disruptions of labor wreaked havoc, other groups organized for the specific purpose of removing Mendieta. Although Grau had departed, his followers met on February 8 and formed the Partido Revolucionario Cubano, commonly referred to as the Auténticos. As the party of the "authentic" revolution, it advocated social and economic reform, but the driving force behind the movement was political, for the party's principal objective was to place Grau in the presidency at the next general elections. Caffery recognized the importance of the ex-president's influence and carefully watched the party's operations. After observing its activities for a month, he concluded that Grau still had tremendous popular appeal and that even without his direction, the party was steadily increasing its membership. While the leadership disavowed the use of terrorism, Caffery thought that the Auténticos' persistent attacks against Mendieta's government were inciting others to move in that direction. He hoped that the Mendieta regime would gain popular support before the Auténticos became too powerful, for he feared that Grau's return might stimulate the opposing forces to more aggressive action.[23]

While the Auténticos initiated their campaign against Mendieta, the Communist Party directed its efforts toward the same end.

Because of the widespread poverty and political uncertainty, Cuba was fertile ground for communism. The party's activities centered in Havana through its domination of the island's most powerful left-wing union confederation, the Confederación Obrera de Cuba, led by the Communist activist, Lázaro Peña. But its organization soon spread to the sugar mills, plantations, mines, and public utility companies. Since foreign interests operated many of these enterprises, they were foci for the nationalism and class consciousness that had arisen during Grau's tenure. Reporting the party's activities as early as January 29, 1934, Caffery attributed its power to the desperate economic conditions and hoped that once prosperity returned, the movement would dissipate.[24]

Though the ambassador had accurately identified some of the causes of the party's growth, he failed to grasp the most significant reasons for its impact. The Communist Party had been officially organized in 1925, but Machado quickly outlawed it. Forced to operate secretly, the Communists became identified with the opposition to the tyrant and joined the vanguard of social reform. Not only did the party attract followers from within the labor movement, but it also managed to win support from some leading intellectuals and from an increasing number of young teachers, writers, and professional people.[26] The experts chosen by the United States Foreign Policy Association to study Cuban social and economic conditions in 1934 admitted that the Communist influence was not confined to the small membership that accepted the party's rigid discipline. The party developed its disproportionate strength "through the hundreds of thousands who sympathize more or less clearly with Communist ideas and aims. These have welcomed communism as a redeeming force which might lead them out of the wilderness of poverty and distress which Cuba had become."[26] To demonstrate further the egalitarian nature of the party's appeal, the Communists paid special attention to the Negro's inferior position in Cuban society, holding out to him the hope for greater participation in the island's affairs.[27]

With the opposition mobilizing its forces, a clash with the government was inevitable. The first organized confrontation between the two groups began on March 5, 1934, when the Havana tobacco workers, who had been out of work for several weeks, protested against the government's use of troops to protect strikebreakers loading cigars bound for New York. Dock workers struck in sympathy, followed by telephone employees and by bakery, ice, and milk deliverymen. Unlike the relatively spontaneous upheavals of August 1933, this strike was politically inspired. The Communists, led by the National Confederation of Labor, engineered the movement, and at the peak of the strike more than 200,000 workers participated.[28] At first Mendieta did not know how to respond to the work stoppage, but after the government survived the initial impact, he took drastic action. On March 7 to crush the strike, Mendieta suspended the constitutional guarantees that he had recently sworn to maintain. He also signed the National Defense Act, which was specifically designed to cope with the strike situation and the Communist agitation. Under it any attempt to establish another form of government on the island became a criminal act, and foreigners who perpetrated any offense against the public order would be deported. Following these decrees, the army sent strikebreakers to the docks to load ships. The government promised the striking stevedores that they could return to work without penalty but warned that if they chose not to do so, they would lose their jobs. The government's scheme succeeded; the laborers returned to the docks on March 10, and other businesses resumed normal activity. The government, backed by 500 heavily armed strikebreakers and the army, had won the first round.[29]

Caffery applauded these acts, for he believed that Mendieta must stand firm to avoid being removed from office by Communist agitators. Some disturbances continued but Caffery happily reported the government's survival and noted that commercial activity was increasing. Other American commentators, however, saw no reason for rejoicing. *Newsweek* reported that the strike movement had dissipated but that this lull did not signify a return to stability. Another critic, Clara Porset, reinforced this viewpoint, arguing that Mendieta's regime blocked any constructive reform program and forced laborers to work against their will while Batista and Caffery controlled the government's movements from behind the scenes.[30] The *New Republic* of March 21 summed up the dissenters' frustrations concerning the United States policy toward Cuba: "Looking back over recent months, it is clear that President Roosevelt has not, in relation to Cuba, lived up to his promise not to meddle in the internal affairs of Latin America."[31]

The government not only faced external opposition, it also had to

cope with internal friction. After Mendieta assumed power, the
scramble for patronage began. Caffery wrote, "competition is so
vigorous that many members of the concentration forces are more
interested in job hunting than they are in the welfare of the
Island."[32] Although Mendieta had not participated in this patronage struggle, some of his followers and the A.B.C. were the
worst offenders. The petty bickering over governmental
appointments had created additional animosity within the regime,
and the Auténticos were hoping that it would ultimately cause an
irreparable breach in the government coalition.[33]

In this state of extreme confusion, Caffery wrote that Mendieta's
vacillation was adding to the political uncertainty. Because of the
president's inability to make firm decisions, he was losing popularity and prestige. Caffery did not know what would result from this
indecisiveness; he wrote, "Were it expedient for me to see him
everyday, and were it expedient for me to advise him on all
political subjects, I believe that matters political might work out
better than they do." But, he added, obviously he could not
perform such a role.[34]

Mendieta was painfully aware of the constant criticism leveled
at him for the government's inaction. In response, he announced his
reform proposals on April 18, pledging to remove the last vestiges
of Machado's regime and to adopt a body of advanced social and
economic legislation. Not only would he increase the quota
established by Grau's 50% law, he would deal with unemployment
by distributing state lands to farmers as homesteads and would aid
their settlement with loans through an agricultural bank. Mendieta
even hoped to resolve the vicious patronage battle by initiating
some kind of administrative career civil service. Finally he directed
his attention to agrarian reform, including such areas as protection
of the small sugar planters, agricultural diversification, and
cooperative farming.[35]

The conservative president had outlined a broad and even
radical program, but first peace had to be restored. The provisional
government realized that the only way to acomplish this goal was
to reestablish constitutional legitimacy as quickly as possible. On
April 17 the government decided to hold elections for a constituent
assembly before the end of 1934. On July 10 after almost three
additional months of discussions between the council of state and
the cabinet, the members approved a law extending suffrage to

women and announcing that all Cubans over twenty years of age should register with the electoral census. In order to carry out the decree's provisions, a superior electoral tribunal was established to conduct the census and the elections. To the electorate which totaled 1,650,598, the government announced in late August that elections for a constituent assembly were scheduled for December 30, 1934. With this declaration, the government began to set up the necessary machinery to take the electoral census, and the enumerators started work in late September. In spite of constant delays, the government reported a month later that nine-tenths of the eligible Cubans had been inscribed on the rolls.[36]

The apparent success of the government's efforts soon faded, for ten days later the cabinet unanimously decided to postpone the elections until March 1935. When Mendieta approved the decision, some of the opposition demanded his resignation because he had promised elections before the year's end and had broken his promise. Mendieta answered that honest elections could not be held because political parties were not sufficiently organized and the government did not have adequate time to set up the necessary voting machinery. The president had every intention of fulfilling his election pledge, but he thought that his delay would give the island a better chance to conduct fair elections.[37]

While the country prepared for elections, the various political parties began to take concrete form. Within the government coalition, Miguel Mariano Gómez, son of Cuba's second president and leader of his own political faction, increased his influence in the administration. Another prominent political leader, Mario Menocal, former president of the republic, supported the incumbent regime. Even the Liberal Party, discredited by long association with Machado, renewed its efforts to win respectability. By 1935 politicians had begun to remember its former voting appeal and were vying for its support.[38]

These political factions still backed the government, but Mendieta lost the support of one of his earliest and staunchest adherents. In late June the A.B.C. decided to withdraw from the government coalition. Ever since Mendieta's inauguration, the party had steadily lost influence in government counsels, while the military increased its dominance. Under these conditions, the party felt that it had no choice but to retire from the coalition. At first the A.B.C. refrained from attacking the incumbent regime, but by the end of the year Martínez Saenz had taken his party into the opposition camp.[39]

To counteract this loss of support, the government made overtures to the Auténticos, but when Grau returned to the island in May, such an alliance proved impossible. Caffery reported on June 2 that Grau was already talking of elections before the end of the year in order to dole out patronage to his hungry followers.[40] According to the ambassador, "it is obviously a fact that he is miserable about being out of office."[41] Once Grau resumed his activities, the Auténticos expanded their campaign against the government and demanded its resignation, but on September 27 just when the party seemed to be making progress in its new assault, Grau left the island once again. His followers claimed that the government had not given him adequate guarantees for his personal safety, but the Auténticos neglected to mention that Grau also needed medical attention. They still castigated the government vociferously, but without its leader, the party lost some of its cohesiveness.[42]

Not only was Mendieta confronted by opposition from the organized political parties; the government also faced continued resistance from the students. Early in May the university students voted to return to classes and banish communism from the premises, but by fall, they had reversed their moderate course. On the first anniversary of the sergeants' revolt, the students expressed their discontent with the government by burning Batista in effigy. Later in the month, student groups became even more extreme and declared that if Mendieta did not resign, they would fight the regime with every means at their disposal. Since Grau had granted the university autonomy, Mendieta refused to intervene in the hostile demonstrations. While the student agitated, educational activity remained at a virtual standstill, as it had during Machado's last days.[43]

Students were not the only ones to manifest open resistance to the government. On August 21 Batista crushed an attempted coup d'etat by two former military allies. Besides this direct assault on the military, strikes continued to plague the island. On August 11 postal and telegraph employees walked off their jobs, demanding payment of salary arrears. Repeating its actions in the March strike, the government employed troops and strikebreakers to continue service and threatened strikers with dismissal if they did not return to work. Some employees began trickling back to their posts, but the vast majority refused to accept Mendieta's ultimatum and stopped the restoration of telegraph and postal service by a campaign of sabotage and by stealing essential equipment. By the end of the month the government and the employees finally reached an agreement, but on the strikers' terms. Although service returned to normal, Mendieta had to abandon his promise to fire all those who refused to go back to their posts after the government's directive, and this cost him still more prestige.[44]

The Communists decided to capitalize on the disorder by taking independent action, and they planned an ambitious general strike for October 8. Led by the National Confederation of Labor, they succeeded in paralyzing most of Havana's transportation network for a time, but the government's troop deployment and the hostility of rival labor unions spelled doom for their effort. The Communist scheme failed, but not before one person died and fifteen more were wounded in what proved to be needless bloodshed.[45]

These continuing crises in all quarters necessitated frequent alignments in the cabinet, but the government coalition remained surprisingly consistent. The traditional political parties plus the military alliance clearly held political power. With the exception of the A.B.C., the groups that Grau had excluded from his government now occupied the presidential palace. The old politicians had replaced the revolutionary advocates; more conservative Cuban leadership had triumphed over those who wished to destroy the existing regime.

In spite of the recurrent government crises, the opposition was rendered powerless by the Cuban political tradition of disunity. When the A.B.C. defected from the government coalition, the radicals gained a powerful ally and claimed that the Mendieta regime was composed solely of conservative factions. Even with this additional ammunition, however, the antagonists could not drive Mendieta from office. Like the various factions that had opposed Grau, the new opposition could not unite against a common foe, and every group took its place at a different point on the political spectrum. Divided by political idealogy and by the rival ambitions of their leaders, the antagonistic sectors—Auténticos, A.B.C., Communists, and the multitude of other nameless cliques—could not find the magic formula for cooperation against the Mendieta regime.[46]

Besides the historic antagonism among the opposition factions, each group faced its own internal division and disillusionment. The rivalry for leadership in the A.B.C. was causing an intraparty schism. The latent animosity between the conservative and radical labor unions was impossible to reconcile. Some opposition leaders dejectedly felt that the revolution was dead and only anarchy remained.[47] The *Miami Herald* reflected this growing sense of frustration on December 19: "Cuba is in her normal state of unrest. Soldiers are on duty in Havana following bombing, terrorism and rumors of revolution. The outs forever plot to attain power, the ins scheme to remain in control. Poor Cuba has been the victim of American blunders, her own extravagant and crooked government, and the violence of constant rebellion, plus disruptive economics. Cuba is a problem."[48]

The effects of political chaos appeared in an upsurge of violence. On March 29 the Havana chief of police was nearly assassinated and by late April Caffery reported with disgust that bombing had become a business, for many Cubans had learned how to make explosive devices during Machado's regime and were now putting their knowledge to use again.[49] Caffery reported that "a great many of them [terrorists] have found a means of livelihood in this business and are seemingly ready to place or throw bombs according to a readily obtainable schedule of prices."[50] In such an unstable atmosphere, the slightest provocation could have disastrous results. When the government declared a legal holiday on May 1, 1934, International Labor Day, 10,000 demonstrators marched in a Havana parade. Someone fired a shot and nervous soldiers began firing into the crowd while the marchers scurried for cover. Even tragic incidents like this one did not drive Mendieta to act. While he refused to punish violators of the peace, conditions grew still worse.[51]

Mendieta remained steadfastly opposed to drastic prosecution of terrorism until June 15, when it directly threatened him. That afternoon at a luncheon honoring his administration, the president rose to address his audience and a bomb planted in a stairway directly behind him exploded. Two soldiers were killed, five marines wounded, and Mendieta and a cabinet members were slightly injured by bomb fragments. That evening he enacted one of the most drastic public order laws in the republic's history. The Decree-Law of Social Defense and Public Order imposed the death penalty on those who injured anyone in a terrorist attack. It prohibited the manufacture and sale of explosives and levied severe penalties on anyone who provoked political disorder, attended unauthorized political gatherings, or injured—or even in-sulted—government officials. To enforce this broad decree, the administration established a special urgency court, which was authorized to act without regard for ordinary rules of evidence or procedure. Once this tribunal handed down a sentence, no appeal to any other court was permitted.[52]

Mendieta had finally taken a step toward halting terrorism, but enforcing the new decree was another matter, and terroristic activity intensified throughout the rest of 1934. During celebration of the first anniversary of the September revolt, over fifty bombs exploded in the capital. Another urgency court was established on September 18 to handle the increasing load of terrorists' trials, but as Caffery explained, the judiciary's internal weaknesses had been largely responsible for the government's inability to cope with problems of violence: "Judges in the past have been so intimidated by threats of personal violence that the majority of the terrorists have almost immediately been set free, and . . . in some cases have been again captured committing further crimes, and again set free."[54] The young radicals had remained free from prosecution for so long that they brazenly defied the law. Although the government threatened to hold suspected terrorists without bail, Caffery concluded that its pronouncements were being brushed aside by the criminals, for Havana's inhabitants "by this time know only too well the Civil Government's lack of virtue of courage."[55]

On November 9 the ambassador reported that he did not know of one incident in which any terrorist of an important political faction had been convicted by the courts,[56] for judges sentenced only those people who had no political connections. Appalled by this state of affairs, Caffery declared on November 12 "that if the Government would round-up all the well-known terrorists in the Island, say a maximum of 200 individuals, and hold them in jail, the terrorists' situation would automatically be cleared up and it would probably not be necessary to kill a single terrorist in order to bring that about."[57] But at this time Mendieta did not wish to answer terrorist action with his own supervised repression.

Only Batista consistently received the ambassador's approval. Caffery believed that many groups in Cuba had changed their opinions of him. Instead of regarding him as the radical upstart who had led the September revolt, in Caffery's opinion, the Cuban public now realized that "no Government, this or any other, could last a day, if opposed by Batista."[58] Even Mendieta openly acknowledged his debt to Batista's support, and on April 16 at Camp Columbia he told his audience that the military commander had saved the country from disorder and anarchy. The alliance between Batista and Mendieta, forged by necessity, had become almost a symbiotic relationship, whereby the president relied on the power of the military to quell disorders and Batista depended on Mendieta's popularity to keep Grau out of the presidency.[59]

As a result of this alliance, the connection between the civilian and military sectors in the political structure changed radically. The new military establishment markedly increased the size, technology, and training of the armed forces. In their first twelve months under Batista's control, the Cuban armed forces rose from 8,000 to 15,500 enlisted men. In 1932 the military received 15 percent of the national budget, but during the height of the depression in 1935 and 1936, the appropriation rose to 22 percent. The burgeoning strength of the military increased even more when the national police force, numbering 3,000 men, was reorganized by the central goverment to work in harmony with the army. On April 19, 1934, José Pedraza, a close friend of Batista and a fellow conspirator in the sergeants' revolt, was appointed chief of police in Havana to stop the growing terrorism by increasing military supervision.[60]

A shift in Cuban leadership had indeed taken place. Until the collapse of the Machado regime, the government had used the armed forces at its discretion, but with Batista's rise, the military had almost reversed the traditional alignment. Céspedes, Grau, and Hevia had lost their presidencies because of dissatisfaction within the new military leadership. Mendieta's regime established a new relationship. He had failed to act with firmness, and the opposition refused to reconcile itself with the existing government. Both these failures, plus many complex imponderables, had degraded Cuba's political process to its nadir while increasing the military's authority to influence and indeed direct civilian decisions.

Throughout 1934 Caffery and his associates reported on Cuba's domestic turmoil in great detail. In these dispatches several themes

200349

recurred: first, that the civilian government was incapable of restoring domestic tranquillity; second, that the political factions supporting and attacking the government contributed greatly to the domestic disorder by their inability to unite in a constructive program for the nation's problems; and third, that the judicial system instead of creating an atmosphere of law and order, only added to the confusion. If the embassy's dispatches were to be taken at face value, only Batista could receive credit for keeping Cuba from plunging into anarchy. What the American embassy failed to analyze was the cost of the military chieftain's growing authority. While Batista's opponents cried out against the increasing militarism, Caffery and his staff merely noted its stabilizing effects. The ambassador was not alone in his support of the incumbent regime. The Roosevelt administration openly sustained Caffery's position by initiating the program that would remain the basis of American policy toward Cuba for the next quarter of a century.

6

The Good Neighbor Policy
Takes Form

Throughout 1934 United States diplomats were well aware of Mendieta's precarious position. Political ineptitude, economic depression, and terroristic activity replaced the recognition issue and created new anxieties for the Department of State. To compound the policy-makers' problems, the Roosevelt administration was severely criticized for recognizing Mendieta when he had been in office less than a week, especially since he could not restore domestic peace. Why had the United States not recognized Grau in the same short period? Hostile writers had their own simplistic answer. They thought that the administration would not support Grau because he was a radical and hence unsympathetic to American political and economic interests. Mendieta, however, was a conservative and the antithesis of his predecessor. Clearly he was an acceptable choice for the traditionalist policy-makers and thus won Roosevelts's blessings easily.

Although this argument had some validity, critics ignored a fundamental question in the issue of Cuban recognition. They concentrated on the differences between the two politicians and overlooked the relationship between recognition and the more general issue of nonintervention in Latin America. Welles had rigidly maintained that the United States could not support a government that had seized power illegally. Arguing from this position, he had advocated and received permission to implement the nonrecognition policy. This crucial decision was not seriously debated at the time within the administration, but after the United States signed the nonintervention agreement at Montevideo and Roosevelt publicly pledged not to intervene in the internal affairs of Latin American states, Hull, Phillips, and Daniels argued forcefully for the end of the nonrecognition policy. They reasoned that if Roosevelt hoped to gain the confidence of the Latin American nations, his policy would have to be consistent, and thus the United States would have to end its special relationship with Cuba.

Critics of the State Department's Cuban policy were not aware of this internal struggle. Even after Welles returned to Washington, everything seemed the same, but behind the scenes, Caffery was working energetically for a change. When Grau finally resigned, the new envoy argued for recognition on two basic premises: that it was essential to restore the island's political stability, and that without official relations, the United States could not carry out the Good Neighbor concept in Cuba. Caffery justified recognizing the Mendieta government, therefore, as easily as Welles has justified nonrecognition of Grau.

Unfortunately for the Cubans, recognition was not a panacea for all their domestic ills; the Roosevelt administration realized this fact and acted to help restore economic stability. Only nine days after Mendieta's inauguration the United States made its first effort to help the island. Remembering his conversation with Ambassador Cintas about the extent of starvation on the island, Roosevelt had the Surplus Relief Corporation grant Cuba a liberal credit of approximately $2 million in foodstuffs. After a short delay, however, Mendieta rejected the offer because Cuban merchants protested that it would injure their trade.[1]

When this idea failed to meet with a favorable response, Welles proposed another plan. Early in the Céspedes regime, he had proposed a direct loan to' pay Cuban public employees' back salaries, but officials of the United States Treasury declared that there was no machinery to grant such economic assistance. In the interim, the Roosevelt administration had created the First Export-Import Bank to foster trade between the United States and the Soviet Union, but this program failed to materialize. Using the still-intact structure, the president announced the creation of the Second Export-Import Bank to provide credits and stimulate trade with Cuba. On the last day of April the bank loaned Cuba $4 million to purchase silver bullion for coinage into pesos which it could use to pay government employees' salary arrears and to fix a minimum wage for them. During the next year Cuba received two similar grants, but except for granting these loans, the bank did not play a significant role in stimulating United States-Latin American trade until the advent of World War II.[2]

These gestures showed Roosevelt's intention of assisting the island's economic revival. Luckily Mendieta assumed the presidency at the start of the *zafra*. Although the economic acitivity of the harvest helped to alleviate some of the desperate conditions, the Cubans called for the United States to enlarge its market for sugar, the island's principal export and producer of revenue. The islanders claimed that only with larger sugar sales would the depression end, and as early as January 25 Caffery urged the immediate establishment of a Cuban sugar quota to stop further domestic disorders: "Masses of the Cuban population are now in dire want and obviously an easy prey for communist agitators. Even the present satisfactory Government would not be able to stand very long against starving masses of people."[3] The ambassador tried to persuade American sugar companies on the island to make optimistic declarations about the prospects for a large sugar crop, but they refused despite urging from the United States press and from Cuban commentators, all of whom also directly correlated stability with American preferential tariff.[4]

During the grinding season Cuban commercial activity intensified, and Caffery filed daily reports on the number of mills that participated in the harvest, clearly showing that as more mills took part, tangible signs of economic improvement were plainly visible: increased auto sales, a mild boom in retail clothing sales, and improvement in the wholesale dry goods business. These signs of economic revival were attributed directly to the increased income of the sugar workers.[5] Late in March, as the grinding season slackened, Caffery conferred with the Cuban secretaries of state, finance, and agriculture, who had a simple message for him. Without an adequate sugar quota and an increased preferential tariff, they said, "no prospect will exist of restoring peace and tranquility to this country."[6]

Because of this critical situation, Mendieta appealed directly to Roosevelt on February 5 for a sugar quota and a tariff reduction to stimulate the sugar industry by creating an incentive to hire workers and increase wages. Three days later Roosevelt responded to this request by sending a message to Congress asking that sugar be added to the list of basic commodities under the Agricultural Adjustment Act for United States domestic, territorial, Cuban, and other foreign producers. When Cuban officials heard the news, they expressed their appreciation.[7]

Passed in 1933, the A.A.A. had authorized the secretary of agriculture to enter into voluntary marketing agreements with producers of basic farm commodities, but sugar was not originally classified as a basic article. During the summer the secretary asked the various members of the sugar industry to meet in Washington and devise some formal program, but they could not reach agreement. When the industry failed in its efforts, the administration drafted its own proposal, and on February 8, 1934, Roosevelt asked Congress for sugar legislation. After three months of heated congressional debate, the president signed the Jones-Costigan Act on May 9. The new bill made sugar a basic agricultural commodity under the A.A.A.; thus, the secretary of agriculture could fix quotas on sugar entering the American market. On the same day Roosevelt also lowered the sugar tariff from 2.50 cents to 1.875, and since the Commercial Treaty of 1903 granted Cuba a 20 percent reduction on its sugar entering the United States, the president's action automatically lowered the Cuban sugar duty from 2 cents to 1.50.[8]

Both these actions had a profound effect on the Cuban sugar industry. Because of pressure by domestic and insular suppliers, Cuba received a quota of 1,902,000 short tons, which was approximately half of the average exported between 1922 to 1931 but higher than exports during 1932 and 1933. Even with this sharp reduction, Roosevelt's program of artificially raising the price of sugar entering the American market and guaranteeing a definite allotment to the Cubans helped to halt the decline of the island's principal export.[9]

The United States had now demonstrated its willingness to aid the Mendieta government. But what of the other promises to revise the Permanent Treaty of 1903 with its noxious Platt Amendment and to renegotiate the outdated commercial treaty of the same year? The public actions already taken had been initiated before or shortly after Mendieta's inauguration, but these other complex problems could not even be discussed until recognition was formally accorded. Once this was accomplished, the United States could negotiate directly with the Cuban officials. Caffery presented his credentials on February 28, and he promised Mendieta every possible consideration, especially in trying to improve economic conditions. Mendieta applauded his sentiments, but he went on to suggest that the outmoded political and commercial treaties signed shortly after the Spanish-American War should be revised.[10]

Even as Memdieta spoke, discussions on the Platt Amendment were being conducted in Washington. Originally a rider to the Army Appropriation Bill of 1901, it had been forced on the Cuban Constitutional Convention in June 1901. To emphasize the United States' right of military intervention, both nations signed a political treaty on May 22, 1903, which embodied the Platt Amendment. Later the United States sent troops to the island on three separate occasions—in 1906, 1912, and finally in 1917. During the 1920s, however, agitation for repeal from within the United States and from Cuba increased. Critics conceded that in the period of confusion and readjustment after the Spanish-American War, the United States had had some justification for intervening, since its troops were obliged to maintain stability for investment, to protect foreign residents' lives, and to guard against foreign invasions.[11] By the 1920s, they insisted, the amendment had simply outlived its usefulness, and as early as 1927, Leland Jenks succinctly reflected the growing resentment against what critics considered an archaic policy. Since the United States had become the most powerful nation in the world, wrote Jenks, "our abnormal relations with Cuba are becoming more of a liability than an asset in our efforts to defend ourselves by securing the good will of our Hispanic neighbors."[12]

While the Hoover administration refused to take action on the question, the abrogation of the Platt Amendment won new converts. In April 1930, Senator Thomas J. Walsh, the Montana Democrat who had become a national figure through his investigation of the Teapot Dome scandal, urged the United States either to abandon the Platt Amendment or to intervene militarily in order to conduct free elections. In the same month a prominent Cuban politician Cosme de la Torriente advocated the negotiation of a new political treaty in which the United States would offer its support in case of foreign attack and Cuba would reciprocate by continuing to allow the United States to operate the Guantánamo naval base for the defense of the Panama Canal.[13] Even Ambassador Guggenheim openly opposed the extension of the Platt Amendment once he left his post, holding "that Cuba must work out her own salvation regardless of the mistakes that she may make.

I am in complete agreement with the dictum that it is far better for Cuba to make her own mistakes than to have our Government make mistakes for her."[14] In spite of this growing campaign against the Platt Amendment, Secretary Stimson still would not consider its abrogation.

Once Roosevelt took office, the proponents of a change in Cuban policy intensified their attack. Two weeks after Machado fled, the *New Republic* praised the president for not landing troops and offered him some additional advice on carrying out foreign policy: "If there is to be a New Deal in regard to Latin America . . . , abrogation of the Platt Amendment should be the first card played."[15] After the sergeants' revolt, Jorge Mañach, a leading member of the A.B.C., echoed this sentiment, claiming that the amendment blocked Cuba's sovereignty. Other Cuban nationalists used the Platt Amendment in the same way to heighten xenophobia, thereby offering their countrymen a patriotic bond and expanding anti-American feeling in an effort to force the repeal of the odious amendment.[16]

In the United States, critics responded favorably to these Cuban cries for independence. In December 1933, the *New Republic* repeated its call for abrogation, and in early 1934, the *Nation* advised Roosevelt to scrap the entire political treaty.[17] Scholars too protested against the existing policy. Hubert Herring wrote that the "time has gone forever when we can have neighbors who are half slave and half free. That has been the status for thirty five years and it has produced nothing but disaster."[18] Graham Stuart, a prominent political scientist specializing in United States-Latin American relations, reviewed the amendment's history and concluded a "new deal in our relations with Cuba is required and the Platt Amendment should be revised materially or junked, and the latter would be preferable. The right to intervene still exists under international law and no special treaty provision is necessary."[19]

There was also considerable opposition to the Platt Amendment among prominent politicians. Key Pittman, Democrat from Nevada and chairman of the Senate Foreign Relations Committee, told reporters on August 10, 1933, that he favored scrapping the Monroe Doctrine in the interest of amity between the United States and Latin America. Renunciation of the doctrine, he added, would assure Latin America that the United States was sincere in its commitment to nonintervention.[20] Pittman spoke in generalities; a month later Senator Borah, the ranking Republican on the committee, came out explicitly in favor of abrogating the Platt Amendment as a policy long repudiated by the American public. According to Borah, the amendment "was a mistake in the first place and it has never benefited the people in either Cuba or the United States."[21]

Sensing the growing hostility toward intervention, Roosevelt cautiously placed his administration on the side of abrogation. Although he refused to recognize Grau, Roosevelt announced in the Warm Springs declaration of November 1933 that once Cuba had a stable government, the United States would be willing to renegotiate the Permanent Treaty. Even this assurance did not stop debate. On January 18, 1934, Congressmen Hamilton Fish of New York, a Republican member of the House Committee on Foreign Affairs, called for the abrogation of the Platt Amendment, and eleven days later he submitted a resolution advocating its repeal or revision. His action corresponded to a similar Senate resolution, made five days earlier, stating that the Platt Amendment was being examined to determine whether it should be repealed. When both houses of Congress requested information on the current status of the amendment, Hull told the chairmen of both foreign relations committees that the State Department was giving the matter its careful consideration.[22]

While agitation within the United States increased, the Cuban ambassador to the United Stated, Manuel Márquez Sterling, conducted his own campaign. After a distinguished career as a journalist, he had been appointed ambassador to Mexico in 1929, but he resigned two years later in protest against Machado's oppressive regime. He moved to Washington, where he continued his voluntary exile until Céspedes selected him as ambassador to the United States on August 17, 1933, giving him the primary mission of abrogating the Platt Amendment. Before the new appointee had a chance to carry out his assignment, the sergeants' revolt destroyed any possibility of reaching an agreement. The implementation of the nonrecognition policy obliged Márquez Sterling to await the moment when some government would win recognition.[23]

Even though he held no official position, the Cuban diplomat continued his efforts. While the Montevideo Conference was in progress, he went to see William Phillips about press articles which intimated that the United States was considering the abandonment of the Platt Amendment. The acting secretary referred his visitor to the Warm Springs declaration and also informed him that no official steps could be taken until the United States recognized a Cuban government. Continuing his lobbying, Márquez Sterling requested and received a private interview with Roosevelt on December 20, and before he returned to Cuba as Grau's designate secretary of state, he frequently spoke with Welles about the island's problems. Márquez Sterling finally left for Cuba on January 10, only to see his plans altered again by another change in the presidency. Nevertheless the trip was not wasted. He spoke with Caffery about repeal and also consulted Mendieta and his chief advisers. After these talks, he took up formal ambassadorial duties in Washington, presenting his credentials on the last day of January.[24]

After a delay of over four months, Márquez Sterling resumed his original task and began discussing abrogation with Welles again on February 1. Afer several preliminary talks, Welles officially asked the ambassador on March 30 to renegotiate the Permanent Treaty. Márquez Sterling's persistence was finally having results, for Welles was equally convinced that the United States' right of military intervention had to be eliminated. At Welles's insistence, formal talks between the two men began on April 2. After two weeks of conferences, Welles presented Márquez Sterling with a revised treaty, which he immediately sent to Secretary of State Cosme de la Torriente, hoping for a prompt reply. Instead the Cuban secretary hesitated, and without instrucions from his government, Márquez Sterling suggested his own changes on May 1. When the Cuban government finally sent a response on May 12, the assistant secretary and the ambassador quickly resolved the differences in the drafts, and by May 22, they had finished the final document. Two men, working for only four months but with minimal friction, had found the formula that would end more than three decades of heated debate.[25]

With the negotiations completed, Roosevelt transmitted the revised treaty to the Senate for ratification on May 29. In his message to the Senate, the president announced, "By the consummation of this treaty, this Government will make it clear that it not only opposes the policy of armed intervention, but that it renounces those rights of intervention and interference in Cuba which have been bestowed upon it by treaty."[26] With this strong presidential support in addition to the prevailing sentiment against the Platt Amendment, the treaty immediately went to the Senate Foreign Relations Committee, which unanimously approved it without any changes. It was a brief document containing five sections: the cancellation of the original treaty, the confirmation of the first intervention's legality, American retention of the Guantá-namo naval base, measures for protection against epidemics and contagious diseases, and finally the means for ratification.[27]

Key Pittman asked the Senate to ratify the treaty on May 31, and after only a mild expression of doubt by Simon D. Fess of Ohio, the senators ratified the new treaty without so much as a roll-call vote. Once the United States Senate had approved the revised treaty, Cuban ratification quickly followed on June 4, and five days later both nations exchanged ratifications.[28] Two days later, Mendieta told an audience that Cuba had become a republic on May 20, 1902, but that the Platt Amendment had limited complete sovereignty. "Thus, on May 29, 1934, the work of May 20, 1902, was completed. Cuba was free, independent, and sovereign!"[29]

Even before final abrogation was approved by either country, Hull optimistically predicted a new era in Cuban-American relations. On the day the treaty went to the Senate, the secretary told reporters that a new spirit of hemispheric relations had been born at Montevideo and that now the abrogation of the Platt Amendment provided a concrete accomplishment under Roosevelt's leadership.[30] Prominent Cuban politicans, newspapers, and individuals also rejoiced.[31] Ruby Hart Phillips described the outpouring of emotions: "Church bells rang; sirens and whistles were blown; crowds gathered in front of the Presidential Palace where the municipal band played the national anthem."[32] Along with the Cubans, Latin American governments and presses ap-peared unanimous in their praise. Since the United States' most serious obstacle in gaining Latin American coooperation was its interventionist policy, the abrogation of the Platt Amendment created friendlier relations not only between two nations, but over the rest of the hemisphere as well. With this single step, the Roosevelt administration had immeasurably enhanced its prestige in projecting its Good Neighbor image throughout Latin Amer-ica.[33]

The American news media also applauded the new treaty.

Charles Hackett, who had closely watched and commented on Cuban events since the outbreak of violence in August 1933, stated that the Roosevelt administration had demonstrated its sincerity in opposing armed intervention,[34] and he later added that "the new treaty . . . gave Cuba its full sovereignty for the first time."[35] *The Christian Century* greeted "this abrogation with joy,"[36] and even the critical *Nation* expressed pleased surprise at the ease with which the new treaty had passed.[37] Lester Woolsey declared that Cuba had gained full sovereignty after thirty years of American tutelage. Not only had the Cubans won their independence, but the Roosevelt government had clearly illustrated its peaceful intentions. In fact, the "whole history of the United States in Cuba has been one of magnanimity toward a small country, unexampled in the annals of international relations, and sufficient, it is believed, to satisfy the most delicate sensibilities."[38]

Not all writers could agree with this remarkable statement, especially remembering the three military interventions, the island's strategic importance, and the vast economic holdings of American citizens. In the midst of Cuba's national celebration, the *Miami Herald* warned the islanders that the United States still remained "just as interested in the welfare of Cuba, just as ready to protect life should that become necessary."[39] Later in the month, the *New Republic* granted that although the Platt Amendment had been repealed, "the shadow of our influence in Cuba is still a strong one."[40] Finally in late June the liberal *World Tomorrow* added that abolition did not end the amendment's implications. The United States, it pointed out, could still direct Cuba's destiny through the threat of intervention or other political and economic pressures.[41]

Although most American observers were convinced that the abrogation of the Platt Amendment completely fulfilled the promise of the Good Neighbor Policy, events on the island immediately before and after the celebrated episode proved that the United States had not significantly altered its Cuban policy. The presence of American warships in Cuban waters furnished the first evidence of inconsistency between the announced and actual policies. Roosevelt had ordered the first vessels to the island when Machado fled, and at the end of January 1934, twenty-five American ships were still assigned to the Cuban waters. On February 1, Rear Admiral C. S. Freeman, who was in charge of the squadron, discussed with Caffery the removal of some ships and decided to keep some forces, including a vessel in Havana harbor, ready for emergency action.[42] One month later Admiral Freeman proposed that the American vessels be removed as quickly as possible; but Caffery reflected, "in view of the existing communist menace here, I did not desire to put myself on record as fixing any definite date for withdrawal from Havana harbor."[43] On April 9 the admiral told the ambassador that a time limit should be set for the warships' withdrawal. This time Caffery replied that the ships should remain throughout the summer because if they left too soon their departure might suggest to the Cubans that the United States thought the Mendieta government a failure. Such an impression "might consequently be followed by disorders throughout the Island."[44]

The ships remained as Caffery had requested, furnishing assurances to Cubans that the United States supported the existing regime. Even the abrogation of the Platt Amendment did not sway Caffery. The day after Roosevelt sent the new political treaty to the Senate for ratification, the Navy Department asked to withdraw the cruiser *Richmond* from Cuban waters, "as a longer stay would be contradictory to convention terms."[45] Three days after the exchange of ratifications and the Cubans' joyous celebration, Caffery argued in favor of keeping the *Richmond* at her present station. When he conferred with Mendieta and Cosme de la Torriente, they agreed that the time was not appropriate for the removal of the American naval presence. Caffery's superiors agreed. In a memorandum of June 18 Welles wrote that he and Navy Department officials had reached an understanding that no action would be taken towards the ships' withdrawal, and Roosevelt also approved the proposal.[46]

One month later Admiral Freeman again pressed the ambassador about the vessels in Cuban waters, reiterating that the navy wanted to reduce its task force and reassign its units. Caffery answered that some ships might leave, but he still insisted that a light cruiser should remain in Havana harbor and a marine battalion be ready for immediate action. Finally on September 1, 1934, the last of the squadron left Havana harbor. The fleet had remained in the area since August 1933; the Platt Amendment had been officially abrogated in June 1934, but with the advice of the ambassador, the consent of the Cuban government, and support from Welles and Roosevelt, the ships continued to cruise in the area for an additional three months.[47] The critics who believed that American naval forces could operate freely without a formal treaty had been proven correct.

The debate over the withdrawal of the ships went beyond communiqués within the United States government. Whether they lay just over the horizon or anchored in Havana harbor, American warships created tension. Cuba had witnessed three previous landings of American troops, and the people protested against the presence of the ships. On July 6 the Cuban newspaper *Ahora* claimed that they had remained to protect United States business interests. Ever since Machado fled, American warships had steamed in Cuban waters, "as if to remind us we are not altogether free, despite our will." But, the paper continued, no matter what American corporations do, Cuba will be independent: "Because we do not want to feel ashamed in our own land, we demand from our provisional government that it make an immediate effort toward the withdrawal of the sentinel, whose only mission seems to be to restrain the acts of men who want to be free."[48] Ten days later the Society of Cuban Women sent a telegram to the Department of State urging the ships' removal. The society appreciated the Good Neighbor idea, but the women were apprehensive about the American warships in Cuban ports and requested their immediate evacuation.[49]

Even the experts sent out by the Foreign Policy Association to study social and economic conditions in Cuba could not condone the inconsistency of abrogating the Platt Amendment while allowing American ships to stay in Cuban waters. According to their report, the Roosevelt administration "showed commendable restraint in not landing marines in Cuba during the repeated crises of the last two years. Nevertheless, the good effect of this policy on Cuban opinion was to a certain extent dissipated by the fact that American warships remained in Cuban waters for almost a year."[50]

Other incidents also added to the American embassy's problems. On May 24, 1934, just as Caffery was getting ready to leave the embassy, an automobile sped by firing a volley of bullets. The assassins missed their principal target, but one sentry was critically wounded. After this attempt, the Cuban government provided the embassy with soldiers at all times, and Caffery became the first American envoy in Cuba to have a constant bodyguard.[51]

Violence spread through the entire island. The bombings in

Havana had become daily occurrences, and the Cuban authorities could not suppress this terrorism. The American consul general in Havana, C. R. Cameron, thought that the terrorists were smuggling dynamite from Florida to the island. To stop this menace, on June 29 Roosevelt signed a proclamation at Hull's request, making the sale of arms to Cuba unlawful except with the permission of the secretary of state.[52]

The American embassy continued to be a center of controversy. On July 17 Caffery learned that the A.B.C. had stored several hundred rifles and other arms at its old legation building. Although the building had not been used for several years, it was still American property. As soon as he learned of the armaments' existence, Caffery had them shipped to Camp Columbia, but opponents of American policy demanded to know why they were there in the first place. Caffery's silence on the entire episode convinced many Cubans that the arms had originally been intended for use against Grau when Welles was ambassador.[53]

In addition to the hostile critics on the island, Josephus Daniels was becoming increasingly irritated by American policy and policymakers. The United States ambassador to Mexico sympathized with the Cuban revolution's goal of eliminating foreign exploitation, basing his opinion on the assumption that the Cubans were experiencing a social upheaval similar to the Mexican Revolution.[54] Writing to Hull on July 10, he complained bitterly, "I could wish we had as Ambassador in Cuba a man of the new type. Welles and Caffery are of the old school of diplomats, who never saw anything wrong in the sort of diplomacy which cost us the confidence of the people of Pan America in the past years. What we need in all Pan American Embassies and Legations are men of our type, who will change the whole atmosphere and have welcome in their hearts for a New Deal in those countries such as we wish for our own."[55]

While public attention focused on political events, the United States and Cuba moved simultaneously to revitalize commercial intercourse. This activity, though perhaps less spectacular than political diplomacy, had a far greater immediate impact on American policy in Cuba. The Roosevelt administration had already assisted the island's sugar industry with the Jones-Costigan Act and the president's tariff reduction on sugar. These measures helped to revive Cuba's desperate economic plight, but their effect was only temporary. Until Cuba diversified its economy or somehow revived its sugar industry, many of the islanders would face the daily prospect of starvation. The State Department was well aware of this situation and also knew that in order to regain its former trading position with Cuba, the United States would have to lower its sugar duty still further.[56]

The restoration of trade between the two nations was crucial to Cuba's survival, but it was equally important to Hull, who wished to use it as a model for his longstanding plan of lowering international tariff barriers. When he became a member of Roosevelt's cabinet, Hull pressed the president for tariff reform, but domestic considerations made Roosevelt reluctant to raise the subject. Not until March 2, 1934, did Hull gain Roosevelt's lukewarm support for tariff legislation; on that date the president asked Congress to pass the Reciprocal Trade Agreements Act. The secretary fought vigorously in favor of this bill on the grounds that tariff renovation would stimulate domestic recovery. When the act was signed on June 12, Hull expressed his delight; the Roosevelt administration had embarked on a program that was to become the basis of New Deal foreign economic policy.[57]

While the various interest groups debated the merits of the proposed legislation, the United States was already working on a new commercial treaty with Cuba. Welles had originally initiated exploratory talks in Havana, but Grau's presidency stopped the negotiations until after Mendieta's inauguration. Unlike Welles and Márquez Sterling in their negotiations for the abrogation of the Platt Amendment, Caffery and his staff conducted the delicate transactions on the island instead of in Washington for several reasons. The embassy in Havana had commercial data unavailable to the State Department, a broader knowledge of Cuban economic affairs, and easily accessible commercial contacts. With these considerations in mind, Hull approved his ambassador's plan.[58]

Early in February, Caffery and the Cuban officials began to discuss the possibility of a new commercial treaty, and on February 19 serious bargaining started. While the Roosevelt administration was pushing sugar legislation through Congress, the two negotiating teams discussed the various reduction proposals and the form of the agreement. Once the Reciprocal Trade Agreements Act passed in June, the secretary switched from the tentative treaty to a reciprocal trade agreement and pressed for an early completion date. Despite Hull's impatience, the agreement was delayed by continued disagreements over the substance of the tariff reductions and by the resignation of the Cuban secretary of treasury. Nevertheless, by the middle of July the Cubans had received the United States' proposal for reductions. With this phase of the negotiations completed, the Cuban and American delegates met in day and night sessions to finish the agreement, and by August 21, they had succeeded. Hull wanted the first reciprocal trade agreement signed in Washington, so Cosme de la Torriente left Havana to perform the ceremony.[59]

After five months of intensive negotiations, the first reciprocal trade agreement was signed on August 24, 1934. Although it had been concluded under the new legislation, it stood in a separate category from later reciprocal trade agreements, for it continued the special customs treatment begun under the original commercial treaty of 1903. Each nation guaranteed exclusive preferential tariff reductions on certain commodities, no matter what rates either one might grant to third countries. Even though Hull was an avid supporter of the most-favored-nations clause, he abandoned it in this agreement to demonstrate how mutual tariff reductions could restore trade.[60]

Under the agreement the United States received preferential rates of from 20 to 75 percent on 426 items covering a wide range of agricultural and industrial products. In turn, the United States granted tariff preferences ranging from 20 to 50 percent on 35 Cuban articles amounting to 90 percent of Cuba's exports to the United States. Sugar and tobacco received 20 percent margins of preference, but both agricultural articles were subject to United States quota restrictions. The new rate on sugar, for example, was .90 cents, but this duty remained effective only as long as the quota provisions of the Jones-Costigan Act were enforced. Once the legislation became inoperative, the duty would immediately return to its old rate of 1.5 cents. Tobacco was also limited by the United States control program: imports of Cuban tobacco were restricted to 18 percent of the total amount used in the United States for cigars during 1933. While tobacco exports could expand, the depression made large increases very unlikely. The United States also agreed to lower the duty on certain Cuban vegetables and fruits, but these reductions could take effect only during the season when these items were not produced on the mainland. The United

States had ingeniously limited Cuban imports by fastening them to United States internal controls, while its exports to Cuba had no quantitative restrictions.[61]

Even though the immediate effect of the agreement was to revive the island's depressed conditions, its long-range consequences were disastrous. For years Cuban reformers had argued for a diversification program, and with the decline of the sugar market in the 1920s, the government embarked on a deliberate plan to vary its economy. The tariff of 1927 was principally designed to stimulate native production in a broad range of agricultural and industrial goods, but depression and revolution impeded the plan's success. Though highly beneficial in the short run, the 1934 agreement allowed United States products to drive native goods off the market, making diversification even more difficult than before. While the reciprocity agreement underwent some minor changes in subsequent years, the basic structure remained intact. Cuba received a preferential sugar tariff, while the United States gained access to the Cuban market for a wide range of agricultural and industrial commodities.[62]

This inequity did not bother representatives of either nation at the time of the signing. Hull had his first reciprocal trade agreement, and he announced that it benefited both nations. Because of the quota and the earlier tariff reduction, sugar prices on the New York exchange rose steadily from .86 cents at the beginning of March to over 1.50 cents from July to September, and the new agreement assured the continuation of this upward trend. With the economic revival, Cosme de la Torriente echoed Hull's sentiments and thanked the American people and their president for their efforts to help Cuba. Mendieta also sent a personal message of gratitude to Roosevelt, who replied with the hope that the agreement would stimulate the lowering of international trade barriers.[63]

Although the Cuban and American people did not have time to digest the full significance of the new agreement, first reports from the island proved very favorable. On August 26 Matthews reported that a number of large orders for certain American products had already been placed and that Cuban newspapers were praising the Good Neighbor Policy. The local American colony also reacted enthusiastically, and shortly after the signing, the president of the American Chamber of Commerce of Cuba wrote to Hull applauding the new program. While the embassy reported on Cuban enthusiasm, the Department of State assessed sixty-five editorials from all over the United States and found overwhelming support for the agreement except among anti-New Deal journals and those in areas adversely affected by the agreement. Even though reactions were generally favorable, the papers warned that the United States should be careful when negotiating with the larger industrial states.[64]

While the newspapers urged caution in future bargaining, the Department of State carefully watched the flow of trade between the island and the mainland. The agreement became effective on September 3, and the department at once noted beneficial results. Caffery reported a tremendous increase in the shipment of American products to Cuba throughout September and October, and on November 6, Laurence Duggan, chief of the Division of Latin American Affairs, added that the first statistical study of the agreement showed an acceleration of trade.[65]

In order to stimulate United States recovery and win converts to the reciprocal trade program, the department continued compiling and releasing statistics that indicated the expanded movement of goods to Cuba. These press releases may have had positive results in the United States, but the effects in Cuba were just the opposite, for the A.B.C., the Auténticos, and the Communists began to attack the agreement because of its one-sided advantages. Duggan wrote that although these charges might be unfounded, "the fact remains that the releases issued in Washington showing enormous exports to Cuba without emphasizing the corresponding advantages to Cuba have provided ammunition to the opponents of the Mendieta regime."[66]

The embassy quickly responded to demonstrate the agreement's equity. Walter J. Donnelly, the commercial attaché, spoke before the American Chamber of Commerce of Cuba on November 28, noting that American sales to Cuba had increased, but he added that in order to extend this growth, the Roosevelt administration would have to increase Cuban purchasing power. Although Cuba had granted the United States reductions on a wide variety of goods, the American government had given the island a reduction on its sugar duty and a quota which greatly benefited the Cuban economy.[67]

Caffery spoke before the same influential group of businessmen on February 20, 1935, stressing the benefits of the agreement and noting the dramatic trade increase, but he also warned that the advantages had not reached all levels of Cuban society. He cautioned his listeners that the "concentration of purchasing power in the hands of a few is not as desirable as in the hands of many. In Cuba today, the people need food, clothes, and other supplies. It is the lack of these that produces restlessness, agitation and finally revolution." The ambassador hoped that the American firms would increase wages to put more money in the workers' pockets, for a more equitable distribution of wealth would increase the possibility of peace. Hoping to impress this point on his audience, Caffery concluded that such a course of action was "not altruism but sound common sense."[68]

The two basic programs of the Good Neighbor Policy, the new political and reciprocity treaties, had now been put into effect in Cuba, but shortly after the signing of the reciprocity agreement and the sailing of American warships, the paradoxical nature of the United States' intentions came into question during the hearings of the Senate Munitions Committee, better known as the Nye Committee. By the time the committee opened its sessions on September 4, 1934, public opinion was decidedly against munitions-makers. Of the many firms summoned to testify, the most active in selling armaments to Cuba was Federal Laboratories. John W. Young, the company's president, began his testimony before the committee on September 18. He had done a large business in Cuba but had always kept the State Department aware of his dealings. Young had sold machine guns and two armored limousines to the Machado government, and he admitted that in order to do business, he had paid graft to Cuban agents. Young told the committee that he had not sold any arms to the revolutionaries because the State Department would not sanction such dealings; even when Céspedes came to power, Federal Laboratories did not do any businesss.[69]

The emergence of the Grau regime radically changed Young's policy in selling arms to Cuba. He inquired about conducting business with Grau, but the officials at the Latin American Division of the State Department and the Naval Intelligence Bureau told him that he had to devise his own program. Young then went to Havana to examine the situation and talked there with Cuban officials and members of the opposition.[70] Upon returning to

Washington, he again conferred with State Department representatives, who told him that there "was no ruling, no law, no treaty to
their knowledge that could control the situation. I could do
business either way I wanted."[71] Given this leeway, Federal
Laboratories made the most of the situation by selling arms both to
the government and to opposition forces.[72]

After Mendieta was inaugurated, Young's relations with the
government changed again when the Cuban president asked him to
serve as a consultant to help plan, direct, and train a national
police force. Before the hearings, the munitions-maker had already
received $12,000 for himself and two assistants for five or six weeks
in Cuba on the project. Young had also taken the former chief
inspector of the New York State Police, Alberto B. Moore, to
Havana to aid him after the Cuban government had cleared his
visit with the American embassy. One of Young's plans for
modernizing the Cuban police was the use of a new product that
he was trying to sell—tear gas. The Cubans accepted his advice and
on April 23 used this weapon for the first time to disperse about five
hundred demonstrators. When the first bomb exploded, the mob
fled, leaving one person dead from the toxic fumes. According to
the press, the police were jubilant over the results of their
experiment, and Pedraza acclaimed the effectiveness of the gas.[73]

On July 29, 1934, Federal Laboratories sent a memorandum to
its agents about the prospects for increased business. The company
claimed a large expansion of sales, especially in its export trade.
The Cuban government had already purchased over $400,000
worth of gas hand-grenades, tear and sickening gas, gas riot-guns,
Thompson submachine guns, and a fleet of radio patrol-cars and
armored cars equipped for fighting rioters. Federal Laboratories
urged its employees to find new markets for the company's
program: "With conditions of unrest as they are today throughout
the world, you have a real opportunity before you if you only get
back of this thing and push the Federal program."[74] Cubans might
be starving, but a good businessman could always find a market for
his products.

Young's testimony, the delayed removal of the warships, and
Cuba's continued domestic chaos clearly demonstrated that the first
efforts of the Good Neighbor Policy in Cuba had not solved the
island's problems. In spite of this, Roosevelt gave the unmistakable

impression that his administration had embarked upon a new policy. Four years after the abrogation of the Platt Amendment, he stated that the abrogation "was additional definite proof that the United States was opposed to any further armed intervention" in the hemisphere.[75] Secretary Hull affirmed the president's declaration, and indeed he went even further in his memoirs, claiming, "If the case of Cuba was to be the focus of our acts and intentions, a happier one could scarcely have been chosen."[76]

Even more than the president and his secretary of state, Sumner Welles led the movement to convince the American public that the United States had changed its fundamental relations with Cuba. Through all types of media—personal appearances, radio addresses, pamphlets, and later his memoirs—Welles was the principal administration spokesman for the Good Neighbor Policy in Cuba.[77] Speaking before the Institute of Public Affairs at the University of Virginia on July 2, 1935, he declared that the "policy of your Government toward Cuba has been for the past 2 years, in the best sense of the word, the policy of the 'good neighbor.' " Not only had the United States canceled its right to intervene, he continued, but also "our relationship with Cuba stands on exactly the same footing as our relationship with any other sovereign independent nation of the world."[78] He spread this message wherever he went and always repeated three main themes: the United States had canceled the Platt Amendment, had renounced its previous intervention privileges, and had stopped interfering in Cuban internal affairs either directly or indirectly.

Although administration spokesmen constantly reiterated these themes, Grau and his supporters doggedly maintained that the United States had not practiced the New Deal in Cuba.[79] Upon his arrival in Panama on August 9, 1935, the ex-president told reporters that the United States gave the interests of American companies in Cuba priority over those of domestic firms. Furthermore, he said, even though the Platt Amendment had been repealed, its spirit still lived in the person of Caffery. Concluding his remarks, Grau asserted that there was "more intervention in Cuba today than ever there was during the days of the Platt Amendment."[80]

There was evidence for such a strong allegation in the concrete actions of the United States, in spite of Roosevelt's publicly applauded Good Neighbor Policy. The American government no longer had the responsibility of preserving order on the island, but if the United States had truly intended to end any possibility of intervention, why did it hold onto the Guantánamo naval station and encircle the island with warships? Critics recognized these inconsistencies: American troops remained on Cuban soil ready for action, and the Cubans were painfully aware of the United States naval presence. Thus, the abrogation of the Platt Amendment was not a generous surrender of American rights but simply the admission that intervention by treaty was no longer useful or desirable.[81]

The fact was that although the Roosevelt administration had formally repudiated political domination, the American ambassador remained the second most influential politician in Cuba after Batista. Although optimistic writers alleged that American political domination had suddenly ended,[82] the past thirty-six years had almost created a set of reflex actions in Cuba. When the Cubans could not solve their internal problems, they forced United States actions; thus, the American ambassador became an integral part of the political process.[83] Up to 1934, Cuban politicians had operated under this system; was there any reason to expect reform overnight?

This political alignment was closely associated with economic actions. The Eximbank loans, the Jones-Costigan Act, the lowering of the Cuban sugar tariff, and the reciprocal trade agreement have given authors reason to praise Roosevelt for his assistance in alleviating Cuba's abysmal economic situation, but in fact, Cuba paid a tremendous price. Signing the agreement damaged the island's diversification program severely. The lowering of duties on 426 products from the mainland made Cuba even more dependent on American goods. The Cuban government's freedom to sign commercial treaties with other nations was also greatly impaired. Finally, the trade agreement helped to continue the status quo against any reformist alternatives.[84]

This unwholesome arrangement was compounded by yet another condition imposed by the United States. Even with the reciprocal trade agreement, Cuba's sugar and tobacco markets were not guaranteed. If the United States altered its agricultural program so as to affect these crops, according to the agreement Cuba would lose her tariff preference and quota. The United States desired a new commercial arrangement in order to restore Caba's purchasing power so that islanders could purchase goods from the mainland. In the process, the United States negotiators had driven a hard bargain which the Cubans felt they could not reject if they were to save their principal industry. Clearly, the new agreement was not a humanitarian gesture to benefit the depressed island; people on the mainland were the primary consideration. Small wonder that three years after the signing Alberto Delgado Montejo wrote, "Cuba does not have its own economy."[85]

These political and economic arrangements remained in operation throughout Roosevelt's long tenure. They were hailed as the first concrete examples of a new Latin American policy, and the president helped to perpetuate this image by using the "Good Neighbor" terminology. Closer examination, however, reveals that Roosevelt and his advisers were not trying to implement a new program, but to discard the outmoded elements of the traditional one. The right to intervene militarily was canceled, and an outdated commercial treaty was revised. The United States still possessed its naval base, American prestige in the person of the ambassador remained, and American economic interests continued to exert a powerful influence. Somehow writers failed to recognize these factors and vastly exaggerated the uniqueness and the impact of these early efforts to initiate a new Latin American policy. Stability, not the adherence to the nebulous platitudes of the Good Neighbor Policy, continued to be the basis of the United States' strategy toward Cuba even in the turbulent year 1934.

7

The Path to Revival:
The End of the Mendieta Regime

Although the Roosevelt administration used the abrogation of the Platt Amendment and the signing of the first reciprocal trade agreement to project its Good Neighbor image, neither action immediately helped to alleviate Cuba's internal troubles. At the start of 1935 Mendieta's regime was still confronted by social unrest, economic depression, and political uncertainty, but gradually the situation improved. Some of the government's actions helped to restore an unsteady political peace; economic recovery followed the rise in sugar prices; and the people appeared to be tired of revolution. These interrelated trends toward peace became more pronounced as the year progressed, but during this period of sporadic revival, it was evident only that the achievement of stability would be a long and painful process.

The extremely low standard of living was one of the Cuban government's principal concerns. The people, especially those living in the interior, suffered in every conceivable way. Education had practically ceased to exist. Most Cubans lacked adequate medical care because they could not afford to pay for doctors' services, and the government did not have the money to send medical teams to the interior. The public health situation had deteriorated to such an extent that health officials began to fear an epidemic of infantile paralysis. People who were able to eke out a living spent about 60 percent of their total income on food. Cyrus Wicker of Miami University, who studied Cuba's economic situation in 1934, reported that starving faces could be seen throughout the island; he estimated that at least 400,000 inhabitants lived in dire poverty.[1] When the British government surveyed the island's economic conditions in early 1935, it confirmed

Wicker's findings, declaring that two-thirds of the population lived "on the marginal line of subsistence."[2] Observers began to compare Cuba's plight in 1935 to the desperate state of affairs that had existed on the island at the close of the Spanish-American War.

The plight of a people living through a depression was not difficult to understand. Cubans wanted money to buy the necessities of life, but in a society with a limited number of jobs, the work force represented the minority; the jobless or those in danger of losing employment were the majority. Grau had given the laborer a minimum wage, an eight-hour day, maternity insurance, and workman's compensation, but he never initiated unemployment insurance. After labor won protection for its members, it retarded economic improvement by blocking the introduction of new machinery in order to prevent further layoffs and dismissals.[3] Conditions were so wretched in 1935 that the Foreign Policy Report suggested that Cuba's only available source of new income was farming. The Cuban government had to push for this program, the report warned, for "Unless the problem of providing food for the masses of the people is solved, there can be little prospect of political stability or ultimate reconstruction."[4]

This conclusion was reasonable but incomplete in that it neglected Cuba's population explosion and the demographic shift to the urban areas. According to the Cuban census of 1899, the island had a population of a little more than 1.5 million. In the next three decades, the island's population rose to almost 4 million because of a growing birth rate, a declining death rate, and immigration, which showed an annual increase of almost 75,000 or 3.43 percent. Although the depression coupled with revolution drastically decreased the growth rate to approximately 8,000 a year from 1931 to 1935, the movement to the cities and towns continued. In 1931, for the first time in Cuban history, city dwellers outnumbered their rural counterparts. Because of this demographic shift, combined with the nation's reliance on sugar and tobacco, farming could not supply the urban majority with enough food.[5]

Political agitation added to the social unrest. Mendieta, still president, was almost killed on New Year's Day when a bomb was thrown at his car but failed to explode. Although other terroristic actions slackened, the continued violence made the civilian government more reliant than ever on Batista's military power. In the midst of this uncertainty, the incumbent administration tried in vain to reach an agreement with the opposition parties. Once these attempts failed, Mendieta became convinced that the only solution to the island's predicament would be the convocation of a constituent assembly.[6]

Although the political situation remained as chaotic as ever, the annual *zafra*, starting on January 15, significantly stimulated commercial activity. To insure a successful harvest, the government detailed troops to the sugar mills so that saboteurs and agitators could not cause any disruptions. These precautions seemed to have a quieting effect, and there was also every reason to believe that the inhabitants were more interested in earning a living than in demonstrating against the government. Violence had not completely abated, but economic revival was the opposition's worst enemy.[7]

In spite of the brightening economic picture, the activity of the student groups still remained unpredictable. Even though the university students staged a strike in early January, the American embassy paid little attention to what it considered just another antigovernment demonstration. Late in the month, however, police coverage of the walkout increased; the police wounded one student and arrested thirteen others for rioting. With this new government affront, the students voted for an indefinite strike, and they even gained faculty support for their right to participate in political affairs. As the movement gained momentum, other groups pledged their cooperation, and by the end of the month, the strike was no longer merely the expression of one faction's disenchantment. More than just another student demonstration, it was gaining new followers each day, and the participants now planned a general strike to topple the regime.[8]

Watching these events from the embassy, on February 26 Caffery lashed out against the government for its ineptitude: "The continued failure of the civil Government to act has increased the responsibility of the army for the preservation of order, and at the same time has encouraged the strike leaders."[9] This time, however, Mendieta surprised the ambassador by publicly attacking his critics, vigorously defending his position, and denouncing the strike movement as unpatriotic and an obstacle to elections. In addition the government tried to prevent additional organizations from joining the strike, while Batista met with his military advisers to discuss the maintenance of order. In the meantime he took the precaution of having extra troops patrol Havana's streets.[10]

By March 1 the strike looked more ominous than ever. Within the government, six cabinet members resigned because of the regime's failure to act against the strikers. From outside, the opposition leaders claimed that they had mobilized over 300,000 followers, united in a desire to overthrow the government. The A.B.C. and the Auténtico parties joined forces and actively sought other organized support in an effort to remove Mendieta. Although the Communist Party operated independently, it avidly supported the strike's political objective. For a brief moment, the leaders of the March 1935 strike hoped that they could duplicate the conditions that had existed in August 1933.[11]

This illusion of unity and the uneasy peace ended on March 6, when five bombs exploded in Havana's customshouse and treasury department, leaving one person dead and eight wounded. The opposition factions, claiming to speak for 500,000 Cubans, called for Mendieta and Batista to resign. The adversaries gained other powerful allies when the unions from five government departments issued a manifesto urging a general strike and declaring that current conditions on the island had not changed since the Machado regime. As terrorism and violence returned to Havana, the students added to the tense situation by beginning to store weapons at the university. While these actions had their usual disruptive effects, the enemies of the regime could neither enlarge their base of support nor unite their existing forces.[12] On March 10 Caffery asserted that the .opposition leaders no longer controlled the strike's direction: "Now it is in nobody's hands: it has become a disorganized movement toward chaos."[13]

This flurry of hostile activity sparked an immediate government response. Acting quickly, the administration suspended all constitutional rights, established the death penalty for antigovernment activity, and placed military governors in the provinces. Soldiers and police moved to strategic points throughout the capital and searched and temporarily occupied the university. In spite of these measures, killings continued, and Mendieta responded by declaring a state of war, which gave the military unprecedented powers.[14] With absolute authority in its hands, the military now answered the opposition's sporadic violence with supervised repression. On

March 12 Caffery, who staunchly supported the government throughout its struggle, reported the discovery of the bodies of nine men who had died in the strike at the hands of the military authorities. He condoned this organized brutality, reasoning, "Now that the military and police are in charge of the situation, it was perhaps too much to hope that there would be no bloodshed whatsoever." Still he sent word to Batista to stop the killings, but by this time the troops had crushed the strike.[15]

Since the government's survival was no longer at stake, the authorities began wholesale arrests. The A.B.C. and Auténtico parties appeared to be disintegrating, as scores of their leaders fled the island.[16] Showing his satisfaction at the collapse of the general strike, Caffery wrote on March 15 that it failed because of its unpopularity with the majority of the Cuban population and because of the army's concerted efforts. The civilian government had declared martial law, but Caffery continued to criticize Cuban politicians: "Although this is the first time since the Provisional Government took office fourteen months ago that a subversive movement has been met with determination, little credit for this can justifiably be claimed by the civilian authorities, whose procrastination during several preceding weeks permitted the movement to gain such dangerous momentum. . . . the prestige of the army in general, and of Colonel Batista in particular, has emerged on a new high level."[17]

Besides giving this glowing tribute to the military, Caffery reported on opposition fragmentation and government solidarity. He cited the end of Havana's curfew, the termination of the state-of-war decree, and the removal of prisoners from military to civilian courts, to illustrate the trend toward political peace. In late March Mendieta made his own declaration on the strike, stating that the movement had not served any constructive purpose. He thanked the armed forces for ending the disorders, and once again he promised that elections would be held in spite of the terrorism. As far as he was concerned, he would hold elections and those who interfered would be excluded. He would then leave office and allow historians to judge his administration.[18]

Before historians had their chance, his predecessor stated that Cuban conditions were abhorrent. Grau indicted the army for cruelly repressing the March strike and claimed that elections could not be held because the government could not protect the voters. Late in March the *New Republic* condemned Batista and compared him to Machado.[19] Hubert Herring continued the attack, relaying descriptions of the government's ruthlessness. He did not understand how the Roosevelt administration could take the position that the Cuban people were loyal to Mendieta. A general strike that included over 500,000 participants and lasted over two weeks was hardly a display of devotion. The government's use of unprecedented military authority, he went on sadly, had resulted in the destruction of the entire movement: "Labor unions have been broken up and their funds conficasted. Many of the ablest and most patriotic leaders of the island have been jailed or forced to flee. It does not augur well for peaceful elections in the near future."[20] Even with the encouraging economic developments, Herring held, Mendieta's pledge of impartial elections would be almost impossible to fulfill.[21]

While critics deplored the Cuban regime's ruthless repression of the strike's leaders, Batista continued his search for Guiteras, who had not only been active in the March upheaval but also continued to defy the regime, evading all the military's traps. He even had the audacity to organize his own band of terrorists, called Joven Cuba. To his enemies, Guiteras remained nothing more than a Communist and a gangster, but to his admirers he personified the hope of a successful revolution. His controversial career, however, ended when one of his followers betrayed his hiding place. Early on the morning of May 8, Batista's troops surrounded him and twenty armed supporters at the ancient El Morrillo fortress on the north coast of Matanzas Province. After a two-hour battle, Guiteras and one follower were dead, eight had been arrested, and the rest fled. According to Hubert Herring, the Mendieta-Batista regime had rid itself of its most dangerous political foe, but the embassy looked on Guiteras as a criminal and declared that he "was regarded as Cuba's Public Enemy No. 1 and that the feeling of relief at his final elimination from the scene is universal among lawabiding elements of all strata of Cuban society."[23] Even though many government supporters greeted the news of his death with a sigh of relief, Guiteras's martyrdom became a symbol for leftist groups throughout the island. Joven Cuba swore to kill everyone connected with its leaders' betrayal and carried out this threat with brutal efficiency over the next two years. Later, to demonstrate his continued hold on Cuba's radicals, they erected a monument on the spot where he died.[24]

Guiteras's death, coupled with the collapse of the principal opposition factions, helped to assure an uneasy political stability. Even during the peak of the strike, Caffery claimed that it was "decidedly unpopular with the public."[25] In support of this statement, the *Miami Herald* told its readers on March 9 that Cuba was experiencing a general strike, but that "the sugar mills are grinding and the tourists are touring, finding Havana fair as ever."[26] The majority seemed weary of the years of revolutionary upheaval. Noting this sentiment, Caffery declared on March 21 that the "feeling of relief at the clearing of the atmosphere is almost universal." The people, he continued, were tired of disorder, and now that the terrorism had been reduced to a minimum, the public seemed more imbued with a respect for law and order. He thought that the Cubans were generally relieved because the agitation had ceased. Concluding his assessment, Caffery added that although the Cuban situation was still unpredictable, he felt "that Cuba today and the Cuban people are happier, more contented, more prosperous, and less harrassed [sic] than they have been in years."[27]

Since his arrival, Caffery had argued that once commercial activity increased, political disturbances would diminish. The strike had interrupted an economic revival, but business continued to show a new vitality. At the close of the *zafra* on April 9, Caffery declared the harvest a tremendous success and gave the army all the credit for keeping the strike from spreading to the sugar fields. The difference between the agitation in the cities and the quiet in the countryside led the ambassador to believe even more firmly that there was a direct correlation between economic prosperity and political tranquillity. As sugar prices rose steadily, exports and imports showed improvement which, in turn, stimulated more bank clearings and a return to buying on credit. Laborers received better wages, and small farmers produced more goods for a public that now had the money to buy them. The increasing revenue allowed the government to spend more money on public projects.[28] Caffery took great pride in this movement and on April 29 proclaimed success for the program that he had helped to formulate: "Politics, in the Cuban mind, has for so long symbolized violence, threats, terrorism, and revolution, that the general public desires only to be left in peace to enjoy the rapidly increasing prosperity, a prosperity which, I am happy to say, it is now being realized is due to the Costigan-Jones legislation and the Trade Agreement."[29]

While some might have argued with the cause and effect relationship posited by Caffery, the economic revival was clearly visible. In 1933 Cuba imported only a little over $22 million worth of goods from the United States and exported just over $57 million worth of its products to the mainland. Two years later, the island's imports had jumped to over $55 million, and its exports had almost doubled in value. The vast expansion was attributed to the Jones-Costigan Act and the reciprocity agreement. Before they went into effect, the price quotation of the New York exchange read 1.23 cents per pound for sugar, while the London market paid .97 cents. In 1935 sugar prices in the American market had increased to 2.33 cents, while the London price moved up only to 1 cent. According to the Royal Bank of Canada, the Cuban sugar industry was in a better position in 1935 than at any time since 1929.[30]

Once Cuban purchasing power increased, American exporters reaped the benefits. Assessing the effects of the new agreement after its first twelve months, the State Department found that the export of United States agricultural commodities to Cuba had expanded by 174 percent and nonagricultural exports by 86 percent. Cuban exports to the mainland had jumped by a phenomenal 281 percent, but this amazing expansion was deceptive. Excluding sugar, Cuban agricultural exports to the mainland increased by only 17 percent, and this growth came mainly from tobacco sales. Although the immediate benefits to Cuba helped alleviate its depression, those who feared the perpetuation of the monoculture had been proven correct.[31]

As long as sugar seemed to be the nation's salvation, Cuban critics who wished to diversify the island's economy could not find an audience. Sugar was the dominant industry, and on February 19, 1935, the Unión Social Económica de Cuba formed to continue the existing commercial relationship. Six months after its founding, a commission of eighteen of its members visited Washington to confer with American officials. They met with Roosevelt on August 12, and he told them that he was happy to see the island showing signs of prosperity. He also called the trade agreement a practical demonstration of the Good Neighbor Policy. Dr. Guillermo Patter-

son y de Jáuregui, a longtime Cuban diplomat and now the
ambassador to the United States, thanked Roosevelt for his role in
helping Cuba move toward recovery. When the commission
returned to Cuba, it received favorable press comment for its
attempts to extend the benefits of the reciprocal trade agreement.
The existence of this lobbying group showed that Cuba's sugar
interests would do everything in their power to continue the
economic accord established in 1934.[32]

Even the increased commercial activity and the restriction of a
tenuous political peace did not stop hostile critics from continuing
their attacks on the Mendieta government. On July 3 Carleton
Beals, whose book *The Crime of Cuba* had damned the Machado
regime, published an article entitled "The New Crime of Cuba."
He described Roosevelt's Cuban policy as a dismal failure whose
"result is that only another Machado is today able to govern Cuba.
His name is Colonel Fulgencio Batista." Welles, he wrote, had
denied recognition to Cuba's only popular regime, and Caffery not
only continued his predecessor's mistakes but also helped to return
the island to the control of the old politicians, whose regime was
modified only by the inclusion of Batista's military forces. Only
after the establishment of a conservative administration did the
United States abrogate the Platt Amendment, because the State
Department could still dominate the island's policies. In Beals's
opinion, Cuba had regressed from the rule of a civilian dictator to
that of a military tyrant: "In the name of the New Deal in Latin
America we have nailed Cuba back on the same old cross."[33]

While some Americans were content to read Beals's condemna-
tion of United States diplomacy, others decided to see conditions
for themselves. On the evening of July 2 a group calling itself the
Commission to Investigate Social and Economic Conditions in
Cuba landed in Havana, planning to spend two weeks studying the
prevailing situation on the island. Seventeen members, led by the
well-known leftist playwright Clifford Odets, had been chosen to
conduct this study, and although they claimed to be unbiased, they
had made several antagonistic statements about the Mendieta
government. As the ship docked, a number of American
newspapermen and Cuban opposition leaders waited for the
passengers to disembark, but others, less friendly, were also on
hand. When the ship was in its berth, Cuban police went on board,
arrested the visitors, and held them for interrogation. The commis-

sion began its study of Cuba inside the Tiscornia detention camp.[34] In the morning Odets phoned Vice-Consul D. D. Edgar, demanding to know why his group was being held. After several hours of probing, the vice-consul learned that the government had denied the delegates entry because they were not tourists and had come only to provoke disorder. He told Odets that he could appeal the decision, but instead the commission decided to leave. On the evening of July 3, they embarked on the same ship that had brought them.[35]

From the time of their incarceration and for the next two days, the Department of State received fifty protests concerning the detention of the commission and the lack of protection by United States officials in Havana. The protests came mainly from leftist organizations, but some were from such prominent writers as Waldo Frank, Lewis Mumford, and Lincoln Steffens.[36] The department's standard reply was that the American representatives in Havana had not been remiss in their duties but had acted promptly once the commission contacted them. Joseph F. McGurk, acting chief of the Division of Latin American Affairs, pointed out that Cuba had the right to determine the admission of aliens, "and that any representations by another government seeking to interfere with or to influence the administration of measures exclusively within domestic competence could only be regarded as unwarranted intrusions upon that sovereignty."[37]

This reasoning did not satisfy Odets, who cabled Caffery on July 5 demanding an "immediate official explanation [of the] outrageous treatment [of the] deportation [of the] American Commission." The ambassador replied on the same day that the Cubans had every right not to allow the commission to enter the island, and he added that Odets had never requested his assistance.[38] Naturally this defense of the Cuban government did not satisfy the commission. Six days after receiving the ambassador's reply, the delegation, now the Provisional Committee for Cuba, passed two resolutions: first, that they were deported on false charges; second, that Caffery had known what was happening to them and that since he had not come to their aid, he should be removed from his post.[39] Ironically, the commission that had originally condemned the ambassador for intervening in Cuban domestic affairs now censured him for not intervening on its behalf.

McGurk, who took charge of the reply, reiterated that a

sovereign nation could admit whomever it wanted, but instead of ending there, he went on to correct some errors in the resolution. First, the group had not been deported for lack of Cuban citizenship; second, it had decided to leave without an investigation even though the consulate had offered one. Diplomatic officials in Washington knew nothing of the commission's project and did not see how their Havana personnel could have acted with greater speed since they too were unaware of the mission. Finally, even though the channels of communication were available, Odets had not contacted the embassy until the following morning. With respect to the part of the resolution demanding Caffery's removal, McGurk concluded, "you are informed that the Ambassador at Habana enjoys the fullest confidence of his Government."[40]

Even this strongly worded statement expressing both support for the ambassador and doubt of the commission's credibility did not end the affair. On August 1 the Provisional Committee for Cuba sent representatives to see Undersecretary Phillips, protesting the unfair handling of their case, and late in October, they even contemplated forming another delegation to return to Cuba.[41] Along with these activities, the commission gained further publicity in the *New Republic*, which claimed that America's Cuban policy had reached a new low point.[42] Beals and Odets also combined to write a short book with the auspicious title *Rifle Rule in Cuba*, alleging that President Mendieta was "merely Caffery's office-boy and Batista his top-sergeant. Both Batista and Caffery travel behind the same machine guns, the machine guns that were trained on a little group of honest American investigators to drive them out of the land. If Batista were not protected by Caffery he could not for one moment have dared to take such unforgettable and unjustifiable action."[43] The commission, the authors contended, had gone to study Cuba's military dictatorship and had found the information it was seeking. The island was indeed ruled by terror and force, and the American embassy supported the repressive regime. Even though Cuba's tyrannical government had put a stop to their study, this did not end comment and exposure but in fact increased critical discussion. The mission was therefore a great propaganda victory, although it had failed to achieve its ultimate goal, since Cuba still suffered from dictatorship and Yankee imperialism.[44]

Each of the involved parties—the commission, the State

Department, and the Cuban government—claimed that it had followed the proper course of action. Possibly the *Miami Herald* best analyzed the affair on the day the delegation returned to the United States. According to the paper, a group went to Cuba to examine conditions there, as if the United States did not have enough problems of its own. American citizens frequently felt the need to probe other nations' troubles, but these individuals "carried with them prejudices and preconceived ideas as to what they wish to find. Hence, there would be no value attached to their effort." Odets insisted that his party was unbiased, but he contradicted himself by declaring that the group's mission was to discover how American interests were subverting the island's independence. The newspaper thought that the only possible result of a mission with such a purpose in mind would be additional enmity between the two countries. When the mission aborted, the paper concluded: "Snoopers from the United States, unfavorable to big business, will hardly contribute anything of importance to the situation and they may stir up a mess. The Cuban government does very well to sit down on them."[45]

Despite such adverse comment, left-wing circles in the United States continued their campaign, and Cuban opposition leaders also attacked the Mendieta regime. Continuing his assault, Grau accepted an invitation to give a series of three lectures in Panama City. He arrived on August 9 and did not even wait to reach his podium. Speaking to reporters at the docks, he stated that the Roosevelt administration had not practiced the New Deal in Cuba. According to him, the interests of American companies came before those of the Cubans; the Platt Amendment had been abrogated, but it still existed in the presence of Caffery. After this preview, he presented his first lecture on August 12. Only forty-two people had attended a prominent American's speech four days earlier, but Grau drew a capacity crowd and received a tremendous ovation for his vehement attack on American policy in Cuba. According to his account, the Cuban people did not control the nation. He informed his audience that the island's economy was weak; capital was in foreign hands; intervention by the United States ambassador continued; and the only possible result of these unsavory conditions would be another popular uprising. Only his program of ending financial imperialism, replacing the old politicians, and disbanding the mercenary army could prevent such an inevitable rebellion, for only with his reforms could the island become a truly independent state.[46]

Such allegations might damage the Cuban government's image abroad, but they did not interfere with Mendieta's course of action. Now, with political and economic stability assured, he returned to his favorite theme of elections. At first he wanted elections for a constituent assembly, but after the March strike, the political leaders on the island united behind a formula for general elections. In early July a new electoral code was promulgated, and Mendieta later decreed that elections would be held on December 15, 1935.[47]

Once these steps were taken, political parties began to regroup. Batista promised that the armed forces would act impartially, and the United States pledged that it would not interfere with the upcoming elections. Even with these guarantees and Caffery's efforts to have the opposition factions participate in the contests, these groups refused to take part.[48] They were certain that elections would be a farce, and Grau went even further: "If we participate, we will be cheated or massacred."[49]

Such statements did not stop the traditionalist politicians from electioneering. By the beginning of November four definite parties had emerged. The largest and best organized, the Conjunto Nacional Democrático, nominated its leader Mario Menocal for the presidency on October 12. His main competition came from two political parties that had decided to combine their forces. Acción Republicana nominated Miguel Mariano Gómez to lead the fusionist ticket, and Federico Laredo Bru of Unión Nacionalista was selected as his vice-presidential candidate. The third most powerful force was the Liberal Party, which had been reformed under the prominent journalist, Ramón Vasconcelos, and on September 30 the party selected journalist, Carlos Manuel de la Cruz to lead the ticket. Finally and least significantly, Conjunción Centralista Nacional chose the ousted ex-president Céspedes to try again for the presidency.[50]

While the parties organized and the political tempo quickened, Mendieta and Batista continued to state that the government would conduct honest and impartial elections. With such constant assurances, the campaign seemed to be proceeding satisfactorily, with the usual political maneuvering. The Menocalistas tried to join forces with the Liberals, but they refused. Once this alliance failed to materialize, the Liberals began to negotiate with the fusionists. In the midst of this complicated political bargaining, Ramón Vasconcelos worked diligently for the new coalition, promising that his party would remove its own presidential ticket to support the fusion candidates, but Manuel de la Cruz refused to resign. Finally, torn by internal feuding, the Liberal Party split. Two provisional assemblies directed by Vasconcelos supported the fusionists, while the other three assemblies stood behind their original choice. As a result of this action, Gómez emerged as the leading contender, Menocal began to fear defeat, and Manuel de la Cruz denounced those of his party who deserted him.[51]

This kaleidoscopic political picture became even more confusing on November 19 when the supreme electoral tribunal ruled that the triparty pact between the Gómez forces and the dissident Liberals was invalid, since the Liberal Party's members must vote for their own presidential nominee. Immediately after this announcement, the fusionists denounced it as politically designed to assist Menocal. They demanded furthermore that the government enact legislation to overrule the tribunal, or they would withdraw from the contest. While the fusionists waited for Mendieta to act, the Menocalistas held that the tribunal's pronouncement must be respected.[52]

With less than a month remaining before the elections, a crisis had arisen which seemed to have no acceptable solution. Mendieta appointed a Cuban commission to devise a compromise, but the political parties rejected its plan. After this idea failed, on November 29 the president invited Dr. Harold W. Dodds, president of Princeton University, to help resolve the impasse. He was well prepared to serve as a technical adviser in electoral matters. Before becoming president of Princeton, he had been a professor of politics there, served as an electoral adviser to Nicaragua from 1922 to 1924, aided in the Tacna-Arica plebiscite between Chile and Peru during 1925, and presided over Nicaragua's national board of elections in 1928. Shortly after his arrival in Havana on December 2, Dodds met with Mendieta, and for the next two days he conferred with the various political factions. After this brief stay, he gave his report to the Cuban government on December 6, suggesting that elections be rescheduled for January 10, 1936, and that the fusionist presidential ticket be allowed to stand in those provinces where the Liberal Party had approved it. Later in the day, the government accepted his proposals.[53]

While Dodds's recommendations were cloaked in electoral-
code jargon, his decision was a clear-cut victory for the fusionists.
They received the news with delight; the opposition reacted with
consternation. On December 8 Menocal and Céspedes announced
jointly that they would not participate in the elections while
Mendieta was in office because of his favoritism toward the
fusionist ticket. The two political leaders stated that they would
reserve their decision only if a new and impartial president not
involved in the political struggle were appointed. Following this
declaration, both men and many of their supporters resigned as
candidates in the elections. The fusionist group naturally deplored
their opponents' stand, but the fact remained that under the
existing circumstances, Mendieta's dream of impartial elections
was crushed.[54]

Faced with virtually no opposition to Gómez and possible
rebellion from other antagonistic factions, Mendieta stated in a
manifesto on December 9 that, in order for elections to be held on
schedule, he would resign. Personally affronted by Menocal's
charge of partiality and frustrated by the intrigue of Cuba's
political parties, Mendieta submitted his resignation to the cabinet
on the morning of December 11. Once his resignation had been
accepted, he left the presidential palace. His ordeal of almost
twenty-three months was finally over.[55]

Mendieta had not been a strong executive. The feuding of his
allies and the antagonism he faced from the opposition baffled the
old politician, who never really seemed to understand how to cope
with Cuba's vast internal problems. The same unstable political
and economic conditions that had plagued Grau also haunted
him—with one tremendous difference. Grau was easily able to
recognize his adversaries—Batista, Caffery, and the old politicians.
Once he identified these individuals, Grau called on the factions
that had supported him in his nationalistic crusade. Mendieta could
not follow his predecessor's tactics. He did not have any definite
program beyond the restoration of peace. Even his supporters
sapped his initiative, for the parties that backed him vied for
political supremacy instead of cooperating to ensure peace. Thus
Batista strove to solidify his position by undermining Mendieta's
presidential authority, and Caffery's critical opinion of Mendieta's
leadership damaged the president's image even more.

Hubert Herring claimed that "Mendieta was a weak man, but honest and of eager goodness of will. Yet he was only a puppet President, for Colonel Fulgencio Batista was the real ruler of the island."[56] Much of this statement is valid, but Mendieta had an importance that transcended the often confusing events of his presidency. His regime was not remembered for a long list of positive acheivements. Given the unparalleled chaos in which it operated, Mendieta's government did not have the political or economic stability to carry out a far-flung program of reform. In spite of this fact, he served a useful purpose by being a conserva- tionist rather than an innovator. Instead of repudiating Grau's programs, he consolidated them. By appearing as the antithesis of his predecessor, he helped form a new synthesis, for only a traditional politician of his stature could have made permanent the many social and economic reforms of the 1933 revolution. Although many of the new laws remained unenforced, they were never repealed. Mendieta left the presidential palace without realizing his personal desire of conducting impartial elections, but this final defeat does not detract from the fact that, whether or not he realized it, he helped bridge the gap between the old generation of 1898 and the new one of 1933.[57]

8

The Winner Loses:
The Impeachment of Gómez

Mendieta's unexpected resignation precipitated another political crisis. While politicians searched for an interim president who would be acceptable to all groups, Secretary of State José A. Barnet y Vingares temporarily assumed executive powers. In the midst of the confusion, the council of state and the cabinet met on the evening of December 11 to select a successor, but they could not reach a decision. While they argued, the Liberal presidential candidate, Manuel de la Cruz, accused the United States of interfering with Cuban domestic politics. The Dodds mission, he argued, had caused Mendieta's downfall and had demonstrated the failure of American diplomacy. Menocal, on the other hand, called the resignation a necessary and patriotic gesture, and the next day his party declared that Barnet should remain as provisional president. This announcement settled the momentary impasse, and at noon on December 13 Barnet took the oath of office, promising impartial elections. The seventy-one-year-old diplomat was well suited to his new role. Since he had been in the foreign service for over thirty-two years, he had not been involved in domestic policies. With his appointment, a serious presidential deadlock was avoided, and just as important, the Menocalistas once more agreed to take part in the elections scheduled for January 10, 1936.[1]

The immediate problem was solved, but the presidential change had not altered the overall political situation. Grau and other opposition leaders reiterated that their groups had no intention of participating in the elections because Batista still controlled the regime. Thus, during the closing weeks of December, the campaign had narrowed down to the same two candidates who had appeared in the early fall—Gómez and Menocal. Both old politicians now intensified their activities and announced their satisfaction with the government's impartiality. Even the Liberal Party's official rejection of its original nominee in order to support Gómez did not cause any delay, for the Menocalistas continued to express their confidence in the government's fairness.[2] Additional assurances of impartial elections came on December 30, when Secretary Hull told reporters that the United States did not have "any preference or prejudice toward any particular electoral candidate, political group or party." The Platt Amendment, he said, had been abrogated, and the Cuban people were solely responsible for their domestic affairs.[3]

The government had made the necessary election preparations by the start of the new year. Not only was this the first presidential race since Machado's election in 1924, but the voters were also choosing congressional and gubernatorial candidates. The 1936 contest featured one other innovation: for the first time in the island's history, women cast ballots. The evening before the voting, two thousand soldiers were dispersed around the countryside to insure orderly polling, and the polls opened early on the morning of January 10.[4] Some minor disorders occurred, but the polling took place with remarkable calm. Chargé Matthews claimed that this was "the quietest election in Cuban history."[5]

The early returns assured the fusion ticket's victory, and when the final results were tabulated, they showed that with 1,650,598 registered voters, Gómez received 515,749 votes and Menocal 420,681. The coalition had triumphed, but even in victory, some ominous signs appeared. Only 61 percent of the eligible voters had exercised their franchise. Although the opposition factions that had not joined in the elections were still a minority, they could use these statistics to support their contention that almost two-fifths of the voting public had given a vote of no confidence to the goverment backed by Batista's military might. This display of continued hostility indicated that the opposition factions would not reconcile their differences with the new regime. Gómez would assume the presidency with the active allegiance of slightly over 30 percent of the voters, and even this figure was deceptive. Shortly after the elections, the victorious coalition was already starting to show signs of cracking; the minority president's support was dwindling to an even greater extent.[6]

The forty-six-year-old victor, Miguel Mariano Gómez y Arias, did not worry immediately about these thorny problems. By winning the election, he followed a family political tradition, for his father was the second president of Cuba. Despite his youth, he had a long career as a politician, serving twelve years in the House of Representatives and twice being elected mayor of Havana during Machado's regime. Even as mayor, the short and slender Gómez displayed his independent nature by attacking the national government's tyrannical rule. Now Gómez was president, and like his predecessors since August 1933 he faced many obstacles. His long association with the traditional politicians weakened his ability to enlarge his base of support, and he also had to preserve his coalition's unity.[7] These were minor anxieties compared to his major problem. Batista had dominated the island's politics since the sergeants' revolt, and even before the elections, the *Nation* had warned, "The United States may attain its desire of having a 'constitutional' President in Cuba, but the island will be no nearer freedom than it was under Machado."[8] The question of whether a civilian would once again take command of the government would be answered only after Gómez's inauguration on May 20.

In the meantime, Barnet had to cope with the immediate issue of United States-Cuban commercial relations. At the peak of the reform movement in December 1933, Grau had decreed an increased sugar quota for the *colonos*, people who cultivated sugarcane but were unable to grind it themselves. This new allotment system damaged the position of American firms. Since Cuban independence, they had purchased huge sugar plantations in order to guarantee their own supply and to lower production costs. Now not only were they forced to process cane for the smaller Cuban farms, but they lost some of their own quota as well. As a result, United States mills claimed that they were being discriminated against, and they grew increasingly irritated at the Cuban government's policies concerning internal quotas. They saw only one recourse: to ask the United States Congress for protection.[9] On October 11, 1935, Duggan expressed his disapproval of such pressure. He said that it "would be most unfortunate for a publicly aired dispute to arise at this time between the foreign interests and domestic interests in the Cuban sugar industry." The issue, he felt, was a domestic one. The larger sugar interests were fighting the smaller ones for quota advantages, and he did not want the State Department to interfere in the struggle.[10]

Duggan was partly correct in his analysis, but he did not see the larger issue implicit in quota regulations. The passage of the Jones-Costigan Act had protected the crops of American domestic producers through the use of quota restrictions. When granted a definite allotment the Roosevelt administration to the Cuban industry, native producers began to agitate for a larger share of the lucrative American market just as domestic growers on the mainland had done. Thus by late 1935 United States sugar interests in Cuba were confronted with an economic squeeze by their fellow sugar-producers at home and by the domestic concerns on the island. All wanted part of the quota, but there was only so much to go around.

The problem of crop distribution grew as the 1936 sugar harvest approached. The State Department was acutely aware of the Cuban government's earlier actions against foreign firms in behalf of its own. According to Arturo Mañas, a Cuban lawyer representing a large number of United States sugar companies on the island, the Cuban officials commonly believed that the American government would not interfere in this issue because it supported the nation's rising living standard. The implication was clear—the Cubans felt that the United States would not protect American sugar interests on the island. Welles spoke to Caffery about the problem, and they decided that the embassy would not take any official action. Instead, the ambassador would continue to press from behind the scenes for equitable treatment of United States companies. Caffery discussed the problem with Mendieta during his presidency, and he agreed to withhold any objectionable decree. In spite of the ambassador's efforts, the sugar people talked of nothing else, and agitation for further crop redistribution grew.[11]

Barnet entered office in the midst of the sugar quota debate. Before he had a chance to take any action, events on the mainland further complicated the issue. On January 6, 1936, the United States Supreme Court declared that a tax on processors of agricultural commodities was unconstitutional when used as a device to control production. This one decision jeopardized Roosevelt's entire agricultural program and immediately caused an adverse reaction in Cuba. Even though Secretary of Agriculture Henry Wallace quickly announced that the decision did not affect the quota provisions of the Jones-Costigan Act, the island's sugar interests were still suspicious.[12]

Wallace had reassured the sugar industry, but at the same time *U.S.* v. *Butler* forced the United States to abandon its cigar-tobacco adjustment program. On March 16 Wallace announced that tobacco duties would be restored to the levels that had existed prior to the reciprocity agreement.[13] Soon after this decision Caffery warned that when the Cubans "come to realize the full significance and import of the announcement we must expect loud protests and expressions of keen disappointment." Adverse climatic conditions, he added, had already damaged the tobacco crop, and the restoration of the earlier tariff duties would emphasize Cuba's loss to an even greater extent.[14] Cuban and American officials discussed the possibility of a restricted supplemental agreement on tobacco, and even though Duggan argued that such a concession would not affect any American group and would only aid Cuban growers, no action was taken.[15]

Although the tobacco growers had a legitimate complaint, their protestations failed to prompt an official government response because of the sugar industry's power to shape and direct economic policy. Despite the loss of the tobacco concession, sugar still represented the island's livelihood, and the industry's spokesmen were not willing to risk their position. If the reciprocal trade agreement were canceled in the hope of regaining the tobacco concession, the sugar industry might lose some of its original reduction, and the producers were not willing to take such a gamble. Thus the Supreme Court's decision affecting United States domestic legislation had grave repercussions in Cuba. It negated the island's second most important concession in the reciprocity agreement, driving the island to increase its dependence on sugar. At the same time, the sugar industry showed its willingness to sacrifice another industry to maintain its own advantage.

While the Roosevelt administration was trying to salvage its agricultural program, the Cuban government was enacting legislation to regulate the sugar industry. If Barnet's interim presidency did anything of importance, it was the enactment of Decree-Law No. 522 on January 18, 1936. This law established quota regulations that would remain in effect for six years. It helped stabilize the industry by ending the struggle between the various factions for quota advantages. Most important to the American interests, it established the Sugar Stabilization Board with nineteen members which would be the controlling group in the regulation of the industry and awarded six of these representatives to the Americans, thus affording them protection against political favoritism and discrimination. Matthews applauded the new law. He informed Duggan on January 24 that he had been working on it since the previous spring. His efforts had paid rich dividends: "Frankly, I am quite delighted with it, and the general concensus of opinion is unquestionably that it is very fair."[16] The only problem he saw was the possibility that other legislation might revise or repeal this decree-law, and throughout the life of the decree, the embassy pressed diligently for its continuation without significant alterations.[17]

Despite Matthews's general optimism, Caffery wanted the United States to consider additional legislation to protect its sugar companies in Cuba. He feared that unless the government took further action the American firms would slowly lose more and more of the Cuban market because of the discriminatory practices of Cuban officials. The island's quota system, the profitable American market, the increased efficiency of the sugar mills, and the length of the dead season (from the end of one *zafra* to the start of the next) all suggested that the Cuban government and its domestic sugar interests would try to improve their position at the expense of the Americans. Although United States producers tried to counteract the efforts to decrease their quota, they were largely unsuccessful. The fierce battle over the passage of Decree-Law No. 522 demonstrated the Cubans' desire to discriminate against American interests even more, but fortunately for the Americans, these efforts failed. The American companies, Caffery claimed, had been treated fairly only at the embassy's insistence, but the Cubans were still trying to gain a larger quota for their mills. On April 22 he urged, "I do not wish to convey the impression that American sugar interests have been guiltless of serious errors in the past or that the maintenance of the 'status quo' is the soundest long-run policy for the economic life of this Republic. I do wish, however, to make it clear that the present protection is due to the Embassy's activity and interest." The only way to protect the gradual elimination of the United States sugar companies from the "very substantial position which they now occupy in Cuba," Caffery reiterated, was for the Roosevelt administration to enact some kind of regulation for their protection.[18]

The ambassador's strong plea met with a negative response from his superiors. Duggan felt that considerable progress had been made with the passage of Decree-Law No. 522 and that Gómez's election assured American companies of fair treatment. As for American legislation, on April 27 he wrote that the embassy's suggestions were "objectionable" because the "United States Government . . . would be directly injected into the quota fight or in determining when an unfair discrimination had resulted, justifying a reduction in the Cuban quota." He also pointed out that the Jones-Costigan Act already gave the secretary of agriculture the power to limit quotas. Although Duggan did not want to use this lever, he did feel that discreet reference to it might be useful when confronting Cuban officials. Even though the direct issue that faced the department was discrimination by the Cuban government, only an improvement in the world situation would help foreign producers. The department, Duggan urged, should work for an international sugar conference to establish a world price that would help relieve the pressure for a place in the American market.[19]

Welles supported Duggan's opinion. Even though the secretary of agriculture had the power to control quotas, the United States would be reluctant to use it on imports from foreign nations. Welles added, "In the long run . . . it is believed that the American sugar interests will secure more favorable treatment as a result of an agreement reached directly by them in cooperation with the Cuban sugar interests and the Cuban Government than by any scheme of control exercised by the Government."[20] Caffery's proposal of economic coercion on the part of the United States had been overruled by his superiors; the State Department had made the point that it would not interfere in Cuba's decision to regulate its sugar crop despite the loud protestations from American sugar firms. At the same time, however, the embassy would continue to press for equitable treatment.

While the officials in Washington debated their role in protecting American sugar interests, they were taking steps to insure their investment by gradually moving out of the industry. In 1929 United Sttes firms had $544 million, or 60 percent of their total capital, invested in sugar, but seven years later this figure had declined to $240 million or 36 percent of the commitment. During this period American companies had slowly begun to take their money out of the sugar business and place it in other areas like public utilities and transportation. Other indications of the trend away from sugar were the decline in American-owned mills and in the percentage of their production. In 1927 American corporations owned seventy-five mills producing 62.5 percent of the entire crop; in 1934, although the number of mills decreased by five, production increased by 5.6 percent. After the Cuban and American governments enacted new sugar legislation, this upward trend ceased, and by 1939 American mill ownership decreased to 65 percent and production slipped to 55 percent of the total Cuban production. American firms quickly realized their tenuous position and were withdrawing from the sugar industry.[21]

Cuba's economic prosperity enabled its citizens to begin to purchase sugar properties. Since 1934 the island had exhibited a commercial recovery attributable in part to the lack of political and labor agitation. Even more important, the United States' tariff on Cuban sugar had allowed the island to benefit from higher prices and a definite market allotment. Although some Cubans argued against this overwhelming reliance on sugar, the island's producers called for the continuation of reciprocity. The State Department published an analysis of trade between the two nations after the first two years of the reciprocal trade agreement; this report confirmed its earlier studies. The United States' gains came from a wide variety of its agricultural and industrial commodities while Cuban sugar alone accounted for the tremendous increase in the value of the island's exports. In 1937 the Department of Commerce issued similar findings. The total foreign trade between the two countries had reached its highest level since 1929, with Cuba ranking first among Latin American nations exporting to the United States and occupying the third spot as a source for United States products going to Latin America.[22]

With this steady economic upswing, Cubans appeared to be losing interest in political agitation. Of course, the rhetorical contest between the old politicians and the reformers continued. The critics still claimed that the revolution was destroyed, while the conservative leaders counseled slow political development. While both sides argued, the same graft and corruption, domination by the army, and some terroristic activity continued. Immediately after the election, hopes for a return to political peace grew, but as the inauguration drew closer, this optimism abated. As soon as Congress convened on April 6, the victorious coalition began to crumble, for instead of acting in a legislative capacity, members of both houses maneuvered for supremacy. The day before the inauguration, Justo Luis Pozo, a leader of the Unión Nacionalista, claimed that once elections were over, fusion ceased to exist and each party was free to take independent action. Gómez added to the fragmentation of the victorious political parties by ignoring the island's economic and political problems. He left Cuba at the end of March and toured the United States for two months, returning home shortly before his inauguration.[23]

The threat of political disintegration did not interfere with the inauguration, however, and on May 20, 1936, the thirty-fourth anniversary of Cuban independent, Gómez became the sixth constitutionally elected president. Early in the evening, the new chief executive went before Congress and read his inaugural message. It was vague and generally inoffensive, but Gómez warned the armed forces that the civilian government was now in charge of the nation's affairs. To emphasize this point, he appeared without Batista at the inauguration. Gómez also showed his independence by selecting a cabinet without consulting the coalition that had placed him in office.[24]

These actions, like his preinauguration absence, were costly political blunders. Instead of considering vital legislation, congressmen preferred to look for ways of securing patronage. When the administration tried to organize a united front to enact important proposals, some parties were willing to cooperate, but there were never enough participants for a working majority. Because of this political inaction, congressional functions were paralyzed, none of the nation's crucial problems were being solved, and the new administration's prestige was already greatly damaged.[25] As 1936 drew to a close, the duly elected executive and legislature were proving their ineptness.

While the politicians were losing stature, Batista was winning new supporters. He had already started to modernize the armed forces by supplying them with new barracks, homes, and hospitals; besides these internal improvements, he publicized the army by touring the provinces. To assure his continued power, he made certain that the new Congress would be composed of men who would listen to his dictates. Only his relationship with Gómez was cloudly. Even before the inauguration, Batista had constantly promised to support the new government. Despite his reassuring statements, there was continual speculation that the two leading political personalities were at odds. No one knew precisely where either man stood. Batista controlled the army and increased his stature, while Gómez fought to restore civilian authority. Both men seemed cordial to each other, but what would happen if and when they clashed?[26]

Such problems probably did not cross Batista's mind when he decided to start 705 rural civic-military schools which had been authorized by Barnet in early 1936. The decree provided that the commander of the army should designate various members of the army to serve as rural schoolteachers. The men chosen for these positions had not made the military their career but were civilians who were inducted into the army before beginning their work. Late in the summer of 1936, about 750 sergeant-teachers arrived in Havana and paraded before Gómez, his cabinet, and Batista. On the third anniversary of the September revolt, the schools opened to 35,000 elementary school children and 20,000 adults in rural areas. The program became extremely popular, but by the end of the year Batista faced a problem. The original decree called for the project to be financed from the military budget, but it was proving more costly than expected. How could Batista continue his rural education plan and at the same time modernize the armed forces?[27]

The military leader found the obvious answer to his problem: he had new legislation introduced in Congress to finance the rural schools program. Under the new bill, each bag of sugar would be taxed nine cents, bringing in an estimated annual revenue of $1.5 million. The bill was introduced in the Senate, and it was passed unanimously on December 4. Up to that moment, the American embassy showed no particular interest; Batista saw no difficulties and left the capital to attend troop maneuvers; and other segments of Cuban society seemed favorable to the nine-cent law. Neither the American ambassador nor the military chieftain saw it as anything more than a means to finance the school project. What they failed to take into account was the fact that the law gave the army official control over rural education and thus took additional power from civilian authorities.[28]

If Batista and Caffery overlooked this crucial issue, Gómez did not. On December 9 with Batista away from Havana, the president, without consulting his friends and advisers, called in the

House leaders and asked them to defeat the bill. If they did not listen to his advice, he warned, he would veto it. Gómez's action surprised Batista. At first the colonel wanted to return and personally lead the fight for its passage, but such a move would immediately precipitate a crisis. Instead he remained at troop maneuvers while friends of both men searched for a compromise.[29]

During the second week of December, the crisis was carefully hidden from the public and press. Congressional leaders looked for a compromise, but neither man would listen. Although the military officers were greatly agitated, Caffery reported that they were not acting unreasonably but were trying to get the necessary votes to override a veto.[30] The Secretary of Agriculture José Gómez Mena saw Caffery on December 15 to present the administration's position and urged him to make a public statement in favor of the veto. The ambassador answered: "I asked the secretary if he realized that such a declaration might involve the probability of our having to land troops back here. I told him that, in my opinion, under no circumstances would my Government authorize me to make such a declaration." He was doing everything possible that he could do personally and informally to urge moderation on the part of the military, and, he declared, "I had very strongly advised them against violence or a violent attitude." The officers told him that they did not intend to take any rash action, and they affirmed furthermore, that "whatever is done by supporters of the bill will be done legally and constitutionally."[31]

Caffery's moderating efforts did not prevent the situation from deteriorating as both men summoned their forces to fight for their respective causes. On December 17 the ambassador wrote, "it is difficult to perceive the possibility of any satisfactory way out of the impasse," but he reassured the department that no revolt would occur because "Colonel Batista has again sent me definite assurance that whatever is done will be entirely constitutional and legal and quite free from violence."[32] The cabinet member who had seen Caffery only two days earlier to win his support for the veto now asked for his cooperation in obtaining Gómez's resignation. Once more Caffery told the minister that he could not join in any such activity.[33] The situation had become so explosive that the ambassador decided to cable Welles about the crisis, telling him, "on numerous occasions since President Gómez's inauguration, I have been influential in patching up disagreements between him and the

1. A Havana street after government troops fired on the mob celebrating the rumored resignation of Machado. Pools of blood are visible in the foreground. August 1933. U.S. Information Agency photo.

2. One of the first photos of President Céspedes and his cabinet. August 1933. U.S. Information Agency photo.

3. The pentarchy. From left: Sergio Carbó, Ramón Grau San Martín, Guillermo Portela, José Irizarri, Porfirio Franca. September 1933. U.S. Information Agency photo.

4. Fulgencio Batista, September 1933. U.S. Information Agency photo.

5. Cuban army and navy officers entrenched in the Hotel Nacional watch the soldiers of the revolutionary army who have surrounded the hotel. September 1933. U.S. Information Agency photo.

6. From left: Batista, Colonel Juan Blas Hernández, and President Grau. Havana, October 1933. U.S. Information Agency photo.

7. Batista giving orders to his soldiers at Camp Columbia after their defeat of the rebels who had tried to overthrow the Grau government. November 1933. U.S. Information Agency photo.

8. President Mendieta shakes hands with Ambassador Caffery after signing the treaty abrogating the Platt Amendment, June 1934. U.S. Information Agency photo.

9. Batista and comrades shortly after the impeachment of Gómez. December 1936. U.S. Information Agency photo.

10. Batista and General Malin Craig, Chief of Staff of the U.S. Army, arriving in Washington, D.C., November 1938. U.S. Information Agency photo.

11. President Roosevelt and high officials greeting Batista on his arrival at Bolling Field, December 1942. U.S. Office of War Information photo.

12. From left: Batista, Cordell Hull, and Dr. Manuel y Santander of Peru lunching at the Pan-American Union, December 1942. U.S. Office of War Information photo.

chief of the army." Caffery approached Gómez on the evening of December 17 and tried in vain to get him to change his position.[34]

At this point, the public became aware of the conflict. By the following day the situation had deteriorated to such an extent that congressmen were openly discussing the possibility of impeaching Gómez if he vetoed the bill. While the politicians were abandoning their civilian leader, Batista traveled around the island winning support for his project. Apart from new support gained by this personal campaign, people in the interior who had benefited from the rural schools program called for passage of the nine-cent law; sugar mill owners and sugar growers, who would have to pay the tax, had endorsed it; and the press and radio voiced their support.[35]

Even though Caffery stated that the rural schools program had many obvious flaws, he also added that the project was popular throughout the nation. If the army had not initiated it, rural inhabitants would not have had any education. In addition, the ambassador thought that the program had directed Batista's attention toward constructive projects, so that he intervened less in other governmental affairs. This point was crucial, for Caffery admitted that "it has been very difficult to keep the army from taking over the Government." Since Gómez had assumed executive power, military officers were being removed from civilian posts that they had held under Mendieta. This loss of positions and patronage was making them increasingly antagonistic to the new regime. In spite of military hostility, the civilian government was being restored, but the conversion, Caffery noted, had been interrupted by Gómez's hasty action. The ambassador believed that he would have to solve the problem: "It is obviously now up to me to try again . . . to endeavor to bring about peace between the Palacio and *Columbia*."[36]

Caffery hoped to avert a crisis, but on December 18 he took the precaution of informing the State Department that Gómez's opponents might impeach him.[37] At this news, Washington officials surveyed the Cuban political situation, realizing that the real issue was not the sugar tax but rather the choice between military and civilian control. The diplomats in the department, however, were more interested in the possible results of the conflict than in its causes: "If Colonel Batista forces the issue along *constitutional lines* and he several times has informed Mr. Caffery that he would take none but legal and constitutional steps," the power would automatically be transferred to the vice-president.[38] But the question that worried Washington diplomats most was whether or not Batista would follow a legalistic formula.

While the department wrestled with the constitutional issue, the Cuban ambassador to the United States, Guillermo Patterson, asked to deliver a personal note from Gómez to Roosevelt as early as possible on December 19.[39] Since Hull was in Buenos Aires attending the Inter-American Conference for the Maintenance of Peace, Patterson refused to see anyone but the president. At 11:00 A.M. he left Roosevelt a brief memorandum on the conditions, stating that the present problem was caused not by a political dispute but by Batista's effort to have the Cuban president removed from office. Gómez stated that he objected to the constitutionality of the rural civic-military schools but that the military refused to allow Congress to decide the issue. The officers had summoned the congressmen to Camp Columbia, where they were informed that if Gómez were not removed, the army would dissolve the legislature. The memorandum ended, "A violence of this nature if successful, would establish a military dictatorship in Cuba with destruciton of democratic principles and would cause a grave state of unrest in the Republic."[40] Although Gómez did not ask directly for Roosevelt's active support, the implication was clear. Ironically, at the same time that he was asking the president of the United States to intervene in the island's domestic affairs, the delegates at Buenos Aires were declaring the illegality of interference and intervention in the affairs of Latin American states.[41]

Gómez's appeal did not persuade Roosevelt to intervene. After discussing the situation with Acting Secretary of State R. Walton Moore, Roosevelt said that he would not intervene in any way, but he hoped that Caffery would point out that the Cuban president's action of calling in congressional leaders to lay before them his opinion of the sugar tax bill was exactly what other democratic presidents did and thus was not to be considered grounds for impeachment. Caffery was to convey this opinion to the appropriate people. When Moore phoned Caffery on December 21 to relay Roosevelt's suggestions, the ambassador declared that he had already used that argument. He then added that the opposition dismissed any conciliatory gesture because it was determined to remove Gómez on any available pretext.[42]

Gómez's opposition was acting with surprising speed to accomplish its objective. One day before debate on the sugar tax bill began, some House members had already drawn up his indictment.[43] On December 15 Caffery urged Batista to stop the impeachment movement, but "Batista made it abundantly clear to me . . . that due to the intense agitation and intense feeling in the Army his own job would be endangered in case he is defeated in this controversy. Therefore he is not as open to reason as he has always been previously up to this time."[44] The movement for impeachment accelerated the following morning when leaders of both houses received petitions for a special session to consider charges against Gómez. During the regular session the House passed the nine-cent tax bill by an overwhelming majority of 106 to 43 and immediatley sent it to Gómez for his expected veto.[45] Now there was no hope of stopping the opposition forces, and Matthews sent the following dispatch: "Mr. Caffery feels that the breach between the two men has developed to such an extent as to make a reconciliation impossible and that sooner or later one or the other will have to give way."[46]

Gómez had lost the initiative. His plan to take power from the military had backfired. Crowds marched through Havana's streets in support of the bill, military officers put pressure on congressmen to vote for impeachment, and the press and radio urged the passage of the bill. On the morning of December 20 a cabinet member saw Caffery and intimated that Gómez's only hope was the United States' "moral intervention," but the ambassador said that this was impossible. Later in the day Gómez even decided to accept a congressional decision to override his veto, but his acquiescence came too late. The opposition was bent on his removal.[47]

The House convened on Monday, December 21, 1936, to await the anticipated veto, and Gómez did not disappoint the members. He based his action on the idea that education should be controlled by the civilian and not the military branch of government: "I cannot fail to note that this law awakens in me fears as to the possible division of the people into irreconcilable classes, separating the Cuban family, until now undivided by religious sentiment, caste, nor race, if the educational system drifts into a separation of civilian life from the military."[48] After the message was read, the House quickly began the procedure for overriding the veto. Caffery hoped that the members would limit themselves to that one act, but he was mistaken. They voted to reconvene later that afternoon so that they might take up the indictment against the president.[49]

For the first time in the history of the republic, Congress was going to try a chief executive. Unfortunately for Gómez, the Cuban Constitution did not specify any definite crimes as grounds for impeachment.[50] Watching these events, Caffery thought that the opposition had the votes for an indictment in the House. He added that even though Gómez had precipitated the crisis, the Congress was acting legally but "with unseemly haste as well as levity and cowardice." He declared, "although the present proceedings have little to recommend them the fact is that the Army and Congress are quite decided to remove President Gomez from office and I see in sight the likelihood of no (repeat no) public protest whatever in the Republic against his removal."[51]

Late that evening the House indicted Gómez for putting pressure on congressmen to support him, coercing Congress by his veto, being inactive, and failing to increase the productivity of the nation. To accuse the president simultaneously of inertia and authoritarianism may seem absurd, but the opposition leaders were not concerned about consistency.[52] One of Gómez's supporters, Eduardo Suárez Rivas, staunchly defended him, contending, "to proceed so lightly in a matter of such gravity as the false accusation of the President of the Republic is not the spontaneous determination of the Representatives freely acting, but rather the result of a military *coup* . . . plotted in the barracks and shrouded in a cloak of legality."[53] Nevertheless, 111 members of the House cast their votes for indictment, while only 45 chose to vote against the charges.[54]

Following the lower chamber's action, the Senate convened the next afternoon to hear the veto message and then the House indictment. First the senators overrode the presidential veto by a vote of twenty-six to six. Such a lopsided count indicated that the opposition forces could easily convict the president, as they needed only a simple majority of the thirty-six senators. The Senate adjourned until the afternoon of December 23 to try the president, and in the interim, the press suggested that Gómez resign. His fate virtually sealed, Gómez waited for the final verdict, and in the early morning of December 24, the Sente officially convicted him by a vote of twenty-two to twelve.[55]

Thus Gómez was the first president to be removed from office by Congress. Upon receiving notification of his conviction, he immediately left the presidential palace for his private residence. After leaving office, he issued a statement claiming that the charges were without foundation and added that he had been betrayed by the very coalition that had supported him only eleven months earlier. He had tried to carry out his duties by vetoing the nine-cent tax because it gave even more power to the military, which already controlled one-third of the national budget. Now, he said, Batista should openly take power. He ended his message without making any reference to the role of the United States. Subsequently he charged Caffery with complicity in his removal, for the ambassador had not only refused to intervene in his behalf, but had also consorted with the military. The ex-president's activities did not end there; over the next year he tried in vain to regain his position by appealing his case through the courts.[56]

While Cuba experienced her constitutional crisis, the *St. Louis Post-Dispatch*, reflecting journalistic opinion in the United States, proclaimed the advent of a military dictatorship. When the confrontation between Gómez and Batista gained publicity on December 19, the paper commended the Cuban president for his stance but added that unless he compromised, the military would remove him from office. Four days later the newspaper warned that as long as the armed forces had supreme power, "true democracy cannot exist." Even though the Cuban Congress operated under the guise of legality, the result was still the "establishment of a military dictatorship bordering on Fascism." Gómez would become another martyr who had tried and failed. After his conviction, the paper declared, "The army is master of Cuba." It had control of the rural education program; now it controlled the executive too. "So Cuba joins the group of militaristic countries where the soldier is schoolmaster."[57]

Other American newspapers and magazines also deplored the defeat of Cuban democracy and compared Batista to Mussolini and Hitler,[58] but the Cubans did not see the impeachment struggle from the same perspective. After Gómez's removal, the people did not demonstrate for his return but instead quietly accepted the congressional action. Mario Lazo, disappointed by the perversion of the democratic process, asked his Cuban friends why the legislative leaders were not satisfied with just overriding the veto, and they answered, "To them the essential thing was that Batista had brought order out of chaos, had given the country stability it so greatly needed, and the issue of military versus civilian rule was secondary. By instinct they were attracted to the young new leader who had met so much success and was already regarded by many as a caudillo."[59] Other writers reflected these sentiments. Cubans were more interested in stability and the rising economic prosperity than in maintaining a democratic facade.[60]

Gómez had chosen an issue with which he hoped to defeat his principal rival, but he made a tremendous blunder in attacking the nine-cent tax and the system of rural education. As a result, the military, supported by a large segment of the laborers and influential leaders in business and government, ousted the president. The impeachment proceedings were constitutionally legal, but the substance of the law was ignored if not negated. Ironically, while Caffery's Cuban and American criticis accused him of intervening in the island's domestic affairs, Gómez went directly to Roosevelt for his assistance, and cabinet members requested support for the ambassador. None of these paradoxical considerations seemed to bother Cuban officials at the time, for the removal of Gómez resolved a more important question. Ever since his first revolt in September 1933, Batista had steadily expanded his authority. When a civilian government returned to power in 1936, no one knew the exact status of the military forces or their commander, but once the president was removed, this issue was settled. Now Batista was the island's undisputed political boss.

Once Cuba's internal conflict had been resolved, another event followed which affected the course of United States-Cuban relations: Jefferson Caffery left his post in March 1937 to assume new duties as ambassador to Brazil.[61] Caffery was by far the most controversial figure appointed to the Cuban ambassadorship during Roosevelt's long tenure. His opponents attacked him from every conceivable vantage point. In early 1935, one critic claimed that Caffery was ruling the island through its own military forces.[62] The *New York Post*, on May 16, 1936, accused him and Batista of establishing a reactionary state, perpetuating the policies of the Coolidge-Hoover era, and "making a joke of the Good Neighbor Policy."[63] Similar protests and demands for Caffery's removal came into the Department of State and the White House throughout his tour of duty. Although his enemies varied in their language, their message was similar. They advocated his immediate removal on the grounds that, as shown by his continual intervention in Cuba's internal affairs, he had refused to implement the Good Neighbor spirit.[64]

Caffery also had his defenders. One American who spent five months on the island in early 1936 wrote to Roosevelt about Caffery's outstanding job. As far as he was concerned, "there is no one better equipped than Mr. Caffery to spread" the Good Neighbor Policy.[65] Mario Lazo later added that the ambassador was "entitled to recognition for a great service rendered to Cuba."[66] Roosevelt and Hull personally defended his conduct,[67] and in his memoirs Hull wrote that "Caffery proved himself one of our outstandingly capable representatives."[68]

In early 1936, Hubert Herring assessed the American ambassador from yet another perspective, showing how difficult it was to analyze his impact. Herring had commented on Cuban affairs since Machado's dictatorship, and he realized the problems that Caffery faced. The opposition forces attacked him for his support of Batista and the old politicians; the government coalition praised him for assisting in the maintenance of constitutional rule. "About the only thing firmly proved by the developing drama is that the American Ambassadorship in Cuba deserves first place on the list of impossible jobs."[69]

Herring's analysis not only showed the wide gulf between Caffery's defenders and his detractors but also illustrated some of the difficulties in assessing his three-year tour of duty. Perhaps Caffery himself gave the most enlightening clue about his Cuban policies. On March 8, 1935, he wrote to Roosevelt that the most successful diplomats were those who had the ability to establish good working relations with officials of the host country.[70] In his Cuban experience, he acted on this principle. When he took charge of the embassy in December 1933, he was acutely aware of the island's chaotic conditions and of Welles's adamant opposition to Grau's regime. As Roosevelt's special representative, he had somehow to change the existing government without invoking the Platt Amendment and also to find a method of reviving the island's depressed economy. To accomplish these goals, Caffery immediately began to discuss the political impasse with Cuban leaders in both the opposition and the administration, but more important, he won Batista's confidence.

In the midst of this complicated political maneuvering, Grau's unexpected resignation and Mendieta's assumption of the presidency partly solved the ambassador's first problem. Even after Roosevelt granted recognition, Caffery still helped to shape Cuba's internal political structure. Distrustful, almost disdainful, of the Cuban political leaders, Caffery formed an intimate working arrangement with Batista, who, he thought, repeatedly saved the island from anarchy. He complemented his close ties with the military leader by his part in negotiating the reciprocity agreement, firmly believing that once foreign trade increased, political unrest would abate. Like Welles, Caffery chose to become an integral part of Cuba's political process. The combination of economic revival with military control restored the stability that Caffery desired.

To assure the success of his program, the envoy continued to influence and even to direct internal policies, often knowing more about what was going to happen than the Cuban president did. In his overt actions, such as supporting Mendieta's shaky government with the presence of American warships, influencing domestic sugar legislation to protect United States companies, and forcing the military to maintain a constitutional facade in the removal of Gómez, Caffery had a fundamental effect on Cuba's internal development. When he left the island, he could claim that its political and economic problems had been partially resolved. But his critics could also rightly attack him for ignoring what they considered to be the Good Neighbor Policy of noninterference in Cuban political and economic affairs. Caffery might have retorted that these charges, though true, were side issues to him. His purpose was to restore stability, and he had accomplished his primary task.

The ambassador was correct in believing that a kind of stability had returned to Cuba. Yet he must share much of the responsibility for perpetuating many of the island's internal difficulties. His disparagement of the civilian leaders and his admiration of Batista drove Cuba's political system into greater disrepute. Although he never advocated military intervention, he used the presence of the warships to support the Mendieta government and thereby maintained his political influence even after the abrogation of the Platt Amendment. He refused to assume the role of official mediator that Welles had taken on, but during the conflict between Batista and Gómez, he showed not only his involvement in the domestic crisis but also his power to direct its outcome. Finally, like his predecessor, he refused to deal with the opposition forces unless they joined the government coalition. Since Caffery held to this position during his tenure, idealistic reformers like Grau could accuse the United States of retarding revolutionary innovation. The Cubans themselves shared the responsibility for the country's failure to achieve political tranquility, but they used Caffery as their scapegoat. Cuban politicans refused to seek a compromise, preferring to make Caffery, like Welles before him, seem responsible for their division. Peace had been achieved, but the price was the further fragmentation of the nation, making a reconciliation between the chief factions impossible to accomplish.

Ironically, while United States policy-makers were contributing to this political deterioration, the Roosevelt administration was claiming success for the Good Neighbor Policy. In the Democratic presidential platform of 1936, the foreign policy plank listed the abrogation of the Platt Amendment as a positive achievement.[71] On August 14, 1936, Roosevelt went so far as to proclaim in his Chautanqua address, "In the whole of the Western hemisphere our good-neighbor policy has produced results that are especially heartening."[72] Roosevelt's Latin American policy stood as a unique exception to the American isolationism of the mid-1930s. He had outlawed military intervention as an instrument of diplomacy, revived trade within the Western Hemisphere, and gained personal stature throughout Latin America for his efforts.[73]

The American public acclaimed this policy, and so did Batista and the island's traditional leadership. As for the Cuban opposition forces, they voiced their consternation. While they never attacked Roosevelt directly, they deplored the policies of his subordinates, Welles and Caffery. They had witnessed the abrogation of the Platt Amendment but saw warships remain at their post; they had watched the subservient action of their Congress in the impeachment of the first constitutionally elected president since the fall of Machado; and they noted the intensification of the sugar monoculture after the signing of the reciprocity agreement. If Roosevelt had envisioned initiating a new program throughout Latin America with the announcement of the Good Neighbor Policy, many Cubans felt that this commitment had not been implemented on the island. As far as they were concerned, the application of the Good Neighbor Policy was merely another way of maintaining the status quo.

9

A Time for Consolidation

For the first time since Machado's ouster there was no question about the presidential succession. Twelve hours after Gómez's removal, Vice-President Federico Laredo Bru took the oath of office at noon on December 24, 1936. Roosevelt assisted this reasonably smooth transfer of political authority by permitting automatic American recognition because the new chief executive had assumed his duties in the constitutionally prescribed manner. The tense situation did not immediately end, however, for some people began to spread rumors that Laredo Bru would shortly resign or be replaced, while others speculated that Gómez would ultimately return to the presidency. In an effort to squelch this idle gossip, Batista and prominent government leaders publicly pledged their support for the new administration, but even this display of solidarity did not stop all of the widespread speculation.[1]

A new man had assumed the presidency, but in many respects, he symbolized the return to the old politics even more than his deposed predecessor. Born in Remedios, Santa Clara Province, Laredo Bru had fought in the War of Independence, entered local politics, and become a prominent leaders of the Unión Nacionalista. After Machado fled, he joined the cabinet of Céspedes, and under the Mendieta regime he became president of the council of state. To seal the fusion pact in 1935, Gómez chose him as his running mate. Now he was president. Unlike Gómez, Laredo Bru demonstrated his political acumen from the outset by declaring, since he realized that he would have to share power with the military, that he was a friend of the armed forces. This statement, coupled with his previous record, helped to calm the potentially explosive situation.[2]

As for Batista, he had gained a stunning political victory with the removal of Gómez. The nine-cent tax easily became law, increasing the prestige of the armed forces to an even greater extent. The Cuban economy was reviving as well, for the sugar harvest was progressing normally with prospects for an excellent crop, and tourism showed a marked increase. Even the students seemed weary of revolution. When the university reopened on April 2, more of them enrolled than ever before, and most seemed content to attend classes rather than participating in political controversies. The only apparent sign of antagonism was the congressional division into militarist and civilian factions. Reconciliation between them would take time, but with the conclusion of the tense political confrontation, the island looked forward to peace.[3]

Even this apparent tranquillity depended on the continued rise in sugar exports. When the industry had been placed in jeopardy, the whole fabric of society was shaken, and uncertainty returned when, on March 1, 1937, Roosevelt proposed a new sugar bill to meet the Supreme Court's earlier objections to the A.A.A. As the bill moved through Congress, the Cubans carefully watched its progress, and while they waited for final passage, the islanders faced a temporary business decline. Adding to the confusion, Gómez's supporters began to spread rumors that the United States was punishing the island for impeaching their leader. This gossip reached such fantastic proportions that on March 25 Matthews reported, "It would be difficult to find any one in Cuba, however well informed, who does not closely associate these two questions [Gómez's impeachment and the United States sugar legislation] in a relationship of cause and effect."[4] The rumors persisted until September 1, when Roosevelt signed the new sugar law. Once the Cubans realized that it was similar to the Jones-Costigan Act, economic uncertainty ended, and business resumed normal activity. Again the Cubans had been forced to realize the extent to which their economic and political stability depended on the domestic sugar program of the United States.[5]

While the Cuban sugar industry lobbied in the United States for a larger quota and a higher price, Cuba was also participating in an international sugar conference in London, hoping to devise an effective program to boost the price of sugar on the world market. On May 6, 1937, Cuba and the other major sugar exporters agreed to limit their exports for a five-year period. Unlike the abortive Chadbourne Plan of 1931, in which only 40 percent had participated, the London agreement won the support of the twenty-one nations that controlled almost 90 percent of the world production. Now Cuba had not only a guaranteed quota on the American market, but also world cooperation, which might assure even greater stability for its principal industry.[6]

While the island concentrated on economic security, Cuban politicians continued to prove their inability to act. Any hopes for congressional cooperation had disintegrated, for upon the removal of Gómez, each party reverted to the traditional struggle for patronage. Pending legislation received little if any attention while the various factions fought, and congressional prestige slipped to a new low. Capitalizing on the failures of the traditional parties, the Auténticos and other opposition parties renewed their demand for the constituent assembly that had been promised by every regime since August 1933. As resentment at congressional ineptness grew, this idea began to gain a large and vocal following.[7]

Batista quickly realized that he was losing ground. If he was going to maintain his undisputed leadership, the government would have to take positive steps. With such a purpose in mind, he granted an interview to a representative of *Diario de la Marina* on June 20 and announced his intention of initiating a broad program for the island's economic and social advancement. Laredo Bru, his cabinet, and prominent congressional leaders enthusiastically offered their cooperation, and what was now labeled the Three-Year Plan became the chief topic of discussion on the island. Some cynically called it Cuba's "300-year plan," but others sincerely predicted that it would be a New Deal for the islanders. The program included the establishment of new regulations on the sugar industry to assist the small grower, proposals for the distribution of government land to squatters, agricultural diversification, educational improvements, and many other long-promised reforms. Batista had again demonstrated his political astuteness by providing something for everyone in one stroke.[8]

Batista had deliberately stolen the Auténticos' avowed platform, for, as he confided to Matthews, one of his chief objectives was to prevent the radical elements from returning to power. He asked the chargé's opinion of his plan, and for the first time he also hinted that he was depending on American economic assistance to carry out his ambitious endeavors.[9] Matthews thought that many of the proposals had merit, but he also foresaw that most of them would never be enacted into law, for, as he wrote on June 28, "The classes and interests which have hitherto dominated Cuba's economic life may, of course, be expected to oppose many of the Colonel's reforms, if not openly at least through quiet methods of sabotage. To hope that they will understand that the adoption of a moderate program of reform at the present time will save them from far more prejudicial . . . measures by a less sympathetic regime is, I fear, to credit the majority with a foresight and vision which they do not possess."[10]

Matthews's pessimism proved to be well founded when Batista's first major reform went to Congress in early July. Entitled Ley de Coordinación Azucarera (Law of Sugar Coordination), its objectives were (1) to guarantee the small sugar-growers a larger share of the crop by transferring a percentage of the quota to them from the wealthier plantation owners and (2) to establish minimum wages and prices for grinding cane. Although the bill quickly won congressional consent and was signed into law on September 3, it was only partially successful during the next two decades. As for the rest of Batista's ambitious reform program, he was forced to abandon it early in 1938 because of economic recession, lack of United States assistance, and the call for the constituent assembly. Part of the Three-Year Plan had been enacted into law, but those that controlled the island's economy also dictated how much of it the government would enforce.[11]

During the struggle over the sugar law, American diplomats showed themselves more alert to the necessity of reform than were the island's sugar interests. Matthews, for example, urged that even though the American companies were adamantly opposed to the law, the embassy should not intervene in their behalf. On July 26 Welles agreed with the chargé's decision, stating that the *colonos* must have fair and equitable treatment "if that highly influential body in Cuban public opinion was to be kept as an inherently conservative and moderating influence in Cuban political and economic life . . . that point of view taken by certain Americans in Cuba to the effect that all advantages were to be obtained by the mill owners and none by the colono was, in my judgment, as short-sighted as it was stupid."[12] Matthews made his government's position quite clear to Cuban authorities. He was certain that the American companies would lose their fight, and he was dismayed because Batista had offered them the fullest possible protection.[13] Even without the embassy's assistance, American interests continued to lobby against the sugar law and the entire program. Their efforts were supported by local businessmen. These men, "representing for the most part the spirit of entrenched greed," wrote Matthews, "will certainly engage in the most determined attempts at undercover sabotage and I believe that they will, as they have always in the past, succeed in keeping their present dominant economic position immune from any serious inroads."[15]

In the midst of the debate over the Three-Year Plan, the United States changed its diplomatic personnel in Havana. A new first secretary, Willard Beaulac, took his post on August 15. He had graduated in the first class of Georgetown University's School of Foreign Service in 1921 and had then joined the diplomatic corps. For the next sixteen years he served in various Latin American posts, gaining an intimate knowledge of the region's customs and language.[16] Two days after Beaulac became first secretary, Ambassador J. Butler Wright arrived. The fifty-five-year-old envoy had spent thirty-six years in the foreign service. Beaulac later described him: "Handsome, charming, debonair, he was a model of manly elegance would would have played his role on Broadway as successfully as he fulfilled it in real life."[17] Perhaps because he had been minister to Uruguay during the Monetevideo Conference, he was firmly committed to nonintervention and noninterference in the internal affairs of Latin American states. Wright was thus by temperament the antithesis of his predecessor. With political and economic security assured on his arrival, not only did he act to ensure the continuation of domestic peace, but he also waged a concerted campaign to end the American ambassador's role of policy adviser to Cuban officials in their domestic decisions.[18]

Wright made his intentions clear, even while presenting his credentials to Laredo Bru on August 23. He stated that he was the first United States ambassador sent to Cuba since the abrogation of the Platt Amendment and added that he wanted to try to fulfill the obligations of the Good Neighbor spirit by cooperating with the Cuban government in mutual endeavors. Three weeks later, addressing the American Club in Havana, he again emphasized the theme of cooperation, telling his audience that he would protect United Stated interests and would simultaneously foster friendlier relations between the two countries.[19] Shortly after assuming his post, he told the Cuban lawyer Mario Lazo that "the State Department had instructed him to deal with the Cuban President in formal fashion. 'We will not be cutting corners, . . . there will be no repetition of the past.' "[20] Wright held to this approach throughout his stay, always conscious of Hull's instructions to follow a strict policy aimed at nonintervention and noninterference. Unlike Caffery, he operated through the usual diplomatic channels, only occasionally dealing directly with Batista. His primary mission was one of public relations, of convincing the Cubans that the United States meant to be a Good Neighbor, while Beaulac and the rest of the staff handled the embassy's daily routine.

Unfortunately for the ambassador, this policy proved more difficult to carry out than to announce. Wright's first detailed assessment of Cuban conditions, dated January 15, 1938, explained the complex problems that confronted him. The economic indicators showed that the island was continuing its business revival. The price of sugar was satisfactory, tobacco exports were increasing, the new sugar legislation aided Cuba's small farmers and laborers, and the tourist trade was thriving. But while the economic situation was improving, the ambassador noted ominous developments in the political sphere. Batista completely dominated domestic affairs, and although he himself appeared genuinely interested in helping the peasants, many of his supporters were concerned only with personal gains. Despite widespread corruption, a large segment of the population still approved of the military's role in the government, but Wright realized that many others opposed the military's predominance and felt that the reforms promised during the Revolution of 1933 would never materialize. The truth, Wright concluded, "is that out of a widespread popular revolt of the masses has come military dominance—more or less benevolent at the time, but nevertheless fairly complete and in a position to be arbitrary. This situation . . . is new in Cuba and one which is psychologically repugnant to the mass of Cubans, who are in general impatient of restraint and all too individualistic." Even though the opposition factions were not satisfied with the present regime, he saw little chance of change, for the island's current political activity could be characterized in one word: apathetic.[21]

Political stability depended on steadily rising sugar exports, but the 1938 *zafra* was disastrous, so the island faced its worst economic crisis in several years. Compounding the government's misfortunes, a ten-month drought in the eastern end of the island killed livestock and caused fires in the sugar fields. When the price of sugar on the American market dropped, the government faced even graver problems, for its revenue drastically declined, and although by the end of the year Laredo Bru was beginning to reduce expenditures, the recession gave the opposition a clear issue with which to attack Batista's policies.[22]

Once the delicate balance between economic prosperity and political stability had been shaken, the apathetic mood changed abruptly. Congress refused to act in the crisis, and when the failure of the harvest was publicized, the call of the opposition groups for a constituent assembly became the principal topic for political discussion. In response to this growing agitation, Batista, Laredo Bru, and the leading government officials announced on May 10 that the government would shortly hold constituent assembly elections in which all parties could participate. After five years of bitter controversy, the opposition finally decided to accept the administration's offer and prepared for the upcoming contest. As more and more political exiles returned, Laredo Bru signed a new electoral census law on July 23, and anticipation of the assembly increased.[23]

While the Cubans tried to settle their internal problems, the American embassy turned its attention to the complex issue of the island's public debt. The Platt Amendment had originally included a provision that allowed the State Department to examine all Cuban foreign loans. As a result, the island's bond issues were floated in the United States, and Americans held the bulk of the securities. Once the depression struck, Machado and Céspedes had continued payment at a reduced level, but Grau shocked the bondholders when he announced the first formal default on the foreign debt in the republic's history. On April 10, 1934, Mendieta reaffirmed his predecessor's decision by signing a decree declaring an indefinite moratorium on all servicing of the foreign debt. During his chaotic administration, the State Department refused to intervene on behalf of its investors, but it did help to sponsor the Foreign Bondholders Protective Council to bargain for payment on the securities. Once the United States abrogated the Platt Amendment, further complications arose. The Roosevelt administration no longer had the responsibility of scrutinizing Cuba's foreign loans, but it did have an obligation to assist American investors who had legitimate claims.[24]

As the island moved slowly toward economic recovery, the
bondholders began pressing Washington to collect Cuba's debt,
which was estimated at $85 million. In July 1936 the Cuban
government invited the council to send representatives, who
discussed the issue without any positive results. In spite of these
early reversals, American investors continued their agitation until
February 14, 1938, when the government enacted a law that
provided for an $85 million bond issue to consolidate and cancel
most of its earlier bonds. Even this measure did not satisfy all the
creditors; Purdy and Henderson Company and Warren Brothers,
both holding bonds of over $15 million, had been excluded from the
settlement.[25]

The State Department did not help them to settle their claims
until Beaulac reported on the Cubans' attitude toward their
remaining debts. Earlier, when a Cuban delegation had visited
Welles to discuss the entire public debt question, they had
somehow gained the impression that if they satisfied most of the
bondholders, the United States would give the regime economic
assistance. Dismayed by this attitude, Beaulac urged a prompt
settlement and informed the Cuban government that the United
States desired equal treatment for all its investors.[26] On October 16
Welles recalled his earlier discussions with the Cuban delegates,
but he categorically denied any bargain: "There has never been
any indication by me of 'additional economic benfits' as a *quid pro
quo* for an adjustment on the part of Cuba with its bondholders."[27]

In spite of Welles's clarification, the Cuban government refused
to reach a settlement with the unpaid bondholders. The island's
recession and the bickering within Congress inhibited any movement toward a final solution. Frustrated by this inaction, Welles not
only reemphasized the necessity of a settlement, but also warned
the Cuban regime that until it balanced its budget, ended
corruption in its treasury department and internal revenue service,
and corrected the laws that affected American interests adversely,
the island could not expect any American assistance. When a
proposed loan from the Eximbank came up for discussion in early
1939, Wright repeated Welles's ultimatum that the bank would not
extend credit until these problems were solved.[28]

Internal conditions on the island had changed radically since the
Mendieta government received the three silver loans from the
bank, and so had American policy. During the early period of

virtual anarchy, the State Department's principal concern was the restoration of stability, and it granted the loans with this purpose in mind. Now that the island's economic and political peace was assured, the United States decided to exert pressure for the repayment of the bondholders' loans. By the end of 1939 the State Department had evolved a new position concerning Cuba and the American bondholders: no economic assistance without a final settlement on the debt and internal reforms.

The bondholders' controversy, combined with the economic recession and the opposition's agitation for the assembly, again placed Batista's position in jeopardy. Having taken credit for Cuba's recent revival, he now faced the brunt of the criticism for the growing uncertainty. At the peak of these attacks, the United States Army's chief of staff, General Malin B. Craig, unexpectedly came to Batista's assistance by inviting him to attend Armistice Day exercises in Washington on November 11, 1938. When the local press heard the news, it placed extraordinary importance upon the event, speculating that Batista would be offered guarantees of economic aid.[29]

Batista left the island on October 29 while the islanders discussed the benefits that he would obtain. Unfortunately for them, the State Department was not contemplating any large grants of economic assistance. On the contrary, Duggan felt that the Cubans had received more benefits from the Good Neighbor Policy than perhaps any other Latin American state and that over the past five years a paradoxical situation had developed. The Cubans had placed innumerable obstacles in the way of American companies, while the American government had not restricted any legitimate activities of Cuban firms on the mainland. "This is not reciprocity," declared Duggan, "nor what in return for its assistance to Cuba the United States has a right to expect from Cuba." He thought that the United States should demand a continuation of Decree-Law No. 522 and a possible revision of the trade agreement. In addition to these measures, he wanted a treaty to assure American companies treatment equal to that of their Cuban counterparts, a debt settlement, and changes in the island's inadequate and inefficient financial structure. Only after the Cuban government acted on these items, he stressed, should the United States consider granting economic assistance.[30]

Batista attended the Armistice Day celebration, spoke with

Roosevelt, and discussed the island's problems with State Department officials. Returning on the gunboat *Cuba* on November 25, he received a hero's welcome. The guns of Cabañas Fortress fired a salute as he landed, thousands lined the waterfront and the route to the presidential palace, Laredo Bru and other prominent politicians received him at the palace, and from the balcony, he watched a four-hour parade in his honor. Afterward he told the enthusiastic crowd that he had gained many benefits from the Roosevelt administration. He stated that there would be a new reciprocity agreement favoring more Cuban goods, hinted that the United States would grant financial assistance, and added that the two nations would cooperate in military affairs.[31]

The military leader did not tell his listeners that these benefits would accrue only after the Cuban government acted on the United States' proposals. One month after Batista's return, Wright informed the State Department that except for Batista's promise not to change Decree-Law No. 522, no other action had been taken.[32] Welles quickly reaffirmed the American position. The United States would not begin trade negotiations until a bondholders' settlement had been reached. If the Cubans did not act on these claims, the United States could only assume that the regime was not cooperating, and therefore the Eximbank would not grant any loans. The undersecretary commented, "The obvious tendency on the part of the Cuban Government to demand further and further commitments by this Government prior to cleaning up its obligations to American citizens should be definitely discouraged." Furthermore, he told Wright to point out that if the Cubans did not act soon, the United States would not give any kind of financial assistance at all. According to Welles, the next move was up to Cuba, not the United States.[33]

Under these conditions, Batista quickly realized that he would not be able to deliver all that he had originally promised on his triumphant return. When he spoke at a banquet on January 9, 1939, he told his audience that although his trip had been successful, Cuba should expect more from her own productivity than from foreign assistance. This announcement plus the obvious lack of United States aid disappointed the Cubans, for although they regarded his visit as a personal victory, he had not helped to alleviate the business slump. Along with these economic disappointments, the regime was faced with the prospect of increased political agitation when Grau returned to Havana on December 9, 1938, ending his self-imposed exile of more than four years. All the local papers carried the news of the return and Grau's announcement that he had come back to participate in the elections for the constituent assembly. Faced with the demands of the United States for internal reforms, the uncertainty of the economic conditions, and the increasing demand for the assembly, Batista's popularity plummeted, and with it Cuba's stability.[34]

While Batista tried to regain his lost prestige, the opposition groups acted to form a united front. On January 5, 1939, Grau, Menocal, Gómez, and Martínez Saenz met and publicly declared that the only way to solve Cuba's domestic problems was to hold elections for the constituent assembly. As the opposition factions increased their pressure, the government tried to make a virtue of necessity. Batista expressed a rather hollow delight that an opposition bloc had formed, and Laredo Bru promised that all political parties would receive full guarantees of impartial elections. Behind the scenes, political activity intensified. Batista vied for support from both the right and the left; the opposition forces organized and reaffirmed their demand for elections; and the political parties began to form coalitions for the upcoming campaign. On April 17 Laredo Bru signed a new electoral code law, and three months later the political parties were organized and ready for the elections.[35] Toward the end of May, one writer described the confusing state of affairs: "Cuba is not all rum and rumba. All the worries of the world can be found here in miniature. The soaring budget, the shrinking national income, the farm surplus, the rising cost of a political peace, the class-concious conflict, indecisive democracy giving way to armed authority."[36]

Batista still controlled the island, but he faced mounting pressure from the United States to settle the problems that he had discussed in Washington. On July 29 Welles reminded the Cuban ambassador to the United States, Pedro Martínez Fraga, that nine months had elapsed since Batista's trip. The Roosevelt administration, he continued, would gladly carry out its program of economic assistance if Cuba would fulfill its obligations. Since the Cuban government had not made any significant reforms, Welles felt that the regime was responding to his outstretched hand of friendship with a kick. Martínez Fraga promised him that the problems would be solved, but Welles, tired of empty pledges, sternly warned him:

"I said that he must bear in mind that if after August 9th or 10th a reasonable period had elapsed and that the assurances he had given me were not carried into practice, he could not possibly wait any longer but must announce the definite suspension of the [trade] agreement negotiations and our inability to continue with the program of economic cooperation upon which he had agreed."[37]

Besides the external pressure from the United States and the opposition's demands for elections, Cuba's economic situation was still deteriorating. Although tourist receipts had doubled since 1934, the price of sugar had declined, and so had tobacco exports. This bleak outlook continued until September 1, 1939, but once the European war began, sugar prices soared. In August 1939 the price-spread for sugar between New York and London was .63 cents per pound, but from August 31 to September 6, the New York quotation jumped from 2.03 to 2.96, and the London price advanced from 1.32 in August to 2.42 in September. Cuban business and political circles now hoped for a prolonged conflict, which would save the island's economy. Following Roosevelt's declaration of neutrality, Laredo Bru signed a similar decree, while the business interests rejoiced at the newfound prosperity.[38]

Hopes for economic salvation soon faded when Roosevelt shattered Cuban dreams by suspending the quota provision of the 1937 Sugar Act on September 11, 1939 because of excessive sugar purchases by both consumers and speculators immediately after outbreak of the war. Since the tariff reduction on Cuban sugar remained in effect only as long as the United States domestic program was in force, the duty was automatically raised from .90 to 1.50 cents per pound. Roosevelt's action, taken as a result of domestic pressure, had also canceled Cuba's principal benefit under the trade agreement. Instead of having an advantage in the American market under the quota system, it had to cope with approximately equal prices on both the world and the American markets.[39]

The Cubans received Roosevelt's action with consternation. It had shattered their dreams of unbounded prosperity created by excessive war profits. Since the American government had not consulted the Cuban government before Roosevelt acted, the first response of the Cuban public was to assume that the United States was retaliating for Cuba's failure to fulfill her obligations. When the Cuban government recovered from its initial shock, there was talk of denouncing the entire agreement. But more prudent counsel prevailed, and on September 19 the Cuban Sugar Stabilization Institute adopted a resolution which declared that the suspension had violated neither the International Sugar Agreement nor the reciprocity agreement. The group hoped, however, that the United States would restore the quota to protect the island's sugar industry.[40]

While the Cubans pressed for a resumption of the quota, Germany attacked Poland, and the United States called for a meeting of foreign ministers in Panama City, at which the participants established a neutrality zone around the Western Hemisphere. Although the Cubans signed the Declaration of Panama, they were more concerned with their sugar problems, and both the delegation and the Cuban public paid closer attention to sugar and tobacco rates than to the question of wartime cooperation. After the meeting ended, the islanders did not seem interested either in its results or in the European conflict.[41]

Even though State Department officials concentrated on the gloomy reports from Europe, they were also aware that something had to be done in Cuba to restore economic stability. Shortly after Roosevelt suspended the sugar quota system, American and Cuban officials began negotiations on a supplemental trade agreement, which was completed on December 18. While the Cubans received a few new concessions, they were principally concerned with the provisions that restored the lower duties on tobacco that had been canceled in March 1936 and with the resumption of the .90 cents per pound duty on sugar. The latter, however, could only be reestablished when Roosevelt revoked his suspension proclamation, and this occurred eight days after the supplemental agreement was signed. Even though the agreement was primarily designed to restore Cuba's lost benefits, the United States received significant reductions on four items and lesser concessions on twelve others.[42]

In essence, the economic relationship between the two nations at the beginning of 1940 closely paralleled that established by the original agreement of 1934, with one major exception. Although the Cubans had regained their two principal concessions, they realized their vulnerability to domestic pressures in the United States. Two events apparently unrelated to United States-Cuban economic relations—the action of the Supreme Court in 1936 and the outbreak of war in 1939—had had widespread repercussions on

Cuba's tobacco and sugar industries. Now that the island's businessmen had witnessed the results the unilateral actions of the Roosevelt administration, they began to express their dissatisfaction with the existing economic arrangement. They argued that while the United States had not given them adequate guarantees for their products, the Cuban government had never taken any steps to impede the privileged position of American exports to the island. These concrete inequities in the reciprocity agreement started widespread agitation for a new agreement almost as soon as the supplemental one was concluded, for nothing in the supplemental agreement protected the Cubans against a repetition of the United States' earlier actions. The island's commercial interests were tired of supporting a so-called reciprocity agreement which was essentially unequal.

The signing of the supplemental reciprocity treaty and the restoration of the sugar quota came too late in the year to aid the government coalition in its struggle to win the constituent assembly elections. Two weeks before the balloting, one observer predicted that the opposition forces had already won thirty to thirty-five delegates out of the seventy-six to be selected. On November 15, 1939, the Cuban people chose the delegates for the long-awaited constituent assembly. The elections were quiet, and the early returns indicated close contest. As late returns began to show the opposition's victory, the opposition leaders praised the government's impartiality, calling the elections the fairest in Cuban history. When the results became final, they showed that the opposition had won forty-one of the seventy-six seats.[43]

The election revealed some interesting developments in Cuban politics. Out of an electorate of 1,611,583, there were 1,044,043 votes cast, or 65 percent of the total. Even with opposition participation, this election drew only slightly over 107,000 more votes than the 1936 elections. If the parties were divided by political leanings, almost 70 percent of the voters had preferred those groups claiming to represent the right, while the reformists or extreme left-wing parties only received 30 percent. Yet this apparent conservatism was deceptive, for the Auténticos, with little discipline or organization, led all parties in the number of voters and delegates to the assembly. Thus, while the established groups demonstrated the power of their organizations, the large Auténtico vote illustrated the success of the party's appeal for

THE CONSTITUENT ASSEMBLY ELECTIONS OF 1939[44]

Party	Leading Figure	Political Leaning	Vote	Delegate(s)
Progovernment				
Liberal	Ramón Vasconcelos	right	179,239	16
Unión Nacionalista	Mendieta	right	125,915	9
Unión Revolucion-aria-Comunista	Blas Roca	left	92,663	6
Conjunto Nacional Democrático	Carlos Saladrigas	right	70,525	3
Realistas	Sergio Carbó	right	36,338	1
Popular Cubano	none	right	9,663	0
			514,343	35
Opposition				
Auténticos	Grau	left	215,050	18
Demócrata Republicano	Menocal	right	163,445	15
Acción Republicano	Gómez	right	78,097	4
A.B.C.	Martínez Saenz	right	64,001	4
Agrario Nacional	Alexander Vergara	left	9,107	0
			529,700	41

reform in the government. Just as interesting as the voting pattern were the coalition alignments. The traditional politicians in the government coalition had accepted Communist support, and within the opposition camp, the reformist-minded Auténticos had aligned themselves with conservatives like Menocal, Gómez, and Martínez Saenz. These various parties had certainly cooperated not along ideological lines but for or against Batista's rule. If the elections proved anything, they gave some vague indication of the colonel's inability to control the island's volatile political parties at the end of 1939.

Illustrating this unusual alignment most graphically was the Communist Party's support of Batista, especially since an alliance between the two seemed so unlikely. The party had criticized him bitterly since 1933 for his repressive tactics and for his refusal to grant it legal status. In addition, the Communists had denounced Batista as a Fascist in order to rally the island against militarism during the Popular Front period of cooperation with other leftist parties in the West. But time altered their relationship. As the elections drew closer, Batista, recognizing the need for political support, arrived at an accord with the Communist Party, and, in return for his financial support and protection, the party agreed to assist him and his platform. The results of the pact quickly became evident. On May 1, 1938 the daily Communist newspaper *Hoy* began publication; on September 13 the party was officially inscribed in Havana Province; and by early 1939 Batista removed restrictions on Communist labor unions. As a result of these actions, the party grew in size and strength. The politicial events that had drawn Batista and the Communist Party together emphasized the main concern of Cuban politicians—ideology played a secondary role to the attainment of power.[45]

Even this additional support did not provide the margin of victory for the government coalition. After the results showed the opposition's triumph, Batista took personal charge of his forces. Although he had not officially announced his presidential aspirations, various politicians had advocated his candidacy since early 1937, while he remained flattered but noncommittal. In the midst of defeat, Batista made the crucial decision to direct the government parties' efforts by ending his self-imposed silence on the presidency. On December 4, 1939, he told newspapermen that he intended to leave the army. Two days later he kept his promise and resigned his commission; he accepted the presidential nomination of the government forces on December 11. Now the officially announced candidate began to prepare the most elaborate and expensive campaign in the nation's history.[46]

In the swirl of political events, an unexpected tragedy affected the conduct of United States-Cuban relations: on December 4, J. Butler Wright died at his post.[47] Wright had been a vocal advocate of noninterference, and, equally significantly, he had carried out his concept of the Good Neighbor Policy by withdrawing the embassy from its involvement in local politics. He had witnessed the partial success of the Three-Year Plan, economic recession, constituent assembly elections, and Cuba's reaction to the Européan war. Even though he constantly reported on the instability of the government's civilian and military leadership, he refrained from intervening in domestic affairs.

Wright's efforts to remove himself from internal conflicts did not seriously affect United States-Cuban economic policy. The State Department demanded a debt settlement for its investors and also the continuation of Decree-Law No. 522 for American sugar companies operating in Cuba. These were minor anxieties compared to basic commercial policy. Although spokesmen for the Roosevelt administration continued to use the trade agreements program as concrete evidence of the Good Neighbor spirit, the Cuban agreement could not be accepted as truly reciprocal. Cuba lost her two chief tariff reductions in the 1934 treaty, but American exporters never experienced any loss. To make matters worse, Cuban officials had not been consulted before their concessions were canceled, nor did the Cuban government have any legal recourse except abrogating the entire agreement. The Roosevelt administration had bound the island's economic destiny so closely to the American domestic agricultural program that Cuba had to suffer from events over which it had no control.

Even though the reciprocity program disappointed the Cubans, the political relationship between the two countries was slowly changing. In one crucial respect Wright had succeeded where Welles and Caffery had failed: he had removed himself from direct participation in local affairs. This was his major contribution, and his reward was the conspicuous lack of criticism from the opposition during his tour of duty. Ironically, while Wright moved away from interference, the State Department under Welles's direction compensated by demanding a bondholder settlement and internal reforms in return for economic assistance. However, even this pressure was slight in comparison to the overt dictation practiced by Roosevelt's first two ambassadors. The abrogation of the Platt Amendment had ended the United States' responsibility for the maintenance of domestic tranquillity, and although the American ambassador was still the second most important figure on the island, he scrupulously avoided any involvement in the direction of local politics.

Wright's job was simplified by the relative domestic peace that prevailed during his three years as ambassador. The reviving though erratic economy had restored some of the island's lost prosperity, and the rise of Batista had assured political stability. The time had come for Cuba to consolidate the internal gains achieved during the Revolution of 1933. To be sure, the opposition could still claim with some justification that the island's economy rested on an unwelcome sugar monoculture and an equally abhorrent military dictator, but Cuba was slowly changing its character. Grau's reforms had become institutionalized, and Batista's rural-civic military schools and the Three-Year Plan were efforts to correct longtime problems. The elections for the constituent assembly had not only proven the government's ability to

hold reasonably fair elections, but also demonstrated the effectiveness of the Auténticos' reformist pronouncements. While the
controlling economic and political interests tried desperately to
maintain the status quo, each government from 1933 to 1940 had
been forced to make concessions to the laborers, the small farmers,
and the students. In this seven-year battle between right and left,
the latter had won some significant concessions. A new decade was
about to begin, bringing another important presidential election, a
constitutional convention, and a world war. As these events
unfolded, the American government reiterated its commitment to
noninterference while the internal changes brought on by the
Revolution of 1933 became more pronounced. Cuba had ended the
turbulent decade of the 1930s; she hoped that the new one would
offer peace and prosperity.

10

Batista Legitimizes His Power

The defeat of the government coalition in the assembly elections brought a temporary lull in political activity while the various parties planned their next moves. Hoping to capitalize on their victory, the winning groups called for a postponement of the general elections on the grounds that they did not have sufficient time to prepare for the campaign. If the government refused their request, they threatened to withdraw from the elections. While these groups agitated for a delay, Batista and his supporters resisted. This new conflict produced a serious deadlock, for the opposition parties dominated the Assembly, while Batista's forces controlled Congress. Neither group could act without the other's consent, but at the beginning of 1940, no one had a solution to the perplexing problem.[1]

While the various factions fought, Laredo Bru remained in the background. He had gained enormous prestige through the successful completion of the supplemental reciprocity agreement with the United States, and he had also proved his durability by remaining in office longer than anyone since Machado. On December 26, 1939, he ended his silence by announcing that he would meet with both sides to devise an acceptable schedule for the general elections. For the next month politicians presented numerous proposals, and finally, on February 4, 1940, they reached an acceptable compromise. The Assembly would be allowed to draft the new constitution and transitory provisions, but until the new president took office, the Congress would continue to legislate. The date for general elections was later postponed from February 28, to July 14, and Laredo Bru, whose term expired on May 2, agreed to remain in office until the inauguration on October 10. Finally, congressmen would be allowed to serve their full terms even though the new constitution reduced the size of the Congress;

thus, the new one would be composed of the incumbents plus the new members, and its inflated membership would slowly be reduced in future congressional elections.[2]

To ensure the acceptance of this program, Grau and Batista had personally participated in the conferences that led to the settlement, and they imposed the agreement on their followers.[3] When the solution was announced, Laredo Bru proclaimed that this compromise was a momentous event "because this is the first time that Cubans by themselves, political opponents, face to face, without outside interference, without being impelled by ambition, have reached an understanding between themselves to conduct their political activities on a plane of the truest democracy." Even Beaulac, who was usually pessimistic about the ability of Cuban politicians to cooperate, added that the public acclaimed the plan and that the outlook for political stability and a successful assembly was "unusually favorable."[4]

Although the embassy refused to become involved in this struggle, Beaulac carefully reported the development of the stalemate and the possibility of a military coup. On January 11 he warned, "If this occurred, it is almost certain that some effort at reprisal would be made, and it is possible that the country would drift into a situation resembling—in some measure, at least—that which pertained prior to the downfall of President Machado."[5] Despite the gravity of the situation, the State Department remained impartial. When Menocal asked Welles to comment on the possible position that the United States might take if the opposition factions withdrew from the elections, the undersecretary refused to speculate. By removing the Roosevelt administration from the conflict, Welles compelled Cuban politicians to resolve their own internal dilemma.[6]

While the Cubans directed their attention to the settlement, the new American ambassador to Cuba, George Messersmith, arrived in Havana on March 2. The fifty-six-year-old envoy had been an author, lecturer, and teacher before joining the consular division of the foreign service in 1914. He then carried out most of his service in Europe; as consul general in Berlin during the rise of Adolf Hitler, he was one of the first to warn against the growing Nazi menace.[7] Beaulac later wrote a vivid description of his new chief: "Serious and grim, Messersmith had no hobby but his work and no recreation except mystery stories and an occasional game of

Chinese checkers. . . . [He] hammered away at every problem until it was solved. He never gave up. He never relaxed. He complained continually about the delicate state of his health while doing the work of three men without apparent fatigue." Messersmith was a meticulous worker who watched every event and reported on it in minute detail. Beaulac called him "the No. 1 letter writer in the service," for he continually wrote to Roosevelt, Hull, and Welles, and sometimes his letters were fifteen typewritten pages single-spaced, with three or four more pages of postscripts. Beaulac admitted that the ambassador's tireless efforts must have been rewarding, for his "greatest merit was that he was always successful."[8]

The new ambassador was hardly settled in his quarters when he began to observe the machinations of Cuban politics. Both Batista and Grau realized that the key to victory was the support of Menocal's conservative party. Each tried desperately to secure the former president's backing, and by the middle of March, Menocal had made his decision. Even though he had aligned his party with Grau in the assembly elections, he now reversed his course and reached an accord with Batista. The Auténticos, of course, hoped to stop such an alliance, and although they succeeded in creating some dissension within Menocal's party, the conservative leader forced his followers to accept his decision. He announced that he had personally approved of the union because it would assure the government parties of a majority in the general elections and would thus give Cuba a conservative government. He expected some defection, but felt this a small price to pay in order to defeat the radical proposals of the Auténticos.[9]

The Batista-Menocal pact was a severe setback for Grau, even though the remaining opposition parties reaffirmed their support for him and he received an unexpected ally from the Liberal Party of Santa Clara Province. This group voted to join him because of its bitterness over Batista's concessions to Menocal in the selection of district candidates. Politicians now busily surveyed the political situation while both presidential candidates began to campaign.[10] Messersmith reported his impression of these events to Hull on March 26: "Cuban politics is pretty rotten, and the tradition is strongly established here that to the victor belongs [sic] the spoils. In this respect the Cubans are in their political life where we were some hundred years ago, and, in many ways, our situation then and theirs now are not very much different except that there is greater venality among Cuban politicians than there was among ours."[11]

While some politicians focused their attention on the elections, the delegates to the Constituent Assembly opened their sessions on February 9. Beaulac, who attended the inaugural ceremonies, reported that the galleries were packed with Auténticos and that when Grau "appeared on the floor of the House the galleries figuratively raised the roof, and the ovation was repeated several times during the course of the afternoon."[12] Other prominent opposition leaders, he continued, also received warm greetings, but not the government supporters. When someone mentioned Batista's name, he was loudly booed, and this "anti-Batista demonstration, which lasted several minutes, was turned into another roof-raising Grau demonstration when the latter waved his hand at the gallery."[13]

To no one's great surprise, the Assembly elected Grau its president. The delegates were then assigned to draft specific articles and went to work energetically.[14] Messersmith expressed his concern that they were acting too hastily, without giving careful consideration to the various proposals. The members, he believed, had exhibited "an amazing amount of demogoguery'" and the most radical suggestions had come from the Auténticos, "compared with whom even the Communists have, at times, been made to appear conservative."[15] The irresponsible efforts to gain a popular following for the approaching general elections made the embassy increasingly concerned lest the proposed draft adversely affect American interests, especially those associated with the moratorium on the public works debt and the limitation on the size of landholdings. Messersmith and Beaulac actively maneuvered for revision among legislators and members of the government. Their efforts had little effect, but embassy officials took their failure calmly, confident that even though the Cuban delegates might incorporate their nationalistic aspirations into the constitution, the government would not take any drastic action in reducing the size of foreign plantations or canceling American bondholders' claims.[16]

While the embassy was busily assessing the various articles, the assembly delegates and government officials traveled on a special train to Guáimaro, a small town in Camagüey Province where the Constitution of 1869 had been proclaimed, in order to sign the new document. It stressed such individual rights as the vote, free speech, and free assembly, it guaranteed autonomy to the university, and it promised universal primary education. The constitution also consolidated the gains of labor since 1933 by recognizing its right to organize, strike, and bargain collectively; there were also provisions for an eight-hour day, a forty-four-hour week, a minimum wage, and social security. Other sections expressed the hope that Cuba might end such vexing problems as large landholdings and internal graft and corruption. The delegates showed their distrust of the president by limiting him to one four-year term and allowing reelection only after an eight-year interval. The autonomy of the Congress and the judiciary was confirmed in the hope that they might help to check presidential domination. In a real sense the 1940 Constitution was a hopeful catalogue of many reforms that had been proposed since the birth of the republic, especially those that had been adopted after 1933. Of the 286 articles, 61 dealt specifically with social and economic issues. In spite of the general optimism that prevailed once the constitution was signed, time proved that it was no panacea for the maladies that beset the Cuban body politic.[17]

One observer watched the constitutional celebration with a skeptical eye. Two days before the polls opened, Messersmith wrote Welles in all too familiar language about the difficulties that he anticipated: "I am on the whole getting more of the opinion that we must take a stronger and firmer stand here, and that if we fail to do so we will be prejudicing seriously the interests of Cuba and ourselves, and not helping the picture of inter-American cooperation on the whole." He feared the possible effects of the European war on the Cuban economy and took exception to the islanders' attitude toward the position of the United States. Because the island was necessary for hemispheric defense, he reported, many Cubans thought that they could intimidate the United States into granting economic assistance. As evidence he cited the hostile constitutional provisions which might be used to cancel the public works debt and to attack those Americans who held large sugar plantations. Even though he approved of the Good Neighbor Policy, he added, "what I do foresee is that with the new situation which we have to face, and with the increasing importance of the factor of self-preservation, we will have to take a stronger stand, not only here but in some of the other American Republics."[18]

As far as the elections were concerned, Messersmith doubted the qualifications of both candidates. Grau, he said, is "not a strong man and not a man of decisions and there is no adequate reason to believe that he would be influenced in his acts by the decent men who are supporting him. There is much more reason to believe that he would follow in the main the worst influences around him."[19] Batista had surrounded himself with "a group of unscrupulous politicians who are interested only in getting out of their position what they can while they are in them."[20]

To assure Batista's victory, in early January his supporters began to place pressure on American sugar companies for campaign contributions, and six months later they devised a plan whereby these firms would give them two cents for each bag of exported sugar.[21] Even though one company gave $60,000 and others added to Batista's coffers, Messersmith declared that most of them "refused to be shaken down."[22] When company representatives came to the embassy for advice, Messersmith told them "that if they chose to participate in Cuban politics to this extent they could not expect help from the Embassy in case they got in trouble with the authorities later on."[23] Besides asking for money, Batista's supporters also hoped that American firms might direct their workers to vote for their candidate. "As most of them met these advances coldly when made by the military," said Messersmith, "it is reasonable to assume that Batista will not love them the more."[24]

The pressure for campaign funds was not confined to sugar companies, for, as the manager of the local branch of the Chase National Bank told Messersmith on June 26, a Batista supporter had requested a million-dollar loan to finance his leader's campaign. When the banker refused, the Cuban expressed anger. Messersmith resented the intimidation of American business firms by Batista's supporters. He warned Welles that the United States must act more vigorously to protect its citizens, for not only did they expect adequate safeguards, but the Cuban people also would welcome a firmer stand by the American government.[25]

As the campaign drew to a close, the cooperative spirit which had made possible the political compromise vanished. The opposition forces charged the military forces with interference on Batista's behalf and demanded that they stop their activities.[26] Five days before the balloting, Messersmith informed the State Department that these allegations were true and added, "Most observers assert that in a fair election Grau would win, but the prevailing opinion is that the election will not be entirely fair and that Batista will win."[27] The embassy warned that throughout the island the bitterness between the opposing blocs had reached critical proportions. The campaign in its closing days had taken on the appearance of a violent struggle.[28]

At the height of the political tension, the Cuban people went to the polls on July 14. Astonishingly, the election was relatively free from violence, for only five people were killed and forty wounded, but the results did not surprise anyone. Batista won by a vote of 805,125 to 583,526. An analysis of the voting showed that about three-quarters of the eligible voters had participated—almost 400,000, or 10 percent more than in 1939. While the opposition media claimed that the military prevented a fair election, other newspapers called it the most orderly in the island's history. The Cuban weekly *Carteles*, which had not been favorable to Batista's candidacy, applied the techniques of the Gallup Poll to the election, showing that an overwhelming percentage of its sample regarded the elections as orderly and the military and police authorities as impartial. They accepted the fact that Batista had won and that his victory represented the will of the majority.[29]

While the embassy was busily assessing the results of Batista's sweeping victory, it was also watching the ominous events in Europe. Impressed by the rumored threat of Nazi penetration in Latin America, Roosevelt gave this issue high priority. Havana had already been selected as the meeting place for a Pan-American Conference of Foreign Ministers, which opened on July 21. Some of the Latin American governments feared the possibility of a Nazi coup in Argentina and Brazil, and the Roosevelt administration moved to counteract such a contingency. The United States had already formulated its own no-transfer policy, and the most significant result of the conference was the acceptance of the Havana declaration, which stated that the Western Hemisphere would not allow any transfer of territory from one European nation to another. While the Cuban press supported this stance, it was disappointed that the island had not received any economic assistance from the United States.[30]

Hull directed his principal efforts to having this declaration passed, but he also had an opportunity to discuss the public works debt issue with Cuban officials. Since the beginning of 1940 the embassy had steadily applied pressure for the payment, and Beaulac urged a prompt settlement because it would benefit Cuba's financial position and help create the proper conditions for American economic aid.[31] Once Messersmith arrived, he too worked for a solution, but he also "did not wish to begin my stay here by being a bill collector. . . ."[32] After the election and conference ended, the State Department and its representatives in Havana renewed their efforts for a settlement. On August 3 Messersmith predicted a quick solution, and a little over one month later, Laredo Bru signed a satisfactory bill ending the issue of the public works debt, which had created so much tension since the start of the depression.[33]

Messersmith thought that Laredo Bru had accomplished a great deal during his presidency for which he had received very little credit: "Now his term is ending on October 10, and the only real brake that there has been on Batista will be gone."[34] The opposition tried to prevent the inauguration by taking numerous electoral disputes to the judiciary, but these tactics failed.[35] The ambassador shared their doubts, for he feared that Batista "has so little background, understands the situation in the United States so little, and is still in the hands of bad advisers here. I do not see that under the best circumstances we can expect too much from him. I fear that he and others will have to learn some bitter lessons before we can expect a reasonable administration here."[36]

Despite this gloomy prediction, at noon on October 10, 1940 Batista became the seventh constitutionally elected president of the republic. The day was a national holiday known as the Grito de Yara, commemorating the first revolutionary outbreak against Spanish domination. A drizzling rain fell while thousands listened as Batista called for national unity and promised support for hemispheric defense. The *Nation* commented that it would wait to see if Batista had been converted from totalitarianism to democracy. *Time* added that the new president said the revolution was over but that Grau suggested that another was about to commence.[37] No matter what anyone said, this was the apex of Batista's career. He had overcome enormous obstacles. Born in poverty and raised without the benefits of a formal education, he had risen from being a drifter to the position of commander in chief of the armed forces. While politicians fell, Batista consolidated his position.

With his elevation to the presidency, his highest expectations must have been fulfilled.

Almost immediately after the inauguration, Batista announced his cabinet selections. Out of the seven parties that supported him, he chose moderate or conservative ministers from five, excluding only the Communist and Popular parties, but he preferred to surround himself with his old military comrades and listen to their advice. When he had been in office only nine days, Messersmith was already writing, "It is incredible to what degree corruption pervades the administration here."[39] *Carteles* reflected the ambassador's impression in its editorial of January 26, 1941, which demanded that Batista replace corrupt politicians with honest men. It realized that graft was a commonly accepted practice in Cuban political life, but it still damned the administration for allowing public officials to neglect their duties while filling their own pockets.[40]

The organized opposition forces also attacked Batista and his officials for their corrupt practices and carefully watched for other issues that might unite the nation against the administration. Confused by the mounting criticism, Batista hesitated, refusing to announce any program or take responsibility for those of the previous regimes. When the first session of the new Congress ended on December 19, it had not even passed the 1941 budget.[41] Political events, according to Messersmith, had proven "Batista's failure to date to assume leadership and responsibility."[42]

Besides the traditional problems of corruption and congressional inaction, the government faced new troubles at the university. Students had played a major role in politics since Machado's overthrow, but when the university reopened in 1937, it did not resume its earlier part in national affairs. Even though the students were not a viable political force in 1940, the campus was still torn by unrest. The generation of 1930 had institutionalized the use of urban violence, and now the university became the center of terroristic activity by students and by other groups that had no connection with the university. Groups of racketeers known as the *bonches* engaged in assassinations, blackmail, and other criminal acts, using the university as their headquarters because the constitution prohibited police from entering its premises. Even though many students and faculty members complained about their new colleagues, the government refused to violate university autonomy. Batista was well aware of the students' potential power, and as long as this movement had no political overtones, he decided to let the university solve its own dilemma.[43]

Batista's troubles extended to his own coalition when some of his allies demanded the expulsion of the Cuban Communist Party, theoretically on the grounds of its stand against hemispheric defense. In fact, the coalition feared the party's growing influence. For the first time in their history, the Communists were part of a victorious coalition. They had elected ten congressmen, more than one hundred members of town councils, and the mayor of the nation's second largest city, Santiago de Cuba. Batista also permitted them to control the ministry of labor, and as their power grew, the other members of the government forces increased their attacks, but the president refused to take any action.[44] Analyzing this perplexing situation on April 29, 1941, Beaulac stated, "There are, of course, obvious inconsistencies in the Cuban Government's public attitude toward Communism and President Batista's personal friendship and loyalty to the Communist leaders."[45]

After Russia entered the war, this conflict seemed to be settled. The Cuban Communists not only abruptly ended their opposition to wartime cooperation, but they also became the most vocal advocates of preparedness. Now that the party had halted its anti-American attacks, Batista thought the rest of his coalition would not have any objection to his selection of a well-known Communist leader, Juan Marinello, to fill a senatorial vacancy. He was mistaken, for the other parties balked and forced him to accept another man. Batista's close relations with the Communist Party had antagonized the rest of his coalition and also created anxiety in the American embassy, but even with this concerted opposition, the president continued to support the party that had offered him its early backing.[46]

The most serious challenge to presidential authority came from the most unexpected source. Almost immediately after assuming office, Batista began to remove the military from the civilian duties that it had assumed after the sergeant's revolt. Early in 1941 Batista authorized civilian officials to take over certain functions, such as the policing of the customshouse, which the navy had carried out since 1933. Batista acted partly because of the widespread and well-publicized naval graft, but also because he did not completely trust the navy's commander, Colonel Angel A. González. At the same time the president changed the lottery system to stop the rampant gambling being directed by the chief of the national police, Colonel Bernardo García. When García protested, Batista forced his resignation.[47]

During the period of mounting tension between the military leaders and Batista, the armed forces were confined to their barracks. On the last day of January, the disenchanted colonels met to discuss the difficult situation. The chief of the army, José Eleuterio Pedraza, who had been a close ally of Batista in the 1933 revolt, was especially distraught over García's removal because he and García were good friends. Showing his open dissatisfaction, Pedraza refused to accept Batista's new chief of police and declared that he would personally assume these duties along with his others. He saw the president the following day and warned him that he could not count on the support of the military. According to Pedraza, the colonels no longer backed Batista, but had instead switched their allegiance to him.[48]

Messersmith recalled in his memoirs that for the first three days of February "the President was practically a prisoner . . . in the Palace."[49] He seemed helpless, but this appearance was deceptive. In fact, he was planning his moves. At 4:00 A.M. on February 3, he reinforced the palace guard and drove to Camp Columbia to confront the military leaders. When he arrived, he demanded and received their pledge of loyalty. By 9:00 A.M. Batista had suspended constitutional guarantees for fifteen days, taken personal command of the armed forces, and had the three seditious colonels arrested.[50] Although Messersmith had warned earlier "that there is real danger of revolution which may or may not involve civil strife,"[51] Batista stopped the rebellion without bloodshed. He quickly reestablished constitutional rule and exiled the three men, but, to show his confidence, he allowed all three to return. None ever participated in military affairs again.[52] Messersmith described the climactic end of the crisis: "The President wanted me to know that everything was in order, that no one had been hurt, and he would be very glad if I were to come over to see him." When Messersmith called on Batista on February 4, the president looked extremely fatigued,[53] and with good reason, for he had just survived the only direct challenge to his authority that took place during his first administration.

The ambassador applauded the maintenance of civilian rule, and the Cuban press and public also appeared unanimous in their approval.[54] American reactions were mixed. The once hostile *Nation* told its readers on February 15 that "during the past two or three years he has reestablished a large measure of practical democracy. His promptness in restoring full civil rights after temporarily suspending them at the time of the arrests, seems to indicate that he means to continue his experiment with the democratic method."[55] Even with such praise, the *New Republic* did not see any change in Batista's methods. On February 17 the magazine reaffirmed its anti-Batista position, stating, "if he has really turned democratic in any degree, we are not aware of concrete evidence of it."[56] But most Americans favored Batista's position, and in August 1941, John Gunther reflected the prevailing sentiment when he declared that "his main accomplishment is the restoration of civil authority."[57]

The failure of the February revolt ended any threat to Batista's political authority, but it did not solve Cuba's economic problems. Even before the elections, Messersmith had reported that Batista was hoping for assistance from the Eximbank, but the ambassador felt that this was not possible until the public works debt had been settled. After Batista won the presidency, Martínez Fraga asked the State Department for a loan to help supplement the Cuban budget. Messersmith opposed the idea both because of Cuba's outstanding obligations and because he believed that the Cuban ambassador had exaggerated the island's financial predicament. Rumors still persisted that the Cuban government would ask for a loan of between $15 million and $65 million. This time Messersmith objected vigorously and recommended that no economic assistance be granted until Cuba had settled with its American creditors, reorganized its treasury department and possibly some other agencies, altered its sugar quota system, and given assurances to American businessmen against discriminatory practices. In addition he advised a careful examination of Cuba's budgetary and tax structures and suggested that tight American controls be placed on any loan.[58]

The Cuban government was acutely aware that the United States would not assist it until a debt settlement was concluded. While the regime proposed the legislation necessary to settle this issue, the government also started to negotiate for a loan. Martínez Fraga, the initiator of the scheme, continued his efforts in

Washington to gain State Department support; meanwhile, a bill authorizing a $50 million loan was introduced in Havana. In quick succession the Cuban Congress passed laws to settle the remainder of the public works debt and to contract the proposed new loan. Cubans received the loan bill with some misgivings. Some hoped for the aid, but many feared that the new administration would use it unwisely.[59] On November 9, Messersmith expressed his concern although he believed that the United States should assist Cuba he added, "but it is even more important that what we do should be done wisely and constructively, rather than in a hurry, no matter how much the Cubans press us."[60]

Despite the controversial nature of the loan, the Cubans continued to lobby for it by sending a delegation to Washington for negotiations, but by the end of the year, the Eximbank had taken a position against such a large grant, and the commission returned home empty-handed. Once the Cuban public learned of the fiasco, Batista received sharp criticism for promoting a scheme that the United States had rejected. To shift the burden of the blame, Martínez Fraga became the scapegoat and was forced to resign. Batista's impetuous action had greatly damaged his new administration's prestige, for he had promoted an idea that he hoped would solve the island's economic problems in one stroke, without consulting either his chief advisers or—even worse—the American ambassador and his government.[61]

Even though Messersmith strongly opposed this loan, he clearly favored some assistance program. On January 8, 1941, he advocated economic aid because Cuba had lost her European sugar market and needed a loan to put additional workers in jobs. Besides this need, the island had to have money for its agricultural diversification and public works programs. Since any loan required close supervision by the Eximbank, Messersmith felt that there would be no chance of corruption.[62] Even more important, the ambassador argued that the United States must help preserve Cuba's political stability: "This is the first constitutional Government which Cuba has had for seven years and we would, I believe, be placing ourselves in an impossible position if we did not give the present Government the support it needs."[63]

Welles concurred, but first he wanted the Cuban government to settle its remaining claims, end discrimination against American sugar mills, reform its fiscal and administrative agencies, and reduce its annual budget. Batista quickly began to act on these items, and Messersmith conceded that Cuba was fulfilling the American prerequisites. In this favorable atmosphere, the State Department recommended a loan of $25 million for agricultural diversification and public works. While Cuban and Eximbank officials discussed the specific terms of the loan, Batista proposed the necessary legislation to Congress, and in early 1942 the agreement was signed. The United States had granted Cuba the necessary money to carry out a large-scale program for internal improvements, but this aid had far broader implications.[64] As J. Lloyd Mecham pointed out, economic assistance programs had definite political overtones. "The Good Neighbor was taking on more and more the character of a security policy."[65]

This economic assistance loan was not implemented quickly enough to alleviate Cuba's economic problems. In late 1940 the Cuban government asked the Eximbank for an immediate loan to finance additional sugar production and thereby stimulate sluggish commerce. Shortly after the start of the new year, the bank granted a loan to finance the production of an additional 400,000 tons of sugar. Besides providing for this increased harvest, the United States set other conditions for assisting the distressed sugar industry by demanding that Decree-Law No. 522 be extended, so as to assure protection to American interests.[66] Writing to Roosevelt on April 19, Messersmith also noted the growing connection between economic assistance and hemispheric defense: "As we are so much interested in the maintenance of the political situation here for defense, as well as economic reasons, our action in this request has been more than justified and, in the measure expected, effective."[67]

Even these negotiations did not end the commercial bargaining between the two nations. After the signing of the supplemental reciprocity agreement in 1939, Cuban business circles became increasingly hostile to its provisions, and on April 15, 1941, the regime formally asked to negotiate a new one. While both countries were discussing the terms, Messersmith expressed his concern over the sugar legislation pending before the United States Congress. Although it was passed by the Senate, the Roosevelt administration then took a strong stand against the bill and had it defeated. While the American legislators were discussing the sugar issue, the uncertainty over their possible action placed the reciprocity negotiations in constant jeopardy.[68]

In spite of these uncertainties, the bargining proceeded rapidly, and by the end of the year, negotiations on the second supplementary agreement were completed. The United States granted reduction on tobacco and beef, but, more important, it lowered the sugar tariff from .90 cents per pound to .75. The Cubans were pleased with these concessions, and in return they lowered their duties on thirty-eight American products. The agreement was signed on December 23, 1941 and went into effect the next month. Even though both nations expressed their approval, the basic commercial relationship between them had not been fundamentally altered. Cuba still depended on the exportation of its sugar to the mainland, while the United States continued to be the island's chief supplier.[69]

Throughout the negotiations, Messersmith argued that the United States should give the Cubans more reductions because the reciprocity agreement had principally benefited American exporters. Reflecting on this episode, he later recalled that Roosevelt and Hull had directed him to negotiate a new agreement because "we had been treating Cuba shabby [sic] for years with regard to her sugar exports to the United States. When we had a good crop in the United States we kept down imports from Cuba, with the corresponding depressing effects in Cuba. When we had a poor crop in the United States, we yelled for Cuban sugar and the Cuban economy was upset by new hopes for sugar exports. We were at all times the principal buyer of Cuban sugar, which was the principal crop of the island, but we were a sporadic buyer." Roosevelt and Hull, he continued, had directed him to correct this inequity and he claimed success: "It was now possible for the Cuban government and for Cuban businessmen to plan on a surer basis. The danger of calamity from year to year which had been staring them in the face was gone."[70]

The new reciprocity agreement was closely connected to another American proposal that did more than anything else to stimulate the sugar industry. Late in 1941, rumors began to spread on the island that the United States was contemplating the purchase of the entire Cuban sugar crop for 1942. When Messersmith asked Cuban officials on October 21 to send a delegation to Washington for contract negotiations, they were not surprised. The delegation arrived on November 8, and the American and Cuban negotiators reached an agreement on January 28, 1942, to sell the entire sugar crop for 2.65 cents per pound because of the wartime emergency and Cuba's economic slump.[71]

This economic assistance and the consolidation of Batista's political power touched off an era of prosperity such as the island had not seen since World War I—yet even these developments did not create a truly stable society. Messersmith constantly expressed his concern over the Cuban politicans' failure to act constructively. After he had spent almost a year at his post, he wrote, "I now had the feeling that the disorganization in the administration had almost reached the stage of parilization [sic]."[72] Batista had removed efficient administrators and replaced them with his political allies, and as a result, the treasury department was disorganized, the Communists controlled the labor industry, and the minister of education was interested only in his own personal gains. On July 11, 1941, Messersmith confided to Welles that he had tried to assist Batista as inconspicuously as possible: "The President and I have an understanding with each other that when we really wish to see each other about matters of importance, we get in touch with each other and we have several places where we can meet unobtrusively and for hours with the knowledge of but a very few persons."[73] The ambassador hoped to convince Batista to alter the composition of his cabinet so as to place more competent officials in government ministries, and on July 16, Batista followed his advice. Messersmith thought that the cabinet changes had improved the administration, but Batista was still faced with congressional inaction and steadily rising living costs because of wartime shortages.[74]

Even though Messersmith continually criticized the Cuban political process, he felt that Batista, his government, and the general public supported the United States in what he considered to be his most important assignment: conditioning the Cubans to the possible outbreak of total war. His constant support for economic assistance to bolster political stability came from the conviction that the United States could not afford chaotic conditions on such a strategically located and economically important island. The embassy carefully reported on the islanders' growing identification with American interests over those of the Axis powers.[75] On June 15, 1940, Messersmith wrote that the European line of defense had almost collapsed and that the new defense perimeter was the Americas: "In these days we have to fight fire with fire and I myself am confident that with some of these countries the interests of the Good Neighbor Policy involves not necessarily the use of the big stick but a much stronger and more definite attitude than we have taken." If Latin America wanted to assure itself a place in the United States market, the ambassador believed that these nations had to cooperate with the American defense position: "I cannot emphasize too strongly what I believe is the necessity for this firm and unequivocal leadership. The American States expect it, and, I believe, want it now. . . ."[76]

The leaders of most Cuban political parties aided Messersmith's anti-Nazi effort by speaking out against European totalitarianism. On September 9, 1940, Laredo Bru started the government's program against the Axis by prohibiting broadcasts of ships' movements in Cuban waters, and eighteen days later the Partido Nazista Cubano was dissolved.[77] The ambassador thought so much of the Cuban cooperative effort that on January 15, 1941, he wrote to Roosevelt, "So far we have been getting one hundred percent cooperation from the Cuban Government in defense matters, and it is my endeavor to keep it so."[78] Two weeks later, Batista ordered the suppression of all totalitarian propaganda in Cuba, including flags, insignia, plays, movies, and radio programs. Even the Spanish community so closely identified with the Falange, the Spanish Fascist party, publicly pledged its support for Batista's regime and his policy of cooperation with the United States. At the end of 1941 the Cuban nation appeared to be solidly behind American defense objectives.[79]

The Cuban government also demonstrated its support of United States policy by entering into secret military talks. Batista and Welles had already discussed military cooperation when Batista visited Washington in 1938, and now Welles wanted to start negotiations on a concrete program. Messersmith, therefore, was to discuss the use of airfields and port facilities and methods of protection and vigilance for the Cuban coastline. In early June and again in late August 1940, military missions arrived in Havana to discuss defensive measures, and at the conclusion of these talks, the Cubans formally gave the United States permission to use the island for its own defensive purposes as well as for the defense of the entire hemisphere.[80]

While the United States was negotiating military agreements with various Latin American states, it also passed the Lend-Lease

Act, on March 11, 1941, to give additional assistance to its allies. Almost immediately after the passage of the act, Cuba submitted a request listing its military needs. While the governments discussed the terms of the aid, Secretary of War Henry L. Stimson suggested that although various Latin American nations were asking for aid, the countries doing the fighting, like Great Britain and China, should have top priority. In spite of this argument, the government felt that it should grant Cuba $7,200,000 worth of military equipment. The agreement was signed on November 7, thus binding the island even closer to the effort for hemispheric defense.[81]

The United States gained other military advantages on the island. Early in the spring of 1941, the State Department requested and received an extension of the agreement that allowed each nation to use the other's airspace. In addition, the War Department and Pan American Airways had made a secret agreement during 1939 to improve airfields in various Latin American nations, and the company was already working on the one at the Camagüey airport. These plans for improving air facilities were complemented by the navy's desire to enlarge its perimeter around Guantánamo naval base for defensive purposes. The navy originally wanted sole jurisdiction, but the State Department argued for joint American-Cuban participation to avoid nationalist outcries. An agreement was concluded which provided for a jointly controlled defense area to be managed by a board of United States and Cuban officers. Although there were minor changes in the formal text, by the end of the year the agreement had been completed.[82]

The United States' programs of economic assistance and military cooperation proved their effectiveness when Japan attacked Pearl Harbor. One day after Roosevelt asked for a declaration of war, the Cuban Congress unanimously passed its own resolution of war against the Japanese, and two days later, it followed the same course of action toward Germany and Italy. Batista quickly evoked emergency wartime powers to freeze enemy funds and requested immediate United States aid to expand the Cuban armed forces; at the same time Messersmith asked the State Department to send another military mission as soon as possible.[83] On December 20 the ambassador reflected his pleasant surprise over the Cuban war response: "I might state that, while I had always felt that the Cuban people would respond to any action we might take with respect to war, I had not anticipated that the public response would be as enthusiastic, general, and gratifying as had been the case."[84]

In the midst of the excitement generated by the entry into World War II, Messersmith was preparing to leave for a new post. Roosevelt had called him in November to inform him that he would replace Josephus Daniels as ambassador to Mexico. Although Messersmith was pleased with his new appointment, he wanted to conclude some unfinished business. Once he had done this, he said good-bye to his Cuban friends and sailed for Miami on December 25.[85] In his memoirs he recorded that he and his wife felt that "our stay there will always remain as one of the happiest ones during our many years of service abroad for our government."[86]

Messersmith had many reasons to be satisfied with the success of his Cuban assignment. He had arrived in Havana during an internal political crisis and had avoided any American involvement. He had witnessed the signing of the 1940 Constitution, and although he was not pleased with some of its provisions, he had tried to use his influence behind the scenes instead of becoming embroiled in a public debate over the articles that adversely affected the United States. Finally, he had watched the presidential elections, Batista's triumph, and the consolidation of Batista's power after the February revolt. In a real sense, his tour of duty, coupled with that of J. Butler Wright, reinforced the American commitment to noninterference in the island's internal political affairs. The promise conveyed by the abrogation of the Platt Amendment was being fulfilled by 1942.

Nevertheless, the withdrawal of the ambassador from Cuba's internal political turmoil had not diminished the overwhelming influence attached to the position. In many respects, Batista's rise to power reinforced Cuba's shaky political stability. Therefore, the United States did not have to assert itself in domestic politics and could rely on other tactics to protect its interests. While offering public assurances that Good Neighbor diplomacy meant noninterference in local politics, the United States used its economic power to influence decisions on the island. During Messersmith's tenure, this tactic was constantly employed to achieve the desired results. Welles maintained, for example, that Cuba would have to settle its public works debt obligations before the United States would consider any kind of economic aid. Even after this issue was resolved, he and Messersmith demanded internal reforms in Cuba's political system before assistance would be granted. Finally, in the contract for the financing of an additional 400,000 tons of the sugar crop, the Eximbank required the renewal of Decree-Law No. 522 in order to protect American sugar interests. The blatant political interference of Welles and Caffery had definitely ended; possibly Batista's ascendancy would have assured this in any event. In its place, the United States employed another—yet just as effective—means of control: economic coercion.

While assistance programs replaced political direction, Messersmith worked steadily for hemispheric solidarity. In his efforts he frequently connected economic prosperity with political stability, and he firmly believed that these interrelated movements would assure Cuban cooperation in the event of war. His beliefs proved correct. When he sailed, he knew that the island was solidly behind the American commitment, directing its efforts against fifth column activity, popularizing the war effort, cooperating with military bases, and selling its entire 1942 sugar crop. Beaulac's assessment of his superior was accurate—Messersmith was always successful.

11

War, Prosperity, and Politics

Batista's unequivocal support for the United States after the Pearl Harbor attack strengthened the American effort to gain hemispheric cooperation, but at the same time, the Cuban declaration of war created new problems for the American embassy. Since Messersmith and Beaulac had already been transferred to new assignments, Chargé d'Affaires Ellis Briggs, who had served under Caffery as his second secretary, temporarily assumed charge of the embassy.[1] Recalling those hectic first days of the war, he described his early difficulties. Although the United States had already purchased Cuba's entire 1942 sugar crop, labor disputes in the sugar fields and strikes on the docks interrupted loading schedules. As if these problems were not enough, the arrival of survivors from ships torpedoed by German submarines gave Cuba the impression that the Axis controlled the shipping lanes. The United States' military forces had to protect the island's 1600-mile unguarded coastline in order to assure the Cubans that they were safe. "The Cuban people were all for the war," declared Briggs, "but they wanted to be convinced we were fighting it."[2]

While the American and Cuban governments focused their attention on the conduct of the war, the island's politicians were preparing for the 1942 congressional elections. Although 431 candidates filed to run for fifty-eight seats, the public showed little interest in the campaign, since no significant issues were at stake. On March 15, 1942, approximately 50 percent of the eligible voters went to the polls. In what the embassy described as remarkably quiet, generally honest, and impartial elections, the government bloc won forty-six of the contests. While the winning coalition celebrated its victory, Grau, disgruntled by the results, denounced the elections because of the government's alleged corruption. While such charges of fraud were typical of the losing side in

Cuban elections, they indicated rising interest in another impending campaign. Even though the presidential elections were over two years away, politicians had begun to speculate on the possible candidates.[3]

In the midst of this internal political maneuvering and wartime activity, Roosevelt sent his last ambassadorial appointee to Havana. Spruille Braden was different in at least one respect from his four predecessors. While they had been career diplomats, he had served as a mining executive in South America for almost twenty years before joining the United States diplomatic mission at the Montevideo Conference in 1933. After participating in that meeting, he became the American delegate to the Chaco Peace Conference, called to end a long and bloody war between Paraguay and Bolivia. Once the belligerents had signed a peace treaty, Braden was appointed ambassador to Colombia. Now he moved to the crucial Cuban post at the age of forty-eight, with nine years experience as a New Deal diplomat. Braden felt that he had gained a certain amount of expertise in that time. He was a firm advocate of the Good Neighbor commitment, but he felt that it should be a reciprocal policy. The United States would give assistance to Latin American states, but they must respond in like fashion.[4] While his Cuban critics accused him of interfering in local affairs, Briggs recalled mainly that Braden was "as competent as he was indestructible . . . ,"[5] and Mario Lazo spoke in similar terms, calling the ambassador "vigorous, tough, forthright to the point of bluntness, and a man of high principles."[6] These widely divergent opinions of Braden made him the most controversial ambassador since Caffery.

Braden arrived in Havana on May 15. While he familiarized himself with his new duties, Batista asked the opposition to support his war program. Hoping for cooperation, he began discussing the possibility of a war cabinet that would include representatives from all the parties. His existing cabinet even resigned to give him greater maneuverability in the selection of new appointees, but his efforts proved futile. Although the opposition leaders favored an Allied victory, they insisted that they could not participate in Batista's corrupt administration. Thus when the president announced the composition of the new cabinet, it contained many of the original members without any participation from the opposition.[7] Batista's efforts to form a united front had weakened the cabinet's prestige, and Briggs felt that the "net effect . . . of futile political maneuvering and jockeying for position has been to augment public disgust with most of the parties and the majority of their leaders."[8]

Despite the internal political discord, the Cuban government vigorously moved against fifth column activity by interning enemy aliens. The police arrested August Luning, a German spy who was using a secret radio to inform submarines of ship movements in Cuban waters. When the government tried him for espionage, his trial aroused intense public interest. He was convicted and then executed on November 10, the only Axis agent to meet such a fate in any Latin American nation during the war. But even though Batista strenuously prosecuted the war effort, many Cubans remained ambivalent. Some criticized the United States' military strategy, while others complained of the economic privations that they had to endure. Although most islanders applauded the successful invasion of North Africa and began to identify themselves with the winning cause, the American embassy was constantly concerned about Cuban apathy toward the war effort.[9]

As opposition to the Axis gained momentum, the Cuban Communist Party vigorously advocated compulsory military conscription and urged a troop commmitment to the European front at the earliest possible date. Inasmuch as Batista was entirely committed to the war effort and was also closely acquainted with many Cuban Communist leaders, their support now made it possible for his government to grant formal recognition to the Soviet Union. On October 16, 1942, the two countries established diplomatic relations' making Cuba the first Latin American nation to recognize Russia' and early in the following year they exchanged ambassadors.[10] The establishment of diplomatic relations and the Communist Party's growing prestige on the island caused grave concern in the American embassy: "Today the Communist Party is becoming an increasingly important factor in the general unrest now taking place with the dislocation of labor and industry under war conditions." While the embassy did not want to exaggerate the party's influence, there was no doubt that it was gaining power because of Batista's active support.[11]

Following the international Communist policy of attracting additional leftist supporters, the Cuban Communist Party changed its name on Janaury 22, 1943 to the Popular Socialist Party. The drive to gain new adherents gained added momentum in March when Batista placed two Communist leaders—Juan Marinello and Carlos Rafael Rodríguez—in his cabinet, as ministers without portfolios. Although neither man had any specific duties, they were the first Communists to be appointed to any Latin American cabinet. The president also allowed the Communists to increase their influence on the ministry of labor and within the union movement. Although he was attacked for these actions, Batista later defended himself by stating that he wanted full cooperation from every political party in the nation. After all, he went on rhetorically, if Roosevelt could meet directly with Stalin, why should not he cooperate with Cuba's Communists?[12]

The opposition added the charge of friendship with communism to its familiar accusations of corruption and inefficiency. Before long, these intensified assaults began to sap the president's popularity. Looking for a way to regain the initiative, Batista used the same tactic that had succeeded so well in 1938—a trip to Washington. Indeed, when the government announced that Roosevelt had invited Batista to see him at the White House, the opposition was stunned. Once again Batista had used American prestige to bolster his shaky domestic position, and he intended to make certain his trip ended successfully. Since his first visit, changed conditions on the island had improved his prospects. On his first trip, he had little if any bargaining power, but now, because of Cuba's strategic and economic importance, American negotiators were ready to support his regime in order to assure the continuation of wartime cooperation.[13]

Batista left for the United States on December 7,[14] and on the same day Welles analyzed the island's problems for Roosevelt. All of Cuba's troubles had been blamed on its president, and as a result, Grau was increasing his popularity at Batista's expense. "Since the overthrow of Batista might plunge the Island during this critical period into chaos," Welles reasoned, "it is essential, if he is to remain in office, that his visit to Washington not be a failure." The undersecretary wanted to assist the island both militarily and economically because only with American support could Batista maintain his undisputed position as the island's political leader.[15]

The following evening Roosevelt gave a banquet in his guest's honor at which he recalled his decision not to send troops to the island in the 1933 crisis. The American president praised Batista for his role in that time of stress and drank a toast to his health. The honored guest then rose and returned the toast, eulogizing Roosevelt for initiating the Good Neighbor Policy and again pledging complete support for the war effort.[16] Once the official functions were completed, Welles and Batista discussed the island's needs in three broad areas: military aid, public works projects, and sugar sales. After the conferences, Welles told Roosevelt, "I believe that in general it will be possible within the limits imposed by war shortages to permit him [Batista] to return to Habana satisfied that the United States has done everything possible to help Cuba in its difficult situation."[17]

Of the three general topics discussed in Washington, the easiest to settle was the request for military assistance. Since Cuba was strategically located in the middle of the Caribbean, the American army and navy both wanted to establish bases there. Besides the large Guantánamo naval installation, the United States hoped to set up new landing fields for training missions and airplane patrols. In the spring of 1942 the American government received permission to build an airfield near San Antonio de los Baños, twenty-five miles south of Havana. Later known as Batista Field, it was intended to train pilots for B-25 bombers. Soon after this agreement was signed, the War Department negotiated another to build an air base at San Julían in Pinar del Río Province. In addition to these major installations, the army developed several auxiliary landing fields, and the navy constructed harbor defenses and patrolled the island's coastline. While the American military forces used Cuba for its strategic purposes, Batista requested additional lend-lease aid to train and equip his own troops. In response to this request, the United States sent rifles and other supplies to the army and patrol boats to the navy. Some Cuban nationals also decided to enlist in the American armed forces.[18]

In spite of all this cooperation, Braden complained constantly about the Cuban war effort. He repeatedly criticized the islanders for their apathetic or hostile attitudes toward the United States' wartime policies. Braden also objected that the Cubans failed to attend to their harbor defenses, forcing American troops to maintain them. He constantly stressed the graft and corruption of the Cuban officials in charge of censorship programs.[19]

While few major difficulties arose over military cooperation, the $25 million economic assistance loan negotiated in 1941 proved a nearly empty gesture. It was originally intended for agricultural diversification and public works projects, but once the United States entered the war, the government simply did not have enough materials to carry out the programs. Welles had promised Batista that some of the public works projects would be completed, but by July 1944 the Eximbank had only disbursed $3,125,000. The United States' inability to fulfill its commitment, combined with the phenomenal prosperity caused by booming sugar sales, made the loan a topic of political controversy. Batista's opposition maintained that Cuba no longer required American economic assistance and that he was only using the money to enhance his personal fortune. With these increasingly bitter outcries against the loan, the American government began to consider its abrogation by the end of Batista's term; it did cancel $15 million of the original agreement shortly after he left office.[20]

While these first two issues were important to the conduct of United States-Cuban relations, the sugar question remained the crucial one. Fortunately for the Cubans, sugar was in shorter supply during the war years than most other foods in the United States. It was the first agricultural commodity to be rationed after the attack on Pearl Harbor, and the only one not removed from ration control before 1946. Such a shortage was unexpected, for during the 1930s sugar had been abundant and its price extremely low. Now, however, the United States had suddenly lost imports from Java and the Philippine Islands, and production was decreasing in Hawaii, Puerto Rico, and at home, thanks to labor shortages and the erection of military installations. At the same time the demand for sugar soared, not only in itself as a basic staple but for its by-products, such as invert sugar and blackstrap molasses, from which came the industrial alcohol needed in unprecedented quantities to make synthetic rubber.[21]

Even before the United States entered the war, the Roosevelt administration mobilized the American economy to assure the production of essential goods. Under the direction of the Reconstruction Finance Corporation, subsidiaries such as the Defense Supplies Corporation and the Commodity Credit Corporation were established in 1940 to procure strategic materials from the Latin American nations. In Cuba this program began with the purchase of the island's entire sugar crop, with the exception of sugar for local consumption and small exports to other Latin American

states. The Defense Supplies Corporation and the Cuban Sugar
Stabilization Institute signed the first contract for the 1942 crop at
a price of 2.65 cents per pound, and the former bought all of Cuba's
sugar by-products for synthetic rubber throughout the war. Although the price for the next two crops remained 2.65 cents, the
Commodity Credit Corporation conducted the negotiations. Along
with these agreements, the United States also agreed to subsidize
sugar producers who bore excess costs resulting from interruptions
in shipping and other difficulties caused by the submarine
menace.[22]

These wartime sugar purchases had a tremendous impact on
United States-Cuban economic relations. The Roosevelt administration had no serious problems in the negotiations for the purchase
of the 1942 sugar crop. Once it was signed, the islanders anticipated a substantial economic upswing, and Wall Street speculators
touched off a mild boom in Cuban stocks. Their optimism was well
founded. While the average price for Cuban sugar was 1.75 cents
per pound in 1941, the 1942 purchase price of 2.65 cents was the
highest since 1926. Along with the rise in price, production jumped
from 2,441,000 tons in 1941 to 3,800,000 in the following year,
which was the largest crop since 1930. As a result of the higher
prices and the enlarged crop, sugar growers experienced their most
prosperous year since 1927.[23]

When negotiations for the 1943 crop began, the Cubans naturally
argued for a contract similar to the previous one, while the State
Department wanted a smaller crop, since there was already a 1.5
million ton carry-over from the 1942 purchase caused by shipping
difficulties. The size of the crop was only one of the negotiators'
problems; Cuban growers also wanted a higher price. Even though
both these issues created a great deal of anxiety during the
bargaining sessions, the United States persuaded the Cubans to
accept the same price and the limitation on production. In calling
for a reduction, American experts had miscalculated the Allies'
sugar needs, but after they realized their error, the United States
asked the Cubans to increase their output. The islanders gladly
complied with this request, and as a result, the Cuban producers
had another banner year.[24]

With the commencement of bargaining for the 1944 crop, the
Cubans repeated their calls for higher prices, but negotiations
proceeded fairly smoothly nevertheless. Considering the evident

critical sugar shortage, the United States asked the Cubans for the largest possible crop, and as a result, the 1944 harvest was the third largest in the island's history. Even though the islanders acceded to the American requests, the Cubans began to raise new issues in the negotiations. Remembering the devastating consequences of the "dance of the millions" after World War I, when sugar prices plunged drastically and the island entered a prolonged depression, they wanted to discuss plans for the postwar readjustment period. Besides these long-range problems, the Cubans were also worried about the inflation created by the increasing prosperity and the shortage of consumer goods. Although these issues were cause for real concern, the American negotiators refused to discuss postwar readjustment since they had no idea what the United States Congress would do with regard to sugar legislation. This complicated problem was left for the next Cuban president to resolve.[25]

The Cubans benefited from the purchase of their sugar crops during the war, but it is equally true that Batista made a concrete contribution to the Allies' victory by his willingness to cooperate. In spite of strong domestic pressure to raise the price of sugar and increase production, he not only fulfilled his commitment to supply the United States with the island's sugar production but also held to the 2.65-cent price throughout his term of office. Even when the United States negotiators misjudged in 1943, Batista accepted their request for a smaller crop, and when the United States experts recognized their mistake and reversed their position, he likewise changed his.

In the midst of this growing prosperity based on sugar sales, the Cuban government did not concern itself solely with the island's main export but continually turned its attention to the problem of diversification. On February 4, 1942, Batista used his emergency wartime powers to decree that every sugar producer who held more than 165 acres must devote a portion of his land to the production of other vital foodstuffs such as rice, corn, and beans. To further this aim, the United States agreed to purchase all the surplus beans, peanuts, and corn produced in 1943 and 1944 and also shipped seed and farm machinery to the island. Even with this aid, the Cubans made little progress toward agricultural diversification. Farmers would not shift to new crops when the old ones were so lucrative; they did not use the machinery to its fullest advantage; and direct government aid was highly inadequate. Not for the first time, Cuban sugar and tobacco proved to be curses as well as blessings. Because the island was so well-suited to the production of these crops and because they were bringing such high prices during the war, neither the government nor the island's commercial interests provided the necessary inducements for agricultural diversification.[26]

Although the farming program proved a disappointment, other programs were more encouraging. Batista signed several broad decrees to increase industrial enterprises. In March 1944 he suspended import duties on various kinds of machinery, tools, and other equipment not produced on the island, hoping to foster the growth of new industries. Probably the greatest success came with the expanded production of minerals vital to the war effort. The construction of the Nicaro Nickel Company with American capital stimulated the mining of Cuban nickel, and other scarce minerals, such as manganese and chromium, were also developed. Even though these efforts were not as successful as they might have been, and after the war the diversification programs began to lapse with the revival of American exports to the island and the reestablishment of import duties.[27]

Both Messersmith and Braden were acutely aware of the need for Cuban diversification and of the obstacles in its way. Many people who did not recognize the efforts that the embassy personnel made during the war to assist in diversiffication charged the United States with retarding this program. In his memoirs, Messersmith not only defended the American effort but also chided those critics in both Latin America and the United States for their failure to recognize the State Deprtment's efforts:

> . . . we took a very real interest in putting the Cuban economy on a sounder basis. There is much talk these days of the Point Four program as though we had not been thinking of these things before the program was inaugurated. In more than one country for many years, as is shown by the foregoing with respect to Cuba, we were endeavoring to take practical steps to aid in stabilizing the economies. Those in our country who are so vociferous about our neglecting our Latin neighbors and those among our Latin neighbors who are even more vociferous about our neglecting them are talking out of a lack of knowledge or to cover up deficiencies of their own. If

in some of these Latin countries as much effort had been made
by the governments and leaders of opinion in these countries
to aid in the improvement of the economies of the countries as
we did in the United States to aid, the situation would be very
much improved in many of these countries.[28]

Despite the lack of progress in the diversification programs,
Batista's cooperation in military operations and sugar sales greatly
assisted the American war effort. But although United States-Cuban relations functioned smoothly in these two crucial areas,
Braden constantly complained that Batista refused to act on
routine matters affecting both nations. Writing on May 19, 1943, he
showed his growing annoyance: "This inertia with respect to his
functions as Chief Executive, taken in conjunction with the
corruption which now prevails in Cuba . . . is slowly paralyzing
the present administration as a functioning organization, and it is
becoming increasingly difficult to make any progress whatever with
respect to even the most routine questions."[29] Braden reported that
he could not get the Cuban officials to act promptly on such items
as fuel rationing, labor disruptions in ship loading, taxation of
American agencies, and censorship of mail, radio, and cables.[30] By
late 1943 Braden was convinced that Batista was taking advantage
of the United States: "I believe that the Cuban Government has
regarded the Good Neighbor Policy thus far as a down-hill pull on a
one-way street, and that the sooner they realize that traffic likewise
moves in the opposite direction, the better it will be for Cuban-
American relations."[31]

While the widespread corruption and inefficiency in routine
matters irritated Braden, one incident in early 1943 created grave
concern at the embassy. On January 20 the Tinguaro sugar mill, the
third largest mill in Cuba, owned by the Cuban-American Sugar
Company, was damaged by fire. The company exaggerated the
destruction, estimating that the mill would cost $1.5 million to
repair, while it minimized the social consequences of closing the
mill, alleging that it employed only 200 workers. These claims
were in direct conflict with the accounts of local newspaper, which
stated that the mill needed only $150,000 for rebuilding and that it
had 600 employees. While the Cuban government wanted the mill
rebuilt, the company refused to rebuild unless the regime would
guarantee that the mill could operate on a profitable basis.[32]

The issue of repairing the sugar mill soon became a hotly debated political topic. Batista warned the company in early February that he was contemplating government action. When the company refused to act, he appointed a government interventor to reconstruct the mill at the company's expense. Braden had participated in the futile negotiations to settle the problem. He blamed the company for its failure either to devise a rebuilding program or to sell the mill, but he also thought that the Cuban government had acted imprudently. In any case, the ambassador opposed the seizure and demanded that if the Cubans expropriated the mill, the American-owned company should receive prompt and adequate compensation. While the Cubans were considering the embassy's note, Batista seized a Cuban-owned Bacardi Rum plant on October 5 because of the company's refusal to obey a government directive to settle a labor dispute.[33] On the same day Braden wrote to the State Department, "these seizures may be among the most important events that have occurred since my arrival."[34]

As a result of the government's action, the latent antagonism between the labor and business sectors came to the surface. While the island's commercial interests censured the regime for its intervention, Braden urged a settlement. Finally both cases were resolved. In the American case, a group of Cubans bought the sugar mill, and the government's intervention ended on March 15, 1944. Even though the two cases were settled, Braden thought that these incidents had further embittered class feeling, frightened foreign investment, and encouraged irresponsible radical groups to create additional animosity in the island's labor relations.[35]

Although the Tinguaro intervention created tension between business and labor, it did not damage Cuba's economic growth. Unfortunately for the islanders, however, this prosperity did not solve their political problems. Almost immediately after the 1942 congressional elections, speculation over the presidential elections, still two years off, began to intensify. Once Batista had assured the island's political leaders that he would not stand for reelection, a scramble for the nomination began within the government coalition between Vice-President Gustavo Cuervo Rubio and Carlos Saladrigas.[36] While they fought for support, Grau was already preparing his campaign for the opposition. Late in the year, Batista told Braden of his fear that Grau might succeed him: "It would be better to have the Communists or anybody else than Grau and his crowd around him in their inefficiency and total inability. And yet he is the only Cuban who stands out as a leader with a following and, therefore, the only one who would seem able to win the elections."[37] Braden must have considered such a prediction highly exaggerated, for shortly after he arrived in Havana, he met Grau and described him as a sincere idealist, though he added, "at no time did I have the feeling that I was speaking to a really important man."[38]

While the ambassador analyzed the political conditions on the island, Cuban officials were trying to determine the State Department's position in the upcoming elections. On August 6, 1942, Cuervo Rubio saw Welles in Washington and asked him to comment on his possible candidacy, but the undersecretary told him that the United States refused to interfere "in any manner or form with the domestic concerns of the people of other American Republics and that under no circumstances would the Government of the United States indicate any preference either by support or opposition to any Cuban citizen who might run for the presidency of Cuba."[39] Later in the year, Braden reiterated this position, but Cuban politicians remained unconvinced. The history of interference by the United States in Cuban domestic affairs had conditioned the island's politicians to anticipate the State Department's intentions toward their internal affairs.[40]

The growing speculation over the embassy's attitude and the struggle within the government factions for the presidential nomination were further complicated by the need for a new electoral code and census. As usual, Congress procrastinated on both vital pieces of legislation until Batista demanded action. On June 1, 1943, it passed the new electoral code, requiring all eligible Cubans to vote and to carry an identification card. Besides the enfranchisement sections, the act set June 1, 1944 as the date for elections and October 10 for the president's inauguration. Once the new code was promulgated, the government took a census, which determined that 2,259,514 of Cuba's 4,624,998 citizens were eligible voters. Each citizen was then given the opportunity to register with one of the various political parties. When the registration ended, the government factions claimed twice as many members as the opposition forces. The government claims of numerical superiority did not disturb Grau's supporters for they believed that Batista's officials had interfered in both the census and the affiliations to ensure the government's victory in the presidential elections.[41] Under these circumstances, the opposition saw little if any likelihood of impartial elections, and Braden concurred: "In short, such elections cannot represent democracy triumphant, but only democracy dishonored."[42]

The prospects of certain victory stimulated the battle for the presidential nomination that was being fought in the government coalition throughout 1943, with Cuervo Rubio and Saladrigas the leading candidates. When Batista promised to support the latter, Cuervo Rubio deserted the government coalition to form his own party. Now the contest had narrowed down to a choice between Grau and Saladrigas. The embassy believed that the charismatic Auténtico leader was the more popular candidate and would win in honest elections, but Batista controlled the electoral machinery and had personally selected Saladrigas as his successor. Saladrigas was a forty-five-year-old conservative lawyer from Havana, a founder of the A.B.C. who had played an active role in the Revolution of 1933. During the next ten years, he had held several cabinet posts and had served as Batista's first prime minister. Now the tall and slender politician not only had to unite the diverse elements within the government coalition, but he also had to prove that he, like Grau, could gain a popular following.[43]

By the middle of 1943 the contest between the two men had developed into a struggle between a continuation of the past and the expectation of the future. The underlying question became whether the Cuban people wanted a continuation of Batista's blatantly venal regime or would take their chances with the Auténticos, who promised honest government. Government dishonesty had become a commonly accepted practice with the birth of the Cuban republic, and many of the political leaders expected to enhance their personal fortunes while they occupied their posts. During the depression, widespread graft abated simply for the lack of revenue, but the prosperity of the war years had changed the situation. Corruption had become so pervasive that even a public conditioned to such practices was demanding reform. Local businessmen were organizing to improve public services and to promote honest and efficient government, which officials had either ignored or neglected.[44] Reviewing the events of 1943, the editor of *Carteles* declared "if 1942 was bad, 1943 shows a more deplorable balance of unlawful acts and deficiencies in Cuban life . . . . public evils have become even worse, while there is no sign of improvement to avoid further deterioration."[45]

On May 29, 1943, Braden wrote angrily, "Corruption has never before been so rampant, so organized, or so profitable for those at the top. It has never before caused such widespread disgust."[46] To prove these charges, the ambassador reported that Batista and other government officials were having money deposited in the United States. Even though the State Department agreed that Cuban graft was overwhelming, it was more interested in wartime cooperation than in reforming Cuban politicians. When the department surveyed the situation, it concluded that "the internal political situation of Cuban is unsatisfactory; that it is more apt to deteriorate than to improve until the next President is inaugurated; but that the situation does not appear to offer a serious threat of social or political disturbances or bloodshed."[47]

While the State Department focused its attention on hemispheric cooperation, Braden felt that the Good Neighbor Policy demanded honesty on the island. Concerning himself especially with the Cuban politicians' efforts to have Americans contribute to the government coalition's campaign fund, Braden saw Batista on July 27, 1943 and told him that the United States' commitment to nonintervention meant that American companies and individuals should not contribute either to political parties or to individual candidates: "I will not tolerate their intervention in Cuban elections in any way, shape or manner . . . . they must not contribute even a five-cent piece to a Cuban candidate."[48] In a speech before the American Chamber of Commerce of Cuba on September 22, he publicly repeated his position as an official pronouncement of American policy on the island.[49]

The fundamental reason for the ambassador's forceful warnings was not just the dismal record of Batista's regime; Braden was just as much interested in the United States' alleged relationship to corruption and Cuban politics. According to him, the Cubans blamed the American government for allowing graft to flourish while the Platt Amendment was in effect so he had designed this policy to stop charges that Americans were involved in the regime's dishonesty. After he had formally announced his program, Braden felt that the Cubans were finally realizing that they and not the American residents were responsible for their government's activities. The United States, the ambassador declared, had to show the Cubans that the Good Neighbor Policy was an effort to end past mistakes "and that we shall be compelled to desist from granting favors to the Cuban Government until they have demonstrated a spirit of complete reciprocity and, above all, of honesty."[50]

Braden was convinced that he was following a properly neutral course of action, but Batista and his supporters felt that the ambassador was actively working against them, and tension between the Cuban government and the embassy mounted. In June 1943, the antiadministration newspaper *Prensa Libre* reported that Braden and Batista were at odds. Late in the year, Braden was warned that some of Batista's advisers were advocating his removal because of his efforts to stop their illicit practices. The rumor was true; at the end of 1943 Batista requested his recall.[51]

Replying to this request on January 5, 1944, Hull regretted the controversy over Braden's activities, but he thought that he should not be removed. Braden and Batista should try to reconcile their differences somehow, for Hull did not want to see the wartime cooperation between the two nations placed in jeopardy. He "said that in any event there should be no abrupt change with the almost certain wide publicity that would break out, but that the next best thing, in case there can be no healing of this breach, would be for the matter to rest quietly for a time and then let the normal transfers among our diplomats take care of the situation."[52] Hull's suggestion settled the conflict. Braden remained at his post, but his relations with Batista improved only slightly.[53]

Braden's problems with Batista did not interrupt the presidential campaign. At the beginning of 1944, the embassy predicted that Saladrigas would win the election. Even defections to Grau and the charge that he was Batista's handpicked successor did not negate the government candidate's growing advantages. Supporters of the regime had slowly united behind what they considered his certain victory. Batista might protest his impartiality, but he controlled the armed forces, an almost unlimited supply of funds, and the electoral machinery—and he was using all of these to propel his friend into office. Besides these political factors, the economic boom continued unabated despite accusations of widespread corruption. As a result of the political and economic state of affairs, the opposition was becoming increasingly disillusioned. *El Mundo* was already calling Saladrigas "the almost elected President," and Braden scheduled a visit to Washington for Saladrigas after the elections to discuss the problems confronting both nations.[54]

As the elections drew closer, the embassy made Saladrigas a six- or five-to-one favorite. Grau was more popular, but Batista had done everything in his power to assure the Auténtico leader's defeat. To increase his lead, Saladrigas toured the provinces in the middle of May, but his attempt to gain new supporters backfired because he lacked the charismatic appeal that his opponent possessed. At the start of the electioneering, Braden saw no chance for an Auténtico victory, but after a time he expressed some cautious doubt as Grau's popularity mounted at Saladrigas's expense. The campaigning was to end on May 25, but now the embassy would not even try to predict a winner.[55] Four days later the ambassador added that the "wave of popular support for Grau continues to grow astonishingly and Saladrigas's supporters are patently worried."[56]

Although there were several outbreaks of violence on the last day of May, order and quiet prevailed when the voters went to the polls on June 1. The expectation of government coercion proved unfounded, for Batista carried out his pledge of holding impartial elections. When the balloting ended, every sign indicated a close race, and the public already believed that Grau had won. The rumors of his victory became official the following afternoon, when Saladrigas publicly conceded. Grau's followers greeted his triumph with unbounded enthusiasm. Crowds gathered to cheer in front of their leader's home; cars filled with Auténticos raced through the streets proclaiming their victory; and some supporters comman-deered streetcars and buses to rejoice.[57] One reporter commented, "the masses have a blind faith that Doctor Grau can cure all their ills. They idolize him with a fanatic frenzy that must be seen to be believed."[58] What the reporter did not realize was that Grau's victory was more than a personal triumph. He had coined the phrase "Cuba for the Cubans" ten years earlier; now his supporters were giving him the chance to turn his slogan into a concrete program. In the minds of many Cubans, his election promised the fulfillment of the 1933 Revolution.

The final election results were almost anticlimactic. The affiliation process which had shown that there were two govern-ment supporters for every opposition member proved meaningless.

In an election in which more Cubans went to the polls than ever before, Grau received 1,042,874 votes or 54 percent, while Saladrigas had 837,230. But even though the Auténticos had won the presidency, their victory was far from complete, for the government coalition still controlled the Congress, and Batista had won the widespread praise for his conduct in holding fair elections. Grau had won the presidency, but Batista had not been discredited.[59]

While the Auténticos were celebrating Grau's victory, Braden was reporting on the Cuban reaction to the American embassy's activities during the campaign. Even though he repeatedly reminded the Cubans that the United States would not intervene in the election, Braden contended that they would not accept this fact because the "custom of believing in United States intervention and pressure in Cuba is so ingrained that it is difficult for the man-in-the-street to accept fully that our country is in no way interfering in Cuban affairs." With the elections over, the United States was receiving some of the credit for the generally honest elections. The ambassador added that his noncontribution policy had been vindicated since if he had allowed Americans to contribute to Saladrigas's campaign fund, the embassy would have been in an awkward position after Grau's triumph. Now, according to the ambassador, the embassy could easily maintain the same position in future elections.[60]

While the embassy was analyzing the election results, Grau was acting as if he were already in office. On June 8 before the Rotary Club and promised reforms such as the establishment of a real civil service and the dismissal of corrupt officials. Braden felt that the president-elect had made a costly political blunder by announcing his intention of removing dishonest government employees. To dismiss all of them would take a Herculean effort, and the ambassador thought that Grau's declaration only placed the recipients and their patrons on their guard. By taking such a stance, Grau had demonstrated a poor sense of timing and a failure to appreciate the realities of Cuban politics.[61]

Grau was not the only one who demonstrated his lack of tact; his enemies created additional tension. Once Batista accepted the Auténtico victory, General Manuel Benítez Valdés, his fellow conspirator in the sergeants' revolt, denounced the president in the vilest of terms as a traitor because he had permitted Grau to win.

To silence these caustic attacks, Batista relieved Benítez of his duties, confined him to his house, and later forced him to leave the island. Even though one malcontent was gone, rumors persisted that the armed forces were dissatisfied with Grau's election, but Batista had made his position clear. He would hold firm power until October 10, and on that date he would turn over the government to his successor.[62]

While Benítez reflected the discontent within the military, the national police exhibited similar anxieties. Grau's victory signaled a change in political authority that allowed the extremists who associated with the Auténticos to expand their activities. Rumors began to spread after the elections that the radicals were going to use the new regime to take revenge on the police who had repressed them, and this speculation quickly proved to be correct. From the election to the inauguration, the extremists conducted their own personal vendetta by assassinating five policemen and two civilians and wounding five more people. As a result of these attacks, some police were already fleeing the island, while other Batistianos, fearing retaliation after the inaguration, refused to interfere with the extremists' activities. The public soon clamored for an end to terrorism, and Grau responded by asking the radicals to halt their attacks, but all this pressure was wasted. Urban violence had returned to the island after a nine-year lull.[63]

Grau added to his troubles when he announced his plan to remove Communist influence from labor unions. At first the party strongly objected to this hostile declaration, but the Communist leadership quickly reversed its position, stating that it supported most of the new president's programs. Although most Auténticos continued their unabated attacks on the Communists, Grau diminished his because of the need to broaden his political base. He recognized that the Communist Party had polled over 120,000 votes, or slightly more than 4 percent of the total electorate, which had resulted in the election of three senators and four representatives. In late July, the president-elect and the Communist leaders began to discuss a political bargain, and on September 13, an agreement was reached in which the party pledged its support for the new administration in return for Grau's cooperation. Even though the Communist Party and Grau had opposed each other since 1933, circumstances now changed their political relationship.

Once again power considerations and not ideology proved more important than past antagonisms in making political decisions.[64]

While Grau directed his attention to internal conditions, he was also establishing friendly relations with the American ambassador. Three days after the elections, the two men discussed the possibility of an official visit to Washington, and, after an agenda was arranged, Grau left Havana on August 29.[65] Two days later Roosevelt welcomed his guest and recalled the 1933 Cuban crisis, claiming that Grau had assisted in the repeal of the Platt Amendment. Since that time, Roosevelt added, there had been "no trouble at all" between the two nations.[66] The next afternoon, Hull spoke before the governing board of the Pan American Union, calling Grau the great benefactor of the Cuban people. Responding to these flattering comments, Grau endorsed Roosevelt's Good Neighbor concept, which, he said, was "a policy in splendid harmony with Cuban ideals."[67] Although none of the concrete problems confronting the two nations were settled during the visit, it was still a success. When Grau returned to Havana on September 9, the cordiality with which he was treated made it seem his first presidency had been forgotten.[68]

While preparations for the change of political leadership in Cuba continued, Batista summarized his accomplishments on the eleventh anniversary of the sergeants' revolt. He felt that his main contribtuions were the restoration of political stability and economic prosperity; he hoped that the incoming administration would enact the reforms that Congress had failed to consider under his administration; and he also hinted that he might return to seek the presidency. What he failed to mention was that the cooperative spirit that had existed between him and Grau immediately after the elections had vanished because pilfering from the treasury by members of the Batista government had assumed mammoth proportions. The nation's financial situation had become so bad by the inauguration that the new government was only assured of one thing—there would be no money in the treasury when Grau took office.[69]

Grau had returned to the island in plenty of time for his inauguration, but the enthusiasm for the new regime, which had been widespread immediately after the election, began to fade. Law enforcement was in a chaotic state: extremists sought retribution; Batistianos who feared for their lives were leaving the island; the armed forces' loyalty was questionable despite promises of support; labor groups dominated by Communists might oppose the new regime; and inflation was steadily growing worse. As if these anxieties were not enough, the newly elected Congress convened on September 18 and immediately began to argue about its role in the government. Braden further complicated Grau's problems when he spoke before a group of Cuban industrialists on October 4, warning them that they must diversify agriculturally and modernize their sugar industry. If they did not listen to his advice, Braden predicted, they would surely suffer in the postwar years.[70]

Some observers feared another period of violence similar to the one that had followed Machado's exodus, but Braden dismissed this possibility. Batista had not been a repressive ruler, and he had won a large popular following for his role in restoring stability. Braden's optimism was guarded, however, for he was not certain "that Grau could and would forcefully dominate the situation. Unfortunately, his unwillingness or inability this far to control the radical elements among his followers is disquieting."[71]

In the midst of these contradictory currents, the inauguration proceeded on schedule. In fulfillment of a campaign pledge, Grau disclosed his private assets on October 6 and promised a similar disclosure at the end of his term to prove that he had not used his office to increase his personal wealth.[72] Four days later, Grau was inaugurated as large, well-mannered, festive crowds watched what Braden called the island's "first democratic electoral triumph."[73] Immediately after the ceremony, Grau held his initial cabinet meeting, and that evening he addressed Congress. He gave a concise statement of his domestic program, which included suppression of graft, reorganization of the fiscal system, crop diversification, industrial development, and expansion of the rural schools program.[74] Braden believed that every political faction acclaimed the speech, and even wary businessmen were expressing more confidence in the new regime: "Thus at the present moment Dr. Grau appears to be supported not only by the large and rather inarticulate mass of his unconditional supporters, but by all Cuban political opinion. Only the future will show whether Dr. Grau knows how to make the most of this unique opportunity."[75]

Braden's optimism notwithstanding, Grau quickly confronted a multitude of problems. A devastating hurricane swept across the island, and the new administration had to spend considerable time coping with the catastrophe. Grau was also in need of revenue, since Batista's officials had emptied the treasury before they left office. But the new president himself was responsible for many of his troubles. He had relentlessly attacked Batista's governments for their undisciplined and inefficient operations; now the Batista coalition began to criticize the new regime on the same grounds. While some of Grau's appointees were men of integrity and ability, they lacked experience in public affairs. The president's egocentric personality, his nepotistic appointments, and the demogoguery of the extremist elements in his party added substance to his opponents' complaints. Grau created a chaotic situation in the government ministries by his wholesale firing of employees; he reasoned that Batista's corrupt appointees had to be replaced and that even if some efficient administrators were removed, this was a small price to pay for honest government.[76]

In a similar manner Grau damaged the effectiveness of the armed forces and the police. One of his first acts was to replace the chief of police in each province, and the new chiefs in turn removed Batista's officials and replaced them with their own appointees. In Havana alone Grau removed over four hundred noncommissioned officers and dismissed or retired numerous patrolmen. With the confusion created by the appointment of new policemen and their fear that they would lose their jobs if they interfered with the extremists' retaliatory violence against Batistianos, law enforcement deteriorated.[77]

Grau's concerted campaign against the military forces added to the disintegration of order. Before the inauguration, rumors of military plots to overthrow him had spread across the island, and now he actively moved to prevent a coup d'etat by attacking the military establishment. By November 7 he had removed twenty-seven officers and shifted or retired the military commanders in all the island's provinces. The animosity between the regime and the armed forces grew even worse when General Francisco Tabernilla Dolz, commander of Cabañas fortress, was dismissed from the army at the end of December for failure to authorize the transfer of four officers. Grau believed that this action would end his military problems, but during the conflict he had weakened the armed forces to such an extent that the principal support on which

Cuban stability had rested for the past eleven years was beginning
to collapse. Once Grau directly questioned the authority of the
armed forces and the national police, their ability to maintain
order was placed in serious jeopardy, and urban violence, which
had lain dormant since 1935, was spreading across the island.[78]

Despite these apparent difficulties, Braden continued to report
that Grau was doing a "splendid job" and that the United States
commitment to "do all that we legitimately can to assist him, was
wise and one which should be continued."[79] The embassy listed
many signs that pointed toward an effective administration, but
Braden's favorable analysis was based primarily on Grau's attitude.[80] After the notorious corruption of the previous regime, the
new one intended to restore honesty in the government. Braden
summarized his views on the fundamental differences between the
two presidents' political attitudes on December 19: "Batista looked
upon the government as a private prerogative, to be exploited for
the benefit of himself and his henchmen. Grau is fired up with a
zeal to improve the lot of the average Cuban and thus far has
shown a determination to exercise the powers of government as a
public trust for the good of the Cuban people. If he continues in
that line, he cannot fail—despite the mistakes which he will
inevitably make—to start the country along a better and happier
road than it was traveling on October 10, 1944."[81]

Although Braden called for the United States to support Grau in
his efforts to form an honest government, the policy of wartime
cooperation initiated by Batista was not continued by his successor.
Braden explained that Grau had the best intentions of cooperating
with the United States, but that his government's inefficiency and
his own inability to delegate responsibility hampered bilateral
negotiations. The Cuban government, for example, had not paid its
debts to American nationals or its debts for lend-lease assistance.
Furthermore, Grau would not sign an agreement on the reciprocal
use of strategic airfields when the American military command
asked for the use of bases after the war. Instead, he demanded the
return of the American-operated installations six months after the
war ended to furnish a visible proof of Cuban sovereignty as soon as
the island no longer needed American military protection.[82]

The bargaining for the 1945 sugar contract also revealed a
change in the Cuban negotiators' position. When the Americans
offered a continuation of the 2.65 cents per pound for sugar, the

Cubans balked. They not only want a substantially higher price, but they also argued for a long-term contract that would protect the sugar industry after the war. At first the American experts refused to discuss either demand, but because of the acute sugar shortage, they finally broke the deadlock by signing a one-year contract that increased the sugar price to 3.10 cents per pound. The contract was signed on April 26, 1945, but the Cubans continued to pressure the American negotiators for guarantees to protect the island against a depression like that which had followed World War I. Even though the Cubans had cause to worry, the United States experts could not act on a long-term contract because they did not know what would happen to sugar legislation after the war ended. The quota regulation enacted in 1934 had now become firmly established as part of United States-Cuban relations; no matter how diligently the Cubans pressed, long-range protection for the island's sugar industry depended on the unilateral action of the United States Congress.[83]

The first Batista era had ended. The unique aspects of Grau's administration and the questions of postwar relations brought forth new problems for both nations to resolve. In the midst of these changes, Roosevelt's last ambassador left Havana after the 1945 sugar contract was signed.[84] Braden had spent almost three years at his post, arriving during the bleakest months of the war and leaving with assurances of an Allied victory. During his stay he had vigorously pushed the American war effort in defense programs, sugar sales, and economic assistance. Although he achieved a great deal, Braden constantly complained about the lack of cooperation on the island. Not only did the Batista regime refuse to act on anything except essential matters, but the local inhabitants also remained ambivalent toward the Allied cause throughout the war years.

While Braden succeeded in his handling of the most crucial problems relating to military and economic affairs, the same cannot be said of his actions in the political arena. His hostility toward the corruption of Batista's government blurred his vision in the conduct of his assignment. Believing that the United States should work actively against dishonesty, Braden opposed the Batista government for its corrupt practices and conceived the idea of the noncontribution policy to stop United States citizens from participating in local politics. While the ambassador argued that his policy was consistent with the Good Neighbor spirit, Batista and his supporters felt that Braden's own outspoken position against the regime constituted interference in domestic politics and violated a basic tenet of Roosevelt's Latin American policy. Even though the ambassador was unquestionably correct in his charge of blatant graft, his crusading efforts in the cause of morality impeded his effectiveness when dealing with Batista. Like Welles and Caffery before him, he failed to anticipate the controversy that would arise once the American ambassador took an active stand on a domestic issue.

Braden had allowed his personal feelings to interfere with his ambassadorial duties, and this attitude carried over to Grau's administration. Unlike his strained dealings with Batista, the ambassador's relations with Grau were cordial because of the new president's pledge to create an honest administration. Apparently able to ignore most of the adverse criticism toward the incoming regime, Braden optimistically reported that Grau was carrying out his promise, and that he was therefore entitled to all the assistance the United States could give him. Unfortunately for Cuba, Grau did not accomplish his stated objective. His inability to delegate authority, his nepotistic appointments, the increase in urban violence, and the chaos created by his wholesale firing of government personnel made it almost impossible for him to run an efficient regime. In addition to these problems, after the Auténticos tasted power, they followed the corrupt practices of their predecessors. The first era of Batista had ended, but the Cuban people quickly realized that Grau's promises were not being fulfilled. The expectations raised by the Auténtico victory ended in bitter disillusionment.

12

The End of Two Eras

Grau's return to the presidency in late 1944 marked more than the end of Batista's first era, for Good Neighbor diplomacy was also drawing to a close. Welles had been forced to resign his post in late 1943, and soon after Roosevelt won his fourth term, Hull left the State Department because of failing health. Two principal architects of the United States' hemispheric policy were gone, but the president's reelection seemed to assure the program's continuation. Then, suddenly, on April 12, 1945 Roosevelt died of a cerebral hemmorhage, and an era in American diplomacy ended.[1]

Roosevelt had entered the White House at a time of extraordinary confusion, and nowhere on the international scene were his problems more complicated than in Cuba. The Hoover administration had left a legacy of inaction in its dealings with the troubled island. In the interest of stability for American investment the Republican administration had tried to ignore Machado's brutality, but when the depression hurt American interests and the anarchic conditions on the island grew worse, businessmen, along with the rest of Hoover's critics, called for the restoration of economic and political stability. Unwilling to take any decisive action, Hoover preferred to pass the problems on to his successor.

Observing the tense Cuban situation, Roosevelt selected Welles as his representative to Havana. Already known for his expertise in Latin American affairs, the new ambassador arrived in Cuba determined to restore stability. At first he thought that a new commercial treaty was the answer, but he soon realized that a political settlement must come first. He hoped that the mediation talks which he presided over would end the crisis, but the dictator's downfall abruptly changed the political situation. Improvising quickly, Welles chose Céspedes for the interim presidency in the belief that he would maintain order, but this scheme was proven a failure by the sergeants' revolt. The sergeants and their student allies overthrew the existing regime and replaced it with a highly nationalistic government which refused to accept mediation as a means of ending the island's political strife.

Shocked by the revolt, Welles believed that his primary duty was to support the legitimacy of Céspedes. In the five days between the coup d'etat and Grau's accession to the presidency, Welles actively supported the deposed coalition's attempts at a counterrevolution backed by American military intervention. But this decision, far from precipitating the new regime's collapse, aided its consolidation. While the ambassador pressed for intervention, the opposition waited, thereby giving the new goverment time to rally its forces in the name of Cuban nationalism. Exploiting the ambassador's alignment with the Céspedes coalition, the revolutionary forces took the initiative from the constitutional government by declaring that they alone represented the cause of Cuban sovereignty against American imperialism.

Welles had somehow underestimated the appeal of the revolutionaries and had exaggerated the deposed government's cohesiveness. Feeling that the Céspedes coalition must return to authority if constitutionality and stability were to prevail, he advocated military intervention. When Roosevelt and Hull flatly rejected that alternative, Welles argued for nonrecognition, alleging that Grau's government did not have the support of the Cuban majority. This request easily won Roosevelt's assent. Although he did not realize the implications of his action at the time, Roosevelt was assuring the eventual collapse of the revolutionary regime by withdrawing the moral support of the United States government and destroying any possibility of economic assistance.

Even though Welles later realized that he had been mistaken in calling for intervention, his initial hostility to Grau formed the basis of American policy toward the Grau government. Unfortunately for Welles, his close identification with stability and constitutionalism impaired his effectiveness as American ambassador. To the traditional leadership he was the champion of legality, to the revolutionary bloc the arch-enemy of revolutionary aspirations. Under incredibly chaotic conditions, Welles had unrealistically committed himself to the restoration of stability, and not surprisingly, each proposal he made to restore order was rejected. Early in December 1933 he made one last desperate attempt to bring peace, but that effort also failed. Welles finally left the island unable to accomplish his impossible objective.

The revolutionary regime prematurely greeted his departure as a victory, not realizing that its policies of opposition and nonrecognition remained unchanged. Unlike his predecessor, Caffery not only worked with Grau's opposition but also turned his attention to eroding the regime's internal support. Once the new envoy gained Batista's confidence, the revolutionary government was doomed and Grau had to resign. His downfall aptly complemented Welles's departure. Whereas Welles had tried to turn anarchy into stability, Grau had sought to make revolutionary change a permanent part of the Cuban political tradition in only four months.

Grau's resignation led to the formation of the Mendieta government, which won recognition after only five days in power, and an uneasy peace eventually returned to the island. In the midst of these events, first Welles and then Caffery took sides in Cuba's internal political conflict, winning praise from the Mendieta-Batista factions and enduring enmity from Cubans who blamed them for destroying the revolution. George F. Kennan cogently summarized the results of this type of American ambassadorial intervention during a series of lectures in 1954: "Let us recognize that even benevolence, when addressed to a foreign people, represents a form of intervention into their internal affairs, and always receives, at best, a divided reception."[2] Diplomatic novices such as Hull and Daniels recognized this danger by consistently opposing both direct military intervention and indirect political interference through the nonrecognition policy.[3] Their views, as well as those of the seasoned diplomat William Phillips, were in direct conflict with those of the first two American ambassadors to Cuba.

Faced with mounting criticism of American intentions toward Cuba, Roosevelt had obviously confused by this divided counsel. At the start of his term, he felt that a new commercial treaty would end the chaos on the island; next he tried his personal touch, recommending to the Cuban ambassador that Machado resign because of Cuba's economic plight. Neither of these simplistic solutions could possibly resolve the increasingly anarchical conditions on the island. After the dictator fled, Welles requested warships to check any possibility of widespread violence, and without considering that he might be charged with indirect military intervention, Roosevelt responded favorably. When the issue of naval encirclement was raised, the president minimized it and declared that the ships were there only to remove American nationals, should that become necessary. The confused actions taken during Grau's presidency showed that Roosevelt still had not clearly formulated a consistent policy. To Welles he promised warships and nonrecognition; to Hull he pledged nonintervention. The commitments were contradictory, but while Roosevelt was evolving his final program, they kept the allegiance of his two principal advisors.

Even during these hectic days, Roosevelt was slowly coming to the conclusion that military intervention was not in the best interests of the United States. In September he refused to fulfill Welles's troop request; in the Warm Springs declaration of November, he hinted that the United States was prepared to renegotiate the Permanent Treaty; in December he allowed Hull to sign the Montevideo declaration; and later in the month at the Woodrow Wilson banquet, he announced that the United States was unlaterally opposed to the use of its military forces in Latin American states. These steps, devised in large part to meet the Cuban crisis, became the principal tenets of the Good Neighbor commitment. By 1934 Roosevelt had placed his administration on the side of nonintervention.

Although the broad commitment had been made, the United States' unique relationship with Cuba appeared to be an exception. The hasty recognition of the Mendieta government gave the impression that the United States was intervening in support of the conservative regime. There was no doubt that Caffery's favorable reaction to Mendieta's accession speeded up Roosevelt's decision for quick recognition, but equally important was Roosevelt's relief that the United States was ending a policy that had caused monumental bilateral and hemispheric complications. Roosevelt's decision to recognize Mendieta after only five days in office was a practical corollary to the nonintervention pledge—a tacit admission that nonrecognition was a form of intervention.

Almost immediately after formal relations were restored, both countries started negotiations to abrogate the Platt Amendment. Widely acclaimed as the first visible fulfillment of the United States' promise to end its interventionist practices, the cancellation had a mixed reception in the country most directly associated with its enforcement. Even after the abrogation, American warships remained at their stations, evidence that the United States was still actively supporting the Mendieta government. Not only did the American sentinels stay, but the symbol of the American military presence, the Guantánamo naval base, persisted as an invasion of Cuban sovereignty. In addition, Caffery's close friendship with Batista made it clear that the American ambassador retained the same powers that he had exercised since the conclusion of the Spanish-American War.

Caffery's overt interference during the impeachment of Gómez intensified the controversial nature of Good Neighbor diplomacy, but with Caffery's departure, Hull was determined to change the image of the American ambassador. Convinced that the first two envoys had violated the nonintervention doctrine, he chose as their replacement Wright, who was gifted as a public relations man, and was firmly committed to the Good Neighbor spirit—he had participated at the Montevideo conference—and who refused to be drawn into domestic controversies. His sudden death in late 1939 brought a new representative but no change in policy. Even Braden's interference in the 1944 elections did not seriously contradict the American position. His actions were prompted more by his overzealous desire to keep Americans from participating in the corruption of the Cuban government than by a policy of meddling in the presidential campaign. His final statement on the noncontribution policy showed how closely he associated it with the Good Neighbor commitment. According to him, now that the policy had been enforced, future ambassadors would be able to keep Americans from contributing to local elections.

The three men who served as ambassadors from 1937 to 1945 took an unequivocal stand in support of Good Neighbor diplomacy, and by the end of their tours, the State Department firmly maintained that the American ambassador had to abstain from any involvement in Cuba's domestic politics. The efforts of these three men helped to promote the Good Neighbor image, and yet the Cubans were never convinced that the historic American interference had ended. No matter what rhetoric the United States employed to support its case, Cubans had been conditioned to act on the assumption that the American ambassador was an integral part of the domestic political process, and the slightest rumor of interference reinforced their beliefs.

The complexities of Good Neighbor diplomacy in Cuba extended to hemispheric gatherings. At the Montevideo Conference, the Cuban delegation bitterly attacked American intervention, and while the United States pleasantly surprised the Latin Americans by signing the nonintervention declaration, Hull made Cuba an exception because of the existing treaty. Later, Latin Americans in general and especially the Cubans conveniently ignored this exception and damned the United States for violating a pledge that it had never made. The Buenos Aires Conference provided another vivid example of the dichotomy between American and Cuban attitudes toward the Good Neighbor Policy. While the Cuban delegation voted with the United States for the reaffirmation of the nonintervention pledge without any exceptions, Gómez was asking Roosevelt to intervene on his behalf to stop impeachment proceedings. Again at the Lima, Panama, and Havana meetings, the Cubans supported the United States' proposals for hemispheric defense, but while they were cooperating on these matters, they were busily engaged in discussing their economic problems with American representatives. There was no doubt that the Roosevelt administration was extremely successful in promoting hemispheric goodwill through these conferences, but the motives for Cuban support were often tied to the immediate issues confronting Cuban-American relations.

Somehow writers have failed to appreciate the complicated nature of Good Neighbor diplomacy and have instead been satisfied to lavish praise on the Roosevelt administration's successes in hemispheric relations without examining the conflict between the administration's rhetoric and its actions. In Cuba the policy was begun not by initiating new programs but by discarding some of the outmoded ones. For example, the Permanent Treaty was revised, excluding the Platt Amendment but retaining the valuable naval base. The commercial treaty was also renegotiated in the form of a special reciprocal trade agreement in order to stimulate the flow of trade between the two nations, but the economic relationship remained fundamentally unaltered. Stability for the island, leading to its expanded commercial interaction with the United States, continued to be the principal objective of the Democratic administration, just as it had been under previous administrations. What changed were the tactics.[4]

Perhaps Beaulac best described the subtle shift in policy. He thought that American intervention had done some good in preserving order, but that it did not benefit the American image. The Montevideo spirit, he maintained, was a positive step toward hemispheric solidarity: "Mutual confidence and respect among the free nations of the Western Hemisphere is more important to the cause of democracy than is the precise degree of democracy that may exist at a given time in a politically immature country. To the extent that interventions tend to detract from mutal confidence and respect, they tend to damage the cause of democracy in the Americas, and therefore throughout the world." Beaulac thought that the Latin American nations had to solve their own problems without United States intervention, but this did not rule out economic aid or other forms of technical assistance.[5]

If American diplomatic policy toward Cuba was confusing, so was the island's internal development. Machado had been overthrown because economic depression and political oppression brought forth widespread popular hostility to his rule. Cubans from all segments of society united to topple the dictator, but once he was gone, unanimity vanished. There were still strikes and violence throughout the island, but with Welles's backing the traditional leadership placed Céspedes in the presidency to restore domestic tranquillity. Machado's removal, then, was not the trigger for the Revolution of 1933.

What ignited the spark of revolutionary upheaval was a series of events prompted by years of frustration in which the insensitive Cuban leadership had ignored unjust political, economic, and social conditions. Machado symbolized these inequities, but Céspedes confirmed the failure of the traditional politicians to inaugurate a far-flung program for the nation's betterment. While the politicians groped for a solution to complex problems, the cries for reform grew steadily louder. The sergeants' revolt released a wave of unprecedented nationalistic feeling. The new military establishment and its student allies literally took control from the generation of 1898 and placed it in their own hands.

Grau and his cohorts—especially Guiteras, with his nationalistic sentiments—gratified the nation's pent-up desires for reform. The reforms were all made in a four-months period during which there were constant strikes as well as two serious rebellions. Far from having a carefully developed program, the Grau regime enacted reforms without the slightest attention to consistency. The eight-hour day, university autonomy, labor's right to organize, the 50% law, and the expropriation of Machado's landholdings vividly illustrate this lack of coordination. The revolution's platform was action; there was no need to catalogue the deeds in logical sequence.

The revolution took shape only after the rush of legislation had ended, and perhaps its fundamental problem lay in its very disorganization. As events unfolded, the revolution did not seem to have logical direction. Grau and his associates acted to correct economic and social injustices as they confronted them, never announcing a concrete list of priorities. When Grau resigned, the revolutionaries were frustrated because they had not finished the work that they had started. Yet at the start of Grau's regime, no one had predicted or even dared to guess what the final outcome would be.

Those hectic months of frantic activity brought momentous advances in the nation's laws, but when Grau left the presidency, bitterness replaced the enthusiasm of the people. Just as Machado was identified with the evils in Cuban society, so Grau became the apostle of rising expectations. After his resignation, he and his adherents denounced Batista's rule. No matter what positive actions Batista took, they were not enough. Since Grau's administration had ended, the reformers could no longer shape the nation's destiny. But if anyone can be accused of having cutting short the Revolution of 1933, its chief supporters must take an equal place with its detractors. Those who made the revolution also frustrated it by refusing to recognize its positive achievements while exaggerating the negative aspects of Batista's rule over the next decade.

Ironically, the consolidation of the revolution came from the forces that the revolutionaries attacked the most vigorously. When Batista and the traditional politicians gained authority, they were forced to support the revolution's accomplishments and to make further innovations. Recognizing the popular support for his opposition's charges that he had thwarted revolutionary goals, Batista strove to parry those assaults by identifying himself with the reform movement. This awareness, in part, drove him to promote the rural school project, initiate the Three-Year Plan, assist in calling together the constitutional convention, praise the Constitution of 1940, and finally allow his rival to recapture the presidency.[6]

Even though Batista was personally receptive to change, his rule retarded political evolution through the party system. When the traditional politicians aligned themselves with Batista to overthrow Grau, they surrendered the power of the civilian sector to make political decisions and placed that responsibility in the military domain. As a result Mendieta and his successors were puppets for the military commander's manipulations. If anyone doubted that a fundamental change had occurred, it was clearly apparent when a subservient Congress openly obeyed the military's injunction to impeach Gómez. After the removal of Gómez, no one could any longer question Batista's absolute authority.

Besides the domination of the military, there were other signs of political retardation. Cabinet crises and congressional ineptitude plagued the governments throughout Batista's era. Two vaguely defined political groupings emerged. The government coalition was conservative, and the Auténticos were radical. Neither side would cooperate with the other, and as a result of this rigidity, political reconciliation became almost impossible. One other ingredient was added to Cuban politics. During Machado's brutal reign, urban terrorism had become a weapon against the government. Although the violence subsided after Guiteras's death, Grau's election unleashed its fury once more, so that the Revolution of 1933 might be said to have institutionalized terrorism.

Not only did Grau and Batista dominate Cuban politics during the Good Neighbor period, they also symbolized the way the system functioned. Grau became a living martyr to Cuban nationalism, and his primary attribute was his greatest liability. Embittered by Batista's defection to the conservative forces, Grau adamantly refused to cooperate with the government in any way. To him the Auténticos represented the only hope of honest government, and therefore, no member of his party should cooperate with the corrupt governmental practices. Such rigidity not only encourged the polarization of politics, but it also deprived any Auténticos from gaining valuable experience in government operations. Even though Grau favored an Allied victory, he still refused to allow Auténtico participation in Batista's wartime cabinet. Insensitive to anything but his cause, Grau felt that once he returned to the presidential palace, honest and efficient government would reappear automatically.

Against this sort of opposition, Batista maintained his supremacy for twelve turbulent years, thanks to his political acumen. By supporting the reforms proposed by the opposition, Batista kept his antagonists divided. By modernizing the armed forces, allowing traditional politicians to remain at their posts, and providing stability for commercial interests, he maintained his own coalition. While these tactics assured his success for a time, they could not eliminate his basic weakness—namely, that he was not a politician but a military leader.

This fact caused a metamorphosis in the island's political structure. Instead of relying on the civilian sector to maintain order, the very process of government became a military function. Even the revolt of February 1941, in which Batista matched his strength against that of three seditious colonels, was not the triumph of democracy over authoritarianism but, more accurately, a discharge of the military forces' debt to its commander in chief. When the crisis arose, Batista did not appeal to the nation for support but instead drove to Camp Columbia to demand recompense for his services in expanding the role of the armed forces.

At no time was Batista's base of stability more evident than when Grau returned to the presidency. When Grau attacked the military establishment, he shook the foundation of Cuban stability, and domestic chaos resulted. The military control over the civilian government would respond only to Batista's direction. Having tampered with that relationship, Grau needed to fill the void and find some other means to maintain peace, but he never found a solution. The order that Batista had forged began to crack, and with it, Cuban stability.[7]

While Cuba changed its political system and the United States altered its relationship to the island's internal affairs, both nations also directed their attention to commercial interaction. The Hoover administration had always maintained that it wanted stability on the island to protect American investment, but this policy was never carried out. Instead the Republican president signed the Hawley-Smoot Tariff, which raised the sugar duty, thus pushing the Cuban economy into a steeper slide.

Under the Roosevelt administration some of the inconsistencies in foreign economic policy were resolved. The goal of stability for American investment never changed; what did change was the means for achieving the desired results. During Roosevelt's presidency, the executive branch of government was beginning to realize that foreign economic policy required better coordination. This was not apparent when Welles arrived in Cuba, for his principal economic goal was to renegotiate the outdated commercial treaty of 1903. Because of Cuba's political instability, the ambassador later proposed additional economic assistance in the form of a direct loan from the United States to the Céspedes regime, so that it could pay government employees. Neither suggestion became effective while Welles was ambassador. Grau's ascendency and the nonrecognition policy brought the bargaining for a new commercial treaty to a halt, and the direct loan could not be extended because the United States had not established any agency to grant economic assistance.

Although Welles was not in Havana to see either of his proposals carried out, both became basic programs of New Deal economic diplomacy. One further expedient that the ambassador had not proposed also occupied a significant place in United States-Cuban commercial relations. The Roosevelt administration had already enacted the A.A.A., which protected basic domestic agricultural commodities, but the program had not included sugar. Responding to pressure from sugar producers for protection, Roosevelt signed the Jones-Costigan Act, establishing quotas for domestic, insular and foreign interests. Now, for the first time in its history, Cuba had an assured market in the United States.

These unilateral American actions were then incorporated into a bilateral trade agreement. In June 1934 Hull won his hard-fought battle for the executive reciprocal trade agreements program, and two months later, the United States and Cuba signed the first agreement under the new act. In removing tariff legislation from the jurisdiction of Congress, Hull had argued that the program would stimulate economic recovery. State Deparment officials were acutely aware of this need in the Cuban negotiations, and at the same time, they also realized that Cuba's political stability depended on an economic revival. As a result of these considerations, the final agreement aided both countries in their immediate goals by giving the United States over four hundred concessions and granting additional advantages to Cuban tobacco and sugar. The first agreement was thus a practical example of the way Hull's reciprocity program enabled the United States to coordinate its national interest with its Cuban policy.

While these actions greatly stimulated commercial intercourse, they bound the Cubans even closer to the American market and to American domestic legislation. The crops that gave the island its principal advantages under the reciprocity agreement—sugar and tobacco—were both subject to unilateral quota regulations. Under these circumstances, the Cubans had to suffer from events beyond their control. The United States Supreme Court decision in 1936 affecting the A.A.A. canceled the tobacco concession, and Roosevelt's temporary suspension of the sugar quota at the outbreak of the European war caused grave repercussions on the island. As the war drew closer, New Deal agricultural policy, Hull's trade program, and Hitler's ambitions steadily increased the flow of trade between Cuba and the United States, and the island's overwhelming reliance on the American market became even more pronounced than it had been before 1933.

Along with commercial measures, the United States initiated a new loan policy toward Cuba. Before Roosevelt became president, all loans from the United States came from private financing, and the government scrutinized them under the terms of the Permanent Treaty. New Deal foreign economic policy significantly altered this relationship by replacing private initiative with direct government assistance. The Eximbank silver loans to the Mendieta regime not only enabled it to pay government employees but also added to the island's stability, which was more important to the State Department. This action, taken before any of the other commercial programs, marked the true beginning of American economic assistance to promote the interests of the United States in Cuba.

When political peace returned and the economy began to revive, the American assistance policy responded accordingly. Before any loans were granted, the State Department demanded a settlement for its bondholders and later added other prerequisites such as reforms in Cuba's monetary and fiscal systems and the extension of Decree-Law No. 522 to protect American sugar companies. By formulating its economic assistance program in this way, the American government passed judgment on the validity of the Cuban requests and also determined the island's internal policies toward American bondholders and sugar interests.

As total war drew closer to the hemisphere, the United States improvised still another method for granting aid. At the start of his presidency Batista needed American assistance to assure the island's stability. Welles realized that the United States must cooperate with the Cuban president not only because he favored the Allied cause but also because he was able to maintain order on the strategically located island. Through its Eximbank loans and later through lend-lease aid, the Roosevelt administration guaranteed the island's internal order and thus the Cuban government's wartime cooperation. Through coordination of its various economic assistance and commercial programs in Cuba, the United States came to understand that there were effective substitutes for the defunct Platt Amendment. Economic policies were just as effective and more subtle in attaining the desired results.

While the United States was changing its economic policies toward the successive Cuban regimes, the latter were searching for new commercial programs. Although their monetary and fiscal systems remained in a confused state, the Cuban regimes did act decisively in relation to the sugar industry. Decree-Law No. 522 established the Sugar Stabilization Institute to direct the island's sugar program, and the Law of Sugar Coordination set wages and quotas for the industry. In the realm of international cooperation, the London agreement, which had the support of 90 percent of the world's producers, replaced the ineffective Chadbourne Plan. Even in these actions that affected internal regulations, the American embassy played a vital role. Since American companies controlled a large amount of the sugar production, the embassy lobbied actively for fair and equitable treatment of American nationals. Political intervention had abated, but this did not stop American diplomats from directing internal decisions to protect their citizens' economic interests.

Cubans realized their predicament with regard to sugar monoculture and the alienation of their property. Fernando Ortíz y Fernández cogently summed up his countrymen's sentiments when he wrote in 1940, "we sons of free Cuba have sometimes asked ourselves whether our officials and politicians are serving the interests of our people or those of some anonymous sugar corporation, playing the part of deputized guards of the great Cuban sugar mill at the order of foreign owners."[9] Ramiro Guerra y Sánchez echoed these feelings, seeing the foreign sugar plantation as the greatest danger to Cuban sovereignty: "The latifundium is taking over all the sources of wealth, and its economic power becomes daily more formidable and irresistible."[10] Foreign domination of the sugar industry had replaced the Platt Amendment as the symbol of American imperialism. More was implicit in this argument than American control of the island's principal export for since American interests directed commercial policy on the island, they retarded the dream of a diversified economy. Critics of American policy in Cuba had shifted their focus from political intervention to economic exploitation, but their basic point had not changed radically. Their arguments against American encroachment upon the island's sovereignty were supported by the growth of nationalistic sentiment over four decades.[11]

While critics were demanding an end to economic imperialism the number of sugar mills owned by Americans decreased from sixty-six in 1939 to thirty-six in 1958, and during that period their production dropped from 55.07 percent of the national total to 36.65 percent.[12] Although the clamor of nationalists may have had some effect on the American decision to withdraw from the sugar industry, there were other reasons for the sale of their properties. During the "dance of the millions," Cubans had used their sugar properties as collateral for expansion loans from the American banks, and when the depression struck in 1920–21, the borrowers forfeited their lands. Since the large American sugar companies survived the collapse of the early 1920s and American bankers were forced to take over Cuban properties, these interests gained overwhelming control of the industry. When prosperity returned during the war, American bankers resold the sugar mills to Cuban buyers, moving out of an industry that they never intended to enter.[13]

Prosperous wartime conditions generated the sale of American sugar properties, but domestic legislation in both countries assisted in this transfer. American owners realized that the American and Cuban quota systems curtailed American profits to benefit the domestic producers in both nations, and as a result, they moved into new industries, retaining their most lucrative sugar properties. But even the steady decline of American participation in the sugar industry did not stop the charges of economic imperialism. Rather than search for internal causes and possible alternatives to reliance on the sugar monoculture, Cuban critics preferred to make the United States the scapegoat for the island's economic dilemma.[14]

Despite this preoccupation with the adverse effect of American investment on the Cuban economy, no one could doubt that conditions on the island had vastly improved since the bleak days of August 1933. Reform in the traditional political system had been slow, but the Cuban government had extended participation in public affairs by granting suffrage to women and modernizing the electoral code. Starting in 1936, the number of people who voted in presidential elections constantly increased; this trend was climaxed in 1944 by Grau's surprising victory and Batista's equally astonishing acceptance of his rival's triumph.

While the Cuban nation hailed these political events as signs that the island was maturing politically, the economy also experienced a phenomenal boom during the war years. Even though this growth was based primarily on sugar sales, the commercial revival stimulated the return of sugar properties to Cuban ownership, aided agricultural diversification, and increased production in the cattle and mining industries and in light industry. The island still faced perplexing problems, but at the close of the war, other nations were in far worse predicaments. The era that had begun with economic depression and political anarchy ended with a reasonably smooth transfer of authority and with prosperity.[15]

Despite these positive signs, many acute problems in Cuban society had not been solved. Many politicians still viewed their jobs as sinecures; urban terrorism increased; the Auténticos never carried out their promises to end corrupt governmental practices. In the economic realm, sugar remained the basis of the island's prosperity, and high wartime profits inhibited moves toward diversification. A form of stability had returned to Cuba by the end of the war, but political immaturity and economic imbalance remained.[16]

For twelve years the Roosevelt administration had been instrumental in shaping Cuba's internal development. Paradoxically, Good Neighbor diplomacy on the island, far from stopping attacks against American activity, actually intensified them. Welles had assisted in the ouster of Machado, and, with the aid of the nonrecognition policy, played as crucial a role in Grau's downfall. Even after he left his ambassadorial post, he continued to direct American policy toward the island from the State Department. Caffery unquestionably contributed to the rise of Batista in his quest for an absolute authority, and he did much to evolve the New Deal's commercial policy toward the island. No matter what the next three ambassadors did, their actions had been determined, in

large part, by what occurred in the early years of the Good
Neighbor Policy's development. The Platt Amendment was gone,
but Batista effectively replaced it in the maintenance of order. The
economy revived, but this was due to unilateral actions taken by
the United States. Stability, the goal of American diplomacy in
Cuba, had been assured, but the price was the continuation of both
the sugar monoculture and the rule of the island's traditional
political forces. In the process of the evolution of the Good
Neighbor Policy in Cuba, opposition forces rightly charged the
United States with maintaining the status quo, and these attacks
became part of a growing tradition of anti-American feeling.[17]

But if the United States is to be blamed for supporting the
continuation of past inequities on the island, the Cubans themselves
were more responsible for their own stagnation. During the Good
Neighbor period, Cuban politicians split into two diametrically
opposed groups. While the Auténticos accentuated all that was
negative and capitalized on each government mistake, the ruling
factions refrained from taking responsible action. In 1944 Grau
promised reform, and the Cuban majority responded to his call. No
longer able to play the role of critic, the Auténtico forces proved
that they had no magical potion to cure the ills of the Cuban body
politic—nor, indeed, did they have a positive program of any sort.
Grau and his associates never reached their lofty goals, and with
their failure, the hope that they personified faded, to be finally
extinguished by Batista's second coup d'etat in 1952. The tragic
irony of the 1933 Revolution was that its two leading personalities
were responsible not only for its rise but also for its fall. Their
successes became part of the island's growing nationalistic heritage; their failures set the stage for a revolution from the next
generation.

Notes

CHAPTER 2

1. Harry F. Guggenheim *The United States and Cuba* (New York: Macmillan Co., 1934), pp. 235–36; Emilio Roig de Leuchsenring, *Historia de la Enmienda Platt: Una interpretación de la realidad* (Havana: Cultural, 1935), 2:173–210.

2. Raymond L. Buell et al, *Problems of New Cuba* (New York: Foreign Policy Association, 1935), pp.52–53; The American Chamber of Commerce of Cuba, *Silver Jubilee Review 1919–1944* (Havana: Seane, Fernandez y Cia), appendix; U.S. Tariff Commission, *The Foreign Trade of Latin America*, Part II: *Commercial Policies and Trade Relations of Individual Latin American Countries*, Section 18: *Cuba* (1940), p.31.

3. Alberto Arrendondo, *Cuba: tierra indefensa* (Havana: Seane, Fernandez y Cia, 1944), pp. 461–68;. Russell H. Fitzgibbon, *Cuba and the United States 1900–1935* (New York: Russell and Russell, 1964), pp. 191–92; Ruby H. Phillips, *Cuban Sideshow* (Havana: Cuban Press, 1935), p.10; Guggenheim, *U. S. and Cuba*, pp.171–72; Russell B. Porter, "Cuba under President Machado," *Current History*, 38 (April 1933):31–32; Ernest Gruening, "Cuba under the Machado Regime," *Current History*, 34 (May 1931):214–16; U. S. Department of State, *Foreign Relations of the United States* (1933), vol. 5, *The American Republics* (1952), p. 274.

4. Buell, *Problems of New Cuba*, pp. 10, 186–87; Francis V. Jackman, "America's Cuban Policy during the Period of the Machado Regime" (Ph.D. dissertation, Catholic University, 1964), pp. 188–89; Stewart C. Blasier, "The Cuban and Chilean Communist Parties: Instruments of Soviet Policy (1935–1948)" (Ph.D. dissertation, Columbia University, 1954), p. 20; Paul K. Krauss," "Communist Policy in Cuba, 1933–46" (Master's thesis, Columbia University, 1950), pp. 6–7; Guggenheim, *U.S. and Cuba*, pp. 168–69.

5. Ibid., 176–91; Phillips, *Cuban Sideshow*, pp. 12, 25–26; Sumner Welles, *The Time for Decision* (New York: Harper Brothers, 1944), p. 194; Albert Lamar Schweyer, *How President Machado Fell* (Havana: Montalvo Cardenas, 1938), pp. 21–43 (earlier published as *Comó cayó el Presidente Machado* [Madrid: Espasa-Calpe, 1934]); Edmund A. Chester, *A Sergeant Named Batista* (New York: Henry Holt & Co., 1954), p.31; Jackman, "America's Cuban Policy during Machado," pp. 178, 191–93.

6. Welles, *Time for Decision*, pp. 191–92; Bryce Wood, *The Making of the Good Neighbor Policy* (New York: Columbia University Press, 1961), p.129; E. David Cronon, "Interpreting the Good Neighbor Policy: The Cuban Crisis of 1933," *The Hispanic American Historical Review* 39 (November 1959):538.

7. *New Republic* 74 (April 26, 1933): 291; Charles W. Hackett, "Guerilla Warfare in Cuba," *Current History* 38 (July 1933):469; *Chicago Tribune*, April 25, 1933, and May 1, 1933; *Miami Herald*, April 24, 1933; Phillips, *Cuban Sideshow*, p. 15; Porter, "Cuba under Machado," p. 14.

8. Samuel I. Rosenman, ed., *The Public Papers and Addresses of Franklin D. Roosevelt* (New York: Random House, 1938), 2:129–32.

9. Lamar Schweyer, *How Machado Fell*, pp. 61–64; U.S. Department of State, *Latin American Series* No. 11, Sumner Welles, "Two Years of the 'Good Neighbor' Policy," (1935), pp.1–6.

10. Cordell Hull, *The Memoirs of Cordell Hull* (New York: Macmillan Co., 1948), 1:3–163,

313; Harold B. Hinton, *Cordell Hull* (Garden City, New York: Doubleday, Doran & Co., 1942), pp. 1–217; Julius Pratt, "Cordell Hull, 1933–1944," in Robert H. Ferrell, ed., *The American Secretaries of State and Their Diplomacy* (New York: Cooper Square Publishers, 1964) 12:1–31.

11. Wood, *The Making of the Good Neighbor Policy*, p. 61.

12. Jackman, "America's Cuban Policy during Machado," pp. 35–36, 173; Majorie Dent Candee, ed., *Current Biography Yearbook,* 1956 (New York: H. W. Wilson Co., 1956–57), pp. 237–38; Alexander DeConde, *Herbert Hoover's Latin-American Policy* (Stanford, Calif.: Stanford University Press, 1951), p.104; *Foreign Relations* (1933) 5:270–92; Lamar Schweyer, *How Machado Fell,* pp.58–60.

13. Harry Guggenheim to Phillip Jessup, March 15, 1933, Box 14, Philip Jessup Papers, Library of Congress, Manuscript Division, Washington, D.C.

14. Charles W. Hackett, "The Cuban Terror," *Current History* 38 (June 1933):341–43; Edward Reed to Cordell Hull, April 3, 1933, 123 Guggenheim, Harry F./117, Record Group 59, General Records of the Department of State, State Decimal File, 1933–44, National Archives, Washington, D.C.; Sumner Welles to Norman Davis, October 22 and November 19, 1932, Box 63, Norman Davis Papers, Library of Congress, Manuscript Division, Washington, D.C.; *Foreign Relations* (1933) 5:277–78; William Phillips, *Ventures in Diplomacy* (Boston: Beacon Press, 1952), p.186; Laurence Duggan, *The Americas: The Search for Hemispheric Security* (New York: Henry Holt & Co., 1948), p.60; interview with Adolf A. Berle, January 2, 1969; Dexter Perkins, *The New Age of Franklin D. Roosevelt, 1932–45* Chicago: University of Chicago Press, 1957), p.86; Pratt, "Cordell Hull," p.18.

15. *Who's Who in America* (1960–61); Peter F. Krogh, "The United States, Cuba and Sumner Welles: 1933" (Ph.D dissertation, Fletcher School of Law and Diplomacy, 1966), pp.80–83.

16. Ibid., 83–88, 140–44; Welles to Davis, April 29, 1926, Davis to Welles, April 30, 1926, Welles to Davis, May 4, 1926, and Davis to Welles, May 7, 1926, Box 63, Davis Papers.

17. Krogh, "U.S., Cuba and Welles," pp.159–76; Welles to Davis, April 6, 1931, Box 63, Davis Papers.

18. Memorandum probably from Welles to Roosevelt, March 3, 1933, PSF–Cuba–1933, Franklin Delano Roosevelt Library, Hyde Park, New York; see also Charles C. Griffin, ed., "Welles to Roosevelt: A Memorandum of Inter-American Relations," *The Hispanic American Historical Review* 34 (May 1954):190–92.

19. Hudson Strode, *The Pageant of Cuba* (New York: Harrison Smith and Robert Haas, 1934), p.296; *Foreign Relations* (1933) 5:278; *Miami Herald,* April 27, 1933.

20. Welles to Samuel Guy Inman, April 24, 1933, Box 13, Samuel Guy Inman Papers, Library of Congress, Manuscript Division, Washington, D.C.

21. *Foreign Relations* (1933) 5:282–85; U.S. Department of State, *Latin American Series* No. 7, Sumner Welles, "Relations between the United States and Cuba" (1934), pp.6–7; according to Adolf A. Berle, the writing of the instructions was a combined effort (interview with Adolf A. Berle, January 2, 1969), For opposing view see Wood, *The Making of the Good Neighbor Policy,* p.59 and Pratt, "Cordell Hull," p.144.

22. *Foreign Relations* (1933) 5:286; *Miami Herald,* May 8, 1933; Strode, *Pageant of Cuba,* p. 292; Lamar Schweyer, *How Machado Fell,* pp.67–73; Rafael Porro Fuentes, who was a student at the University of Havana, gave me his impressions of Welles and the general situation (interview with Rafael Porro Fuentes, January 1, 1969); Hull to Reed, May 4, 1933, 123 W 451/97; Welles, *Time for Decision,* p.193.

23. Strode, *Pageant of Cuba,* p.297; Hackett, "Guerilla Warfare in Cuba," p.469.

24. Lamar Schweyer, *How Machado Fell,* pp. 64–67; Alfred Fabre-Luce, *Révolution à Cuba* (Paris: Editions de "Pamphlet," 1934), pp.33–34.

25. *Foreign Relations* (1933) 5:287–88; Lamar Schweyer, *How Machado Fell,* pp.73–76; Welles to Hull, May 25, 1933, 837.00/3553; Welles to Hull, May 11, 1933, 123 W 451/105.

26. *Foreign Relations* (1933) 5:288–89.

27. Ibid., p.290.

28. Ibid., pp.288–91, 293–94, 296; Welles, "Two Years of the 'Good Neighbor' Policy," p.7.

29. Welles to Roosevelt, May 18, 1933, O.F.–470–Sumner Welles, FDRL.

30. Ibid.; Edgar B. Nixon, ed., *Franklin D. Roosevelt and Foreign Affairs* (Cambridge, Mass.: Belknap Press of Harvard University Press, 1969) 1:140–42.

31. *Foreign Relations* (1933) 5:292, 295–296; *Miami Herald*, May 25, 1933.

32. *Foreign Relations* (1933) 5:296–97; Welles to Hull, June 1, 1933, 837.00/3536.

33. *Foreign·Relations* (1933) 5:297–98.

34. Ibid., p.299.

35. Ibid., pp. 299–300.

36. Ibid., pp. 300–03; *New Republic* 75 (June 21, 1933):139; *Miami Herald,* June 3, 1933.

37. Phillips, *Ventures in Diplomacy,* pp.3–187; Hull, *Memoirs,* 1:160–61; Pratt, "Cordell Hull," p.17; Hinton, *Hull,* p.222; Memorandum of a phone conversation between Phillips and Cintas, June 7, 1933, 837.00/3541; Memorandum of a press conference of Phillips, June 7, 1933, 837.00/3560.

38. Welles to Hull, June 8, 1933, 837.00/3542; *Foreign Relations* (1933) 5:305–7; Welles to Hull, June 12, 1933, 837.00/3547; Welles to Hull, June 13, 1933, 837.00/3548.

39. Ramiro Guerra y Sánchez et al., *Historia de la Nación Cubana* (Havana: Editorial Historia de la Nación Cubana, 1952), 8:78–80; Welles to Hull, June 16, 1933, 837.00/3558; *Foreign Relations* (1933) 5:307–10; Welles to Hull, June 16, 1933, 837.00/3552; Phillips, *Cuban Sideshow,* pp.13, 82–83; Buell, *Problems of New Cuba,* pp.10–11; Strode, *Pageant of Cuba,* pp. 284–85; Ulpiano Vega Cobiellas, *Los doctores Ramón Grau San Martín y Carlos Saladrigas Zayas* (Havana: Lex, 1944), pp.10–12; Charles W. Hackett, "Cuban Peace Prospects," *Current History* 38 (August 1933):594–95.

40. Hubert Herring, "Machado Prepares to Go," *Nation* 136 (June 28, 1933):725–26.

41. *Foreign Relations* (1933) 5:310.

42. Memorandum of a phone conversation between Caffery and Welles, June 2, 1933, 611.3731/502.

43. Ibid.; *Foreign Relations* (1933) 5:304, 306; Nixon, *FDR and Foreign Affairs* 1:143–44, 181; Elliot Roosevelt, ed., *F.D.R.: His Personal Letters* (New York: Duell, Sloan, and Pearce, 1947–50) 1:350.

44. *Foreign Relations* (1933) 5:568–77.

45. Ibid., pp.312–13.

46. *Miami Herald*, June 22, 1933; *Foreign Relations* (1933) 5:313–14; Welles to Hull, June 23, 1933, 837.00/3561; Roosevelt to Welles, June 24, 1933, O. F.–470–Sumner Welles, FDRL; Elliot Roosevelt, *FDR,* 1:354.

47. *New Republic* 75 (June 28, 1933):165–66; see also "America's New Envoy as a Mediator in Cuba," *The Literary Digest* 116 (July 1, 1933):7.

48. Luis E. Aguilar, "Cuba 1933: The Frustrated Revolution" (Ph.D. dissertation, American University, 1967), pp.130–36.

49. Russell Fitzgibbon and H. Max Healey, "Cuban Elections of 1936," *American Political Science Review* 30 (August 1936):724; Phillips, *Cuban Sideshow* pp.28–29; Buell, *Problems of New Cuba,* p.11.

50. Lamar Schweyer, *How Machado Fell,* pp.51–54 and 76–82; Arrendondo, *Cuba,* pp.480–84; Blasier, "Cuban and Chilean Communist Parties," pp.19–20; Buell, *Problems of New Cuba,* pp.187, 196–98; Lowry Nelson, *Rural Cuba* (Minneapolis: University of Minnesota Press, 1950), pp.147–48; Aguilar, "Cuba 1933," p.149; *Foreign Relations* (1933) 5:298–99, 303, 304, 307, 318–19; Mario Riera Hernández, *Cuba política, 1899–1955* (Havana: Impresora Modela, 1955), pp.408–11.

51. Lamar Schweyer, *How Machado Fell,* pp. 87–88; *Foreign Relations* (1933) 5:316.

52. Rosenman, *Public Papers*, 2:236; see also *Foreign Relations* (1933):5:311.

53. Ibid., p. 317; Welles to Hull, July 1, 1933, 837.00/3569; Memorandum of a press conference of Phillips, July 16, 1933, 837.00/3571.

54. Welles to Hull, July 5, 1933, 837.00/3571.

55. *Foreign Relations* (1933) 5:318–19, 323–25; Welles to Hull, July 14, 1933, 837.00/3578; Welles to Hull, July 21, 1933, 123 W 451/110; Welles to Hull, July 8, 1933, 123 W 451/11; Lamar Schweyer, *How Machado Fell*, pp. 83–95; Welles, "Relations between the United States and Cuba," p.7; Nixon, *F.D.R. and Foreign Affairs* 1:314–17.

56. *Foreign Relations* (1933) 5:320–22, 326, 327.

57. Memorandum of a conversation between Phillips and Cintas, July 25, 1933, 837.00/3582½.

58. Lamar Schweyer, *How Machado Fell*, pp. 88–120; Aguilar, "Cuba 1933," pp.132–37; Phillips, *Cuban Sideshow*, p.41; *Foreign Relations* (1933) 5:327–28; "Opening the Jails in Cuba," *The Literary Digest* 116 (August 5, 1933):12.

59. *Foreign Relations* (1933) 5:329–30; Welles to Hull, July 28, 1933, 837.00/3592; *Miami Herald*, July 28, 1933.

60. *Foreign Relations* (1933) 5:301, 322, 332.

61. Aguilar, "Cuba 1933," pp.141–46; *Miami Herald*, July 28, August 2, and 3, 1933; Strode, *Pageant of Cuba*, pp. 298–99; Hubert Herring, "The Downfall of Machado," *Current History* 39 (October 1933):14–15; Charles W. Hackett, "American Mediation in Cuba," *Current History* 39 (September 1933):726.

62. Buell, *Problems of New Cuba*, p.182; see also *Miami Herald*, August 4, 1933.

63. Ibid., and August 5, 1933.

64. Philips, *Cuban Sideshow*, p.47.

65. *Foreign Relations* (1933) 5:332–35; Welles to Hull, August 3, 1933, 837.00/3595; Welles to Hull, August 4, 1933, 837.00/3565; Arredondo, *Cuba*, pp.484–87; *Baltimore Sun*, August 5, 1933; *Miami Herald*, August 7, 1933.

66. Welles to Hull, August 4, 1933, 837.00/3599; Lamar Schweyer, *How Machado Fell*, pp.145–46; *Foreign Relations* (1933) 5:336–37.

67. Ibid., pp. 337–38; Wood, *The Making of the Good Neighbor Policy*, p.62.

68. Phillips, *Cuban Sideshow*, pp.53–54; *Baltimore Sun*, August 9, 1933; *Chicago Tribune*, August 8, 1933; *Miami Herald*, August 8, 1933; Welles to Roosevelt, August 8, 1933, O.F.–470–Sumner Welles, FDRL; Herring, "Downfall of Machado," p.15.

69. *Chicago Tribune*, August 8, 1933; *Miami Herald*, August 9, 1933; *Foreign Relations* (1933) 5:338, 340–43; Cronon, "Interpreting the Good Neighbor Policy," pp.539–41; Lamar Schweyer, *How Machado Fell*, pp.153–60.

70. *Foreign Relations* (1933) 5:339–40, 346–47; Welles to Hull, August 9, 1933, 837.00/3625; *Chicago Tribune*, August 9, 1933; *Miami Herald*, August 10, 1933; Juan Bosch, *Cuba: la isla fascinante* (Santiago, Chile: Editorial Universitaria, 1955) pp.135–36.

71. *Foreign Relations* (1933) 5:340.

72. Ibid., pp.344–45.

73. Lamar Schweyer, *How Machado Fell*, pp.177–82; *Foreign Relations* (1933) 5:347–48; *Chicago Tribune*, August 10, 1933; *Miami Herald*, August 10, 1933; Nixon, *F. D. R. and Foreign Affairs*, 1:349–52.

74. Rosenman, *Public Papers*, 2:319.

75. Phillips, *Cuban Sideshow*, p.56.

76. Ibid., p.55; *Chicago Tribune*, August 10, 1933; *Miami Herald*, August 10, and 11, 1933.

77. *Foreign Relations* (1933) 5:349–54; *Miami Herald*, August 9, and 11, 1933.

78. Ibid., August 10, 1933; Josephus Daniel to Hull, August 9, 1933, Josephus Daniels Papers, Box 750, Manuscripts Division, Library of Congress, Washington, D.C.; *Foreign Relations* (1933) 5:350–51; *Miami Herald*, August 11, 1933; *Chicago Tribune*, August 11,

1933; Lamar Schweyer, *How Machado Fell*, pp.111–21; "Machado's Fall and the Problem of Intervention in Cuba," *The Literary Digest* 116 (August 19, 1933):7; for Roosevelt's isolationism see Lorraine L. Freeman, "Isolationist Carry-Over, 1933–1937" (Master's thesis, University of Buffalo, 1955), pp.123–25.

79. *Baltimore Sun*, August 11, 1933.

80. *Foreign Relations* (1933) 5:296, 355–56; *Miami Herald*, May 24, and 26, 1933.

81. *Foreign Relations* (1933) 5:355–56.

82. Ibid., p.356.

83. Phillips, *Cuban Sideshow*, pp.60–61; *Foreign Relations* (1933) 5:356–58.

84. Wood, *The Making of the Good Neighbor Policy*, p.69; Strode, *Pageant of Cuba*, pp.302–3; Lamar Schweyer, *How Machado Fell*, pp.192–206; *Miami Herald*, August 12, 1933; Phillips, *Cuban Sideshow*, pp.60–61; Welles, "Two Years of the 'Good Neighbor' Policy," pp.9–10.

85. Lamar Schweyer, *How Machado Fell*, pp.207–18; Herring, "Downfall of Machado," pp.14, 16; Strode, *Pageant of Cuba*, pp.306–7; Riera, *Cuba Política*, pp.412–14; Machado died in Miami of cancer on March 29, 1939, never having returned to Cuba.

86. *Foreign Relations* (1933) 5:358–59; Cronon, "Interpreting the Good Neighbor Policy," p.544; *Chicago Tribune*, August 12, 1933; Aguilar, "Cuba 1933," pp.146–47; Welles, "Relations between the United States and Cuba," pp.7–8; Buell, *Problems of New Cuba*, p.12.

87. *St. Louis Post-Dispatch*, August 17, 1933; *Baltimore Sun*, August 20, 1933; "Cuba and the Future," *Nation* 137 (August 23, 1933):199; "Cuban Crisis Resolved," *Commonweal* 18 (August 25, 1933):397; Buell, *Problems of New Cuba*, p.497; Charles E. Thomson, "The Cuban Revolution: Fall of Machado," *Foreign Policy Reports* 11 (December 18, 1935):258; Jackman, "America's Cuban Policy during Machado," pp.102–10; Herring, "Downfall of Machado," p.24; Guerra y Sánchez, *Historia de la Nación Cubana* 8:81; Fitzgibbon, *Cuba and U.S.*, p.197; Memorandum of a phone conversation between Hull, Phillips, Caffery, and Welles, August 14, 1933, 837.00/3646½.

CHAPTER 3

1. Strode, *Pageant of Cuba*, p.306; *Chicago Tribune*, August 14, and 15, 1933.

2. Phillips, *Cuban Sideshow*, p.66.

3. Lamar Schweyer, *How Machado Fell*, pp.218–27; Maria V. Moran, "Church and State in Cuba" (Master's thesis, Columbia University, 1950), pp.67–68; Chester, *Sergeant Named Batista*, pp.51–52; *Miami Herald*, August 20, and 21, 1933; *Chicago Tribune*, August 22, 1933.

4. Ibid., August 15, 1933; *St. Louis Post-Dispatch*, August 15, 1933; *Baltimore Sun*, August 24, 1933; Hubert Herring, "Cuba Cleans House," *Nation* 137 (August 30, 1933):233–34; Welles, "Relations between U.S. and Cuba," p.8.

5. *Miami Herald*, August 20, 1933.

6. Roosevelt to U.S. Navy, August 13, 1933 and Memorandum by Hull, August 13, 1933, PSF–Cuba–1933, FDRL; Rosenman, *Public Papers*, 2:322–24.

7. *Foreign Relations* (1933) 5:363; Memorandum of a phone conversation between Hull, Phillips, Caffery, and Welles, August 14, 1933, 837.00/3646½; Memorandum of a press conference by Hull, August 14, 1933, 837.00/3675; Memorandum of a phone conversation between Hull, Caffery, and Welles, August 15, 1933, 837.00/3646½; William Leahy Diary, August 28, 1933, Box 8, William Leahy Papers, Library of Congress, Manuscript Division, Washington, D.C.; Hinton, *Hull*, p.240.; *Miami Herald*, August 14, and 15, 1933; *Chicago Tribune*, August 15, 1933.

8. Buell, *Problems of New Cuba*, pp.183–85; Nelson, *Rural Cuba*, pp.148–49; Welles to

Hull, August 16, 1933, 837.00/3669; Welles to Hull, August 22, 1933, 837.00/3695; *Miami Herald*, August 22, 1933; *Foreign Relations* (1933) 5:376–78; Welles to Hull, August 20, 1933, 837.00/3684; Robert Bowers claims that Welles and the State Department corresponded to show a clear link between Moscow and Cuba, but I did not find any such evidence. In fact, Welles minimized the Communists' role. After the sergeants' revolt, Bowers says that Hull worked diligently to link Communist penetration in Cuba. Again I found no evidence of this allegation. (Robert E. Bowers, "Hull, Russian Subversion in Cuba and Recognition of the U. S. S. R.," *The Journal of American History* 53 (December 1966):542–54.

   9. *Miami Herald*, August 15, 20, 21, and 23, 1933; Phillips, *Cuban Sideshow*, pp. 104–5; *Chicago Tribune*, August 23, 1933.

   10. *Foreign Relations* (1933) 5:369–71.

   11. Luis J. Bustamante, *Encyclopedia Popular Cubana* (Cienfuegos, Cuba: Imprenta y Libreris "La Moderna," 194[?]–48), vol. C–Ch. p.471; Riera, *Cuba Política*, pp.415–16; Fitzgibbon, *Cuba and U.S.*, p.277; *Chicago Tribune*, August 19, 1933.

   12. H. Max Healey, "The Impeachment and Removal of Dr. M. M. Gómez," December, 1936" (Master's thesis, Indiana University, 1939), p.11; Phillips, *Cuban Sideshow*, pp.72–73; Fitzgibbon, *Cuba and U.S.*, p.197.

   13. Ibid.; "Sumner Welles: Cuban Job Done, He Plans Another," *Newsweek* 2 (August 26, 1933):16; Lamar Schweyer, *How Machado Fell*, pp.183–92; Chester, *Sergeant Named Batista*, pp.52–53; Ricardo Adam y Silva, *La gran mentira, 4 de septiembre de 1933* (Havana: Lex, 1947), p.116; Arredondo, *Cuba*, p.488; Krogh, "U.S., Cuba, and Welles," pp.83–88; interview with Rafael Porro Fuentes, January 1, 1969.

   14. Memorandum by Welles, March 1, 1921, Cuban Elections 1919–1921 (Crowder Correspondence), U.S. Department of State, Record Group 59, Files of Latin American Affairs Division, Box 7.

   15. Welles to Inman, October 30, 1933, Box 13, Inman Papers.

   16. *Foreign Relations* (1933) 5:369–71.

   17. Ibid., p.364.

   18. Herring, "Downfall of Machado," pp.19–20; Phillips, *Cuban Sideshow*, pp.84–85; Aguilar, "Cuba 1933," pp.150–55; Hubert Herring, "Can Cuba Save Herself?" *Current History* 39 (March 1934):152; Emilio Roig de Leuchsenring, ed., *Curso de Introducción a la Historia de Cuba* (Havana: Municipio de la Habana, 1938), 3:463–65; Arredondo, *Cuba*, pp.488–90.

   19. *Foreign Relations* (1933) 5:360–61; *Miami Herald*, August 14, and 16, 1933; August 16, 1933; *Baltimore Sun*, August 14, 1933; *Chicago Tribune*, August 16, 1933; "Cuba Steps into the Dawn of a New Day," *The Literary Digest* 116 (August 26, 1933):12; Phillips, *Cuban Sideshow*, p.81.

   20. *Foreign Relations* (1933) 5:578.

   21. Ibid., pp.578–82; Welles to Roosevelt, August 20, 1933, O.F. 470 Sumner Welles, FDRL; Welles to Roosevelt, August 20, 1933, PSF–Cuba–1933, FDRL.

   22. *Foreign Relations* (1933) 5:582–88.

   23. Ibid., pp.365–67, 371–73; *Miami Herald*, August 15, 16, and 17, 1933; *Chicago Tribune*, August 17, 1933; Herring, "Downfall of Machado," p.21.

   24. Buell, *Problems of New Cuba*, p.12; *Foreign Relations* (1933) 5:373–76; Riera, *Cuba Política*, p.415; Aguilar, "Cuba 1933," p.19; Wyatt MacGaffey and Clifford Barnett, *Twentieth Century Cuba* (New York: Doubleday Anchor Books, 1965), pp.125–28; Fitzgibbon and Healey, "Cuban Elections of 1936," pp. 725–26; *Miami Herald*, August 25, 26, 29, and 30, 1933; *Chicago Tribune*, August 26, 1933; Welles, "Relations between U.S. and Cuba," p. 9.

   25. *Miami Herald*, August 19, 1933; *Foreign Relations* (1933) 5:367–68.

   26. Ibid., p.368.

   27. Ibid., pp.368–69.

28. Ibid., 367–69, 371; Welles to Davis, September 4, 1933, Box 12, Davis papers.

29. *Miami Herald*, August 28, September 2 and 4, 1933; Welles, "Relations between the U.S. and Cuba," p.9; Charles Thomson, "The Cuban Revolution: The Fall of Machado," pp.259–60.

30. Cronon, "Interpreting the Good Neighbor Policy," pp.544–46; Aguilar, "Cuba 1933," pp.148–50; Herring, "Downfall of Machado," pp.21–24; Phillips, *Cuban Sideshow*, pp.81–82, 86.

31. Carleton Beals, *The Crime of Cuba* (Philadelphia: J. B. Lippincott Co., 1933), p.250; Aguilar, "Cuba 1933," p. 98; Phillips, *Cuban Sideshow*, pp.86–87.

32. Ibid., p.101.

33. Ibid., pp.70, 90–91; Chester, *Sergeant Named Batista*, pp.55–57.

34. *Foreign Relations* (1933) 5:378–79; Healey, "Impeachment of Gómez," p.13.

35. Phillips, *Cuban Sideshow*, p.93.

36. Aguilar, "Cuba 1933," pp.155–56; Edwin Lieuwen, *Arms and Politics in Latin America*, rev. ed. (New York: Frederick A. Praeger, 1961), pp.97–98; Chester, *Sergeant Named Batista*, pp.48–49; Phillips, *Cuban Sideshow*, pp.110, 112, 167–68; Fitzgibbon, *Cuba and U.S.*, pp.197–98; Buell, *Problems of New Cuba*, p.13.

37. Aguilar, "Cuba 1933," pp.156–61; Phillips, *Cuban Sideshow*, pp.111–12; Welles, *Time for Decision*, p.197; Thomson, "The Cuban Revolution: The Fall of Machado," pp.262–63; Chester, *Sergeant Named Batista*, pp.65–66; *Foreign Relations* (1933) 5:381–82; Phillips, *Cuban Sideshow*, pp.114–15; Fulgencio Batista, *Cuba Betrayed* (New York; Vantage Press, 1962), pp.317–18; Bosch, *Cuba*, pp.136–37.

38. *Foreign Relations* (1933) 5:379.

39. Ibid., pp.379–80, 382; Fabre-Luce, *Révolution à Cuba*, pp.57–68.

40. *Foreign Relations* (1933) 5:379, 382–84; *Chicago Tribune*, September 6, 1933; *Miami Herald*, September 7, 1933; Herring, "Can Cuba Save Herself?" 151–52.

41. *Foreign Relations* (1933) 5:382–83; Leahy Diary, Sept. 5, 1933, Box 8, Leahy Papers.

42. *Foreign Relations* (1933) 5:383; Fulgencio Batista, *The Growth and Decline of the Cuban Republic* (New York: Devin-Adair Co., 1964), pp.9–10; Chester, *Sergeant Named Batista*, pp.83–84; Phillips, *Cuban Sideshow*, p.114; Adam y Silva, *La gran mentira*, p.187.

43. Bustamante, *Enciclopedia Cubana* (Havana: Molina y Cia., 194[?]-48), vol. B, pp.195–96; Healey, "Impeachment of Gómez," pp.135–37; Riera, *Cuba Política*, pp.416, 527–28; Chester, *Sergeant Named Batista*, pp.1–34; Strode, *Pageant of Cuba*, pp.315–16; Adam y Silva, *La gran mentira*, p.120; Phillips, *Cuban Sideshow*, pp.166–67.

44. *Foreign Relations* (1933) 5:384; Chester, *Sergeant Named Batista*, pp.66–67, 80–81; Batista, *Cuba Betrayed*, 202–3; "Cuba: Sudden Revolt of Sergeants Puts a Professor in the Presidency," *Newsweek* 2 (September 16, 1933):5; *Miami Herald*, September 6, 1933; *Chicago Tribune*, September 8, 1933; Phillips, *Cuban Sideshow*, pp.116–17.

45. *Foreign Relations* (1933) 5:384; Chester, *Sergeant Named Batista*, p.82.

46. *Foreign Relations* (1933) 5:389–90; Memorandum of press conference by Hull, September 5, 1933, 837.00/3858; Memorandum of press conference by Hull, September 6, 1933, 837.00/3859; *Miami Herald*, September 6, 1933.

47. *Foreign Relations* (1933) 5:390–92.

48. Ibid., pp.396–97.

49. Ibid., pp.397–98.

50. Ibid., p.398; Chester, *Sergeant Named Batista*, pp.84–85.

51. *Foreign Relations* (1933) 5:400–406; *Miami Herald*, September 8, 1933.

52. *Foreign Relations* (1933) 5:406.

53. Ibid., p.402.

54. Ibid., p.404.

55. Ibid., pp.402–4; Cronon, "Interpreting the Good Neighbor Policy," pp.546–53; Welles, "Relations between U.S. and Cuba," pp.12–13.

56. *Foreign Relations* (1933) 5:406.
57. Ibid.
58. Wood maintains that Welles's refusal to recognize Grau was difficult to understand, but the American ambassador's advocacy of limited intervention to restore Céspedes to power was even more perplexing, since Welles had previously been opposed to armed intervention (Wood, *The Making of the Good Neighbor Policy*, pp.96–97). I maintain that Welles's call for limited intervention was not inconsistent with the ambassador's previous policies. Although he opposed military intervention, he qualified his position. During the Cuban crisis, Céspedes was illegally ousted, and thus Welles logically recommended intervention to restore the constitutional regime which was his fundamental concern.
59. *Chicago Tribune*, September 8, 1933.
60. *Miami Herald*, September 7, and 8, 1933.
61. Herminio Portell Vilá to James A. Robertson, September 10, 1933, Box 46, James A. Robertson Papers, Library of Congress, Manuscript Division, Washington, D.C.
62. *Foreign Relations* (1933) 5:399–400, 406–8.
63. *Miami Herald*, September 7, and 8, 1933; *Chicago Tribune*, September 7, and 12, 1933; *Baltimore Sun*, September 8, 1933; A statement by Secretary of the Navy Claude Swanson, September 7, 1933, O.F. 159–A, Cuba 1933, FDRL.
64. *Chicago Tribune*, September 9, 1933.
65. Ibid.; Riera, *Cuba Política*, pp. 417–19; Chester, *Sergeant Named Batista*, pp. 96–97; Batista, *The Growth and Decline*, p.8.
66. *Foreign Relations* (1933) 5:392–94, 404–5, 433–35; Strode, *Pageant of Cuba*, p.317; Memorandum of press conference by Hull, September 7, 1933, 837.00/3931; Hull to Daniels, September 12, 1933, Cordell Hull Papers, Box 34, Folder 63, Manuscript Division, Library of Congress, Washington, D.C.
67. Daniels Papers, Diary 1933–42, Box 6, September 6, 1933; *Foreign Relations* (1933) 5:394–95, 401, 409, 413–16, 402–22, 428–31, 437; Cronon, "Interpreting the Good Neighbor Policy," pp.541–44; Carroll Kilpatrick, ed., *Roosevelt and Daniels: A Friendship in Politics* (Chapel Hill: University of North Carolina Press, 1952), pp.145–47; E. David Cronin, *Josephus Daniels in Mexico* (Madison: University of Wisconsin Press, 1960), pp. 67–72.
68. *Foreign Relations* (1933) 5:413; Hull to Daniels, September 14, 1933, Hull Papers, Box 34, Folder 63.
69. Harold L. Ickes, *The Secret Diary of Harold L. Ickes: The First Thousand Days, 1933–1936* (New York: Simon and Schuster, 1953), 1:87.
70. Orders for the U.S.S. *J. F. Talbott*, September 8, 1933, O.F., 159–Cuba–1933, FDRL.
71. Ickes, *The Secret Diary*, 1:87.
72. *Miami Herald*, September 6, 8, and 9, 1933; *Chicago Tribune*, September 6, 7, and 8, 1933; *Baltimore Sun*, September 6, 7, and 9, 1933.
73. "Testing Our Intervention Policy in Cuba," *The Literary Digest* 116 (September 16, 1933):7; "What Do We Want in Cuba," *The Christian Century*, 50 (September 20, 1933):1166–68; "Our Job in Cuba," *Nation*, 137 (September 20, 1933):312–13; "Cuban Hurricane," *New Republic* 76 (September 20, 1933):143–44.
74. *St. Louis Post-Dispatch*, September 6, 1933.

CHAPTER 4

1. Aguilar, "Cuba 1933," pp.161–64; *Foreign Relations* (1933) 5:410–11, 414; Chester, *Sergeant Named Batista*, p.101; Phillips, *Cuban Sideshow*, p.129.
2. Ibid., pp.123–29; International Bank for Reconstruction and Development, *Report on Cuba* (Washington, D.C.: International Bank for Reconstruction and Development, 1951),

pp.65–66; Erna Fergusson, *Cuba* (New York: Alfred A. Knopf, 1946), p.283; Buell, *Problems of New Cuba*, p.201; Henry C. Wallich, *Monetary Problems of an Export Economy* (Cambridge, Mass.: Harvard University Press) pp.10, 12.

3. Aguilar, "Cuba 1933," pp.165–67; Guerra y Sánchez, *Historia de la Nación* Cubana, 8:82–83; *Miami Herald*, September 9, 1933; *Baltimore Sun*, September 11, 1933; Chester, *Sergeant Named Batista*, p.98; Phillips, *Cuban Sideshow*, pp.124–25.

4. Ibid., p.125; Bustamante, *Enciclopedia Popular Cubana*, vol. D–M, p.234; Ronald Hilton, ed., *Who's Who in Latin America*, Part VII, "Cuba, Dominican Republic, and Haiti" (Stanford, Calif. Stanford University Press, 1951), p.22; R. Hart Phillips, "Return Engagement," *Inter-American*, 3 (December 1944):16–18, 42; Vega Cobiellas, *Grau y Saladrigas*, pp.13–30; "Cuba's New President," *Bulletin of the Pan American Union* 78 (September 1944):490–91.

5. Ibid., pp.491–92; Herring, "Can Cuba Save Herself?" pp.152–54; Charles E. Thomson, "The Cuban Revolution: Reform and Reaction," *Foreign Policy Reports*, 11 (January 1, 1936):236–69; *Miami Herald*, September 11, 1933; Phillips, *Cuban Sideshow*, p.125.

6. Portell Vilá to Robertson, September 10, 1933, Box 46, Robertson Papers.

7. Aguilar, "Cuba 1933," pp.167–68; *Foreign Relations* (1933) 5:416; William S. Stokes, "The Cuban Revolution and the Presidential Elections of 1948," *The Hispanic American Historical Review*, 31 (February 1951):60.

8. Aguilar, "Cuba 1933," pp.169–70; Phillips, *Cuban Sideshow*, p.275; interview with Rafael Porro Fuentes, January 1, 1969.

9. Aguilar, "Cuba 1933," pp.169–70; Phillips, *Cuban Sideshow*, p.275; Mario Lazo, *Dagger in the Heart: American Policy Failures in Cuba* (New York: Funk & Wagnalls, 1968), p.45.

10. *Foreign Relations* (1933) 5:416–18.

11. Ibid. pp.410–11, 416–18; Chester, *Sergeant Named Batista*, p.72.

12. *Foreign Relations* (1933) 5:422–24.

13. Ibid., p.424.

14. Welles to Hull, September 12, 1933, 711.37/187; *Miami Herald*, September 12, 1933; *St. Louis Post-Dispatch*, September 15, 1933.

15. Order to the U.S.S. *Taylor*, September 18, 1933, O.F. 159–Cuba–1933, FDRL: Ickes, *The Secret Diary*, 1:92–93; Radio address by Caffery, September 16, 1933, 837.00/4351; Daniels to Hull, September 18, 1933, Box 34, Folder 63, Hull Papers; Daniels to Hull, September 20, 1933, and Daniels to Hull, September 25, 1933, Box 750, Daniels Papers; *Miami Herald*, September 16, 1933.

16. *Foreign Relations* (1933) 5:443–45.

17. Ibid., p.445; *Miami Herald*, September 18, 1933.

18. *Foreign Relations* (1933) 5:450–53, 457–59; Phone conversation between Hull and Welles, September 20, 1933, 837.00/3987; Welles to Hull, September 29, 1933, 837.00/4060.

19. *Foreign Relations* (1933) 5:447–48.

20. Hull to Davis, September 20, 1933, Box 12, Davis Papers.

21. Howe to Barrett, September 20, 1933, Ac 12,830 Box 2, John Barrett Papers, Library of Congress, Manuscript Division, Washington, D.C.

22. *Foreign Relations* (1933) 5:425–26, 431–32, 435–36, 438–43, 445–46, 448–49, 454–57, and 459–62; Welles to Hull, September 12, 1933, 837.00/3922; Memorandum by Wilson, September 18, 1933, 837.00/4008½; Welles to Hull, September 24, 1933, 837.00/4005; *Baltimore Sun*, September 14, 1933; *Miami Herald*, September 14, 21, 22, 25, and 26, 1933; *Chicago Tribune*, September 16, 18, 19, 23, and 25, 1933.

23. Phillips, *Cuban Sideshow*, pp.135–37, 147, 151, 154–55; *Chicago Tribune*, September 15, 27, and 30, 1933, and October 2, 1933; *Miami Herald*, September 15, 23, 27, and 30, 1933, and October 2, 1933; *Baltimore Sun*, October 2, 1933; Welles to Hull, September 23, 1933, 837.00/4002; Office of Naval Operations, September 25, 1933, 837.00/4088; Office of Naval

Operations, October 1, 1933, 837.00/4117; *New Republic,* 76 (September 27, 1933):168; Lazo, *Dagger in the Heart,* p.46.

24. Buell, *Problems of New Cuba,* p.13; *Chicago Tribune,* September 15 and 28, 1933; *Miami Herald,* September 15, 19, and 20, 1933.

25. Ibid., September 22, 1933.

26. Chester, *Sergeant Named Batista,* pp.100–101; *Foreign Relations* (1933) 5:407, 411–12, 418–19, 426–28; interview with Adolf A. Berle, January 2, 1969; Strode, *Pageant of Cuba,* pp.318–19.

27. *Foreign Relations* (1933) 5:418–19; Phillips, *Cuban Sideshow,* pp.126, 141; *Chicago Tribune,* September 11, 1933.

28. Ibid., September 12, 1933.

29. *Foreign Relations* (1933) 5:428; *Chicago Tribune,* September 13, 1933; *Miami Herald,* September 12, 13, and 14, 1933.

30. *Foreign Relations* (1933) 5:463–68; Caffery to Hull, October 2, 1933, O.F. 159–Cuba–1933, FDRL; Welles to Roosevelt, October 3, 1933, O.F. 470–Sumner Welles, FDRL. *Chicago Tribune,* October 3, 1933; *Miami Herald,* October 3 and 4, 1933; Chester, *Sergeant Named Batista,* p.113; Phillips, *Cuban Sideshow,* pp.158–60.

31. *Baltimore Sun,* October 4, 1933; *Miami Herald,* October 3, 1933.

32. Daniels to Hull, October 3, 1933, Daniels Papers, Box 750.

33. *Foreign Relations* (1933) 5:485–87, 515–16; Phillips, *Cuban Sideshow,* p.169; Chester, *Sergeant Named Batista,* p.103.

34. Herring, "Can Cuba Save Herself?" p.156.

35. *Foreign Relations* (1933) 5:469–72; Chester, *Sergeant Named Batista,* p.114.

36. *Foreign Relations* (1933) 5:472; *Miami Herald,* October 5, 1933.

37. *Foreign Relations* (1933) 5:473.

38. Ibid., pp.473–74, 487–91; Chester, *Sergeant Named Batista,* p.116.

39. *Foreign Relations* (1933) 5:475–77; Chester, *Sergeant Named Batista,* pp.117–21, 124; Buell, *Problems of New Cuba,* pp.152, 155–56; *Miami Herald,* October 12, 1933.

40. *Foreign Relations* (1933) 5:491–92, 496–97, 505, 512–13; *Miami Herald,* October 18 and 31, 1933; *Chicago Tribune,* October 24, 1933.

41. *Foreign Relations* (1933) 5:477.

42. Ibid., pp.477–78; Memorandum on political conditions in Cuba, October 10, 1933, O.F. 159–Cuba–1933, FDRL; *Miami Herald,* October 9 and 10, 1933.

43. *Foreign Relations* (1933) 5:460, 478–83; *Miami Herald,* September 28 and 29, 1933; *Chicago Tribune,* September 29, 1933, and October 10, 12, and 14, 1933.

44. *Foreign Relations* (1933) 5:492–94; *Miami Herald,* October 20, 1933.

45. Welles to Inman, October 30, 1933, Box 13, Inman Papers.

46. *Foreign Relations* (1933) 5:491, 499–509; *Miami Herald,* November 1 and 3, 1933; *Chicago Tribune,* November 2, 1933.

47. Ibid., October 23, 26, 27, and 30, 1933; *Miami Herald,* October 23, 24, 25, 28, and 30, 1933, and November 2, 1933; Welles to Hull, October 31, 1933, 837.00/4330.

48. *Foreign Relations* (1933) 5:509–15; Chester, *Sergeant Named Batista,* pp.125–26; *Miami Herald,* November 4 and 6, 1933.

49. William Phillips Diary, November 6 and 7, 1933, William Phillips Diary, The Houghton Library, Harvard University, Cambridge, Mass., *Foreign Relations* (1933) 5:515.

50. Phillips Diary, November 6, 1933.

51. *Foreign Relations* (1933) 5:517–20; Chester, *Sergeant Named Batista,* pp.131, 140; Phillips, *Cuban Sideshow,* pp.105, 212; Navy to White House, November 9, 1933, O.F. 159–Cuba–1933, FDRL; *Miami Herald,* November 7, 9, and 10, 1933; *Chicago Tribune,* September 20, 21, 22, and 26, 1933; J. Lloyd Mecham, "Minority Rule in Cuba," *Current History,* 39 (December 1933):344–45; Charles W. Hackett, "Cuba Lives Through Another Revolt," *Current History,* 39 (January 1934): 462–63; Lazo, *Dagger in the Heart,* p.47.

52. Hackett, "Cuba Lives Through Another Revolt," p.463; *Miami Herald*, November 9, 10, and 16, 1933; *St. Louis Post-Dispatch*, November 10, 1933; *Chicago Tribune*, November 13, 1933.

53. Buell, *Problems of New Cuba*, p.201; IBRD, *Cuba*, pp.154–56; U.S. Department of Labor, Bureau of Labor Statistics, Foreign Labor Information, *Labor in Cuba* (1957), pp.16–17; *Miami Herald*, November 22, 1933; Welles to Hull, December 6, 1933, 837.00/4477.

54. *Foreign Relations* (1933) 5:520–21; Welles to Hull, November 14, 1933, 837.00/4422; Phillips Diary, November 14 and 16, 1933.

55. Welles to Hull, November 16, 1933, 123 W. 451/137; *Foreign Relations* (1933) 5:523; Phillips Diary, November 14 and 16, 1933.

56. Phillips Diary, November 20, 1933.

57. Ibid., November 21, 1933.

58. Ibid., November 22 and 23, 1933; Welles and Phillips to Roosevelt, November 22, 1933, O.F. 159–Cuba–1933, FDRL.

59. Phillips Diary, November 23, 1933.

60. *Foreign Relations* (1933) 5:525–26; Rosenman, *Public Papers*, 2:499–501; Memorandum of a press conference by Phillips, November 24, 1933, 837.00/4482; Hackett, "Cuba Lives Through Another Revolt," 463–64; *Miami Herald*, November 24, 1933; *Chicago Tribune*, November 25, 1933.

61. Phillips, *Cuban Sideshow*, pp.224–26, 228; *Foreign Relations* (1933) 5:528; Phillips Diary, November 27, 1933; Roosevelt to Phillips, November 27, 1933, O.F. 470–Sumner Welles, FDRL; *Chicago Tribune*, November 25 and 30, 1933; *Miami Herald*, November 21 and 23, 1933; "Welles Replaced in Cuba," *The Literary Digest* 116 (December 2, 1933); 8; "Will Roosevelt Wreck Cuba?" *The World Tomorrow* 16 (December 7, 1933); 651–52; *New Republic* 77 (December 6, 1933); 85; "Yanqui Imperialismo," *New Republic* 77 (December 6, 1933); 89–90.

62. *Foreign Relations* (1933) 5:522–23, 527, 529–31; Charles W. Hackett, "Cuba Swings to the Left," *Current History* 39 (February 1934); 539–40; Phillips, *Cuban Sideshow*, p.230; *Miami Herald*, November 24, 28, and 29, 1933, and December 2, 1933.

63. *Foreign Relations* (1933) 5:524, 531–35; Chester, *Sergeant Named Batista*, p.148; Alfred Betancourt to Hull, November 5, 1933, Box 35, Folder 65, Hull Papers.

64. *Foreign Relations* (1933) 5:535–36.

65. Phillips, *Cuban Sideshow*, pp.233–34; Buell, *Problems of New Cuba*, pp.397–411; IBRD, *Cuba*, p.325; *Miami Herald*, December 5, 1933.

66. Phillips, *Cuban Sideshow*, pp.235–36; Buell, *Problems of New Cuba*, pp.402–6; Chester, *Sergeant Named Batista*, pp.148–49; *Miami Herald*, December 7, 8, and 11, 1933.

67. Phillips Diary, December 6, 1933.

68. Hackett, "Cuba Swings to the Left," pp.592–93.

69. *Foreign Relations* (1933) 5:536–38.

70. Phillips Diary, December 9, 1933.

71. *Foreign Relations* (1933) 5:536–41; Phillips Diary, December 11, 1933; *Miami Herald*, December 12, 1933.

72. Phillips Diary, December 12, 1933.

73. Ibid., December 13 and 15, 1933. Phillips, *Cuban Sideshow*, p.240; *Miami Herald*, December 14, 1933; Memorandum by T. N. Gimperling, Lt. Col. Infantry, Military Attaché, December 15, 1933, 123 W 451/171; Pratt, "Cordell Hull," p.177.

74. *Foreign Relations*, (1933) 5:468, 474–76, 483–85, 507–8, 526, 529; U.S. Department of State, *Foreign Relations of the United States* (1934), vol. 4, *The American Republics* (1952), pp.93–94; Phillips Diary, November 23, 1933; *Chicago Tribune*, October 6 and 13, 1933.

75. Phillips Diary, November 11, 1933; *Miami Herald*, November 17, 1933.

76. Phillips Diary, November 25, 1933.

77. Ibid.

78. *Foreign Relations* (1933) 5:527–28 533; Hull to Phillips, November 29, 1933, 837.01/50.

79. Charles E. Thomson, "The Seventh Pan-American Conference," *Foreign Policy Reports* 9 (June 6, 1934): 89–96; Hull, *Memoirs,* 1:351; Gregory B. Wolfe, "The Seventh International Conference of American States: A Case Study in Inter-American Relations with Special Attention to Public Opinion" (Ph.D. dissertation, Fletcher School of Law and Diplomacy, 1961), p.139; Phillips, *Cuban Sideshow,* p.230; H. Freeman Matthews to Hull, May 25, 1937, 837.00/8025; Stokes, "The Cuban Revolution," pp.58–59.

80. Jonathan Mitchell, "Pan-American Prelude," *New Republic,* 77 (December 27, 1933): 192.

81. *Miami Herald,* December 14, 1933.

82. Seventh International Conference of American States, *Minutes and Antecedents with General Index* (Montevideo, 1933), pp.99–100; Herminio Portell Vilá, *Cuba y la Conferencia de Montevideo* (Havana: "Heraldo Cristiano," 1934), pp.1–43; Herminio Portell Vilá, *The Nonintervention Pact of Montevideo and American Intervention in Cuba* (Havana: Molina and Co., 1935), pp.9–11; interview with Herminio Portell Vilá, January 23, 1969; Hull to Phillips, December 18, 1933, 837.00/4538; Aguilar, "Cuba 1933," 192–93; Hinton, *Hull,* pp.260–61.

83. Seventh International Conference, *Minutes and Antecedents,* p.105.

84. Ibid., p.106; for Portell Vilá on the origins of the Platt Amendment see Herminio Portell Vilá, *Historia de Cuba en sus relaciones con los Estados Unidos,* 4 vols. (Havana: J. Montero, 1938–41).

85. Welles to Hull, December 5, 1933, 123 W 431/73; U.S. Department of State, *Biographic Registry* (1945), p.188; interview with H. Freeman Matthews, October 31, 1968.

86. Matthews to Hull, December 13, 1933, 123 B. 764/102; *Biographic Registry,* p.35; interview with Ellis O. Briggs, November 16, 1968.

87. Ellis O. Briggs, *Farewell to Foggy Bottom* (New York: David McKay Co., 1964), p.217.

88. *Foreign Relations* (1933) 5:286, 543; State Department Order, July 12, 1933, 123 C 11/332; Welles to Hull, August 23, 1933, 123 C 11/337; Memorandum by Gimperling, December 18, 1933, 123 C 11/383; Biography of Caffery, O.F. 884 Jefferson Caffery, FDRL; Phillips, *Cuban Sideshow,* p.247; *Miami Herald,* December 19, 1933, and August 19, 1933; Caffery to Roosevelt, March 8, 1935, P.P.F. 2331 Jefferson Caffery, FDRL.

89. *Foreign Relations* (1933) 5:544–46; Chargé d'Affaires *ad interim,* Samuel S. Dickson to Hull, December 28, 1933, 837.00/4571; *Miami Herald,* December 15, 18, 22, and 27, 1933. Memorandum for Roosevelt, December 27, 1933, O.F. 159–Cuba–1934, FDRL.

90. Phillips Diary, December 28, 1933. Freeman, "Isolationist Carry-Over, 1933–1937," pp.15–16, 65–67; Rosenman, *Public Papers,* 2:544–49.

91. Ibid., p.545.

92. Charles A. Beard, *American Foreign Policy in the Making: A Study in Responsibilities* (New Haven: Yale University Press, 1946), p.155.

93. *Foreign Relations* (1934) 4:95.

94. Ibid., p.96.

95. Ibid.

96. Ibid., p.97.

97. Ibid., pp.97–98; Chester, *Sergeant Named Batista,* pp.128–29, 150; Riera, *Cuba Política,* 420–22; Welles, "Two Years of the 'Good Neighbor' Policy," pp.10–11; Bosch, *Cuba,* pp.139–40; Healey, "Impeachment of Gómez," pp.15–18, 103; Briggs, *Farewell to Foggy Bottom,* p.217.

98. *Foreign Relations* (1933) 4:98–101; Phillips, *Cuban Sideshow,* pp.273–75; *Miami Herald,* January 15, 1934; Phillips Diary, December 27, 1933; Hubert Herring, "Another

Chance for Cuba," *Current History*, 39 (March 1934): 656–57; Buell, *Problems of New Cuba*, pp. 406–11.

99.   Ibid., pp.14–15, 208–14; Healey, "Impeachment of Gómez," pp.14–15; Aguilar, "Cuba 1933," pp.170–73; Roig de Leuchsenring, ed., *Curso de Introducción a la Historia de Cuba*, 3:465–66.

100.   Guerra y Sánchez, *Historia de la Nación Cubana*, pp.82–83; Ramón Eduardo Ruiz, *Cuba: The Making of a Revolution* (Amherst, Mass.: University of Massachusetts Press, 1968), pp.12–14; C.A.M. Hennessey, "The Roots of Cuban Nationalism," *International Affairs*, 39 (July 1963):358; Bosch, *Cuba*, pp.137–39.

101.   Herring, "Another Chance for Cuba," p.657.

102.   Aguilar, "Cuba 1933," pp.164–65; Herring, "Another Chance for Cuba," p.568; Hubert Herring, "Cuban Whirlwind," *The Christian Century* 51 (February 7, 1934): 180.

103.   Aguilar, "Cuba 1933," pp.176–85; Buell, *Problems of New Cuba*, p.14; Robert J. Alexander, *Communism in Latin America* (New Brunswick, N.J.: Rutgers University Press, 1957), pp.22, 273, 275; Blaiser, "The Cuban and Chilean Communist Parties," p.22; Wood, *The Making of the Good Neighbor Policy*, p.84; Welles, "Relations between the U.S. and Cuba," pp.10–11; Edward O. Guerrant, *Roosevelt's Good Neighbor Policy* (Albuquerque: University of New Mexico Press, 1950), p.28.

104.   Duggan, *The Americas*, p.62.

105.   Welles, "Relations between the U.S. and Cuba," p.12; William S. Stokes, "The Welles Mission to Cuba," *Central America and Mexico* 1 (December 1953): 15–17.

106.   Portell Vilá, *The Nonintervention Pact*, pp.11–12; Roig de Leuchsenring, *Historia de la Enmienda Platt*, pp.1-41; Lamar Schweyer, *How Machado Fell*, pp.7–19; Guerrant, *Roosevelt's Good Neighbor Policy*, p.5; Buell, *Problems of New Cuba*, pp.497–98; Krogh, "U.S., Cuba, and Welles," pp.1–2.

107.   Guerrant, *Roosevelt's Good Neighbor Policy*, pp.27–29; Donald F. Whitehead, "The Making of Foreign Policy During President Roosevelt's First Term" (Ph.D. dissertation, University of Chicago, 1951) p.220; Cronon, "Interpreting the Good Neighbor Policy," pp.565–67; William E. Leuchtenburg, *Franklin D. Roosevelt and the New Deal, 1932–1940* (New York: Harper and Row, 1963), p.208.

108.   Herring, "Another Chance for Cuba," p.657.

109.   Among those critical of Welles are: Carleton Beals, *America South* (Philadelphia: J.P. Lippincott Co., 1938), p. 480; Chester, *Sergeant Named Batista*, pp.80, 93; William A. Williams, *The United States, Cuba, and Castro* (New York: Monthly Review Press, 1962), pp.9–13; Wood, *The Making of the Good Neighbor Policy*, pp. 71–72; Krogh, "U.S., Cuba, and Welles," pp.7–8.

CHAPTER 5

1.   *Foreign Relations* (1934) 5:100–101; Dickson to Hull, January 16, 1934, 837.00/6661; Phillips, *Cuban Sideshow*, pp.275–76; "Cuba: Hevia Takes Presidency After Two Changes of Mind," *Newsweek* 3 (January 20, 1934):16; Thomson, "The Cuban Revolution: Reform and Reaction," p.269.

2.   *Miami Herald*, January 1, 1934.

3.   Herring, Another Chance for Cuba," pp.658–59; *Foreign Relations* (1934) 5:102; Phillips to Hull, January 16, 1934, 837.00/4655; Phillips, *Cuban Sideshow*, pp.278–80, 284; Bustamante, *Enciclopedia Poplar Cubana*, Vol. D–M, p.354; Hilton, *Who's Who in Latin America*, pp.23–24.

4.   *Foreign Relations* (1934) 5:103–5; Caffery to Hull, January 17, 1934, 837.00/4629;

Memorandum of press conference of Phillips, January 18, 1934, 837.00/4699; Phillips, *Cuban Sideshow*, pp.285–86; Chester, *Sergeant Named Batista*, pp.156–57; Whitehead, "The Making of Foreign Policy during Roosevelt's First Term," p.226; *Miami Herald*, January 17, 1934.

5. Ibid.

6. Guerra y Sánchez, *Historia de la Nación Cubana*, pp.83–84; *Foreign Relations* (1934) 5:105; Phillips, *Cuban Sideshow*, p.264.

7. Ibid. p.289.

8. Bustamante, *Enciclopedia Popular Cubana*, Vol. D–M, p.671; Hilton, *Who's Who in Latin America*, p.32; Arrendondo, *Cuba*, pp.474–75; Aguilar, "Cuba 1933," pp.44–47; Healey, "Impeachment of Gómez," pp.18–20.

9. *Foreign Relations* (1934) 5:105–6; Hull to Phillips, January 19, 1934, 837.00/4645; *Miami Herald*, January 18, 19, and 20, 1934; Hull, *Memoirs*, 1:341; Pratt, "Cordell Hull," pp.151–53; Lazo, *Dagger in the Heart*, p.49.

10. *Foreign Relations* (1934) 5:106; Matthews to Hull, January 22, 1934, 837.00/4681; Daniels Papers, Diary 1933–1942, Box 6, January 24–25, 1934; Daniels to Hull, January 26, 1934, 837.00/4706.

11. *Baltimore Sun*, January 16, 1934; *St. Louis Post-Dispatch*, January 19, 1934; *Foreign Relations* (1934) 5:107.

12. Daniels to Roosevelt, January 29, 1934, Daniels Papers, Box 16.

13. *Baltimore Sun*, January 23, 1934; *St. Louis Post-Dispatch*, January 23, and 25, 1934; *Miami Herald*, January 23, 24, 25, and 29, 1934; "Cuba: Mendieta's Inauguration," *Newsweek*, 3 (January 27, 1934):15; "Quick Action Needed in Cuba," *The Christian Century* 51 (January 31, 1934):140; "Mendieta Lacks Cuban Support," *New Republic* 77 (January 31, 1934):319–20; "Cuba and the New Deal," *Nation* 138 (January 31, 1934):116–17; "Havana Bows to Washington," *The World Tomorrow* 17 (February 1, 1934):51–52; "End of Cuban Strife Seen in Our Recognition," *The Literary Digest* 117 (February 3, 1934):11.

14. Phillips, *Cuban Sideshow*, p.293; Caffery to Hull, January 25, 1934, 837.00/4685; *Miami Herald*, February 2, 1934.

15. Ibid.

16. Ibid., January 22, 1934, and February 19, 1934; Caffery to Hull, February 21, 1934, 837.00/4809.

17. Memorandum from Duggan to Welles and Wilson, March 2, 1934, 837.00/4786; Matthews to Hull, February 9, 1934, 837.00/4766; "The New Constitutional Law of Cuba," *Bulletin of the Pan American Union* 68 (May 1934):371–74; Buell, *Problems of New Cuba*, pp.16, 202–08.

18. Chester, *Sergeant Named Batista*, p.157; Phillips, *Cuban Sideshow*, p.292; Buell, *Problems of New Cuba*, pp.188–91, and 499; Herring, "Another Chance for Cuba," pp.658–60; Ruby H. Phillips, *Cuba: Island of Paradox* (New York: McDowelll, Obolensky, 1959), p.160; Caffery to Hull, February 6, 1934, 837.00/4742; *Chicago Tribune*, January 18, 1934.

19. Caffery to Hull, August 9, 1934, 837.00/5326; Caffery to Hull, August 10, 1034, 837.00/5335; Caffery to Hull, August 11, 1934, 837.00/5338; Matthews to Hull, August 16, 1934, 837.00/5356; Matthews to Hull, November 2, 1934, 837.00/5689; Caffery to Hull, November 3, 1934, 837.00/5696.

20. Caffery to Hull, September 18, 1934, 837.00/5456.

21. Caffery to Hull, February 5, 1934, 837.00/4737; Caffery to Hull, February 6, 1934, 837.00/4741; Caffery to Hull, February 7, 1934, 837.00/4743; Caffery to Hull, February 9, 1934, 837.00/4752; Memorandum of press conference by Hull, February 9, 1934, 837.00/4770; *Miami Herald*, February 3 and 8, 1934; *Chicago Tribune*, January 29, 1934, and February 5, 1934; Charles W. Hackett, "Restive Cuban Labor," *Current History* 40 (April 1934):80–82; MacGaffey and Barnett, *Twentieth Century Cuba*, p.163.

22. Phillips, *Cuban Sideshow*, p.307.

23. Matthews to Hull, February 16, 1934, 837.00/4799; Caffery to Hull, March 3, 1934, 837.00/4851; Caffery to Hull, March 14, 1934, 837.00/4929; Stokes, "The Cuban Revolution," pp.38–40; MacGaffey and Barnett, *Twentieth Century Cuba*, pp.150–51.

24. Stokes, "The Cuban Revolution," pp.47–48; Blasier, "The Cuban and Chilean Communist Parties," pp.23, 33; Matthews to Hull, February 26, 1934, 837.00B/118; Caffery to Hull, January 29, 1934, 837.00B/108.

25. Phillips, *Cuba*, p.187; Krauss, "Communist Policy in Cuba," pp.64–68; IBRD, *Cuba*, p.365; Buell, *Problems of New Cuba*, pp.191–95, 198–99, 291–92.

26. Ibid., p.199.

27. Ibid., p.34; Alexander, *Communism in Latin America*, p.10; Edwin Lefevre, "Cuba's Grievances," *The Saturday Evening Post* 206 (January 27, 1934):74, 76.

28. *Miami Herald*, March 3, 1934; Buell, *Problems of New Cuba*, pp.182, 184–86, 416–32; IBRD, *Cuba*, pp.336–39.

29. Caffery to Hull, March 7, 1934, 837.00/4871; Caffery to Hull, March 7, 1934, 837.00/4872; Caffery to Hull, March 8, 1934, 837.00/4876; Caffery to Hull, March 10, 1934, 837.00/4880; Caffery to Hull, March 10, 1934, 837.00/4889; Caffery to Hull, March 19, 1934, 837.00/4892; Caffery to Hull, March 10, 1934, 837.00/4893; Caffery to Hull, March 13, 1934, 837.00/4903; Caffery to Hull, March 13, 1934, 837.00/4906; Caffery to Hull, March 15, 1934, 837.00/4914; *Miami Herald*, March 7 and 12, 1934; *Chicago Tribune*, March 12, 1934; Phillips, *Cuba*, p.161; Charles W. Hackett, "Labor Crisis Averted in Cuba," *Current History* 40 (May 1934):214–15.

30. Caffery to Hull, March 15, 1934, 837.00/4913; Caffery to Hull, March 16, 1934, 837.00/4932; Caffery to Hull, March 17, 1934, 837.00/4924; "President Mendieta Suspends Civil Rights," *Newsweek* 3 (March 17, 1934):17; Clara Porset, "Cuba's Troubled Waters," *Nation* 138 (March 28, 1934):353–54.

31. "Mendieta's Government," *New Republic* 77 (March 21, 1934):142.

32. Caffery to Hull, March 19, 1934, 837.00/4939.

33. Ibid., March 31, 1934, 837.00/4962; Caffery to Hull, April 7, 1934, 837.00/4985; Charles Hackett, "The Cuban Turmoil," *Current History* 40 (June 1934):333–34.

34. Caffery to Hull, April 9, 1934, 837.00/4982.

35. Matthews to Hull, April 18, 1934, 837.00/5005; Matthews to Hull, May 16, 1934, 837.00/5084; *Miami Herald*, May 7, 1934.

36. Caffery to Hull, April 17, 1934, 837.00/5010; Caffery to Hull, April 18, 1934, 837.00/5004; Matthews to Hull, July 11, 1934, 837.00/5272; Caffery to Hull, July 23, 1934, 837.00/5300; *Miami Herald*, July 25, 1934; Matthews to Hull, August 22, 1934, 837.00/5378; Caffery to Hull, September 21, 1934, 837.00/5464; Caffery to Hull, October 27, 1934, 837.00/5650.

37. Caffery to Hull, October 19, 1934, 837.00/5608; Caffery to Hull, November 7, 1934, 837.00/5709; Matthews to Hull, November 12, 1934, 837.00/5729; Caffery to Hull, December 3, 1934, 837.00/5801; Matthews to Hull, December 6, 1934, 837.00/5812; Matthews to Hull, December 6, 1934, 837.00/5813; *Miami Herald*, December 7, 1934; Hubert Herring, "Cuba's Election Campaign," *Current History* 41 (February 1935):602–04.

38. Matthews to Hull, July 5, 1934, 837.00/5252; Caffery to Hull, July 6, 1934, 837.00/5248; Matthews to Hull, July 26, 1934, 837.00/5306; *Miami Herald*, July 6, 1934; Charles Hackett, "Cabinet Trouble in Cuba," *Current History* 40 (September 1934):715; Matthews to Hull, June 12, 1934, 837.00/5134; Caffery to Hull, July 9, 1934, 837.00/5269; Stokes, "The Cuban Revolution," pp.45–47; Caffery to Hull, October 24, 1934, 837.00/5643; Matthews to Hull, November 20, 1934, 837.00/5758; Caffery to Hull, November 21, 1934, 837.00/5765; Caffery to Hull, November 23, 1934, 837.00/5770; Caffery to Hull, December 1, 1934, 837.00/5793; Caffery to Hull, December 7, 1934, 837.00/5817; Caffery to Hull, January 23, 1935, 837.00/5961; *Chicago Tribune*, November 26, 1934.

39. Matthews to Hull, February 2, 1934, 837.00/4732; Caffery to Hull, June 21, 1934, 837.00/5168; Caffery to Hull, June 22, 1934, 837.00/5179; Caffery to Hull, June 22, 1934, 837.00/5177; Caffery to Hull, June 22, 1934, 837.00/5169; Matthews to Hull, June 22, 1934, 837.00/5193; Matthews to Hull, June 23, 1934, 837.00/5188; Matthews to Hull, June 27, 1934, 837.00/5245; Portell Vilá, *The Nonintervention Pact*, p.16; Charles Hackett, "Cabinet Friction in Cuba," *Current History* 40 (August 1934):594–95.

40. Caffery to Hull, May 19, 1934, 837.00/5083; Caffery to Hull, May 25, 1935, 837.00/5092; Caffery to Hull, May 12, 1934, 837.00/5071; Caffery to Hull, May 31, 1934, 837.00/5108; *Miami Herald,* May 15 and 19, 1934.

41. Caffery to Hull, June 2, 1934, 837.00/5117.

42. Caffery to Hull, September 11, 1934, 837.00/5436; Caffery to Hull, September 14, 1934, 837.00/5449; Caffery to Hull, September 28, 1934, 837.00/1 Grau San Martín, Ramon/21, Caffery to Hull, October 15, 1934, 837.00/5588; Caffery to Hull, October 23, 1934, 837.00/5618; Caffery to Hull, October. 24, 1934, 837.00/5637; Matthews to Hull, November 14, 1934, 837.00/5736.

43. Caffery to Hull, May 8, 1934, 837.00/5957; Caffery to Hull, June 13, 1934, 837.00/5137; Matthews to Hull, September 13, 1934, 837.00/5441; Matthews to Hull, September 18, 1934, 837.00/5452; Matthews to Hull, November 2, 1934, 837.00/5683; Matthews to Hull, November 6, 1934, 837.00/5704; *Miami Herald,* May 8, 1934; Charles Hackett, "Continued Unrest in Cuba," *Current History* 41 (November 1934):215–16; Buell, *Problems of New Cuba,* p.16.

44. Matthews to Hull, August 23, 1934, 837.00/5380; Matthews to Hull, August 24, 1934, 837.00/5384; *Chicago Tribune,* August 24, 1934; *Miami Herald,* August 23, 1934; Caffery to Hull, August 11, 1934, 837.00/5329; Caffery to Hull, August 13, 1934, 837.00/5332; Caffery to Hull, August 14, 1934, 837.00/5341; Matthews to Hull, August 17, 1934, 837.00/5360; Matthews to Hull, August 23, 1934, 837.00/5379; Matthews to Hull, August 30, 1934, 837.00/5400; Caffery to Hull, September 4, 1934, 837.00/5408; Charles Hackett, "Cuba and the Good-Neighbor Policy," *Current History* 41 (October 1934):89–90.

45. Caffery to Hull, October 3, 1934, 837.00/5505; Caffery to Hull, October 3, 1934, 837.00/5506; Caffery to Hull, October 3, 1934, 837.00/5510; Matthews to Hull, October 6, 1934, 837.00/5551; Caffery to Hull, October 8, 1934, 837.00/5565; Caffery to Hull, October 8, 1934, 837.00/5535; Caffery to Hull, October 9, 1934, 837.00/5554; Caffery to Hull, October 10, 1934, 837.00/5564; Charles Hackett, "Cuba's Troubles Persist," *Current History* 41 (December 1934):346; *Miami Herald,* October 9, 1934.

46. Matthews to Hull, July 5, 1934, 837.00/5243; Caffery to Hull, July 7, 1934, 837.00/5268; Caffery to Hull, July 27, 1934, 837.00/5312; Caffery to Hull, August 20, 1934, 837.00/5368; Caffery to Hull, October 11, 1934, 837.00/5577; Caffery to Hull, November 2, 1934, 837.00/5700; *Miami Herald,* June 26, 1934, October 30, 1934, and December 13, 1934; Phillips, *Cuba,* p.163; Buell, *Problems of New Cuba,* pp.17–18.

47. Caffery to Hull, April 27, 1934, 837.00/5027; Caffery to Hull, June 15, 1934, 837.00/5153; Buell, *Problems of New Cuba,* p.18.

48. *Miami Herald,* December 19, 1934.

49. Matthews to Hull, April 2, 1934, 837.00/4959; Hackett, "Cuban Turmoil," pp.334–35.

50. Caffery to Hull, April 25, 1934, 837.00/5024.

51. Matthews to Hull, May 2, 1934, 837.00/5042; Matthews to Hull, May 4, 1934, 837.00/5046; Caffery to Hull, May 28, 1934, 837.00/5097; Caffery to Hull, May 29, 1934, 837.00/5100; Charles Hackett, "Cuba's New Sovereignty," *Current History* 40 (July 1934):472–73.

52. Caffery to Hull, June 15, 1934, 837.00/5140; Matthews to Hull, June 16, 1934, 837.00/5157; Matthews to Hull, June 21, 1934, 837.00/5174; *Miami Herald,* June 16, 1934; Phillips, *Cuba,* pp.162–63; Buell, *Problems of New Cuba,* p.16.

53. Matthews to Hull, September 5, 1934, 837.00/5422; Matthews to Hull, September 5, 1934, 837.00/5427; Caffery to Hull, September 7, 1934, 837.00/5431; *Miami Herald,* September 4, 1934; Buell, *Problems of New Cuba*, p.16.

54. Caffery to Hull, September 19, 1934, 837.00/5458.

55. Caffery to Hull, September 24, 1934, 837.00/5476.

56. Caffery to Hull, November 9, 1934, 837.00/5725.

57. Caffery to Hull, November 12, 1934, 837.00/5737.

58. Caffery to Hull, April 2, 1934, 837.00/4964.

59. Matthews to Hull, April 17, 1934, 837.00/4997; Caffery to Hull, May 4, 1934, 837.00/5055; Caffery to Hull, May 28, 1934, 837.00/5098; Caffery to Hull, July 7, 1934, 837.00/5253; Caffery to Hull, September 4, 1934, 837.75/173; Richard Barry, "Cuba Boils Again—With Two Dictators," *The Literary Digest*, 18 (October 20, 1934):17; Lazo, *Dagger in the Heart*, p.52.

60. Matthews to Hull, April 20, 1934, 837.00/5011; Matthews to Hull, April 23, 1934, 837.00/5015; Caffery to Hull, June 15, 1934, 837.00/5152; Buell, *Problems of New Cuba*, pp.16–17; Lieuwen, *Arms and Politics in Latin America*, pp.98–99, 179; MacGaffey and Barnett, *Twentieth Century Cuba*, pp.139–40, 162; Healey, "Impeachment of Gómez," pp.145–52.

CHAPTER 6

1. *Miami Herald*, January 27, 1934, February 6, 1934, and March 9, 1934; Guerrant, *Roosevelt's Good Neighbor Policy*, p.29.

2. David A. Shannon, *Between the Wars: America, 1919–1941* (Boston: Houghton Mifflin Co., 1965), pp.168–69; Rosenman, *Public Papers*, 3:76–81; "Economic Progress in the Americas: Cuba," *Bulletin of the Pan American Union* 70 (Feburary 1936):188–90; Buell, *Problems of New Cuba*, p.16; Fitzgibbon, *Cuba and U.S.*, pp.240–41; Robert F. Smith, *The United States and Cuba: Business and Diplomacy, 1917–1960* (New Haven, Conn.: College and University Press, 1960), pp.144, 163; J. Lloyd Mecham, *A Survey of United States-Latin American Relations* (Boston: Houghton Mifflin Co., 1965), p.122; George C. Coleman, "The Good Neighbor Policy of Franklin D. Roosevelt with Special Reference to Three Inter-American Conferences, 1933–1938" (Ph.D. dissertation, University of Iowa, 1951), pp.202–03; Wallich, *Monetary Problems*, p.75; Memorandum of conversation by Hull, March 1, 1934, O.F. 159—Cuba–1934, FDRL.

3. Caffery to Hull, January 25, 1934, 837.00/4684.

4. Caffery to Hull, January 26, 1934, 837.61351/679; Caffery to Hull, February 3, 1934, 837.00/4727; Caffery to Hull, February 5, 1934, 837.00/4745; *Miami Herald*, January 26, 1934, February 7, 1934, and Febraury 12, 1934.

5. Caffery to Hull, February 16, 1934, 837.00/4789; Caffery to Hull, February 19, 1934, 837.00/4795; Caffery to Hull, February 20, 1934, 837.00/4800; Caffery to Hull, March 19, 1934, 837.00/4930.

6. Caffery to Hull, March 24, 1934, 837.00/4956.

7. *Foreign Relations* (1934) 5:182–83; Rosenman, *Public Papers*, 3:86–90; Caffery to Hull, February 12, 1934, 837.00/4763; Mendieta to Roosevelt, February 20, 1934, PSF—Cuba–1934, FDRL.

8. U.S. Department of Agriculture, Production and Marketing Administration, Information Bulletin No. 111, *The United States Sugar Program* (1953), pp.6–8; U.S. Congress, *Congressional Record*, 73d Cong., 2d Sess., 1934, 78, p.8403; Matthews to Hull, May 10, 1934, 837.61351/742; Buell, *Problems of New Cuba*, pp.259–60; Fitzgibbon, *Cuba and U.S.*, pp.221–23; Power Yung-Chao Chu, "A History of the Hull Trade Program, 1934–1939" (Ph.D. dissertation, Columbia University, 1957), pp.159–63.

9. Hull to Caffery, May 26, 1934, 837.61351/761; U.S. Tariff, *Cuba,* pp.53–54, 61; Duggan, *The Americas,* pp.76–77; Buell, *Problems of New Cuba,* p.61.

10. Caffery to Hull, March 1, 1934, 123 C 11/402.

11. Coleman, "The Good Neighbor Policy of F.D.R.," pp.131–34; Jackman, "America's Cuban Policy During Machado," p.250; Phillip G. Wright, *The Cuban Situation, and Our Treaty Relations* (Washington, D.C.: Brookings Institution, 1931), pp.169–70, 176–78; Leland H. Jenks, *Our Cuban Colony, A Study in Sugar* (New York: Vanguard Press, 1928), p.86.

12. Ibid., pp.307–8.

13. Wood, *The Making of the Good Neighbor Policy,* pp.52, 57–58; DeConde, *Hoover's Latin American Policy,* pp.107–8; Jackman, "America's Cuban Policy During Machado," pp.88–89, 97, 229–30; Cosme de la Torriente, "The Platt Amendment," *Foreign Affairs* 8 (April 1930):378.

14. Guggenheim, *U.S. and Cuba,* pp.242–43; also see Harry F. Guggenheim, "Amending the Platt Amendment," *Foreign Affairs,* 12 (April 1934):448–57.

15. *New Republic,* 76 (August 23, 1933):29.

16. Jorge Mañach, "Revolution in Cuba," *Foreign Affairs,* 12 (October 1933):56; Juan Andres Lliteras, "Relations Between Cuba and the United States," *International Conciliation,* 296 (January 1934):11–12, 20–23; Ruiz, *Cuba,* p.39; Roig de Leuchsenring, *Historia de la Enmienda Platt,* pp. 43–65; *Miami Herald,* December 18, 1933.

17. Mitchell, "Pan American Prelude," p.192; *Nation,* 138 (February 14, 1934):170.

18. Herring, "Another Chance for Cuba," p.660.

19. Graham H. Stuart, "Cuba and the Platt Amendment," *World Affairs Interpreter,* 5 (Spring 1934):53.

20. Selig Adler, *The Uncertain Giant: 1921–1941* (New York: Macmillan Co., 1965), p.157; *Miami Herald,* August 11, 1933.

21. *St. Louis Post-Dispatch,* September 23, 1933.

22. Hull, *Memoirs,* 1:317; *Congressional Record,* 73d Cong., 2d Sess., 1934, 78, p. 1:892–93, p. 8:8415—16; Key Pittman to Hull, January 24, 1934, 711.37/202; I. R. Barnes to Assistant Secretary of State Wilbur J. Carr, January 30, 1934, 711.37/204.

23. Biography of Manuel Márquez Sterling, January 29, 1934, O.F.159–Cuba–1934, FDRL.

24. Phillips Diary, December 14 and 20, 1933; Memorandum of a conversation between Márquez Sterling and Phillips, December 14, 1933, 837.00/4545; *Foreign Relations* (1934), 5:93–95; Memorandum of a conversation by Hull, January 30, 1934, Hull Papers, Box 57, Folder 199.

25. Manuel Márquez Sterling, *Proceso Historico de la Enmienda Platt* (Havana: Imprenta "El Siglo XX," 1941), pp.373–460; *Miami Herald,* March 30, 1934; *Foreign Relations* (1934) 5:185; Memorandum by Welles, May 2, 1934, 711.3711/1; Memorandum from Frederick M. Diven of the Legal Division of the Department of State to Welles, May 2, 1934, 711.3711/2: Cosme de la Torriente, *Cuarenta Años de Mi Vida, 1898–1938* (Havana: Imprenta "El Siglo," 1939), pp.398–402.

26. Rosenman, *Public Papers,* 3:270–71.

27. *Foreign Relations* (1934) 5:183–84.

28. Hull, *Memoirs,* 1:343; *Congressional Record,* 73d Cong., 2d Sess., 1934, 78, pt 9:9839, 9840, 9925–26, 10116; Caffery to Hull, June 6, 1934, 711.3711/35; Caffery to Hull, June 7, 1934, 711.3711/38; Caffery to Hull, June 10, 1934, 837.00/5126; Cosme de la Torriente, *Cuarenta Años de Mi Vida,* pp.386–89.

29. Matthews to Hull, June 12, 1934, 711.3711/48.

30. Department of State Press Release, May 29, 1934, 711.3711/24.

31. Cosme de la Torriente to Hull, May 29, 1934, 711.3711/3; Caffery to Hull, May 30, 1934, 711.3711/4; Saladrigas to Welles, May 29, 1934, 711.3711/16; Céspedes to Welles, May

30, 1934, 711.3711/17; Mendieta to Welles, May 29, 1934, 711.3711/18; Matthews to Hull, May 31, 711.3711/28.

32. Phillips, *Cuba*, p.162.

33. Coleman, "The Good Neighbor Policy of F.D.R." pp.136–39, 151–52; Josephus Daniels, *Shirt-Sleeve Diplomat* (Chapel Hill: University of North Carolina Press, 1947), pp.324–25; Francisco Cuevas Cancino, *Roosevelt y la Buena Vecindad* (Mexico and Buenos Aires: Fondo de Cultura Económica, 1954), p.183; Fitzgibbon, *Cuba and U.S.*, p.261.

34. Hackett, "Cuba's New Sovereignty," pp.471–72.

35. Hackett, "Cuba and the Good Neighbor Policy," p.88.

36. "The End of the Platt Amendment," *The Christian Century*, 51 (June 13, 1934):789.

37. *Nation*, 138 (June 20, 1934):689.

38. Lester H. Woolsey, "The New Cuban Treaty," *American Journal of International Law*, 28 (July 1934):534.

39. *Miami Herald*, June 11, 1934.

40. *New Republic*, 79 (June 27, 1934):166.

41. "Anarchy in Cuba," *The World Tomorrow*, 17 (June 28, 1934):317.

42. Office of Naval Operation, Jan. 28–29, 1934, 837.00/4832; Caffery to Hull, February 1, 1934, 837.00/4730; Memorandum by Wilson, February 21, 1934, 837.00/4829.

43. Caffery to Hull, March 5, 1934, 837.00/4881.

44. Caffery to Hull, April 9, 1934, 837.00/4983.

45. Memorandum by Phillips, June 18, 1934, 837.00/5163.

46. Ibid.; Caffery to Hull, June 12, 1934, 837.00/5128.

47. Caffery to Hull, July 21, 1934, 837.00/5296; Caffery to Hull, September 1, 1934, 837.00/5412.

48. *Miami Herald*, July 7, 1934.

49. Telegram from the Society of Cuban Women, August 17, 1934, 837.00/5354.

50. Buell, *Problems of New Cuba*, p.500.

51. Caffery to Hull, June 1, 1934, 837.00/5110; Hackett, "Cuba's New Sovereignty," p.473; Phillips, *Cuba*, pp.161–62; Lazo, *Dagger in the Heart*, p.41; "New Pact with Cuba Follows Terrorism," *The Literary Digest*, 117 (June 9, 1934):19; *Miami Herald*, May 28 and 29, 1934.

52. Cameron to Hull, June 26, 1934, 837.00/5218; *Foreign Relations* (1934) 5:185–88; Rosenman, *Public Papers*, 3:319–20; This was taken under the power vested in the president to halt shipments of weapons to any nation where domestic violence existed; *Miami Herald*, June 30, 1934; Hackett, "Cabinet Friction in Cuba," p.597.

53. Caffery to Hull, July 17, 1934, 837.00/5280; Caffery to Hull, July 17, 1934, 837.00/5283; Caffery to Hull, July 17, 1934, 837.00/5286; Chester, *Sergeant Named Batista*, p.150; Portell Vilá, *The Nonintervention Pact*, p.16.

54. Daniels Papers, Diary 1933–42, Monday, Jan. 29–Feb. 2, 1934, Box 6.

55. Daniels to Hull, July 10, 1934, Hull Papers, Box 37, Folder 177.

56. Welles, "Two Years of the Good Neighbor," pp.12–16; Guerrant, *Roosevelt's Good Neighbor Policy*, pp.3–4; Wright, *Cuban Situation*, p.185; Great Britain, Department of Overseas Trade, *Economic Conditions in Cuba, April, 1935* (London, 1935), p.1; Lloyd C. Gardner, *Economic Aspects of New Deal Diplomacy* (Madison: University of Wisconsin Press, 1964), pp.47–48.

57. Memorandum by the Treaty Division of the Department of State, December 18, 1933, 611.3731/503½; U.S. Tariff, *Cuba*, pp.76–77; Joe Wilkinson, *Politics and Trade Policy* (Washington, D.C.: Public Affairs Press, 1960), pp.1–4; Pratt, "Cordell Hull," 107–15, 132–38; Arthur Schatz, "Cordell Hull and the Struggle for the Reciprocal Trade Agreements Program, 1932–1940" (Ph.D dissertation, University of Oregon, 1965), pp.153–62; Beard, *America's Foreign Policy*, pp.145–46, 158–60; Roseman, *Public Papers*, 3:113–17; Gardner, *Economic Aspects of New Deal Diplomacy*, pp.16, 22–23.

58. *Foreign Relations* (1934) 5:108–10.

59. Ibid., pp.110–69; Caffery to Hull, March 3, 1934 611.3731/537; Hull to Wallace, June 29, 1934, 611.3731/716A; Memorandum of a conversation between Hull and Márquez Sterling, April 19, 1934, Hull Papers, Box 57, Folder 199; Memorandum by Duggan, July 21, 1934, 611.3731/925; Caffery to Hull, August 17, 1934, 837.00/5366; Cosme de la Torriente, *Cuarenta Años de Mi Vida,* pp.405–14.

60. *Foreign Relations* (1934) 5:169–77; Chu, "Hull's Trade Program," pp.155–57; Schatz, "Cordell Hull," pp.162–68; Hull, *Memoirs,* p.368; Pratt, "Cordell Hull," p.119; Coleman, "The Good Neighbor Policy of F.D.R." pp.176–79; Wood, *The Making of the Good Neighbor Policy,* p.112.

61. Chu, "Hull's Trade Program," pp.158–59; U.S. Tariff, *Cuba,* pp.27–28; Byron White, "Cuba and Puerto Rico Case Study in Comparative Economic Development Policy" (Ph.D dissertation, University of Texas, 1959), p.120; Fitzgibbon, *Cuba and U.S.,* pp.224–25; Buell, *Problems of New Cuba,* pp.61–63, 260–61.

62. U.S. Tariff, *Cuba,* p.11; IBRD, *Cuba,* pp.783–84; Dudley Seers, ed. *Cuba; The Economic and Social Revolution* (Chapel Hill: University of North Carolina Press, 1964), pp.98–99.

63. *Foreign Relations* (1934) 5:177–81; Buell, *Problems of New Cuba,* p.258.

64. Ibid., pp.179–80; Matthews to Hull, August 25, 1934, 611.3731/1013; Matthews to Hull, August 26, 1934, 611.3731/1003; Caffery to Hull, August 31, 1934, 837.00/5414; A letter from Maurice T. McGovern, president of the American Chamber of Commerce of Cuba, to Hull, September 5, 1934, 611.3731/1078; American Chamber of Commerce of Cuba, *Silver Jubilee Review,* p.19; U.S. Department of State, Division of Current Information, Information Series No. 38, September 11, 1934, 611.3731/1095.

65. *Foreign Relations* (1934) 5:181; U.S. Department of State Press Release, September 5, 1934, 611.3731/1079; U.S. Department of State Press Release, September 18, 1934, 611.3731/1131; Caffery to Hull, October 6, 1934, 611.373/1142; Duggan to Welles, November 6, 1934, 611.3731/1176; Caffery to Hull, November 9, 1934, 611.371/1174.

66. Duggan to Welles, November 22, 1934, 611.3731/1216.

67. Address by Donnelly, November 28, 1934, 611.3731/1258.

68. Caffery to Hull, February 21, 1934, 123 C 11/447.

69. For general background on the Nye Committee see Wayne S. Cole, *Senator Gerald P. Nye and American Foreign Relations* (Minneapolis: University of Minnesota Press, 1962), p.3–123 and John E. Wiltz, *In Search of Peace: The Munitions Inquiry, 1934–36* (Baton Rouge: Louisiana State University Press, 1963) pp.23, 59, 73, 164; U.S. Congress, Senate, *Munitions Inquiry,* Hearings before the Special Committee Investigating the Munitions Industries, pursuant to S. R. 206, 73d Cong., 1934–36, pt 7:1616–42, 1829.

70. Ibid., 1643–44, 1829.

71. Ibid., 1644.

72. Ibid., 1644–45.

73. Ibid., 1659–63, 1843–47, and pt 8:2066–67, 2069; Matthews to Hull, April 24, 1934, 837.00/5017; Matthews to Hull, July 11, 1034, 837.00/5273; *Chicago Tribune,* March 10, 1934.

74. U.S. Senate, *Munitions Inquiry,* pt 7:1900.

75. Rosenman, *Public Papers,* 3:271.

76. Hull, *Memoirs,* 1:344.

77. Welles, "Relations between U.S. and Cuba," p.16; U.S. Department of State, *Latin American Series,* No. 8, Sumner Welles, "Inter-American Relations" (1935), pp.2–4, 13; U.S. Department of State, *Latin American Series,* No. 9, Sumner Welles, "The Roosevelt Administration and Its Dealings with the Republics of the Western Hemisphere" (1935), pp.9–10; U.S. Department of State, *Latin American Series,* No. 10, Sumner Welles, "Pan

American Cooperation" (1935), p.5; Welles, "Two Years of the Good Neighbor," pp.11–12; Welles, *Time for Decision*, p.199.

78. U.S. Department of State, *Latin American Series*, No. 12, Sumner Welles, " 'Good Neighbor' in the Caribbean" (1935), pp.7, 12–13.

79. Ramón Grau San Martín, *La Revolución Cubana Ante América* (Mexico: Ediciones de Partido Revolucionaria Cubana, 1936), pp.76–86; for examples of Auténtico progaganda see its bulletins for September 1 and October 1, 1935, O.F. 159–A Cuba 1935, FDRL.

80. George Summerlin in Panama to Hull, August 10, 1935, 837.00/6501.

81. Phillips, *Cuban Sideshow*, pp.315–16; Buell, *Problems of New Cuba*, pp.498–500.

82. For such views see Samuel F. Bemis, *The Latin American Policy of the United States* (New York: Harcourt, Brace, and Co., 1943), p.282; Allan Nevins, *The New Deal and World Affairs: A Chronicle of International Affairs, 1933–1945* (New Haven: Yale University Press, 1950), p.36; Félix Lizaso, *Panorama de la cultura Cubana* (Mexico: Fondo de Cultura Económica, 1949), p.145; more recently see Mecham, *A Survey of United States-Latin American Relations*, p.118.

83. Grau San Martín, *La Revolución Cubana ante América*, p.82; Portell Vilá, *The Nonintervention Pact*, pp.14–16; Roig de Leuchsenring, *Historia de la Enmienda Platt*, pp.67–118; Roig de Leuchsenring, *Curso de introducción*, pp.420–22; Phillips, *Cuban Sideshow*, p.315; Bosch, *Cuba*, p.128; Buell, *Problems of New Cuba*, pp.19, 497–98; MacGaffey and Barnett, *Twentieth Century Cuba*, pp.374–76; Lazo, *Dagger in the Heart*, p.37; David D. Burks, *Cuba under Castro* (New York: Foreign Policy Association, 1964), pp.5–6.

84. Memorandum by Duggan, March 15, 1934, 611.3731/559; Roig de Leuchsenring, *Historia de la Enmienda Platt*, pp.119–72; Roig de Leuchsenring, *Curso de introducción*, p.422; Ramiro Guerra y Sánchez, *Sugar and Society in the Caribbean: An Economic History of Cuban Agriculture* (New Haven: Yale University Press, 1964), pp.157–69; Fitzgibbon, *Cuba and U.S.*, p.277; Chu, "Hull's Trade Program," 164–65; Seers, *Cuba*, pp.13–16.

85. Roig de Leuchsenring, *Curso de introducción*, p.401.

CHAPTER 7

1. Buell, *Problems of New Cuba*, pp.79, 115, 121; Matthews to Hull, July 28, 1934, 837.00/5314; *New Republic*, 78 (April 4, 1934):199.

2. Great Britain, *Economic Conditions in Cuba*, p.18.

3. Ibid., pp.16–18; U.S. Labor, *Labor in Cuba*, p.2.

4. Buell, *Problems of New Cuba*, p.443.

5. Ibid., p.105; Great Britain, *Economic Conditions in Cuba*, p.18; Oficina Nacional de los Censos Demografico y Electoral, *Censos de población, viviendos y electroal 1953* (Havana, 1953), pp.xxxi, 1; the population in 1899 was 1,572,797; in 1909–2,048,980; in 1919–2,889,004; in 1931–3,962,344; White, "Cuba and Puerto Rico," pp.6, 210–11; Gerardo Canet Alvarez in collaboration with Erwin Raisz, *Atlas de Cuba* (Cambridge, Mass.: Harvard University Press, 1949), p.29.

6. Caffery to Hull, January 17, 1935, 837.00/5932; Matthews to Hull, January 18, 1935, 837.00/5940; Caffery to Hull, February 15, 1935, 837.00/6020; Hebert Herring, "The Cuban Turmoil," *Current History*, 41 (January 1935):472–73; Hubert Herring, "Cuba Drifts Toward Dictatorship," *Current History* 41 (March 1935):729–30; *Miami Herald*, January 2, 1935.

7. Matthews to Hull, January 11, 1935, 837.00/5915; Caffery to Hull, January 16, 1935, 837.00/5946; Caffery to Hull, January 23, 1935, 837.00/5962; Caffery to Hull, February 1, 1935, 837.00/5984; Caffery to Hull, February 8, 1935, 837.00/6005.

8. Caffery to Hull, January 25, 1935, 837.00/5972; Matthews to Hull, January 28, 1935,

837.00/5977; Matthews to Hull, January 30, 1935, 837.00/5983; Caffery to Hull, February 7, 1935, 837.00/6003; Matthews to Hull, February 19, 1935, 837.00/6026; Caffery to Hull, February 20, 1935, 837.00/6032; Caffery to Hull, February 21, 1935, 837.00/6035; Matthews to Hull, February 23, 1935, 837.00/6039; Caffery to Hull, February 25, 1935, 837.00/6048; Caffery to Hull, February 27, 1935, 837.00/6068; Matthews to Hull, February 27, 1935, 837.00/6062; *Miami Herald*, February 25, 1935.

9. Caffery to Hull, February 26, 1935, 837.00/6052.

10. Matthews to Hull, March 1, 1935, 837.00/6079; Matthews to Hull, March 1, 1935, 837.00/6080; Matthews to Hull, March 1, 1935, 837.00/6081; Matthews to Hull, March 1, 1935, 837.00/6085; Matthews to Hull, March 2, 1935, 837.00/6092; *Miami Herald*, March 2, 1935.

11. Matthews to Hull, March 1, 1935, 837.00/6087; Blasier, "The Cuban and Chilean Communist Parties," pp.29–30, 35; *Miami Herald*, March 1, 1935.

12. Caffery to Hull, March 7, 1935, 837.00/6113; Phillips, *Cuba*, pp.165–66; Batista, *Cuba Betrayed*, p.203; Hubert Herring, "Dictatorship in Cuba," *Current History* 42 (April 1935):77–78; *Miami Herald*, March 7 and 8, 1935.

13. Caffery to Hull, March 10, 1935, 837.00/6142.

14. Matthews to Hull, March 4, 1935, 837.00/6103; Caffery to Hull, March 9, 1935, 837.00/6136; Caffery to Hull, March 11, 1935, 837.00/6145; Caffery to Hull, March 12, 1935, 837.00/6155; Caffery to Hull, March 12, 1935, 837.00/6160; MacGaffey and Barnett, *Twentieth Century Cuba*, p.27; *Miami Herald*, March 11, 12, and 13, 1935.

15. Caffery to Hull, March 12, 1935, 837.00/6170; also see Caffery to Hull, March 13, 1935, 837.00/6172.

16. Caffery to Hull, March 13, 1935, 837.00/6162; Caffery to Hull, March 14, 1935, 837.00/6167; Caffery to Hull, March 14, 1935, 837.00/6179; *Miami Herald*, March 14 and 15, 1935.

17. Caffery to Hull, March 15, 1935, 837.00/6191.

18. Caffery to Hull, March 22, 1935, 837.00/6213; Caffery to Hull, March 25, 1935, 837.00/6216; Matthews to Hull, March 28, 1935, 837.00/6221; Caffery to Hull, March 29, 1935, 837.00/6240; Matthews to Hull, May 7, 1935, 837.00/6292; Caffery to Hull, June 11, 1935, 837.00/6355.

19. Ramón Grau San Martín, "The Cuban Terror," *Nation* 140 (April 3, 1935):381–82; *New Republic*, 82 (March 27, 1935):170.

20. Hubert Herring, "Cuba's General Strike," *Current History* 42 (May 1935):192.

21. Hubert Herring, "Cuba Under Army Rule," *Current History* 42 (June 1935):303–4.

22. Matthews to Hull, January 4, 1935, 837.00/5880; Caffery to Hull, May 8, 1935, 837.00/6289; Caffery to Hull, May 8, 1935, 837.00/6290; Chester, *Sergeant Named Batista*, pp.158, 160, 163–64; *Miami Herald*, January 5, 1935, and May 9, 1935; Hubert Herring, "Cuba Plans Elections," *Current History* 42 (July 1935):415.

23. Matthews to Hull, May 9, 1935, 837.00/6295.

24. Phillips, *Cuba*, pp.168–69; *New Republic* 83 (May 29, 1935):59; Matthews to Hull, May 28, 1935, 837.00/6324; Caffery to Hull, May 11, 1936, 837.00/7417.

25. Caffery to Hull, March 8, 1935, 837.00/6124.

26. *Miami Herald*, March 9, 1935.

27. Caffery to Hull, March 21, 1935, 837.00/6207.

28. Caffery to Hull, April 9, 1934, 837.61351/1054; Caffery to Hull, April 29, 1935, 837.00/6280.

29. Ibid.

30. American Chamber of Commerce of Cuba, *Silver Jubilee Review*, p.96 and appendix; U.S. Tariff, *Cuba*, pp.30–31, 56, 74; *Miami Herald*, June 11, 1935.

31. Memorandum on the Reciprocal Trade Agreement, January 25, 1936, 611.3731/1391½.

32. Caffery to Hull, February 20, 1935, 837.61351/988; U.S. Department of State Press Release, August 10, 1935, 837.00/6555; Caffery to Hull, August 24, 1935, 837.00/6520; Hull to Roosevelt, December 19, 1934, O.F. 159—Cuba—1934, FDRL; Statement by José Manuel Casanova to Roosevelt, August 10, 1935, O.F. 159—Cuba, FDRL; Memorandum by Hull, January 28, 1935, Box 57, Folder 199, Hull Papers; Rosenman, *Public Papers*, 4:321–22; "Commission of the Social-Economic Union of Cuba Visits Washington," *Bulletin of the Pan American Union*, 69 (September 1935):667–71; *Miami Herald*, August 22, 1935.

33. Carleton Beals, "The New Crime of Cuba," *New Republic* 82 (July 3, 1935):216–19.

34. Cameron to Hull, July 5, 1935, 337.1121 American Commission/49; Caffery to Hull, July 6, 1935, 837.00/6410; *Miami Herald*, July 3, 1935.

35. Cameron to Hull, July 5, 1935, 337.1121 American Commission/49; Caffery to Hull, July 5, 1935, 337.1121 American Commission/54; *Miami Herald*, July 4, 1935.

36. For a typical complaint see The League of American Writers to Hull, July 3, 1935, 337.1121 American Commission/6.

37. Joseph McGurk, acting chief of the Division of Latin American Affairs to The League of American Writers, July 12, 1935, 337.1121 American Commission/6.

38. Caffery to Hull, July 5, 1935, 337.1121 American Commission/54.

39. Provisional Committee for Cuba to Hull, July 11, 1935, 337.1121 American Commission/61.

40. McGurk to Conrad Komorowski of the Provisional Committee for Cuba, July 18, 1935, 337.1121 American Commission/86.

41. Memorandum by Phillips, August 1, 1935, 337.1121 American Commission/104; Komorowski to Phillips, August 5, 1935, 337.1121 American Commission/103; Cameron to Hull, August 31, 1935, 337.1121 American Commission/107; Memorandum to Duggan, October 17, 1935, 337.1121 American Commission/108½; Nixon, *F.D.R. and Foreign Affairs*, 2:591–92.

42. *New Republic* 83 (July 10, 1935):262.

43. Carleton Beals and Clifford Odets, *Rifle Rule in Cuba* (New York: Provisional Committee for Cuba, 1935), p.6.

44. Ibid., pp.11–32.

45. *Miami Herald*, July 4, 1935.

46. George T. Summerlin in Panama to Hull, August 10, 1935, 837.00/6501; Summerlin to Hull, August 13, 1935, 837.00/6496; Grau San Martín, *La Revolución Cubana Ante América*, pp.25–107; for other declarations by the Auténticos see their bulletins for September 1, 1935, and October 1, 1935, in O.F. 159–A Cuba–1935, FDRL; and December 1, 1935 in 837.00/7082.

47. U.S. Department of State, *Foreign Relations of the United States* (1935), vol. 4, *The American Republics* (1953), p.476–77; Caffery to Hull, March 5, 1935, 837.00/6115; Matthews to Hull, March 5, 1935, 837.00/6117; Caffery to Hull, March 6, 1935, 837.00/6116; Caffery to Hull, March 7, 1935, 837.00/6122; Caffery to Hull, March 7, 1935, 837.00/6123; Caffery to Hull, March 12, 1935, 837.00/6159; Caffery to Hull, June 18, 1935, 837.00/6377; Caffery to Hull, July 6, 1935, 837.00/6410; "New Constitution of Cuba," *Bulletin of the Pan American Union*, 69 (October 1935):796–99; Fitzgibbon and Healey, "Cuban Elections of 1936," pp.726–28; Hubert Herring, "Cuba Regains a Constitution," *Current History* 42 (August 1935):526–28.

48. Matthews to Hull, July 30, 1935, 837.00/6467; Welles to Dr. Eduardo Escasena y Quilez, August 1, 1935, 837.00/6472; Matthews to Hull, August 2, 1935, 837.00/6479; Caffery to Hull, July 13, 1935, 837.00/6437; Carleton Beals, "New Machado in Cuba," *Nation* 141 (August 7, 1935):152–54; Hubert Herring, "The Cuban Kettle Simmers," *Current History*, 43 (October 1935):79–80.

49. Summerlin to Hull, August 10, 1935, 837.00/6501.

50. Caffery to Hull, August 17, 1935, 837.00/6508; Caffery to Hull, September 3, 1935,

837.00/6530; Caffery to Hull, September 28, 1935, 837.00/6574; Caffery to Hull, October 3, 1935, 837.00/6571; Third Secretary of the Embassy Carlos J. Warner to Hull, October 13, 1935, 837.00/6595; Caffery to Hull, October 18, 1935, 837.00/6619; Briggs to Hull, October 21, 1935, 837.00/6615; Briggs to Hull, October 22, 1935, 837.00/6617; Caffery to Hull, November 1, 1935, 837.00/6682; Hubert Herring, "Cuba's Political Parties," *Current History* 43 (December 1935):306; Fitzgibbon and Healey, "Cuban Elections of 1936," pp.728–29; Riera, *Cuba Política*, pp.431–33.

51. Caffery to Hull, September 5, 1935, 837.00/6536; Caffery to Hull, September 10, 1935, 837.00/6539; Briggs to Hull, October 8, 1935, 837.00/6584; Briggs to Hull, October 26, 1935, 837.00/6633; Caffery to Hull, October 29, 1935, 837.00/6643; Briggs to Hull, October 30, 1935, 837.00/6650; Caffery to Hull, October 31, 1935, 837.00/6653; Briggs to Hull, October 31, 1935, 837.00/6654; Matthews to Hull, November 6, 1935, 837.00/6673; Matthews to Hull, November 8, 1935, 837.00/6691; Caffery to Hull, November 8, 1935, 837.00/6712; Matthews to Hull, November 9, 1935, 837.00/6701; Matthews to Hull, November 11, 1935, 837.00/6709; Matthews to Hull, November 12, 1935, 837.00/6716; Caffery to Hull, November 15, 1935, 837.00/6748; Matthews to Hull, November 18, 1935, 837.00/6744; Caffery to Hull, November 18, 1935, 837.00/6745.

52. Caffery to Hull, November 12, 1935, 837.00/6761; Caffery to Hull, November 22, 1935, 837.00/6792; Matthews to Hull, November 21, 1935, 837.00/6671; Matthews to Hull, November 23, 1935, 837.00/6784; Matthews to Hull, November 23, 1935, 837.00/6783.

53. Caffery to Hull, November 26, 1935, 837.00/6797; Matthews to Hull, November 27, 1935, 837.00/6798; Matthews to Hull, November 29, 1935, 837.00/6814; Caffery to Hull, November 29, 1935, 837.00/6827; Matthews to Hull, December 3, 1935, 837.00/6829; Matthews to Hull December 4, 1935, 837.00/6831; Dodds's recommendations to Mendieta, December 6, 1935, 837.00/6843; Matthews to Hull, December 7, 1935, 837.00/6854; *Miami Herald*, November 30,. 1935; Fitzgibbon and Healey, "Cuban Elections of 1936," p.730; Hubert Herring, "Cuban Politics," *Current History* 43 (January 1936):415–16.

54. Matthews to Hull, December 7, 1935, 837.00/6851; Caffery to Hull, December 8, 1935, 837.00/6839; Matthews to Hull, December, 9, 1935, 837.00/6863; Matthews to Hull, December 10, 1935, 837.00/6873; Riera, *Cuba Política*, pp.436–38.

55. Matthews to Hull, December 10, 1935, 837.00/6868; Caffery to Hull, December 10, 1935, 837.00/6857; Matthews to Hull, December 11, 1935, 837.00/6879; Fitzgibbon and Healey, "Cuban Elections of 1936," pp.730–31; Healey, "Impeachment of Gómez," pp.23–24; Chester, *Sergeant Named Batista*, p.165; Phillips, *Cuba*, pp.170–71.

56. Hubert Herring, "The Cuban Presidency," *Current History* 43 (February 1936):526.

57. For interpretation of Mendieta see: Charles Thomson, "The Cuban Revolution: Reform and Reaction," pp.269–76; Wood, *The Making of the Good Neighbor Policy*, p.106; Buell, *Problems of New Cuba*, pp.1, 5, 8; Riera, *Cuba Política*, pp. 422–24; John E. Fagg, *Cuba, Haiti, and The Dominican Republic* (Englewood Cliffs, N.J.: Prentice-Hall, 1965), pp. 82–84; Lester D. Langley, *The Cuban Policy of the United States: A Brief History* (New York: John Wiley and Sons, 1968), pp.160–61.

CHAPTER 8

1. Matthews to Hull, February 25, 1935, 837.00/6056; Matthews to Hull, February 28, 1935, 837.00/6083; Matthews to Hull, December 12, 1935, 837.00/6881; Matthews to Hull, December 12, 1935, 837.00/6884; Matthews to Hull, December 13, 1935, 837.00/6890; Matthews to Hull, December 13, 1935, 837.00/6891; Matthews to Hull, December 14, 1935, 837.00/6897; Barnet to Roosevelt, December 16, 1935, 837.001/Barnet, Jose A./4; *Miami Herald*, December 12, 1935; Riera, *Cuba Política*, pp.424–25; Bustamante, *Enciclopedia Popular Cubana*, Vol. B, pp.187–88; Phillips, *Cuba*, p.171.

2. Matthews to Hull, December 16, 1935, 837.00/6907; Memorandum on Cuban Elections, December 19, 1935, 837.00/6938; Caffery to Hull, December 20, 1935, 837.00/6939; Cuban Revolutionary Party, Bulletin No. 6, January 1, 1936, 837.00/7082; *Miami Herald,* December 12 and 19, 1935.

3. U.S. Department of State Press Release, December 30, 1935, 837.00/6988.

4. Matthews to Hull, January 4, 1936, 837.00/6985; Matthews to Hull, January 9, 1936, 837.00/7014; Caffery to Hull, January 10, 1936, 837.00/7031; *Miami Herald,* January 10 and 11, 1936; Riera, *Cuba Política,* p.440.

5. Matthews to Hull, January 11, 1936, 837.00/7027.

6. Matthews to Hull, January 14, 1936, 837.00/7034; Matthews to Hull, January 14, 1936, 837.00/7037; Caffery to Hull, February 28, 1936, 837.00/7224; *Miami Herald,* January 14 and 16, 1936, and February 27, 1936; Fitzgibbon and Healey, "Cuban Elections of 1936," p.731; Phillips, *Cuba* p.172; Riera, *Cuba Política,* pp.435, 444–46; "Cuba's Eighth Rule in Three Years," *The Literary Digest,* 121 (January 18, 1936);16; "President for Cuba," *Business Week,* no. 333 (January 18, 1936);38.

7. Phillips, *Cuba,* pp.173–74; Healey, "Impeachment of Gómez," pp.20–23; *Miami Herald,* May 20, 1036.

8. *Nation,* 141 (December 25, 1935);727.

9. Duggan to Welles, October 10, 1935, 837.61351/1262; Duggan to Welles, October 11, 1935, 837.61351/1259.

10. Ibid.

11. Duggan to Welles, October 10, 1935, 837.61351/1262; Welles to Duggan, October 12, 1935, 837.61351/1260; Caffery to Hull, November 9, 1935, 837.61351/1298; Matthews to Duggan, December 23, 1935, 837.61351/1327½.

12. *United States* v. *Butler,* 297 U.S. 1; Department of Agriculture, *U.S. Sugar Program,* p.8; Duggan to Matthews, January 10, 1936, 837.61351/1345A.

13. Memorandum on Supreme Court Decision, January 13, 1936, 611.3731/1390; Caffery to Hull, March 17, 1936, 611.3731/1404.

14. Ibid.

15. Memorandum on Possible Supplemental Agreement, May 5, 1936, 611.3731/1426.

16. Matthews to Duggan, January 24, 1936, 837.00/7049.

17. Matthews to Hull, January 20, 1936, 837.61351/1349; Matthews to Hull, January 22, 1936, 837.61351/1355; Chargé Willard Beaulac to Hull, April 11, 1938, 837.61351/1964; Beaulac to Hull, October 31, 1938, 837.61351/2029.

18. Caffery to Hull, April 22, 1936, 837.61351/1471.

19. Duggan to Welles, April 27, 1036, 837.61351/1471; also see Duggan to Welles, May 20, 1936, 837.61351/1495½.

20. Welles to Caffery, June 1, 1936, 837.61351/1471.

21. U.S. Tariff, *Cuba,* pp.13–14; Buell, *Problems of New Cuba,* pp.226–28, 432–39; Wallich, *Monetary Problems,* p.6; MacGaffey and Barnett, *Twentieth Century Cuba,* pp.80–81; Jenks, *Our Cuban Colony,* p.284; IBRD, *Cuba,* pp.72, 336–39, 821–22; U.S. Department of Commerce, *Investment in Cuba: Basic Information for United States Businessmen* (1956) p.10.

22. Great Britain, Department of Overseas Trade, *Report on Economic and Commerical Conditions in Cuba* (1937), pp.1–2; Unión Social Economica de Cuba, *Commercial Relations between Cuba and the United States of America* (Havana, 1936), pp.5–44; U.S. Department of State; *Analysis of Cuban-American Trade during the First Two Years under the Reciprocal Trade Agreement* (1937), pp.1–37; U.S. Department of Commerce, Bureau of Foreign and Domestic Commerce, Division of Foreign Trade Statistics, *Trade of the United States with Cuba* (1938), pp.1–3.

23. Matthews to Hull, March 11, 1936, 837.00/7258; Hull to Governor of California, March 27, 1937, 837.001/Gomez, Miguel M./1; Caffery to Hull, April 17, 1936, 837.00/7370;

Gomez's Program in Washington, April 21–23, 1936, 837.001/Gomez, Miguel M./17; Matthews to Hull, May 19, 1936, 837.00/7432; Healey, "Impeachment of Gómez," pp.24–28; Fitzgibbon and Healey, "Cuban Elections of 1936," pp.733–34.

24. Caffery to Hull, May 20, 1936, 837.001/Gomez, Miguel M./22; Matthews to Hull, May 21, 1936, 837.001/Gomez, Miguel M./24; Matthews to Hull, May 21, 1936, 837.00/6435; Matthews to Hull, May 22, 1936, 837.00/7444; Caffery to Hull, May 25, 1936, 837.00/7449; Matthews to Hull, May 26, 1936, 837.00/7454; *Miami Herald*, May 21, 1936; Healey, "Impeachment of Gómez," pp.29–30; Fitzgibbon and Healey, "Cuban Elections of 1936," p.734; "No. 2's No. 6," *Time* 27 (June 1, 1936,);20.

25. Caffery to Hull, June 12, 1936, 837.00/7504; Caffery to Hull, July 2, 1936, 837.00/7546; Caffery to Hull, July 17, 1936, 837.00/7581; Caffery to Hull, July 24, 1936, 837.00/7590; Caffery to Hull, August 21, 1936, 837.00/7623; Caffery to Hull, September 11, 1936, 837.00/7647; Matthews to Hull, November 13, 1936, 837.00/7730; Caffery to Hull, November 27, 1936, 837.00/7746; Healey, "Impeachment of Gómez," p.30; "Latin America," *Newsweek* 8 (July 18, 1936);23–24.

26. Caffery to Hull, February 27, 1936, 837.00/7212; Matthews to Hull, April 21, 1936, 837.00/7364; Matthews to Hull, May 22, 1936, 837.00/7443; Matthews to Hull, June 22, 1936, 837.00/7519; Matthews to Hull, August 3, 1936, 837.00/7601; "Harried Cuba," *The Literary Digest* 122 (August 22, 1936);12–13; "Clash in Cuba," *The Literary Digest* 122 (October 17, 1936);16.

27. Caffery to Hull, August 28, 1936, 837.00/7631; Healey, "Impeachment of Gómez," pp.39–42; Phillips, *Cuba*, pp.177–78.

28. Matthews to Hull, December 5, 1936, 837.61351/1641; Caffery to Hull, December 11, 1936, 837.00/7756; Memorandum by Division of Latin American Affairs, December 19, 1936, 837.00/7770; Healey, "Impeachment of Gómez," pp.42–49, 120–21.

29. Ibid., 49–56; Caffery to Hull, December 12, 1936, 837.61351/1647.

30. Caffery to Hull, December 14, 1936, 837.61351/1650.

31. Caffery to Hull, December 16, 1936, 837.00/7759.

32. Caffery to Hull, December 17, 1936, 837.00/7760.

33. Caffery to Hull, December 17, 1936, 837.00/7766.

34. Caffery to Hull, December 18, 1936, 837.00/7761.

35. Ibid.; Caffery to Hull, December 18, 1936, 837.00/7763; Caffery to Hull, December 18, 1936, 837.00/7764; Caffery to Hull, December 18, 1936, 837.00/7788; "Crisis in Cuba," *The Literary Digest* 122 (December 26, 1936):14–15.

36. Caffery to Hull, December 18, 1936, 837.00/7763.

37. Caffery to Hull, December 18, 1936, 837.00/7762.

38. Memorandum by the Division of Latin American Affairs, December 19, 1936, 837.00/7817.

39. Moore to Caffery, December 18, 1936, 837.00/7770A; Moore to Caffery, December 19, 1936, 837.00/7770B; Healey, "Impleachment of Gómez," pp.113–14.

40. Patterson to Duggan, December 21, 1936, 837.00/7795.

41. Mecham, *A Survey of United States-Latin American Relations*, p.126; Healey, "Impeachment of Gómez," pp.105–6; Coleman, "The Good Neighbor Policy of F.D.R.," pp.235–80.

42. Memorandum between Roosevelt and Moore and Phone Conversation between Moore and Caffery, December 21, 1936, 837.00/7787.

43. Healey, "Impeachment of Gómez," pp.74–92; *Miami Herald*, December 19, 1936.

44. Caffery to Hull, December 19, 1936, 837.00/7765.

45. Healey, "Impeachment of Gómez," pp.56–74; Caffery to Hull, December 19, 1936, 837.00/7772.

46. Memorandum of conversation between Matthews and Duggan, December 19, 1936, 837.00/7785.

47. Caffery to Hull, December 20, 1936, 837.00/7768; Caffery to Hull, December 20, 1936, 837.00/7769; *Miami Herald*, December 21, 1936.

48. Healey, "Impeachment of Gómez," p.169.

49. Caffery to Hull, December 21, 1936, 837.00/7774; Caffery to Hull, December 21, 1936, 837.00/7780; Caffery to Hull, December 21, 1936, 837.00/7775.

50. Healey, "Impeachment of Gómez," pp.121–26.

51. Caffery to Hull, December 21, 1936, 837.00/7773.

52. Caffery to Hull, December 23, 1936, 837.00/7796; Healey, "Impeachment of Gómez," pp.126–29; *Miami Herald*, December 22, 1936.

53. Healey, "Impeachment of Gómez," p.172.

54. Caffery to Hull, December 22, 1936, 837.00/7777.

55. Caffery to Hull, December 22, 1936, 837.00/7776; Caffery to Hull, December 22, 1936, 837.00/7783; Caffery to Hull, December 22, 1936, 837.00/7789; Caffery to Hull, December 24, 1936, 837.00/7791; *Miami Herald*, December 22, 23, and 24, 1936; Healey, "Impeachment of Gómez," p.96; "Ouster in Cuba," *The Literary Digest* 123 (January 2, 1937):13–14.

56. Matthews to Hull, December 28, 1936, 837.00/7812; Beaulac to Hull, January 10, 1938, 837.00/8218; Copia de documentos relativos a la destitución del Presidente de la Republica de Cuba, Dr. Miguel Mariano Gómez, May 4, 1939, 837.001/Gomez, Miguel M./24½; Duggan to Welles, January 4, 1937, 710.Peace/907–26/27; Adam y Silva, *La gran mentira*, pp.443–46; Phillips, *Cuba*, p.179; Healey, "Impeachment of Gómez," pp.109–12, 114–16.

57. *St. Louis Post-Dispatch*, December 19, 23, and 26, 1936.

58. *Baltimore Sun*, December 21 and 27, 1936; *Miami Herald*, December 23, 1936; "Cuba: Batista Puts Non-Smoker in Position of Domino Player," *Newsweek* 9 (January 2, 1937):12.

59. Lazo, *Dagger in the Heart*, p.54.

60. Riera, *Cuba Política*, pp.441–44; Healey, "Impeachment of Gómez," preface, pp.1–3, 130–33, 163; for a briefer account of Gómez's impeachment see Wood, *The Making of the Good Neighbor Policy*, pp.113–15.

61. Matthews to Hull, March 9, 1937, 123 C 11/507; Hull to Caffery, July 13, 1937, 123 C 11/535.

62. A Letter from Paul Vanorden Shaw to Roosevelt, January 9, 1935, 123 C 11/452.

63. *New York Post*, May 16, 1936.

64. For examples see Letter from Thomas E. Reedy to Duncan U. Fletcher, Senator from Florida, March 29, 1935, 837.00/6228; Letter from International Committee for Political Prisoners to Hull, June 18, 1935, 837.00/6407; Fernando Ortiz to Hull, November 28, 1935, 711.37/250; Letter from publisher of the *New York Post*, J. David Stern, to Marvin H. McIntyre, July 3, 1935, O.F. 159–A Cuba–1935, FDRL; Letter from the Hollywood Chapter of the American League Against War and Fascism to Roosevelt, May 20, 1936, O.F. 884 Jefferson Caffery, FDRL.

65. Letter from Sidney M. Sternback to Roosevelt, May 2, 1936, O.F. 884 Jefferson Caffery, FDRL.

66. Lazo, *Dagger in the Heart*, p.56.

67. Nixon, *F.D.R. and Foreign Affairs*, 2:592; Letter from Hull to Daniel W. Hoan, Mayor of Milwaukee, October 26, 1935, 837.00/6635.

68. Hull, *Memoirs*, 1:341.

69. Hubert Herring, "Cuba Under a New President," *Current History* 43 (March 1936);636–37.

70. Nixon, *F.D.R. and Foreign Affairs*, 2:435–37, and Roosevelt's reply, 2:450.

71. Ibid., 3:327–28.

72. Rosenman, *Public Papers*, 5:286.

73. Leuchtenburg, *F.D.R. and the New Deal*, pp.207–10, 221; Gardner, *Economic Aspects of New Deal Diplomacy*, pp.61–63; Whitehead, "The Making of Foreign Policy during Roosevelt's First Term," 227–28, 242–46.

CHAPTER 9

1. Caffery to Hull, December 24, 1936, 837.00/7797; Memorandum of a Conversation between Matthews and Duggan, December 24, 1936, 837.001/Laredo Bru, Federico/2; Caffery to Hull, December 24, 1936, 837.00/7798; Caffery to Hull, December 28, 1936, 837.00/7800; Caffery to Hull, December 28, 1936, 837.00/7804; Matthews to Hull, December 29, 1936, 837.00/7809; Caffery to Hull, December 31, 1936, 837.00/7815; *Miami Herald*, December 25, 1936.

2. Healey, "Impeachment of Gómez," pp.96–101; Phillips, *Cuba*, pp.181–82; Riera, *Cuba Política*, p.489; Guerra y Sánchez, *Historia de la Nación Cubana*, pp.85–87.

3. Chester, *Sergeant Named Batista*, p.167; Caffery to Hull, January 8, 1937, 837.00/7826; Matthews to Hull, January 15, 1937, 837.00/7828; Matthews to Hull, January 15, 1937, 837.00/7833; Matthews to Hull, January 23, 1937, 837.00/7836; Matthews to Hull, March 10, 1937, 837.00/7878; Matthews to Hull, April 2, 1937, 837.00/7929.

4. Matthews to Hull, March 25, 1937, 837.00/7897.

5. Caffery to Hull, March 5, 1937, 837.00/7875; Matthews to Hull, March 19, 1937, 837.00/7893; Matthews to Duggan, March 22, 1937, 837.61351/1767½; Matthews to Hull, March 25, 1937, 837.00/7897; Matthews to Hull, March 25, 1937, 837.00/7904; Matthews to Hull, April 9, 1937, 837.00/7945; Matthews to Hull, May 18, 1937, 837.00/8018; Memorandum on the Cuban Sugar Situation, November 5, 1937, 611.3731/1607; Department of Agriculture, *U.S. Sugar Program*, pp.8–9.

6. U.S. Department of Agriculture, Minneman, P.G., *The Agriculture of ·Cuba* (1943), p.42; IBRD, *Cuba*, pp.812–14; U.S. Tariff Commission, *Economic Controls and Commercial Policy in Cuba* (1946), p.5; Cuba, Economica y Financiera, *Anuario Azucarero de Cuba 1941* (Havana: Editora Mercantil Cubana, 1941), p.113; Guerra y Sánchez, *Sugar and Society*, pp.171–92.

7. Matthews to Hull, March 30, 1937, 837.00/7895½; Matthews to Hull, April 1, 1937, 837.00/7915; Matthews to Hull, May 18, 1937, 837.00/8018; Matthews to Hull, May 21, 1937, 837.00/8024; Matthews to Hull, May 28, 1937, 837.00/8035; Matthews to Duggan, June 23, 1937, 837.00/8055½.

8. Matthews to Hull, June 21, 1937, 837.00/8055; Matthews to Hull, July 1, 1937, 837.00/8070; Matthews to Hull, July 30, 1937, 837.00/8018; Raymond Buell to Duggan, August 9, 1937, 837.00/8131; *Cuba's Three Year Plan* (Havana: Cultural, S.A., 1938); U.S. Tariff, *Cuba*, p.12; Healey, "Impeachment of Gómez," pp.141–43; Phillips, *Cuba*, pp.183–84; Juan Clemente Zamora y López, *The New Deal* (Havana: "El Score" Herederos de F. Rodriguez, 1937), pp.22–23; Quentin Reynolds, "Astonished Dictator," *Collier's* 99 (June 19, 1937):12, 76–78; *New Republic* 42 (August 11, 1937):2; "Cuba: Spring Fever," *Time* 29 (April 26, 1937):21–23; Rosenman, *Public Papers*, 6:157–60.

9. Matthews to Duggan, July 8, 1937, 837.00/8081½; Matthews to Duggan, August 13, 1937, 837.00/8132.

10. Matthews to Hull, June 28, 1937, 837.00/8063.

11. Matthews to Hull, July 16, 1937, 837.00/8087; Beaulac to Hull, April 11, 1937, 837.61351/1964; Memorandum of a conversation between Welles and Pedro Martínez Fraga, May 5, 1938, 837.00/8273; Second Secretary of the Embassy Edward P. Lawton to Hull, May 7, 1938, 837.00/8258; *Caribbean Land Tenure Symposium* (Washington, D.C.: Caribbean Research Council, 1946), pp.7–8, 263–65; Ramiro Guerra y Sánchez, "Sugar:

Index of Cuban-American Cooperation," *Foreign Affairs* 20 (July 1942):749–53; Great Britain, *Report on Economic and Commercial Conditions in Cuba*, pp.14–16; Phillips, *Cuba*, pp.186–87; Lazo, *Dagger in the Heart*, p.85.

12. Matthews to Duggan, July 24, 1937, 837.00/8086½.

13. Matthews to Hull, August 3, 1937, 837.61351/1857½.

14. Beaulac to Hull, September 23, 1937, 837.00/8157½.

15. Matthews to Hull, July 26, 1937, 837.00/8095.

16. Matthews to Hull, August 16, 1937, 123 B 384/179; U.S. Department of State, *Biographic Register* (October 1, 1945), pp. 17–18; Willard Beaulac, *Career Ambassador* (New York: Macmillan Co., 1951):1–147; interview with Willard Beaulac, December 18, 1968.

17. Beaulac, *Career Ambassador*, pp.147–48.

18. Hull to Roosevelt, June 28, 1937, 123 C 11/447; Hull to Wright, July 13, 1937, 123 W 931/438; Matthews to Hull, August 17, 1937, 123 W 931/447; Biography of J. Butler Wright, O.F. 895 J. Butler Wright, FDRL; Phillip Bonsal to William Culbertson, July 19, 1938, Box 17, Willaim Culbertson Papers, Library of Congress, Manuscript Division, Washington, D.C.; for a highly critical view see: Hull to Senator Kenneth D. McKellar, March 20, 1937, Box 40, Folder 98, Hull Papers.

19. Wright to Hull, August 23, 1937, 123 W 931/449; Wright to Hull, September 15, 1937, 123 W 931/451; Wright to Hull, September 27, 1937, 837.011/295; Welles to Wright, October 16, 1937, 837.011/295; Wright to Hull, November 6, 1937, 837.00/8194; Social-Economic Union of Cuba, *A Frontierless Fourth of July* (Havana, 1938):75–80.

20. Lazo, *Dagger in the Heart*, pp.56–57.

21. Wright to Hull, January 15, 1938, 837.00/8226.

22. Beaulac to Hull, March 26, 1938, 837.00/8245; Beaulac to Hull, September 22, 1938, 837.00/8318; Beaulac to Hull, April 8, 1938, 837.61351/1956.

23. Beaulac to Hull, April 14, 1938, 837.00/8250; Lawton to Hull, May 14, 1938, 837.00/8259; Wright to Hull, May 27, 1938, 837.00/8264; Wright to Hull, June 13, 1938, 837.00/8271; Beaulac to Hull, July 23, 1938, 837.00/8283; Beaulac to Hull, September 22, 1938, 837.00/8318.

24. Fitzgibbon, *Cuba and U.S.*, pp.228–49; Mecham, *A Survey of United States-Latin American Relations*, pp.122–23.

25. U.S. Department of State, *Foreign Relations of the United States* (1938), vol. 5, *The American Republics* (1956), pp.475–79; Lawton to Hull, February 11, 1938, 837.00/8231; Beaulac to Hull, February 18, 1938, 837.00/8232; Beaulac to Hull, March 19, 1938, 837.00/8243; Beaulac to Hull, September 22, 1938, 837.00/8318; Foreign Bondholders Protective Council, Inc., *Annual Reports*, 1936 (New York: Foreign Bondholders Protective Council, Inc., 1937), p.310; *Annual Reports*, 1937, pp.262–63; *Annual Reports*, 1938, p.337; "Message of the President of Cuba," *Bulletin of the Pan American Union* 72 (August 1938):483–86.

26. *Foreign Relations* (1938) 5:479–80.

27. Ibid., p.480.

28. Ibid., pp.481–90; U.S. Department of State, *Foreign Relations of the United States* (1939), vol. 5, *The American Republics* (1957), pp.522–24; Welles to Wright, June 23, 1939, 611.3731/2087; for an assessment of Cuba's financial situation in 1939 see Roswell Magill and Carl Shoup, *The Cuban Fiscal System 1939* (New York, 1939).

29. Beaulac to Hull, October 26, 1938, 837.00/8344; Beaulac to Hull, October 29, 1938, 837.00/8345; Wright to Hull, November 2, 1938, 837.00/8348; Beaulac to Hull, November 5, 1938, 837.00/8349; Chester, *Sergeant Named Batista*, p.173.

30. Memorandum by Duggan, November 9, 1938, 711.37/289.

31. Second Secretary of the Embassy Sidney E. O'Donoghue to Hull, November 26, 1938, 837.00/8355; Chester, *Sergeant Named Batista*, pp.173–74; Phillips,*Cuba*, pp.187–88; Lazo, *Dagger in the Heart*, p.57; Arthur Pincus, "Cuba's Puppet Democracy," *Nation* 147

(December 17, 1938):658–60; "Strong-Man Tourist," *Newsweek* 12 (November 21, 1938):15–16.

32. Wright to Welles, December 29, 1938, 711.37/299CF.

33. Welles to Wright, January 4, 1939, 711.37/299CF.

34. Lawton to Hull, January 10, 1039, 837.00/8375; Wright to Hull, December 10, 1938, 837.00/8361; Lawton to Hull, December 13, 1938, 837.00/8363.

35. Lawton to Hull, January 6, 1939, 837.00/8372; Lawton to Hull, January 7, 1939, 837.00/8373; Beaulac to Hull, April 22, 1939, 837.00/8433; Wright to Hull, June 1, 1939, 837.00/8474; Wright to Hull, June 19, 1939, 837.00/8490.

36. J. P. McEvoy, "Not All Rum and Rumba," *The Saturday Evening Post* 211 (May 20, 1939):82.

37. Memorandum by Welles, July 29, 1939, 711.37/306; also see Memorandum of conversation between Welles and Martínez Fraga, July 31, 1939, 711.37/307.

38. IBRD, *Cuba*, pp.762, 766–67, 769; American Chamber of Commerce of Cuba, *Silver Jubilee*, Appendix; Minneman, *Agriculture of Cuba*, p.3; U.S. Department of Agriculture, Bureau of Agricultural Economics, *Sugar During World War and in the 1939 European War* (1940), pp.2–4; Beaulac to Hull, September 2, 1939, 837.61351/2169; Beaulac to Hull, September 9, 1939, 837.00/8534; Beaulac to Hull, September 11, 1939, 837.00/8535.

39. Memorandum from Philip Bonsal to Briggs and Duggan, September 11, 1939, 837.61351/2177; Hull to Wright, September 11, 1939, 837.51/2469A; Memorandum by Briggs, September 12, 1939, 837.61351/2178; Wright to Hull, September 13, 1939, 837.61351/2178; Wright to Hull, September 13, 1939, 837.61351/2173; Department of Agriculture, *Sugar During World War II*, pp.4, 10.

40. Beaulac to Hull, September 16, 1939, 837.00/8536; Wright to Hull, September 23, 1939, 837.00/8543.

41. William L. Langer and S. Everett Gleason, *The Challenge to Isolation 1937–1940* (New York: Harper and Brothers, 1952), pp.50–51, 129–36, 206–18; Mecham, *A Survey of United States-Latin American Relations*, pp.133–34; Wright to Hull, September 19, 1939, 740.00111 A.R./324; Lawton to Hull, September 30, 1939, 837.00/8547; Beaulac to Hull, October 14, 1939, 837.00/8555; Beaulac to Hull, October 21, 1939, 837.00/8561.

42. *Foreign Relations* (1938) 5:472–74; Bonsal to Hull, June 28, 1939, 611.3731/2109; Memorandum by Wright and Beaulac, October 13, 1939, 611.3731/2226; U.S. Department of State, *Biographic Register* (October 1, 1945), pp.29–30; Memorandum from Bonsal to Duggan, October 13, 1939, 611.6135/569; Memorandum on the Supplemental Trade Agreement, December 13, 1939, 611.3731/2238½; U.S. Department of State Press Release, December 18, 1939, 611.3731/2216; U.S. Tariff, *Cuba*, pp.28–29; Department of Agriculture, *Sugar During World War II*, p.15; for different positions on the agreement see U.S. Department of State Press Release, December 18, 1939, 711.37/320; James S. Carson, *Cuba–Gateway to Latin America* (New York, 1939), pp.1–3; The American Chamber of Commerce of Cuba, *Protect Your Trade with Cuba*, pp.15–18; Asociación de Colonos de Cuba, *Cuba's Tragedy* (Havana: Molina y Cia, 1940), pp.3–10; Asociación Nacional de Hacendados de Cuba, *El Trado de Reciprocidad de 1934* (Havana: Asociación Nacional de Hacendados de Cuba, 1939), pp.3–78; Ramon Conroy to Senator Key Pittman, January 8, 1940, Sen 76A–F9, Committee on Foreign Relations, Cuba, Record Group 46, National Archives, Washington, D.C.; Pedro Martínez Fraga, *Speech Delivered at the Opening of the Cuban Pavillon, New York World's Fair, on May 20, 1939* (Washington, D.C., 1939), pp.9–13.

43. Second Secretary of the Embassy Ralph Miller to Hull, October 28, 1939, 837.00/8567; Beaulac to Hull, Novmeber 13, 1939, 837.00/8581; Beaulac to Hull, November 14, 1939, 837.00/8583; Beaulac to Hull, Novmeber 16, 1939, 837.00/8585; Wright to Hull, November 16, 1939, 837.00/8585; Wright to Hull, November 16, 1939, 837.00/8584; Riera, *Cuba Política*, pp.475–82; Batista, *Cuba Betrayed*, p.206; Chester, *Sergeant Named Batista*,

p.175; Martínez Fraga, *Speech*, pp.5–7; "Batista Backfire," *Time* 34 (December 4, 1939):30, 32.

44. Beaulac to Hull, March 6, 1940, 837.00/8696; Lawton to Hull, December 14, 1938, 837.00/8365, Riera, *Cuba Política*, pp.473–74.

45. Alexander, *Communism in Latin America*, pp.19, 23, 69–70, 278–79; Blasier, "The Cuban and Chilean Communist Parties," iii–iv, 1–2, 8, 32, 50–52, 54; Krauss, "Communist Policy in Cuba," pp.7–11; Lawton to Hull, January 23, 1939, 837.00/8382; Beaulac to Hull, April 19, 1939, 837.00/8430; Wright to Hull, November 10, 1939, 837.00/1939.

46. Matthews to Hull, February 18, 1937, 837.00/7857; Matthews to Hull, February 27, 1937, 837.00/7866; Matthews to Duggan, August 4, 1937, 837.00/8119½; Wright to Hull, May 5, 1938, 837.00/8257; Beaulac to Hull, August 16, 1939, 837.00/8524; Wright to Hull, September 5, 1939, 837.00/8532; Beaulac to Hull, October 26, 1939, 837.00/8566; Beaulac to Hull, November 24, 1939, 837.00/8599; Beaulac to Hull, December 2, 1939, 837.00/8594; Beaulac to Hull, December 4, 1939, 837.00/8597; Beaulac to Hull, December 11, 1939, 837.00/8599; Beaulac to Hull, December 15, 1939, 837.00/8608; Beaulac to Hull, January 6, 1940, 837.00/8622; Phillips, *Cuba*, pp.195–96; Blasier, "The Cuban and Chilean Communist Parties," p.57; Batista, *Cuba Betrayed*, p.328.

47. Beaulac to Hull, December 4, 1939, 123 W 931/500.

CHAPTER 10

1. Beaulac to Hull, December 12, 1939, 837.00/8600; Beaulac to Hull, December 12, 1939, 837.00/8601; Beaulac to Hull, December 13, 1939, 837.00/8602.

2. Beaulac to Hull, December 27, 1939, 837.00/8613; Beaulac to Hull, December 28, 1939, 837.00/8614; Beaulac to Hull, January 2, 1940, 837.00/8616; Beaulac to Hull, January 4, 1940, 837.00/8618; Beaulac to Hull, January 5, 1940, 837.00/8619; Beaulac to Hull, January 13, 1940, 837.00/8639; Ambassador George Messersmith to Hull, March 16, 1940, 837.00/8706; Messersmith to Hull, April 5, 1940, 837.00/8743; Messersmith to Hull, May 22, 1940, 837.00/8775; Riera, *Cuba Política*, pp.483–88.

3. Beaulac to Hull, February 6, 1940, 837.00/8665; Lawton to Hull, February 6, 1940, 837.00/8666; Messersmith to Hull, March 27, 1940, 837.00/8728; Messersmith to Hull, April 6, 1940, 837.00/8742; Beaulac to Hull, May 15, 1940, 837.00/8768; Beaulac to Hull, May 18, 1940, 837.00/8771.

4. Beaulac to Hull, February 8, 1940, 837.00/8667.

5. U.S. Department of State, *Foreign Relations of the United States* (1940), vol. 5, *The American Republics* (1961), pp.738–40.

6. Ibid., 741–42.

7. Hull to Senator Key Pittman, January 4, 1940, 123 M 561/538; Roosevelt to Laredo Bru, January 12, 1940, 123 M 561/543; Beaulac to Hull, January 12, 1940, 837.00/8637; Beaulac to Hull, March 2, 1940, 837.00/8686; Messersmith to Hull, March 8, 1940, 123 M 561/547; Biography of George Messersmith, O.F. 896 George Messersmith, FDRL; Max Freedman, *Roosevelt and Frankfurter: Their Correspondence 1928–1945* (Boston: Little, Brown and Co., 1967), p.209; George F. Kennan, *Memoirs (1925–1950)* (New York: Bantam Books, 1969), p.68–69.

8. Beaulac, *Career Ambassador*, pp.147–50; Interview with Willard Beaulac, December 18, 1968.

9. Beaulac to Hull, March 11, 1940, 837.00/8697; Messersmith to Hull, March 14, 1940, 837.00/8699; Messersmith to Hull, March 15, 1940, 837.00/8702; Messersmith to Hull, March 16, 1940, 837.00/8707; Messersmith to Hull, March 18, 1940, 837.00/8711;

Messersmith to Hull, March 21, 1940, 837.00/8724; Messersmith to Hull, March 26, 1940, 837.00/8733; Messersmith to Hull, March 27, 1940, 837.00/8730; Messersmith to Hull, April 1, 1940, 837.00/8739.

10. Messersmith to Hull, March 19, 1940, 837.00/8714; Messersmith to Hull, April 25, 1940, 837.00/8755; Messersmith to Hull, April 26, 1940, 837.00/8756; Messersmith to Hull, June 12, 1940, 837.00/8785; Phillips, *Cuba*, p.198.

11. Messersmith to Hull, March 26, 1940, Hull Papers, Box 46, Folder 128.

12. Briggs to Hull, January 19, 1944, 837.00/9542; Beaulac to Hull, January 5, 1940, 837.00/8621; Beaulac to Hull, February 10, 1940, 837.011/339; Beaulac to Hull, February 10, 1940, 837.00/8669.

13. Beaulac to Hull, February 10, 1940, 837.011/340.

14. Beaulac to Hull, February 17, 1940, 837.00/8677; Beaulac to Hull, February 23, 1940, 837.00/8681; Alexander, *Communism in Latin America*, p.281.

15. Messersmith to Hull, April 3, 1940, 837.011/359.

16. *Foreign Relations* (1940) 5:763–70; Messersmith to Hull, April 3, 1940, 837.011/359; Messersmith to Hull, April 11, 1940, 837.011/366; Messersmith to Hull, April 12, 1940, 837.00/8750; Messersmith to Hull, May 2, 1940, 837.011/378; Messersmith to Hull, June 26, 1940, 837.011/443; Interview with Willard Beaulac, December 18, 1968.

17. Messersmith to Hull, June 26, 1940, 837.011/443; Messersmith to Hull, July 6, 1940, 837.00/8801; *Cuban Constitution of 1940*, pp.1–52; Jose Manuel Cortina y Corrales, *El regimen de la nacionalidad en la Constitución Cubana de 1940* (Havana: Editorial Carasa, 1941), pp. 5–43; "Cuba's Constitution," *Business Week*, no. 580 (October 12, 1940); 63–64; Bosch, *Cuba*, pp. 140–41; Ruiz, *Cuba*, pp. 102–5; Lazo, *Dagger in the Heart*, pp. 58–61; MacGaffey and Barnett, *Twentieth Century Cuba*, pp.128–34; Williams, *U.S., Cuba, and Castro*, pp.56–58; Gustavo y Sanchez, Gutierrez, *El desarrollo económico de Cuba* (Havana: Junta Nacional de Economía), p.5.

18. Messersmith to Welles, July 12, 1940, 711.37/342; Messersmith to Felix Franfurter. May 31, 1940, Box 83, Felix Frankfurter Papers, Library of Congress, Manuscript Division, Washington, D.C.; Messersmith to Leland Harrison, May 31, 1940, Box 29, Leland Harrison Papers, Library of Congress, Manuscript Division, Washington, D.C.

19. Messersmith to Welles, July 12, 1940, 711.37/342.

20. Ibid.

21. Beaulac to Hull, January 17, 1940, 837.00/8644; Messersmith to Hull, June 21, 1940, 837.00/8788.

22. Messersmith to Welles, July 12, 1940, 711.37/342.

23. Messersmith to Hull, June 21, 1940, 837.00/8788.

24. Messersmith to Welles, July 12, 1940, 711.37/342.

25. Messersmith to Hull, June 27, 1940, 837.00/8794; Messersmith to Welles, July 12, 1940, 711.37/342.

26. Messersmith to Hull, July 3, 1940, 837.00/8800.

27. Messersmith to Hull, July 9, 1940, 837.00/8802.

28. Messersmith to Hull, July 11, 1940, 837.00/8803; Messersmith to Hull, July 13, 1940, 837.00/8807.

29. Messersmith to Hull, July 15, 1940, 837.00/8806; Messersmith to Hull, July 16, 1940, 837.00/8808; Messersmith to Hull, July 31, 1941,. 837.00/9010; Memorandum by Bonsal, August 2, 1940, 837.00 Elections/142; Riera, *Cuba Política*, pp.491–512; Lazo, *Dagger in the Heart*, p.61; Phillips, *Cuba*, p.199; Blasier, "The Cuban and Chilean Communist Parties," p. 57; Batista, *Cuba Betrayed*, p.206; Batista, *The Growth and Decline*, p.17; Chester, *Sergeant Named Batista*, p.179.

30. Messersmith to Hull, August 3, 1940, 837.00/8812; Langer and Gleason, *Challenge to Isolation*, pp.607–37, 688–702; Mecham, *A Survey of United States-Latin American*

Relations, pp.134–35; Phillips, *Cuba*, pp.199–201; Alton Frye, *Nazi Germany and the American Hemisphere, 1933–1944* (New Haven: Yale University Press, 1967), p.130.

31. *Foreign Relations* (1940) 5:743–49; Beaulac to Hull, February 23, 1940, 837.00/8681.

32. Messersmith to Hull, March 26, 1940, Hull Papers, Box 46, Folder 146.

33. *Foreign Relations* (1940) 5:750–62; Messersmith to Hull, June 28, 1940, 711.37/336; Messersmith to Hull, June 29, 1940, 837.00/8795; Foreign Bondholders Protective Council, *Reports for Years 1941 Through 1944*, pp.xvi, 355; George Messersmith Memoirs, Box IX, Vol. II, No. 1, Road Debt Settlement, MS M584g, George Messersmith Papers, University of Delaware Library, Special Collections Division, Newark, Delaware.

34. Messersmith to Hull, October 3, 1940, Hull Papers, Box 48, Folder 139.

35. Messersmith to Hull, August 5, 1940, 837.00/8813; Beaulac to Hull, September 24, 1940, 837.00/8847; Beaulac to Hull, September 26, 1940, 837.00/8849; Messersmith to Hull, October 8, 1940, 837.00/8661.

36. Messersmith to Welles, October 8, 1940, 837.00/8860½.

37. Messersmith to Hull, October 10, 1940, 837.00/8862; Messersmith to Hull, October 11, 1940, 837.001/Batista, Fulgencio/15; Riera, *Cuba Política*, pp.489–91; Phillips, *Cuba*, p.205; *Nation* 151 (October 19, 1940); 151; "President Batista," *Time* 36 (October 21, 1940): 40.

38. Messersmith to Hull, August 15, 1940, 837.00/8822; Messersmith to Hull, October 16, 1940, 837.00/8871; Messersmith to Hull, October 19, 1940, 837.00/8878; Messersmith to Hull, October 29, 1940, 837.00/8881; Messersmith Memoirs, Box IX, Vol. II, No. 3, Havana–Graft, MS M584g; Phillips, *Cuba*, p.206.

39. Messersmith to Hull, October 19, 1940, Hull Papers, Box 48, Folder 139.

40. Messersmith to Hull, January 29, 1941, 837.00/8927.

41. Messersmith to Hull, November 13, 1940, 837.00/8887; Messersmith to Hull, November 20, 1940, 837.00/8893; Messersmith to Hull, December 19, 1940, 837.00/8911; Messersmith to Hull, December 28, 1940, 837.00/8912.

42. Messersmith to Hull, December 21, 1940, 837.00/8910.

43. Beaulac to Hull, March 9, 1940, 837.00/8694; Messersmith to Hull, March 16, 1940, 837.00/8706; Messersmith to Hull, June 28, 1940, 837.00/8799; Messersmith to Hull, August 24, 1940, 837.00/8825; Messersmith to Hull, October 1, 1940, 837.00/8855; Messersmith to Hull, October 5, 1940, 837.00/8858; Messersmith to Hull, December 11, 1940, 837.00/8907; Jaime Suchlicki, *University Students and Revolution in Cuba, 1920–1968* (Coral Gables, Fla: University of Miami Press, 1969), pp.47–48.

44. Lawton to Hull, February 17, 1940, 837.00/8678; Messersmith to Hull, May 4, 1940, 837.00/8764; Messersmith to Hull, June 11, 1940, 837.00/8784; Messersmith to Hull, June 26, 1940, 837.00/8792; Messersmith to Welles, January 31, 1941, 837.61351/2419; Messersmith to Hull, March 20, 1941, 837.00/8954; Beaulac to Hull, April 26, 1941, 837.00/8969; Blasier, "The Cuban and Chilean Communist Parties," pp.56–58; Alexander, *Communism in Latin America*, p.282; Phillips, *Cuba*, pp.206–7.

45. Beaulac to Hull, April 29, 1941, 837.00B/330CF.

46. Beaulac to Hull, May 3, 1941, 837.00/8977; Second Secretary of the Embassy Ralph Miller to Hull, August 2, 1941, 837.00/9009; Briggs to Hull, September 16, 1941, 837.00/9035; Messersmith to Welles, October 21, 1941, 837.00/9049; for Welles's reply see Welles to Messersmith, October 28, 1941, 837.00/9050; Blasier, "The Cuban and Chilean Communist Parties," pp.2–3, 48–49, 53; Alexander, *Communism in Latin America*, pp. 25, 39; Salvador Diaz Verson, *El Nazismo en Cuba* (Havana: Obrapia, 1944), pp.18–24.

47. Beaulac to Hull, January 31, 1940, 837.00/8661; Messersmith to Hull, February 3, 1941, 837.00/8939; Messersmith to Hull, February 5, 1941, 837.00/8931.

48. Messersmith to Welles, February 1, 1941, 837.00/8928; Messersmith to Hull, February 3, 1941, 837.00/8939.

49. Messersmith Memoirs, Box IX, Vol. II, No. 5, Havana–Abortive Revolution, MS M584g.

50. Phillips, *Cuba,* p.208; Chester, *Sergeant Named Batista,* p.190; Lazo, *Dagger in the Heart,* pp.61–62; Batista, *Cuba Betrayed,* pp.207–8, 212; John Gunther, "Batista: The Stenographer Who Became Dictator," *Reader's Digest,* 39 (August 1941):61–65; "Genteel Revolution," *Time,* 137 (February 17, 1941):28; "Strong Man Act," *Newsweek,* 17 (February 17, 1941):34–35.

51. Messersmith to Hull, February 3, 1941, 837.00/8939.

52. Messersmith to Hull, February 4, 1941, 837.00 Revolutions/477; Messersmith to Welles, February 6, 1941, 837.00/8981; Messersmith to Hull, February 8, 1941, 837.00/8930; Briggs to Hull, May 5, 1942, 837.00/9114; Messersmith to Hull, March 1, 1941, Hull Papers, Box 49, Folder 144; Chester, *Sergeant Named Batista,* p.191.

53. Messersmith Memoirs, Box IX, Vol. II, No. 5, Havana–Abortive Revolution, MS M584g; Messersmith to Breckinridge Long, February 26, 1941, Box 138, Breckinridge Long Papers, Library of Congress, Manuscript Division, Washington, D.C.

54. Messersmith to Hull, February 7, 1941, 837.00/8933.

55. *Nation,* 152 (February 15, 1941):171.

56. "Batista of Cuba," *New Republic* 104 (February 17, 1941):197.

57. Gunther, "Batista," p.65.

58. *Foreign Relations* (1940) 5:772–77; Messersmith to Welles, July 12, 1940, 711.37/342.

59. *Foreign Relations* (1940) 5:778–84; Beaulac to Hull, September 14, 1940, 837.00/8841; Beaulac to Hull, September 21, 1940, 837.00/8844; Messersmith to Hull, October 19, 1940, 837.00/8873.

60. Messersmith to Hull, November 9, 1940, Hull Papers, Box 48, Folder 140.

61. Messersmith to Hull, November 30, 1940, 837.00/8897; Messersmith to Hull, December 11, 1940, 837.00/8905; Messersmith to Hull, December 14, 1940, 837.00/8908; Memorandum of a Conversation by Hull, December 17, 1940, Hull Papers, Box 57, Folder 199; *Foreign Relations* (1940) 5:784–91; U.S. Department of State, *Foreign Relations of the United States* (1941), vol. 7, *The American Republics* (1962), pp.127–28.

62. Ibid., pp.128–33.

63. Ibid., p.131.

64. Ibid., pp.133–89; U.S. Department of State, *Foreign Relations of the United States* (1942), vol. 6, *The American Republics* (1963), pp.290–95; Messersmith to Hull, May 10, 1941, 837.00/8980; Messersmith to Hull, August 8, 1941, 837.00/9022; Messersmith to Hull, November 22, 1941, 837.00/9057; Messersmith to Hull, November 29, 1941, 837.00/9060; Briggs to Hull, April 11, 1942, 837.00/9109.

65. Mecham, *A Survey of United States-Latin American Relations,* p.143.

66. *Foreign Relations* (1941), 7:136–41, 227–3); Messersmith to Hull, January 31, 1941, 837.61351/2419; Messersmith to Hull, February 1, 1941, 837.00/8926; Messersmith to Hull, March 22, 1941, 837.00/8953; Messersmith to Hull, March 1, 1941, Hull Papers Box 49, Folder 144; Percy W. Bidwell, *Economic Defense of Latin American* (Boston: World Peace Foundation, 1941), pp.14, 22; Phillips, *Cuba,* pp.193, 207; interview with Dr. Arturo M. Mañas, December 22, 1969.

67. Messersmith to Roosevelt, April 19, 1941, O.F. 896 George Messersmith, FDRL.

68. *Foreign Relations* (1941) 7:197–227; Messersmith to Hull, May 21, 1941, 611.3731/2327; Messersmith to Welles, June 11, 1941, 611.3731/2328; U.S. Department of State Press Release, July 26, 1941, 611.3731/2345; Memorandum by Bonsal, September 22, 1941, 611.3731/2436; Briggs to Hull, October 2, 1941, 611.3731/2430; Messersmith to Welles, December 11, 1941, 611.3731/2607; Briggs to Hull, December 27, 1941, 837.00/9071; for the problems concerning the United States sugar legislation see Messersmith to Hull, March 15, 1940, 837.00/8720; Messersmith to Hull, June 7, 1941, 837.00/8992; Messersmith to Hull, June 21, 1941, 837.00/8994; Assistant Secretary Francis B. Sayre to

Senator Joseph O'Mahoney, August 2, 1939, Hull Papers, Box 45, Folder 119; Messersmith to Hull, March 26, 1940, Hull Papers, Box 46, Folder 146; Messersmith to Hull, April 10, 1940, Hull Papers, Box 46, Folder 129; Messersmith to Hull, June 5, 1941, Hull Papers, Box 49, Folder 145; Hull to Senator Walter F. George, June 7, 1941, Hull Papers, Box 49, Folder 145; Rosenman, *Public Papers*, 8:228–31.

69. U.S. Department of State Press Release, December 23, 1941, 611.3731/2616; Memorandum by Hull, February 18, 1942, 611.6135/914; U.S. Tariff, *Economic Controls and Commercial Policy in Cuba*, p.33; Minneman, *Agriculture of Cuba*, pp.42–60,81, 135–38; "Supplementary Trade Agreement between the United States and Cuba," *Bulletin of the Pan American Union* 76 (March 1942):169–72.

70. Messersmith Memoirs, Box IX, Vol. II, No. 2, Cuban Agreement on Sugar Quota, MS M584g.

71. *Foreign Relations* (1941) 7:237–52; *Foreign Relations* (1942) 6:315–28; Briggs to Hull, October 4, 1941, 8300/9037; Messersmith to Hull, November 6, 1941, 837.00/9052; Messersmith to Hull, January 31, 1942, 837.00/9097; Messersmith to Hull, October 27, 1941, Hull Papers, Box 49, Folder 147; Phillips, *Cuba*, p.212; Arthur P. Whitaker, ed., *Inter-American Affairs,* 1941 (New York: Columbia University Press, 1942), 1:82–83, Chester, *Sergeant Named Batista*, p.197; Guerra y Sánchez, "Sugar: Index of Cuban-American Cooperation," pp.743–56.

72. Messersmith to Welles, July 1, 1941, 837.00/9012.

73. Messersmith to Welles, July 11, 1941, 837.001/Batista, Fulgencio/37.

74. Messersmith to Hull, July 17, 1941, 837.00/9003; Messersmith to Welles, July 17, 1941, 837.00/9013; Messersmith to Hull, October 11, 1941, 837.00/9041; Messersmith to Hull, November 15, 1941, 837.00/9054; Messersmith to Hull, November 15, 1941, 837.00/9062.

75. Messersmith to Hull, May 25, 1940, 837.00/8777; Messersmith to Hull, May 25, 1940, 837.00/8778; Welles to Messersmith, July 22, 1940, 711.37/342.

76. Messersmith to Hull, June 15, 1940, Hull Papers, Box 47, Folder 134.

77. Beaulac to Hull, August 29, 1940, 837.00/8830; Messersmith to Hull, September 3, 1940, 711.37/343; Beaulac to Hull, September 24, 1940, 837.00/8853; Beaulac to Hull, September 28, 1940, 837.00/8851; Messersmith to Hull, December 12, 1940, 711.37/349; Phillips, *Cuba*, p.193.

78. Messersmith to Roosevelt, January 15, 1941, O.F. 896 George Messersmith, FDRL; for Roosevelt's reply see Roosevelt to Messersmith, February 7, 1941, O.F. 896 George Messersmith, FDRL.

79. Messersmith to Hull, January 16, 1941, 837.00/8920; Messersmith to Hull, January 22, 1941, 837.00/8922; Messersmith to Hull, January 25, 1941, 837.00/8925; Messersmith to Hull, February 8, 1941, 837.00/8930; Messersmith to Hull, February 15, 1941, 837.00/8938; Messersmith to Hull, April 19, 1941, 837.00/8968; Messersmith to Hull, May 23, 1941, 123 M 561/606; Messersmith to Welles, June 11, 1941, 611.3731/2329; Messersmith to Hull, July 5, 1941, 837.00/8999; Briggs to Hull, August 29, 1941, 837.00/9047; Messersmith to Welles, October 22, 1941, 837.00/9050; Roosevelt to Messersmith, May 5, 1941, O.F. 896 George Messersmith, FDRL; Messersmith to Hull, October 31, 1941, Hull Papers, Box 49, Folder 147; Selig Adler, *The Isolationist Impulse: Its Twentieth Century Reaction* (New York and London: Abelard-Schuman, 1957), pp.239–359; Frye, *Nazi Germany and the American Hemisphere*, p.166; Guerrant, *Roosevelt's Good Neighbor Policy*, p.170; Phillips, *Cuba*, pp.207–8; Diaz Verson, *El Nazismo en Cuba*, p.48a; *Nation* 153 (August 16, 1941):130; H. Rutledge Southworth and Willard R. Espy, "Franco in the Caribbean," *Nation* 151 (November 23, 1941):500–502.

80. *Foreign Relations* (1940) 5:94–100; Mecham, *A Survey of United States-Latin American Relations*, pp.141, 150–51; William L. Langer and S. Everett Gleason, *The Undeclared War, 1940–1941* (New York: Harper and Brothers, 1953), pp.147–74; Stetson

Conn and Byron Fairchild, *The Framework of Hemisphere Defense* (Washington, D.C.: 1960), pp.67, 213.

81. *Foreign Relations* (1941) 7:97–107, 109, 116–25; Secretary of War Henry L. Stimson to Hull, April 7, 1941, Hull Papers, Box 49, Folder 144; Mecham, *A Survey of United States-Latin American Relations;* Langer and Gleason, *The Undeclared War*, pp.593–624.

82. *Foreign Relations* (1941) 7:101–3, 107–14; Conn and Fairchild, *The Framework of Hemisphere Defense*, p.249; Cosme de la Torriente, "Cuba, America, and the War," *Foreign Affairs* 19 (October 1940):145–55.

83. *Foreign Relations* (1941) 7:112–13, 125–26; Messersmith to Hull, December 6, 1941, 837.00/9063; Messersmith to Hull, December 13, 1941, 837.00/9067; Roosevelt to Batista, December 10, 1941, O.F. 159 Cuba 1941, FDRL; Phillips, *Cuba*, pp.211–12; Diaz Verson, *El Nazismo en Cuba*, p.20a; Mecham, *A Survey of United States-Latin American Relations*, p.145; U.S. Tariff, *Economic Controls and Commercial Policy in Cuba*, 35; Whitaker, *Inter-American Affairs, 1941*, p.72; Lazo, *Dagger in the Heart*, p.62; Ellis O. Briggs, *Shots Heard Round the World* (New York: Viking Press, 1957), p.56.

84. Messersmith to Hull, December 20, 1941, 837.00/9068.

85. Messersmith to Welles, November 28, 1941, 123 M 561/627; Welles to Messersmith, December 6, 1941 123 M 561/628; Welles to Messersmith, December 12, 1941, 123 M 561/633; Messersmith to Hull, December 23, 1941, 123 M 561/629; Briggs to Hull, December 25, 1941, 123 M 561/630; Messersmith Memoirs, Box IX, Vol. II, No. 7, Transfer and Travel to Mexico–1941, MS M584g; Messersmith to Frankfurter, December 2, 1941, Box 83, Frankfurter Papers.

86. Messersmith Memoirs, Box IX, Vol. II, No. 4, Havana–Batista, MS M584g.

CHAPTER 11

1. Messersmith to Hull, May 22, 1941, 123 B 384/278; Messersmith to Hull, July 18, 1941, 123 B 764/244; Beaulac, *Career Ambassador*, pp.150–52; Whitaker, *Inter-American Affairs, 1941*, pp.172–75; interview with Ellis Briggs, November 16, 1968.

2. Briggs, *Shots Heard Round the World*, p.56.

3. Second Secretary of the Embassy Sidney E. O'Donoghue to Hull, March 3, 1942, 837.00/9084; Briggs to Hull, March 7, 1942, 837.00/9096; Briggs to Hull, March 14, 1942, 837.00/9098; Briggs to Hull, March 15, 1942, 837.00/9097; O'Donoghue to Hull, March 17, 1942, 837.00/9100; Briggs to Hull, March 17, 1942, 837.00/9099; O'Donoghue to Hull, March 20, 1942, 837.00/9102; Briggs to Hull, April 11, 1942, 837.00/9118; *Memorandum of the Division of the American Republics*, May 25, 1942, 837.00/9153; Riera, *Cuba Política*, pp.513–20; Blasier, "The Cuban and Chilean Communist Parties," p.79.

4. Briggs to Hull, May 15, 1942, 123 Braden, Spruille/221; Biography of Spruille Braden, December 16, 1941, O.F. 3193 Spruille Braden, FDRL; Braden to Hull, May 22, 1942, 837.00/9119; Braden to Hull, May 26, 1942, 123 Braden Spruille/240; telephone conversation with Spruille Braden, July 21, 1969; Briggs, *Farewell to Foggy Bottom*, p.181.

5. Briggs, *Shot Heard Round the World*. p.56.

6. Lazo, *Dagger in the Heart*, p.65.

7. Briggs to Hull, July 24, 1942, 836.00/9143; Briggs to Hull, July 27, 1942, 837.00/9149; Briggs to Hull, August 1, 1942, 837.00/9152; Memorandum of Phone Conversation by Braden, August 11, 1942, 837.00/9149; Briggs to Hull, August 1, 1942, 837.00/9152; Memorandum of Phone Conversation by Braden, August 11, 1942, 837.00/9163; Braden to Welles, August 13, 1942, 837.002/495; Braden to Hull, August 18, 1942, 837.00/9162; Blasier, "The Cuban and Chilean Communist Parties," 79; Harry B. Murkland, "Cuba's

National Unity Move," *Current History* 3 (September 1942):51–52; Harry B. Murkland, "Cuba's New Government," *Current History* 3 (October 1942):144–45.

8. Briggs to Hull, August 15, 1942, 837.00/9161.

9. Briggs to Hull, January 10, 1942, 837.00/9073; Briggs to Hull, February 28, 1942, 837.00/9091; Briggs to Hull, April 18, 1942, 837.00/9110; Briggs to Hull, May 9, 1942, 837.00/9115; Second Secretary of the Embassy Eugene Hinkle to Hull, September 19, 1942, 837.00/9188; Hinkle to Hull, November 16, 1942, 837.00/9208; Second Secretary of the Embassy Robert Joyce to Hull, December 3, 1942, 837.00/9213; Briggs to Hull, February 27, 1943, 837.00/9208; Phillips, *Cuba*, pp.214–15, 218–19; Chester, *Sergeant Named Batista*, pp.194, 196; Allan Chase, *Falange: The Axis Secret Army in the Americas* (New York: G. P. Putnam's Sons, 1943), pp.57–58, 77–78, 92, 101–2, 101–4, 115–9, 261; Diaz Verson, *El Nazismo en Cuba*, pp.25–42; see also Spruille Braden, *Diplomats and Demagogues: The Memoirs of Spruille Braden* (New York: Arlington House, 1971), pp.287–88.

10. Hinkle to Hull, April 13, 1943, 837.00/9269; Blasier, "The Cuban and Chilean Communist Parties," pp.71, 78–79, 84, 140–42; Krauss, "Communist Policy in Cuba," pp.ii, 14–63; Whitaker, *Inter-American Affairs, 1942*, pp.35–36.

11. Chargé d'Affaires ad interim Alfred F. Nufer to Hull, December 9, 1942, 83700/371 CF.

12. Braden to Welles, March 19, 1943, 837.00/9623; Hinkle to Hull, May 3, 1943, 837.00/9278; Phillips, *Cuba*, pp.219–20; Blasier, "The Cuban and Chilean Communist Parties," pp.1, 77, 80; Alexander, *Communism in Latin America*, pp.44, 280, 283–84; U.S. Labor, *Labor in Cuba*, pp.3–4; Lazo, *Dagger in the Heart*, pp.62–63; Stokes, "The 'Cuban Revolution' and the Presidential Elections of 1948," pp.60–61; Batista, *Cuba Betrayed*, pp.163, 230; Batista, *The Growth and Decline*, pp.15–16.

13. Braden to Hull, July 10, 1942, 837.001/ Batista, Fulgencio/40; Memorandum of a conversation between the Cuban ambassador to the United States, Aurelio F. Concheso, and Welles, October 26, 1942, 837.24/977; Braden to Hull, November 13, 1942, 837.001/Batista, Fulgencio/42; Braden to Welles, November 13, 1942, 837.001/Batista, Fulgencio/72; Memorandum of a conversation between Duggan and Concheso, November 28, 1942, 837.001/Batista, Fulgencio/52; Duggan to Welles, November 28, 1942, 837.001/Batista, Fulgencio/52; U.S. Department of State Press Release, December 5, 1942, 837.001/Batista, Fulgencio/64.

14. Hinkle to Hull, December 8, 1942, 837.001/9215.

15. Welles to Roosevelt, December 7, 1942, 837.001/Batista, Fulgencio/80.

16. Batista's visit, December 7, 1942, O.F. 159–Cuba–1942, FDRL; Roosevelt's toast to Batista, December 8, 1942, PSF–Cuba–1942, FDRL; Batista's toast to Roosevelt, December 8, 1942, PSF–Cuba–1942, FDRL; Conversation between Hull and Batista, December 10, 1942, 837.001/Batista, Fulgencio/80; Rosenman, *Public Papers*, 11:530–31.

17. Welles to Roosevelt, December 12, 1942, PSF–Cuba–1942, FDRL; also see Hinkle to Hull, December 12, 1942, 837.00/9217; Hinkle to Hull, December 21, 1942, 837.00/9221; Hinkle to Hull, February 13, 1942, 837.00/9242.

18. Briggs to Hull, April 8, 1942, 837.00/9108; Braden to Hull, June 4, 1942, 837.00/9123; O'Donoghue to Hull, June 6, 1942, 837..00/9122; Briggs to Hull, July 18, 1942, 837.00/9140; *Foreign Relations* (1943) 6:253–89; U.S. Department of State, *Foreign Relations of the United States* (1944), vol. 7, *The American Republics* (1967), pp.892–905; Chester, *Sergeant Named Batista*, pp.192–93, 199; Lazo, *Dagger in the Heart*, pp.63–64; Phillips, *Cuba*, pp.216, 218, 221; R. Hart Phillips, "Cuba Goes to War," *Inter-American* (May 1943):22–26.

19. Briggs to Hull, January 9, 1943, 837.00/9232; Hinkle to Hull, February 19, 1943, 837.00/9245; Briggs to Hull, March 22, 1943, 837.00/9254; Briggs to Hull, March 25, 1943, 837.00/9256; Joyce to Hull, April 1, 1943, 837.00/9260; Hinkle to Hull, May 22, 1943, 837.00/9292; U.S. Department of State, *Foreign Relations of the United States* (1943), vol. 6, *The American Republics* (1965), pp.135–51; *Foreign Relations* (1944) 7:905–12, 914–18.

20. Briggs to Hull, September 7, 1942, 837.00/9174; Hinkle to Hull, June 13, 1944, 837.00/9658; Chairman of the War Production Board Donald M. Nelson to Roosevelt, December 21, 1942, PSF–Cuba–1942, FDRL; *Foreign Relations* (1942) 6:314; *Foreign Relations* (1943) 6:240–59; *Foreign Relations* (1944) 7:972–89.

21. Department of Agriculture, *Sugar during World War II*, pp.1, 4–5, 12–16, 22.

22. Ibid., pp.8–9, 12, 16–18; Mecham, *A Survey of United States-Latin American Relations*, p.153.

23. Briggs to Hull, February 21, 1942, 837.00/9090; Briggs to Hull, April 9, 1942, 837.00/9107; Briggs to Hull, June 26, 1942, 837.00/9129; "Cuba's Bonanza," *Business Week*, no. 655 (March 21, 1942):86; "High Jinks in Cuba," *Time* 75 (June 15, 1942):78–80; "Cuba's Business Trends," *Foreign Commerce Weekly* 7 (May 16, 1942):6–7, 35–36; Whitaker, *Inter-American Affairs, 1942*, pp.64–66, 68–69, 73–76, 87.

24. Braden to Hull, June 18, 1942, 711.370/380; Briggs to Hull, September 12, 1942, 837.00/9185; Briggs to Hull, October 3, 1942, 837.00/9195; Phillip Bonsal to Messersmith, October 12, 1942, 837.00/9–2942; Memorandum from Duggan to Bonsal and Welles, October 31, 1942, 837.00/9205; *Foreign Relations* (1942) 6:329–43; *Foreign Relations* (1943) 6:151–66; Latin American Economic Institute, *Economic Problems of the Caribbean Area* (New York: Latin American Economic Institute, 1943), pp.9–12; Antonio Barro y Segura, *The Truth about Sugar in Cuba* (Havana: Ucar, Garcia and Cia, 1943), pp.12–41; Alfred F. Nufer, "Cuba in 1943," *Foreign Commerce Weekly* 15 (May 13, 1943):14–15.

25. Hinkle to Hull, August 28, 1943, 837.00/9348; Hinkle to Hull, January 26, 1943, Hull Papers, Box 57, Folder 199; Memorandum of a Conversation by Hull, December 23, 1943, Hull Papers, Box 57, Folder 199; *Foreign Relations* (1943) 6:166–85; "Cuba's Economy in 1944," *Foreign Commerce Weekly* 19 (May 12, 1945):8, 9, 46, 47.

26. Briggs to Hull, February 14, 1942, 837.00/9086; *Foreign Relations* (1943) 6:223–39; *Foreign Relations* (1944) 7:934–35; U.S. Tariff, *Economic Controls and Commercial Policy in Cuba*, pp.5, 46; Minneman, *Agriculture of Cuba*, pp.138–40; L.A. Economic Institute, *Economic Problems of Carribbean Area*, pp.12–13.

27. Minneman, *Agriculture of Cuba*, p.13; U.S. Tariff, *Economic Controls and Commercial Policy in Cuba*, pp.31–32, 40; U.S. Department of State, The Anglo-American Caribbean Commission, *The Caribbean Islands and the War: A Record of Progress in Facing Stern Realities* (1943), pp.49–56; IBRD, *Cuba*, pp.131–34; "Cuba," *Commercial Pan American* 12 (May 1944):110–12.

28. Messersmith Memories, Box IX, Vol. II, No. 2 "Cuban Agreement on Sugar Quota," MS M584g.

29. Braden to Hull, May 19, 1943, 837.00/9290.

30. Braden to Hull, August 14, 1943, 837.00/9336; Braden to Hull, October 6, 1943, 837.00/9364; *Foreign Relations* (1942) 6:356; *Foreign Relations* (1943) 6:211–22, 259–79; *Foreign Relations* (1944) 7:919–38, 990–1012.

31. Braden to Hull, November 10, 1943, 837.00/9391.

32. *Foreign Relations* (1943) 6:197–204.

33. Ibid., pp.204–9; U.S. Labor, *Labor in Cuba*, p.11.

34. Braden to Hull, October 5, 1943, 837.00/9365.

35. Ibid.; Hinkle to Hull, October 11, 1943, 837.00/9367; Hinkle to Hull, October 18, 1943, 837.00/9370; Braden to Hull, October 20, 1943, 837.00/9376; *Foreign Relations* (1943) 6:209–11.

36. Briggs to Hull, April 1, 1942, 837.00/9106; Braden to Hull, May 23, 1942, 837.00/9121.

37. Braden to Hull, October 21, 1942, 837.00/9199.

38. Braden to Hull, July 16, 1942, 837.00/9138.

39. Conversation between Cuervo Rubio and Welles, August 6, 1942, 837.00/9171.

40. Braden to Hull, October 21, 1942, 837.00/9199.

41. Braden to Hull, December 1, 1942, 837.00/9212; Braden to Hull, January 21, 1943, 837.00/9234; Hinkle to Hull, April 26, 1943, 837.00/9247; Briggs to Hull, April 26, 1943, 837.00/9275; Briggs to Hull, June 11, 1943, 837.00/9306; Hinkle to Hull, September 20, 1943, 837.00/9356; Braden to Hull, September 24, 1943, 837.00/9357; Braden to Hull, November 1, 1943, 837.00/9373; Briggs to Hull, November 3, 1943, 837.00/9385.

42. Braden to Hull, November 5, 1943, 837.00/9387.

43. Braden to Hull, April 1, 1943, 837.00/9261; Braden to Welles, May 3, 1943, 837.00/9289; Braden to Hull, May 13, 1943, 837.00/9283; Briggs to Hull, May 18, 1943, 837.00/9288; Braden to Hull, May 21, 1943, 837.00/9291; Braden to Hull, August 20, 1943, 837.00/9343; Hinkle to Hull, August 21, 1943, 837.00/9344; Braden to Hull, October 16, 1943, 837.00/9373; Vega Cobiellas, *Grau y Saladrigas*, pp.73–74; Lazo, *Dagger in the Heart*, p.64; "Cuba's Mr. A," *Newsweek* 23 (May 1, 1944):54.

44. Briggs to Hull, March 1, 1943, 837.00/9249; Braden to Hull, March 9, 1943, 837.00/9251; Braden to Hull, December 3, 1943, 837.00/9503; Braden to Hull, December 4, 1943, 837.00/9510; Braden to Hull, December 30, 1943, 837.00/9528; Briggs to Hull, January 19, 1944, 837.00/9533.

45. Briggs to Hull, January 4, 1944, 837.00/9533.

46. Braden to Hull, May 29, 1943, 837.00/9298.

47. Memorandum of the Division of the American Republics, June 5, 1943, 837.00/9309; also see Memorandum of the Division of the American Republics, January 18, 1944, 837.00/9429.

48. Braden to Hull, August 3, 1943, 837.00/9334.

49. Hinkle to Hull, September 27, 1943, 837.00/9358; Braden to Hull, October 4, 1943, 123 Braden, Spruille/346.

50. Braden to Hull, November 22, 1943, 837.00/9398.

51. Braden to Hull, May 12, 1943, 123 Braden, Spruille/309; Braden to Hull, June 4, 1943, 123 Braden, Spruille/318; Braden to Hull, June 4, 1943, 123 Braden, Spruille/319; Memorandum by Duggan, June 4, 1943, 123 Braden, Spruille/325; Braden to Hull, December 21, 1943, 123 Braden, Spruille/357; Braden to Hull, December 14, 1943, Box 53, Folder 164, Hull Papers.

52. Memorandum of a Conversation by Hull, January 5, 1944, Hull Papers, Box 57, Folder 199.

53. Braden to Hull, March 10, 1944, Hull Papers, Box 53, Folder 166; Briggs to Hull, March 13, 1944, Hull Papers, Box 53, Folder 166; Memorandum of a Conversation by Hull, September 13, 1944, Hull Papers, Box 57, Folder 199; telephone Conversation with Philip Bonsal, November 21, 1969.

54. Braden to Hull, January 15, 1944, 837.00/9539; Hinkle to Hull, January 24, 1944, 837.00/9541; Braden to Hull, February 25, 1944, 837.00/9556; Counselor of the Embassy Allan Dawson to Hull, April 25, 1944, 837.00/9590; Braden to Hull, May 2, 1944, 837.00/9594.

55. Dawson to Hull, May 10, 1944, 837.00/9602; Dawson to Hull, May 12, 1944, 837.00/9601; Braden to Hull, May 17, 1944, 837.00/9610; Braden to Hull, May 19, 1944, 837.00/9613; Dawson to Hull, May 17, 1944, 837.00/9609; Braden to Hull, May 22, 1944, 837.00/9614; Dawson to Hull, May 23, 1944, 837.00/9615; Dawson to Hull, May 24, 1944, 837.00/9616; Braden to Hull, May 26, 1944, 837.00/9622 ; Braden to Hull, May 27, 1944, 837.00/9621; Dawson to Hull, May 30, 1944, 837.00/9626.

56. Braden to Hull, May 29, 1944, 837.00/9620.

57. Braden to Hull, May 31, 1944, 837.00/9623; Braden to Hull, June 2, 1944, 837.00/9624; Braden to Hull, June 2, 1944, 837.00/9625; Braden to Hull, June 2, 1944, 837.00/9632; Braden to Hull, June 2, 1944, 837.00/9633; Dawson to Hull, June 3, 1944, 837.00/9637; Dawson to Hull, June 6, 1944, 837.00/9638; Braden to Hull, June 9, 1944, 837.00/9646; Dawson to Hull, June 12, 1944, 837.00/9649; Nufer to Hull, August 24, 1944,

837.00/8–2444; Riera, *Ruba Política*, pp. 521–46; Bosch, *Cuba*, pp. 141–46; Blasier, "The Cuban and Chilean Communist Parties," p.79; Phillips, *Cuba*, pp.222–23; Chester, *Sergeant Named Batista*, p.201; Fergusson, *Cuba*, p.116; Vega Cobiellas, *Grau y Saladrigas*, pp.155–80; Batista, *The Growth and Decline*, p.17; "Cuban Upset," *Newsweek* 23 (June 12, 1944):52; "Evolution of a Dictator," *Time* 43 (June 12, 1944):37–38; 'Paper Revolution," *Inter-American* 3 (July 1944):3–4.

58. J. P. McEvoy, "Cuba's Masterpiece of Vice Versa," *The Saturday Evening Post* 217 (September 30, 1944):105.

59. Braden to Hull, June 2, 1944, 837.00/9631; Dawson to Hull, June 6, 1944, 837.00/9638; Dawson to Hull, June 12, 1944, 837.00/9649; Nufer to Hull, August 24, 1944, 837.00/8–2444; Riera, *Cuba Política*, pp.521–46.

60. Braden to Hull, June 3, 1944, 711.37/398.

61. Braden to Hull, June 9, 1944, 837.00/9651; Braden to Hull, June 10, 1944, 837.00/9659.

62. Braden to Hull, June 9, 1944, 837.00/9640; Braden to Hull, June 11, 1944, 837.00/9644; Braden to Hull, June 12, 1944, 837.00/9657; Braden to Hull, June 13, 1944, 837.00/9655; Messersmith to McGuirk, September 15, 1944, 837.00/9–1244; Braden to Hull, November 22, 1944, 837.00/11–2244; "Cuba Elects Grau," *Life* 16 (Jane 26, 1944):81–84; "Plot Foiled," *Time* 44 (August 7, 1944):38; Braden, *Diplomats and Demagogues*, pp.298–300.

63. Nufer to Hull, August 14, 1944, 837.00/8–1444 CF: Nufer to Hull, August 14, 1944, 837.00/8–1444; Nufer to Hull, August 23, 1944, 837.00/8–2344; Nufer to Hull, September 1, 1944, 837.00/9–144; Nufer to Hull, September 25, 1944, 837.00/9–2544; Braden to Hull, November 8, 1944, 837.00/11–844; Braden to Hull, November 9, 1944, 837.00/11–944 CF; Braden to Hull, November 10, 1944, 837.00/11–844; Braden to Hull, November 13, 1944, 837.00/11–1344.

64. Braden to Hull, June 9, 1944, 837.00/9652 CF; Braden to Hull, June 16, 1944, 837.00/9665; Braden to Hull, July 21, 1944, 837.00/7–2144; Second Secretary of the Embassy Garret Ackerson to Hull, August 1, 1944, 837.00/8–144; Nufer to Hull, August 2, 1944, 837.00/8–244; Nufer to Hull, August 18, 1944, 837.00/8–1844; Ackerson to Hull, September 14, 1944, 837.00/9–1444; Report by Mecham, October 14, 1944, AC–LA Documents 12–23, Notter File, Box 191, Record Group 59, General Records of the Department of State, National Archives, Washington, D.C.; Phillips, *Cuba*, p.229, Blasier, "The Cuban and Chilean Communist Parties," pp.36, 75, 77–82, 94; Krauss, "Communist Policy in Cuba," pp.11–13; Alexander, *Communism in Latin America*, pp.284, 286.

65. Braden to Hull, June 3, 1944, 837.00/9634; Memorandum from John Cabot to Duggan, June 16, 1944, 837.001/Grau San Martin, Ramon/6–1644; Braden to Hull, July 3, 1944, 837.001/Grau San Martin, Ramon/7–344; Nufer to Hull, August 26, 1944, 837.001/Grau San Martin, Ramon/8–2644.

66. Rosenman, *Public Papers,* 13:253.

67. "Ramon Grau San Martin Visits the United States," *Bulletin of the Pan American Union* 78 (November 1944):601–4.

68. Ackerson to Hull, September 12, 1944, 837.00/9–1244; Donald M. Dozer, *Are We Good Neighbors?* (Gainesville: University of Florida Press, 1959), p.110.

69. Dawson to Hull, June 7, 1944, 837.00/9643; Ackerson to Hull, June 27, 1944, 837.00/6–2744; Ackerson to Hull, July 11, 1944, 837.00/7–1144; Nufer to Hull, July 15, 1944, 837.002/7–1544; Ackerson to Hull, July 18, 1944, 837.00/7–1844; Nufer to Hull, August 4, 1944, 837.00/8–444; Ackerson to Hull, September 11, 1944, 837.00/9–1144; *Foreign Relations* (1944) 7:913.

70. Ackerson to Hull, August 29, 1944, 837.00/8–2944; Nufer to Hull, September 27, 1944, 837.00/9–2744; Nufer to Hull, October 5, 1944, 837.00/10–544; Braden to Hull,

October 7, 1944, 837.00/10–744; Braden to Hull, November 4, 1944, 123 Braden Spruille/352.

71. Braden to Hull, October 4, 1944, 837.00/10–444.

72. Braden to Hull, October 5, 1944, 837.00/10–544; Second Secretary of the Embassy Harold Montamat to Hull, October 11, 1944, 837.00/10–1144.

73. Montamat to Hull, October 9, 1944, 837.001/Grau San Martin, Ramon/10–944; Braden to Hull, October 10, 1944, 837.001/Grau San Martin, Ramon/10–1944; Braden to Hull, October 19, 1944, 837.001/Grau San Martin, Ramon/10–1444; Montamat to Hull, October 19, 1944, 837.00/10–1944.

74. Braden to Hull, October 14, 1944, 837.001/Grau San Martin, Ramon/10–1444; Braden to Hull, November 3, 1944, 837.001/Grau San Martin, Ramon/11–344.

75. Braden to Hull, October 14, 1944, 837.001/Grau San Martin/10–1444.

76. Braden to Hull, October 23, 1944, 837.00/10–2344; Braden to Secretary of State Edward Stettinius, December 10, 1944, 837.00/12–1044; Braden to Stettinius, December 28, 1944, 837.00/12–2844; Chester, *Sergeant Named Batista*, p.202.

77. Counselor of the Embassy John Muccio to Hull, November 14, 1944, 837.00/11–1444; Muccio to Hull, November 27, 1944, 837.00/11–2744; "Cuban Housecleaning," *Newsweek* 24 (November 20, 1944):65.

78. Braden to Hull, November 6, 1944, 837.00/11–644; Muccio to Hull, November 8, 1944, 837.00/11–844; Braden to Stettinius, December 21, 1944, 837.00/12–2144; Braden to Stettinius, December 29, 1944, 837.00/12–2944; "New Broom in Cuba," *The Inter-American* 3 (December 1944):9–10.

79. Braden to Stettinius, December 19, 1944, 837.00/12–1044.

80. Montamat to Hull, October 25, 1944, 837.00/10–2544; Muccio to Hull, November 1, 1944, 837.00/11–144; Braden to Stettinius, December 10, 1944, 837.00/12–1944.

81. Braden to Stettinius, December 19, 1944, 837.00/12–1944.

82. U.S. Department of State, *Foreign Relations of the United States* (1945), vol. 9, *The American Republics* (1969), pp.896–916, 959.

83. Nufer to Hull, July 15, 1944, 837.61351/7–544; Braden to Hull, July 22, 1944, 837.61351/7–2244; Director, Sugar Division to War Food Administrator Marvin Jones, August 31, September 1, 6, 15, 16, 20, and 21, October 31, November 1, 3, 8, 9, and 16, 1944, Reports from March 20, 1944: War Food Administration, Correspondence 1944, Reports—Reports 3, Record Group 16, National Archives, Washington, D.C.; Director Sugar Division, to Jones, March 2 and 6, 1945, Meetings from January 1, 1945 to April 30, 1945, WFA Correspondence 1945, Meetings—Meetings 7, Record Group 16, National Archives, Washington, D.C.; *Foreign Relations* (1944)7:938–58; *Foreign Relations* (1945) 9:917–55; Department of Agriculture, *Sugar during World War II*, pp.16, 21; Department of Agriculture, *U.S. Sugar Program*, p.9; Ministerio de Hacienda, *Comercio Exterior, 1935–39 a 1944* (Havana: P. Fernandez y Cia, 1947), pp.xi–xxx.

84. *The Havana Post*, April 26, 1945.

CHAPTER 12

1. Hull, *Memoirs*, 2:1227–31, 1719, 1721.

2. George F. Kennan, *Realities of American Foreign Policy* (New York: W. W. Norton and Co., 1966), p.57.

3. Hull had E. Wilder Spaulding, director of the Division of Research and Publication of the Department of State, collect the documents dealing with the Cuban crisis from May to December 1933 to show his nonintervention position. Memorandum from Spaulding to Hull, August 28, 1941, Hull Papers, Box 49, Folder 146.

4. Dozer, *Are We Good Neighbors?* p.109; Duggan, *The Americas,* p.5; Mecham, *A Survey of United States-Latin American Relations,* pp.124–25; Nevins and Hacker, *The United States and Its Place in World Affairs,* p.384; Shannon, *Between the Wars,* pp.170–71; Adler, *The Uncertain Giant,* p.124; Walter Johnson, *1600 Pennsylvania Avenue* (Boston: Little, Brown and Co., 1960), pp.106–7; Guerrant, *Roosevelt's Good Neighbor Policy,* pp.1, 17; Coleman, "The Good Neighbor Policy of F.D.R.," pp.390, 401–4; Cronon, *Josephus Daniels in Mexico,* pp.vii–ix; Healey, "Impeachment of Gómez," pp.103, 116–18.

5. Beaulac, *Career Ambassador,* p.259; also see Ellis O. Briggs, *Anatomy of Diplomacy* (New York: David McKay Co., 1968), pp.184–201.

6. For positive assessments of Batista see: Batista, *Cuba Betrayed,* pp.209–11, 218–19; Phillips, *Cuba,* p.190; Chester, *Sergeant Named Batista,* pp.169, 262; Nelson, *Rural Cuba,* p.8; Aguilar, "Cuba 1933," pp.202–5; Healey, "Impeachment of Gómez," pp.152–54 157–58; Hennessy, "The Roots of Cuban Nationalism," p.353.

7. For negative assessments of Batista see: Adama y Silva, *La gran mentira,* pp.476–77; Bosch, *Cuba,* pp.139–40; MacGaffey and Barnett, *Twentieth Century Cuba,* pp.190–91; Seers, *Cuba,* pp.169–70, 174; IBRD, *Cuba,* p.404; Nelson, *Rural Cuba,* pp.235, 239.

8. For Cuba's failure to develop wise economic policies see: IBRD, *Cuba,* pp.57, 530–34, 562–63; MacGaffey and Barnett, *Twentieth Century Cuba,* pp.190–91; Seers, *Cuba,* pp. 12–13; White, "Cuba and Puerto Rico," p.38.

9. Fernando Ortiz y Fernández, trans. by Harriet de Onís, *Cuban Counterpoint: Tobacco and Sugar* (New York: Alfred A. Knopf, 1947), p.70.

10. Guerra y Sánchez, *Sugar and Society,* p.99.

11. For divergent views on diversification see: IBRD, *Cuba,* pp.94–96; Buell, *Problems of New Cuba,* pp.472–73; Seers, *Cuba,* pp.69–71; Nelson, *Rural Cuba,* p.106. Thomas Barbour, *A Naturalist in Cuba* (Boston: Little, Brown and Co., 1945), p.279; J. Merle Davis, *The Cuban Church in a Sugar Economy* (New York: Internation Missionary Council, 1942), pp.77–78; MacGaffey and Barnett, *Twentieth Century Cuba,* p.70; Fergusson, *Cuba,* p.247.

12. The Cuban Economic Research Project, *A Study on Cuba* (Coral Gables, Florida: University of Miami Press, 1965), p.523; for other figures see: MacGaffey and Barnett, *Twentieth Century Cuba,* pp.74–75; Gutíerrez, *El Desarrollo Económico de Cuba,* pp.89–91; Camara de Comercio de Cuba, *Directorio Oficial de Exportación, Producción y Turismo* (Havana: Camara de Comercio de la Republica de Cuba, 1941), p.55.

13. Wallich, *Monetary Problems,* pp. 67–68.

14. One example of a successful American sugar operation is discussed in *Some Facts Regarding the Development and Operation of the United States Fruit Company Sugar Properties in the Republic of Cuba* (Preston, Oriente: Cultural, 1944), pp.1–105 and in Barbour, *A Naturalist in Cuba,* pp.267–68; for a defense of American business practices see: IBRD, *Cuba,* pp. 734–35; Lazo, *Dagger in the Heart,* p.93; Fergusson, *Cuba,* p.245.

15. For assessments of Cuba at the end of the war see: Cuban Economic Research Council, *A Study on Cuba,* pp.619–22; Nelson, *Rural Cuba,* pp.20–21, 140, 145, 219; IBRD, *Cuba,* pp.13, 39–40.

16. For Cuba's internal problems at the end of the war see: MacGaffey and Barnett, *Twentieth Century Cuba,* p.175; IBRD, *Cuba,* pp.134, 136, 441, 453; Davis, *Cuban Church in a Sugar Economy,* pp.31–32, 36, 40–41.

17. For the dichotomy in United States-Cuban relations before and after the war see: Buell, *Problems of New Cuba,* p.268; Phillips, *Cuban Sideshow,* p.317; Healey, "Impeachment of Gómez," pp.144–45; Davis, *Cuban Church in a Sugar Economy,* pp.23, 28–29, 33–34, 78; Barbour, *A Naturalist in Cuba,* p.13; Fergusson, *Cuba,* pp.19–20, 122–23, 136, 241; White, "Cuba and Puerto Rico," p.99; Ruiz, *Cuba,* pp.8, 114; Seers, *Cuba,* pp.10–11; Burks, *Cuba under Castro,* p.5.

Bibliography

PUBLIC DOCUMENTS

Unpublished Material

UNITED STATES

Record Group 16, War Food Administration—Correspondence 1944; Reports—Reports 3, National Archives, Washington, D.C.

Record Group 16, War Food Administration—Correspondence, 1945; Meetings—Meeting 7, National Archives, Washington, D.C.

Record Group 46, Senate, Committee on Foreign Relations, National Archives, Washington, D.C.

Record Group 59, General Records of the Department of State, State Decimal File, 1933–1944, National Archives, Washington, D.C.

Published Material

CUBA

Camara de Comercio de la Republica de Cuba. *Directorio Oficial de Exportación e Importación, Producción y Turismo.* Havana: Camara de Comercio de la Republica de Cuba, 1941.

Constitution of 1940.

Cuba Económica y Financiera. *Anuario Azucarero de Cuba 1941.* Havana: Editora Mercantil Cubana, 1941.

Ministerio de Hacienda. *Comercio Exterior 1935–39 a 1944.* Havana: P. Fernandez y Cia, 1947.

Oficina Nacional de los Censos Demografico y Electoral. *Censes de población, viviendas y electoral 1953.* Havana, 1953.

GREAT BRITAIN

Department of Overseas Trade. *Economic Conditions in Cuba, April, 1935.* London, 1935.

_____ . *Report on Economic and Commercial Conditions in Cuba, August, 1937.* London, 1937.

INTER-AMERICAN CONFERENCE

Seventh International Conference of American States. *Minutes and Antecedents with General Index.* Montevideo, Uruguay, 1933.

UNITED STATES

Congressional Record. Vol. 78.

Senate. *Munitions Industry,* Hearings before the Special Committee Investigating the Munitions Industry, pursuant to S. R. 206 (73 Cong.), 73d Cong. 2d Sess., 74 Cong. 2 Sess. 39 parts; Washington, D.C., 1934–36.

Department of Agriculture. Bureau of Agricultural Economics, *Sugar During the World War and in the 1939 European War.* 1940.

———— . Agriculture Information Bulletin No. 111, Production and Marketing Administration. *The United States Sugar Program.* 1953.

———— . Minneman, P. G. *The Agriculture of Cuba.* 1943.

Department of Commerce. Bureau of Foreign and Domestic Commerce. Division of Foreign Trade Statistics. *Trade of the United States with Cuba.* 1938.

———— . *Investment in Cuba: Basic Information for United States Businessmen.* 1956.

Department of Labor. Bureau of Labor Statistics. Foreign Labor Information. *Labor in Cuba.* 1957.

Department of State. *Analysis of Cuban-American Trade during the First Two Years under the Reciprocal Trade Agreement.* 1937

———— . The Anglo-American Caribbean Commission. *The Caribbean Islands and the War: A Record of Progress in Facing Stern Realities.* 1943.

———— . *Biographic Registry.* 1945.

———— . *Foreign Relations of the United States,* 1933. Vol. 5. *The American Republics.* 1952.

———— . ————, 1934. Vol. 5. *The American Republics.* 1952.

———— . ————, 1935. Vol. 4. *The American Republics.* 1953.

———— . ————, 1938. Vol. 5. *The American Republics.* 1956.

———— . ————, 1939. Vol. 5. *The American Republics.* 1957.

———— . ————, 1940. Vol. 5. *The American Republics.* 1961.

———— . ————, 1941. Vol. 7. *The American Republics.* 1962.

———— . ————, 1942. Vol. 6. *The American Republics.* 1963.

———— . ————, 1943. Vol. 5. *The American Republics.* 1965.

———— . ————, 1944. Vol. 7. *The American Republics.* 1967.

———— . ————, 1945. Vol. 9. *The American Republics.* 1969.

———— . *Latin American Series.* No. 12. Sumner Welles, " 'Good Neighbor' Policy in the Caribbean." 1935.

———— . ————, No. 8. Sumner Welles, "Inter-American Relations." 1935.

———— . ————, No. 10. Sumner Welles, "Pan-American Cooperation." 1935.

———— . ————, No. 7. Sumner Welles, "Relations between the United States and Cuba." 1934.

_____ . _____ , No. 9. Sumner Welles, "The Roosevelt Administration and Its Dealings with the Republics of the Western Hemisphere." 1935.

_____ . _____ , No. 11. Sumner Welles, "Two Years of the 'Good Neighbor' Policy." 1935.

Tariff Commission. *Economic Controls and Commercial Policy in Cuba.* 1946.

_____ . *The Foreign Trade of Latin America.* Part II: *Commercial Policies and Trade Relations of Individual Latin American Countries*, Section 18: *Cuba* 1940.

MANUSCRIPT COLLECTIONS

John Barrett Papers. Library of Congress. Manuscript Division. Washington, D.C.

William Culbertson Papers. Library of Congress. Manuscript Division. Washington, D.C.

Josephus Daniels Papers. Library of Congress. Manuscript Division, Washington, D.C.

Norman Davis Papers. Library of Congress. Manuscript Division. Washington, D.C.

Felix Frankfurter Papers. Library of Congress. Manuscript Division. Washington, D.C.

Leland Harrison Papers. Library of Congress. Manuscript Division. Washington, D.C.

Cordell Hull Papers. Library of Congress. Manuscript Division. Washington, D.C.

Samuel Inman Papers. Library of Congress. Manuscript Division. Washington, D.C.

Philip Jessup Papers. Library of Congress. Manuscript Division. Washington, D.C.

William Leahy Papers. Library of Congress. Manuscript Division. Washington, D.C.

Breckinridge Long Papers. Library of Congress. Manuscript Division. Washington, D.C.

George Messersmith Papers. University of Delaware. Special Collections. Newark, Delaware.

William Phillips Papers. The Houghton Library. Harvard University. Cambridge, Massachusetts.

James Robertson Papers. Library of Congress. Manuscript Division. Washington, D.C.

Franklin Roosevelt Papers. Franklin Delano Roosevelt Library. Hyde Park, New York.

ORAL INTERVIEWS

Personal interview with Ambassador Willard Beaulac, Washington, D.C. December 18, 1968.

Personal interview with Ambassador Adolf Berle, New York, N.Y. January 2, 1969.

Telephone conversation with Ambassador Philip Bonsal, Washington, D.C. November 21, 1969.
Telephone conversation with Ambassador Spruille Braden, New York, N.Y. July 21, 1969.
Personal interview with Ambassador Ellis Briggs, Washington, D.C. November 16, 1968.
Personal interview with Dr. Arturo M. Mañas, New York, N.Y. December 22, 1969.
Personal interview with Ambassador H. Freeman Matthews, Washington, D.C. October 31, 1968.
Personal interview with Dr. Rafael Porro Fuentes, Demarest, N.J. January 1, 1969.
Personal interview with Dr. Herminio Portell Vilá, Washington, D.C. January 23, 1969.

BOOKS

Adam y Silva, Ricardo. *La gran mentira, 4 de septiembre de 1933.* Havana: Lex, 1947.
Adler, Selig. *The Isolationist Impulse: Its Twentieth Century Reaction.* New York and London: Abelard-Schuman, 1957.
———. *The Uncertain Giant: 1921–1941.* New York: Macmillan Co., 1965.
Aguilar, Luis. *Cuba 1933: Prologue to Revolution.* Ithaca N.Y.: Cornell University Press, 1972.
Alexander, Robert J. *Communism in Latin America.* New Brunswick, N.J.: Rutgers University Press, 1957.
Alienes y Urosa, Julián. *Características fundamentales de la economía cubana.* Havana: Banco Nacional, 1950.
———. *Tesis sobre el desarrollo económico de Cuba.* Havana: Asociación Nacional de Industriales de Cuba, 1952.
The American Chamber of Commerce of Cuba. *Protect Your Trade with Cuba.* U.S.A., 1939.
———. *Silver Jubilee Review 1919–1944.* Havana: Seane, Fernandez y Cia, 1944.
Arrendondo, Alberto. *Cuba: Tierra indefensa.* Havana: Editorial Lex, 1945.
Asociación de Colonos de Cuba. *Cuba's Tragedy.* Havana: Molina y Cia, 1940.
Asociación Nacional de Hacendados de Cuba. *El Tratado de Reciprocidad de 1934.* Havana: Asociación Nacional de Hacendados de Cuba, 1939.
Barbour, Thomas. *A Naturalist in Cuba.* Boston: Little, Brown and Co., 1945.
Barro y Segura, Antonio. *The Truth about Sugar in Cuba.* Havana: Ucar, García y Cia, 1943.
Batista y Zaldívar, Fulgencio. *Cuba Betrayed.* New York: Vantage Press, 1962.
———. *Ideario de Batista.* Havana: Prensa Indoamericano, 1940.
———. *The Growth and Decline of the Cuban Republic.* New York: Devin-Adair Co., 1964.
———. *Revolución social o politica reformista.* Havana: Prensa Indoamericano, 1944.

Beals, Carleton, *America South*. Philadelphia: J. P. Lippincott Co., 1938.

———. *The Crime of Cuba*. Philadelphia: J. P. Lippincott Co., 1933.

——— and Clifford Odets. *Rifle Rule in Cuba*. New York: Provisional Committee for Cuba, 1935.

Beard, Charles A. *American Foreign Policy in the Making: A Study in Responsibilities*. New Haven: Yale University Press, 1946.

Beaulac, Willard L. *Career Ambassador*. New York: Macmillan Co., 1951.

———. *Career Diplomat*. New York: Macmillan Co., 1964.

Bemis, Samuel F. *The Latin American Policy of the United States*. New York: Harcourt, Brace, and Co., 1943.

Bosch, Juan. *Cuba: la isla fascinante*. Santiago, Chile: Editorial Universitaria, 1955.

Braden, Spruille. *Diplomats and Demogogues: The Memoirs of Spruille Braden*. New York: Arlington House, 1971.

Bradley, Hugh. *Havana, Cinderella's City*. New York: Doubleday, Doran & Co., 1941.

Briggs, Ellis O. *Anatomy of Diplomacy*. New York: David McKay Co., 1968.

———. *Farewell to Foggy Bottom*. New York: David McKay Co., 1964.

———. *Shots Heard Round the World*. New York: Viking Press, 1957.

Brinton, Crane. *Anatomy of Revolution*. New York: Prentice-Hall, 1952.

Buell, Raymond L. et. al. *Problems of New Cuba*. New York: Foreign Policy Association, 1935.

Burks, David D. *Cuba under Castro*. New York: Foreign Policy Association, 1964.

Bustamante, Luis J. *Enciclopedia Popular Cubana*. 5 vols. Cienfuegos and Havana: Imprente y Libreria La Moderna and Molina y Ca., 1947–48.

Campa y Caraveda, Miguel Angel. *Un año de política exterior cubana, 1939–1940*. Havana: Sociedad colombista panamerica, 1941.

Canet Alvarez, Gerardo, in collaboration with Erwin Raisz. *Atlas de Cuba*. Cambridge, Mass.: Harvard University Press, 1949.

Capestany Abreu, Manuel. *Roosevelt Cuidadano Eminente de America*. Havana: Edicion Oficial del Senado, 1941.

Caribbean Land Tenure Symposium. Washington, D.C.: Caribbean Research Council, 1946.

Carson, James S. *Cuba—Gateway to Latin Amerca*. New York, 1939.

Chase, Allan. *Falange: The Axis Secret Army in the Americas*. New York: G. P. Putnam's Sons, 1943.

Chester, Edmund A. *A Sergeant Named Batista*. New York: Henry Holt & Co., 1954.

Cole, Wayne S. *Senator Gerald P. Nye and American Foreign Relations*. Minneapolis: University of Minnesota Press, 1962.

Conn, Stetson, and Byron Fairchild. *The Framework of Hemisphere Defense*. Washington, D.C., 1960.

Cronon, E. David. *Josephus Daniels in Mexico*. Madison: University of Wisconsin Press, 1960.

Cuba's Three Year Plan. Havana: Cultural, 1938.

Cuevas Cancino, Francisco. *Roosevelt y la Buena Vecindad*. Mexico and Buenos Aires: Fondo de Cultura Económica, 1954.

Daniels, Josephus, *Shirt-Sleeve Diplomat*. Chapel Hill: University of North Carolina Press, 1947.

Davis, J. Merle. *The Cuban Church in a Sugar Economy*. New York: International Missionary Council, 1942.

De la Torriente y Peraza, Cosme. *Cuarenta Años de Mi Vida, 1898–1938*. Havana: Imprenta "El Siglo XX," 1939.

DeConde, Alexander. *Herbert Hoover's Latin-American Policy*. Stanford, Calif.: Stanford University Press, 1951.

Dewart, Leslie. *Christianity and Revolution: The Lesson of Cuba*. New York: Herder and Herder, 1963.

Díaz Versón, Salvador. *El Nazismo en Cuba*. Havana: Obrapía, 1944.

Dozer, Donald M. *Are We Good Neighbors?* Gainesville: University of Florida Press, 1959.

Duggan, Laurence. *The Americas: The Search for Hemisphere Security*. New York: Henry Holt & Co., 1948.

Fabre-Luce, Alfred, *Révolution à Cuba*. Paris: Editions de "Pamphlet," 1934.

Fagg, John E. *Cuba, Haiti, and the Dominican Republic*. Englewood Cliffs, N.J.: Prentice-Hall, 1965.

Fergusson, Erna. *Cuba*. New York: Alfred A. Knopf, 1946.

Ferrell, Robert. *American Diplomacy in the Great Depression*. New Haven: Yale University Press, 1957.

Fitzgibbon, Russell H. *Cuba and the United States 1900–1935*. New York: Russell and Russell, 1964.

Foreign Bondholders Protective Council, Inc. *Annual Reports, 1936–1945*. New York: Foreign Bondholders Protective Council, 1937–45.

Freedman, Max. *Roosevelt and Frankfurter: Their Correspondence 1928–1945*. Boston: Little, Brown and Co., 1967.

Frye, Alton. *Nazi Germany and the American Hemisphere, 1933–1944*. New Haven: Yale University Press, 1967.

Gardner, Lloyd C. *Economic Aspects of New Deal Diplomacy*. Madison: University of Wisconsin Press, 1964.

Goldenberg, Boris. *The Cuban Revolution and Latin America*. New York and Washington: Frederick A. Praeger, 1965.

Graebner, Norman A., ed. *An Uncertain Tradition: American Secretaries of State in the Twentieth Century*. New York: McGraw-Hill, 1961.

Gran San Martín, Ramón. *La Revolución Cubana Ante América*. México: Ediciones del Partido Revolucionaria Cubana, 1936.

Greenbie, Sydney. *Three Island Nations*. New York: Row, Peterson and Co., 1942.

Guerra y Sánchez, Ramiro et. al. *Historia de la Nación Cubana*. Havana: Editorial Historia de la Nación Cubana, 1952.

————., with foreword by Sidney W. Mintz. *Sugar and Society in the Caribbean: An Economic History of Cuban Agriculture*. New Haven: Yale University Press, 1964.

Guerrant, Edward O. *Roosevelt's Good Neighbor Policy*. Albuquerque: University of New Mexico Press, 1950.

Guggenheim, Harry F. *The United States and Cuba*. New York: Macmillan Co., 1934.

Gutíerrez y Sanchez, Gustavo. *El Dessarrollo Económico de Cuba.* Havana: Junta Nacional de Economía, 1952.

――――. *Presente y futuro de la economia, cubana.* Havana: Junta Nacional de Economía, 1950.

Halvares, Enrique. *Batista: Estudio Polemico.* Havana: Editorial Hermes, 1937.

Hilton, Ronald, ed. *Who's Who in Latin America.* Stanford, Calif.: Stanford University Press, 1951.

Hinton, Harold B. *Cordell Hull.* Garden City, N.Y.: Doubleday, Doran, & Co., 1942.

Hull, Cordell. *The Memoirs of Cordell Hull.* 2 vols. New York: Macmillan Co., 1948.

Ickes, Harold L. *The Secret Diary of Harold L. Ickes: The First Thousand Days, 1933–1936.* New York: Simon and Schuster, 1953.

International Bank for Reconstruction and Development. *Report on Cuba.* Washington, D.C.: International Bank for Reconstruction and Development, 1951.

James, Preston. *Latin America.* 3d ed. New York: Odyssey Press, 1959.

Jenks, Leland H. *Our Cuban Colony, A Study in Sugar.* New York: Vanguard Press, 1928.

Jones, Chester L. *The Caribbean Since 1900.* New York: Prentice-Hall, 1936.

Kennan, George F. *Memoirs 1925–1950.* New York: Bantam Books, 1969.

――――. *Realities of American Foreign Policy.* New York: W. W. Norton & Co., 1966.

Kilpatrick, Carroll, ed. *Roosevelt and Daniels: A Friendship in Politics.* Chapel Hill: University of North Carolina Press, 1952.

Lamar Schweyer, Alberto. *Comó Cayó el Presidente Machado.* Madrid: Espasa-Calpe, 1934.

――――. *How President Machado Fell.* Havana: Montalvo Cardenas, 1938.

Langer, William L. and S. Everett Gleason. *The Challenge to Isolation 1937–1940.* New York: Harper and Brothers, 1952.

――――. *The Undeclared War 1940–1941.* New York: Harper and Brothers, 1953.

Langley, Lester D. *The Cuban Policy of the United States: A Brief Hstory.* New York: John Wiley and Sons, 1968.

Latin American Economic Institute. *Economic Problems of the Caribbean Area.* New York: Latin American Economic Institute, 1943.

Lazo, Mario. *Dagger in the Heart: American Policy Failures in Cuba.* New York: Funk & Wagnalls, 1968.

Leuchtenberg, William E. *Franklin D. Roosevelt and the New Deal, 1932–1940.* New York: Harper and Row, 1963.

Lieuwen, Edwin. *Arms and Politics in Latin America.* rev. ed. New York: Frederick A. Praeger, 1961.

Lizaso, Felix. *Panorama de la Cultura Cubana.* Mexico City: Fondo de Cultural Económica, 1949.

MacGaffey, Wyatt and Clifford Barnett. *Twentieth Century Cuba.* New York: Anchor Books, 1965.

Magill, Roswell and Carl Shoup. *The Cuban Fiscal System 1939.* New York, 1939.

Márquez Sterling, Manuel. *Proceso de la Enmienda Platt*. Havana: Imprenta "El Siglo XX,"; 1941.

Martínez Fraga, Pedro. *Speech Delivered at the Opening of the Cuban Pavillion, New York World's Fair, on May 20, 1939*. Washington, D.C., 1939.

Mecham, J. Lloyd. *A Survey of United States-Latin American Relations*. Boston: Houghton Mifflin Co., 1965.

Munro, Dana G. *The United States and the Carribean Area*. Boston: World Peace Foundation, 1934.

Nelson, Lowry. *Rural Cuba*. Minneapolis: University of Minnesota Press, 1950.

Nevins, Allan. *The New Deal and World Affairs: A Chronicle of International Affairs, 1933–1945*. New Haven: Yale University Press, 1950.

———— and Louis Hacker, eds. *The United States and Its Place in World Affairs, 1918–1943*. Boston: D. C. Heath and Co., 1943.

Nixon, Edgar B., ed. *Franklin D. Roosevelt and Foreign Affairs*. Cambridge, Mass.: Belknap Press of Harvard University Press, 1969.

Ortiz y Fernandez, Fernando. *Cuban Counterpoint: Tobacco and Sugar*. Translated by Harriet de Onís. New York: Alfred A. Knopf, 1947.

Pan American Union. *Cuba*. Washington, D.C., 1935.

Perkins, Dexter. *The New Age of Franklin D. Roosevelt, 1933–45*. Chicago: University of Chicago Press, 1957.

————. *The United States and the Caribbean*. Cambridge, Mass.: Harvard University Press, 1947.

Phillips, Ruby H. *Cuba: Island of Paradox*. New York: McDowell, Obolensky, 1959

————. *Cuban Sideshow*. Havana: Cuban Press, 1935.

Phillips, William. *Ventures in Diplomacy*. Boston: Beacon Press, 1952.

Portell Vilá, Herminio. *Cuba y la Conferencia de Montevideo*. Havana: "Heraldo Christiano," 1934.

————. *The Non-Intervention Pact of Montevideo and American Intervention in Cuba*. Havana: Molina and Co., 1935.

————. *Historia de Cuba en sus relaciones con los Estados Unidos*. 4 vols. Havana: J. Montero, 1938–41.

Pratt, Julius. "Cordell Hull, 1933–1944," in *The American Secretaries of State and Their Diplomacy*, edited by Robert H. Ferrell, vol. 12. New York: Cooper Square Publishers, 1964.

Ramon, Ramon. *Cuba: Brief Survey of This Republic*. Havana: "Pan American Columbus Society," 1943.

Riera Hernández, Mario. *Cuba Política, 1899–1955*. Havana: Impresora Modelo, 1955.

Roberts, Walter A. *Havana: The Portrait of a City*. New York: Coward-McCann, 1953.

Roig de Leuchsenring, Emilio, ed. *Curso de Introducción a la Historia de Cuba*. Havana: Municipio de la Havana, 1938.

————. *Historia de la Enmienda Platt: Una Interpretación de la Realidad Cubana*. Havana: Cultural, 1935.

Roosevelt, Elliot, ed. *F.D.R.: His Personal Letters*. 4 vols. New York: Duell, Sloan and Pearce, 1947–50.

Rosenman, Samuel I., ed. *The Public Papers and Addresses of Franklin D. Roosevelt.* Vols. 2–5, New York: Random House, 1938. Vols. 6–8, New York: Macmillan Co., 1941; Vols. 11–13, New York: Harper and Brothers, 1950.

Ruiz, Ramon E. *Cuba: The Making of a Revolution.* Amherst, Mass.: University of Massachusetts Press, 1968.

Seers, Dudley, ed. *Cuba: The Economic and Social Revolution.* Chapel Hill: University of North Carolina Press, 1964.

Smith, Robert F. *The United States and Cuba: Business and Diplomacy, 1917–1960.* New Haven, Conn.: College and University Press, 1960.

Shannon, David A. *Between the Wars: America, 1919–1941.* Boston: Houghton Mifflin Co., 1965.

Some Facts Regarding the Development and Operation of the United Fruit Company Sugar Properties in the Republic of Cuba. Preston, Oriente: Cultural, 1944.

Strode, Hudson. *The Pageant of Cuba.* New York: Harrison Smith and Robert Haas, 1934.

Suchlicki, Jaime. *University Students and Revolution in Cuba 1920–1968.* Coral Gables, Fl.: University of Miami Press, 1969.

The Cuban Economic Research Project. *A Study on Cuba.* Coral Gables, Fl.: University of Miami Press, 1965.

Thomas, Hugh. *Cuba: The Pursuit of Freedom, 1762–1969.* New York: Harper Row, 1971.

Turosienshi, Severin K. *Education in Cuba.* Washington, D.C., 1943.

Unión Social Económica de Cuba. *Commercial Relations between Cuba and the United States of America.* Havana, 1936.

———. *A Frontierless Fourth of July.* Havana, 1938.

Vega Cobiellas, Ulpiano. *Los doctores Ramón Gran San Martin y Carlos Saladrigas Zayas.* Havana: Lex, 1944.

Vilcher de la Maza, Bartolome. *La Tirania de Machado.* Havana: Impresos "Martin," 1933.

Wallich, Henry C. *Monetary Problems of an Export Economy.* Cambridge, Mass.: Harvard University Press, 1950.

Welles, Sumner. *The Time for Decision.* New York: Harper Brothers, 1944.

Whitaker, Arthur P., ed. *Inter-American Affairs 1941–1945.* 5 vols. New York: Columbia University Press, 1942–46.

Wilkinson, Joe R. *Politics and Trade Policy.* Washington, D.C.: Public Affairs Press, 1960.

Wiltz, John E. *In Search of Peace: The Senate Munitions Inquiry, 1934–36.* Baton Rouge: Louisiana State University Press, 1963.

Williams, William A. *The United States, Cuba, and Castro.* New York: Monthly Review Press, 1962.

Wood, Bryce. *The Making of the Good Neighbor Policy.* New York: Columbia University Press, 1961.

Wright, Philip G. *The Cuban Situation and Our Treaty Relations.* Washington, D.C.: Brookings Institution, 1931.

Zamora y López, Juan Clemente. *The New Deal.* Havana: "El Score" Herederos de F. Rodriguez, 1937.

ARTICLES

Albjerg, Victor. "Isolation and the Early New Deal, 1932–1937." *Current History* 35 (October 1958): 204–10.

"America's New Envoy as Mediator in Cuba." *The Literary Digest* 116 (July 1, 1933): 7.

"Anarchy in Cuba." *The World Tomorrow* 17 (June 28, 1934): 317.

Andres Lliteras, Juan. "Relations between Cuba and the United States." *International Conciliation*, 296 (January 1934): 8.

"Batista Backfire." *Time* 34 (December 4, 1939): 30.

Barry, Richard. "Cuba Boils Again—With Two Dictators." *The Literary Digest* 118 (October 20, 1934): 17.

"Batista of Cuba." *New Republic* 104 (February 17, 1941): 197.

Beals, Carleton. "American Diplomacy in Cuba." *Nation* 138 (January 17, 1934): 68–70.

———. "New Machado in Cuba." *Nation* 141 (August 7, 1935): 152–54.

———. "The New Crime of Cuba." *New Republic* 83 (July 3, 1935): 216–19.

Bliven, Bruce. "And Cuba for the Winter." *New Republic* (February 29, 1928): 61–64.

———. "They Have Murdered My Friend." *New Republic* 87 (May 27, 1936): 69–70.

Bowers, Robert E. "Hull, Russian Subversion in Cuba, and Recognition of the U.S.S.R." *The Journal of American History* 53 (December 1966): 542–54.

Buell, Raymond L. "The Caribbean Situation: Cuba and Haiti." *Foreign Policy Reports* 9 (June 21, 1933): 82–92.

Butler, Hugh A. "Our Deep Dark Secrets in Latin America." *Reader's Digest* 43 (December 1943): 21–25.

———. "They Are Still Deep Dark Secrets." *Reader's Digest* 44 (February 1944): 107–11.

"Challenge of the Cuban Kaleidoscope." *The Literary Digest* 116 (September 23, 1933): 7.

"Clash in Cuba." *The Literary Digest* 122 (October 17, 1936): 16.

"Commission of the Social-Economic Union of Cuba Visits Washington." *Bulletin of the Pan American Union* 69 (September 1935): 667–71.

"Crisis in Cuba." *The Literary Digest* 122 (December 26, 1936): 14–15.

Cronon, E. David. "Interpreting the Good Neighbor Policy: The Cuban Crisis of 1933." *The Hispanic American Historical Review* 39 (November 1959): 538–67.

"Cuba." *Commercial Pan America* 13 (May 1944): 87–112.

"Cuba and the Future." *Nation* 137 (August 23, 1933): 199.

"Cuba and the New Deal." *Nation* 138 (January 31, 1934): 116–17.

"Cuba Elects Grau." *Life* 16 (June 26, 1944): 81–84.

"Cuba Steps Into the Dawn of a New Day." *The Literary Digest* 116 (August 26, 1933): 12.

"Cuba: Batista Puts Non-Smoker in Position of Domino Player." *Newsweek* 9 (January 2, 1937): 12.

"Cuba: Bill Against Sugar Money Irks Soldiers, Who Plan Seventh Presidential Upset in 4 Years." *Newsweek* 8 (December 26, 1936): 10.

"Cuba: Hevia Takes Presidency After Two Changes of Mind." *Newsweek* 3 (January 27, 1934): 16.

"Cuba: Mendieta's Inauguration." *Newsweek* 3 (January 27, 1934): 15.

"Cuba: President Mendieta Suspends Civil Rights." *Newsweek* 3 (March 17, 1934): 13.

"Cuba: Spring Fever." *Time* 29 (April 26, 1937): 21–23.

"Cuba: Sudden Revolt of the Sergeants Puts a Professor in the Presidency." *Newsweek* 2 (September 16, 1933): 5–7.

"Cuba's Bonanza." *Business Week* 655 (March 21, 1942): 86.

"Cuba's Business Trends." *Foreign Commerce Weekly* 7 (May 16, 1942): 6.

"Cuba's Constitution." *Business Week*, no. 580 (October 12, 1940): 63–64.

"Cuba's Continuing Revolution." *The Literary Digest* 119 (March 16, 1935): 9.

"Cuba's Economy in 1944." *Foreign Commerce Weekly* 19 (May 12, 1945): 8.

"Cuba's Eighth Ruler in Three Years." *The Literary Digest* 121 (January 18, 1936): 16.

"Cuba's Mr. A." *Newsweek* 23 (May 1, 1944): 54.

"Cuba's New President." *Bulletin of the Pan American Union* 78 (September, 1944): 490–92.

"Cuban Crisis Resolved." *Commonweal* 18 (August 25, 1933): 397.

"Cuban Housecleaning." *Newsweek* 24 (November 20, 1944): 65.

"Cuban Hurricane." *New Republic* 76 (September 20, 1933): 143–44.

"Cuban Upset." *Newsweek* 23 June 12, 1944): 52.

Dane, Vincent. "Havana: 1933." *New Republic* 75 (June 14, 1933): 122–23.

De la Torriente, Cosme. "Cuba, America and the War." *Foreign Affairs* 19 (October 1940): 145–55.

_____. "The Platt Amendment." *Foreign Affairs* 8 (April 1930): 364–78.

DeWilde, John C. "Sugar: An International Problem." *Foreign Policy Reports* 9 (September 27, 1933): 162–72.

"Economic Progress in the Americas: Cuba." *Bulletin of the Pan American Union* 70 (February 1936): 188–90.

"End of Cuban Strife Seen in Our Recognition." *The Literary Digest* 117 (February 3, 1934): 11.

"The End of the Platt Amendment." *The Christian Century* 51 (June 13, 1934): 789.

"Evolution of a Dictator." *Time* 43 (June 12, 1944): 37.

Fitzgibbon, Russell and H. Max Healey. "Cuban Elections of 1936." *The American Political Science Review* 30 (August 1936): 724–35.

"Foreign Policy Association to Organize Commission for Study of Cuban Problems." *Bulletin of the Pan American Union* 68 (June 1934): 457–58.

"Genteel Revolution." *Time* 37 (February 17, 1941): 28.

"Good Neighbor Or Rich Relation?" *New Republic* 82 (March 6, 1935): 89–90.

Grau San Martín, Ramón. "The Cuban Terror." *Nation* 140 (April 3, 1935): 381–82.

Griffin, Charles C., ed. "Welles to Roosevelt: A Memorandum of Inter-American

Relations." *The Hispanic American Historical Review* 34 (May 1954): 190–92.

Gruening, Ernest. "Cuba under the Machado Regime." *Current History* 34 (May 1931): 214–19.

Guerra y Sánchez, Ramiro. "Sugar: Index of Cuban-American Cooperation." *Foreign Affairs* 20 (July 1942): 743–56.

Guggenheim, Harry F. "Amending the Platt Amendment." *Foreign Affairs* 12 (April 1934): 448–57.

Gunther, John. "Batista: The Stenographer Who Became Dictator." *Reader's Digest* 39 (August 1941): 61–65.

Hackett, Charles W. "American Mediation in Cuba." *Current History* 39 (September 1933): 724–26.

———. "Cabinet Friction in Cuba." *Current History* 40 (August 1934): 594–97.

———. "Cabinet Troubles in Cuba." *Current History* 40 (September 1934): 715–16.

———. "Continued Unrest in Cuba." *Current History* 41 (November 1934): 215–17.

———. "Cuba and the Good-Neighbor Policy." *Current History* 41 (October 1934): 88–90.

———. "Cuba Lives Through Another Revolt." *Current History* 39 (January 1934): 462–64.

———. "Cuba Swings to the Left." *Current History* 39 (February 1934): 592–94.

———. "Cuba's Troubles Persist." *Current History* 41 (December 1934): 346.

———. "Cuban Peace Prospects." *Current History* 38 (August 1933): 594–95.

———. "Guerrilla Warfare in Cuba." *Current History* 38 (July 1933): 469–71.

———. "Labor Crisis Averted in Cuba." *Current History* 40 (May 1934): 214–15.

———. "Restive Cuban Labor." *Current History* 40 (April 1934): 80–82.

———. "The Cuban Terror." *Current History* 38 (June 1933): 341–43.

———. "The Cuban Turmoil." *Current History* 40 (June 1934): 333–35.

"Hands Off Cuba." *The World Tomorrow* 16 (September 28, 1933): 534.

'Harried Cuba." *The Literary Digest* 122 (August 22, 1936): 12–13.

"Havana Bows to Washington." *The World Tomorrow* 17 (February 1, 1934): 51–52.

Hennessy, C. A. M. "The Roots of Cuban Nationalism." *International Affairs* (July 1963): 345–59.

Herring, Hubert. "Another Chance for Cuba." *Current History* 39 (March 1934): 656–60.

———. "Can Cuba Save Herself?" *Current History* 39 (November 1933): 151–58.

———. "Cuba Cleans House." *Nation* 137 (August 30, 1933): 233–34.

———. "Cuba Drifts Toward Dictatorship." *Current History* 41 (March 1935): 729–30.

———. "Cuba Plans Elections." *Current History* 42 (July 1935): 415.

———. "Cuba Regains a Constitution." *Current History* 42 (August 1935): 526–28.

———. "Cuba Under Army Rule." *Current History* 42 (June 1935): 303–4.

———. "Cuba's Election Campaign." *Current History* 41 (February 1935): 602–4.

———. "Cuba's General Strike." *Current History* 42 (May 1935): 192.

_____ . "Cuba's Political Parties." *Current History* 43 (December 1935): 306.

_____ . "Cuban Kettle Simmers." *Current History* 43 (October 1935): 79–80.

_____ . "Cuban Politics." *Current History* 43 (January 1936): 415–16.

_____ . "Cuban Whirlwind." *The Christian Century* 51 (February 7, 1934): 179–81.

_____ . "Dictatorship in Cuba." *Current History* 42 (April 1935): 77–78.

_____ . "The Cuban Presidency." *Current History* 43 (February 1936): 526.

_____ . "The Cuban Turmoil." *Current History* 41 (January 1935): 472–73.

_____ . "The Downfall of Machado." *Current History* 39 (October 1933): 14–24.

_____ . "Machado Prepares to Go." *Nation* 136 (June 28, 1933): 725–26.

Hevia, Carlos. "Cuba's Government." *New Republic* 88 (September 9, 1936): 132.

_____ . "What Is Happening in Cuba." *New Republic* 88 (October 21, 1936): 313.

"High Jinks in Cuba." *Time* 78 (June 15, 1942): 39.

Kirchwey, Freda. "Are Intellectuals People?" *Nation* 153 (December 6, 1941): 558–60.

"Latin America." *Newsweek* 8 (July 18, 1936): 23–24.

Lefevre, Edwin. "Cuba's Grievances." *The Saturday Evening Post* 206 (January 27, 1934): 8–9.

_____ . "Soldier and Student Control in Cuba." *The Saturday Evening Post* 206 (January 6, 1934): 5.

"Less Imperialistic?" *The World Tomorrow* 16 (October 12, 1933): 557–58.

Lippmann, Walter. "Second Thoughts on Havana." *Foreign Affairs* 6 (July 1928): 541–54.

Lupien, Alfred L. "Presenting Cuba, Our Good Neighbor." *Bulletin of the Pan American Union* 76 (February 1942): 91–94.

"Machado's Fall and the Problems of Intervention in Cuba." *The Literary Digest* 116 (August 19, 1933): 7.

Mañach, Jorge. "Revolution in Cuba." *Foreign Affairs* 12 (October 1933): 46–56.

McEvoy, J. P. "Cuba's Masterpiece of Vice Versa." *The Saturday Evening Post* 217 (September 30, 1944): 14.

_____ . "Not All Rum and Rumba." *The Saturday Evening Post* 211 (May 20, 1939): 8.

Mecham, J. Lloyd. "Minority Rule in Cuba." *Current History* 39 (December 1933): 344–45.

"Mendieta Government." *New Republic* 77 (March 21, 1934): 142.

"Mendieta Lacks Cuban Support." *New Republic* 77 (January 31, 1934): 319–20.

Mitchell, Jonathan. "Pan-American Prelude." *New Republic* 77 (December 27, 1933): 190–92.

"Message of the President of Cuba." *Bulletin of the Pan American Union* 72 (August 1938): 483–86.

Murkland, Harry B. "Cuba's National Unity Move." *Current Histoy* 3 (September 1942): 51–52.

_____ . "Cuba's New Government." *Current History* 3 (October 1942): 144–45.

"Mr. Welles's Opportunity." *Nation* 136 (May 3, 1933): 489.

"New Broom in Cuba." *Inter-American* 3 (December 1944): 9–10.

"New Constitution of Cuba." *Bulletin of the Pan American Union* 69 (October 1935): 796–99.

"New Constitutional Law of Cuba." *Bulletin of the Pan American Union* 68 (May 1934): 371–74.

"New Pact With Cuba Follows Terrorism." *The Literary Digest* 117 (June 9, 1934): 19.

"No. 2's no.6; New President." *Time* 27 (Juen 1, 1936): 20.

Nufer, Albert F. "Cuba in 1943." *Foreign Commerce Weekly* 15 (May 13, 1944): 14–15.

"Opening the Jails in Cuba." *The Literary Digest* 116 (August 5, 1933): 12.

"Our Cuban Investment." *The Literary Digest* 116 (August 26, 1933): 37.

"Our Job in Cuba." *Nation* 137 (September 20, 1933): 312–13.

"Our Step-Child, Cuba." *New Republic* 58 (May 15, 1929): 345–47.

"Ouster in Cuba." *The Literary Digest* 123 (January 2, 1937): 13–14.

"Paper Revolution." *Inter-American* 3 (July 1944): 3–4.

Phillips, Ruby H. "Cuba Goes to War." *Inter-American* 2 (May 1943): 22–26.

———. "Return Engagement." *Inter-American* 3 (December 1944): 16.

Pincus, Arthur. "Cuba's Puppet Democracy." *Nation* 147 (December 17, 1938): 658–60.

"Plot Foiled." *Time* 44 (August 7, 1944): 38.

Popper, David H. "Latin American Policy of the Roosevelt Administration." *Foreign Policy Reports* 10 (December 19, 1934): 270–80.

Porset, Clara. "Cuba's Troubled Waters." *Nation* 138 (March 28, 1934): 353–54.

Porter, Russell B. "Cuba under President Machado." *Current History* 38 (April 1933): 29–34.

"President Batista." *Time* 36 (October 21, 1940): 40.

"President for Cuba." *Business Week*, no. 333 (January 18, 1936): 38.

"Quick Action Needed in Cuba." *The Christian Century* 51 (January 31, 1934): 140.

"Radicals Climb Into Cuban Saddle." *The World Tomorrow* 16 (September 14, 1933): 509.

"Ramón Grau San Martín Visits the United States." *Bulletin of the Pan American Union* 78 (November 1944): 601–4.

Rayneri, René. "Colonel Batista and Cuba's Future." *Current History* 50 (April 1939): 51.

"Revising Our Caribbean Policy." *New Republic* 65 (January 28, 1931): 286–87.

Reynolds, Quention. "Astonished Dictator." *Collier's* 99 (June 19, 1937): 12.

Roosevelt, Franklin D. "Our Foreign Policy." *Foreign Affairs* 6 (July 1928): 573–86.

Schurz, William L. "Cuba's Economic Isolation." *Current History* 36 (August 1932):545–49.

"Shall Our Sugar Refiners Ruin Cuba?" *Nation* 137 (October 11, 1933): 395.

Shaw, Paul V. " 'Good Neighbor'—and Cuba." *North American Review* 240 (September 1935): 315–41.

Shepherd, William R. "Uncle Sam, Imperialist." *New Republic* 49 (January 26, 1927): 266–69.

Solar, Anthony G. "Cuban Experience." *New Republic* 85 (January 29, 1936): 330–32.

Southworth, H. Rutledge and Willard R. Espy. "Franco in the Carribbean." *Nation* 151 (November 23, 1940): 500–503.

Stokes, William S. "The Cuban Revolution and the Presidential Elections of 1948." *The Hispanic American Historical Review* 31 (February 1951): 37–79.

_____ . "The Welles Mission to Cuba." *Central America and Mexico* 1 (December 1953): 3–21.

Strode, Hudson. "Behind the Cuban Revolt." *New Republic* 77 (October 4, 1933): 204–7.

"Strong Man Act." *Newsweek* 17 (February 17, 1941): 34–35.

"Strong-Man Tourist." *Newsweek* 12 (November 21, 1938): 15–16.

Stuart, Graham H. "Cuba and the Platt Amendment." *World Affairs Interpreter* 5 (Spring 1934): 49–54.

"Sumner Welles: Cuban Job Done, He Plans Another." *Newsweek* 2 (August 26, 1933): 16.

"Supplementary Trade Agreement between the United States and Cuba." *Bulletin of the Pan American Union* 76 (March 1942): 169–72.

"Testing Our Intervention Policy in Cuba." *The Literary Digest* 116 (September 16, 1933): 7.

Thomson, Charles E. "The Cuban Revolution: Fall of Machado." *Foreign Policy Reports* 11 (December 18, 1935): 250–60.

_____ . "The Cuban Revolution: Reform and Reaction." *Foreign Policy Reports* 11 (January 1, 1936): 262–76.

_____ . "The Seventh Pan-American Conference." *Foreign Policy Reports* 10 (June 6, 1943): 86–96.

"Trouble in Cuba." *New Republic* 96 (August 3, 1938): 86.

"Wanted: A New Deal for Cuba." *Nation* 136 (April 9, 1933): 433–34.

"Welles Replaced in Cuba." *The Literary Digest* 116 (December 2, 1933): 8.

"What Do We Want in Cuba?" *The Christian Century* 50 (September 20, 1933): 1166–68.

"What Will Be the Next Move in Cuba?" *The Christian Century* 50 (December 27, 1933): 1629–30.

"Why Not Recognize the Cuban Government?" *The Christian Century* 50 (October 4, 1933): 1228.

"Will Roosevelt Wreck Cuba." *The World Tomorrow* 16 (December 7, 1933): 651–52.

Woolsey, Lester H. "The New Cuban Treaty." *American Journal of International Law* 28 (July 1934): 530–34.

"Yanqui Imperialismo." *New Republic* 77 (December 6, 1933): 89–90.

NEWSPAPERS

The Baltimore Sun, 1933–44.
The Chicago Tribune, 1933–44.
The Miami Herald, 1933–44.

UNPUBLISHED THESES

Aguilar, Luis E. "Cuba 1933: The Frustrated Revolution." Ph.D. dissertation, American University, 1967.

Blasier, Stewart C. "The Cuban and Chilean Communist Parties: Instruments of Soviet Policy (1935–1948)." Ph.D. dissertation, Columbia University, 1954.

Chu, Power Yung-Chao. "A History of the Hull Trade Program, 1934–1939." Ph.D. dissertation, Columbia University, 1957.

Coleman, George C. "The Good Neighbor Policy of Franklin D. Roosevelt with Special Reference to Three Inter-American Conferences, 1933–1938." Ph.D. dissertation, University of Iowa, 1951.

Freeman, Lorraine L. "Isolationist Carry-Over, 1933–1937." Master's thesis, University of Buffalo, 1955.

Healey, H. Max. "The Impeachment and Removal of Dr. M. M. Gómez, December, 1936." Master's thesis, Indiana University, 1939.

Jackman, Francis V. "America's Cuban Policy during the Period of the Machado Regime." Ph.D. dissertation, Catholic University, 1964.

Krauss, Paul H. "Communist Policy in Cuba, 1933–1946." Master's thesis, Columbia University, 1950.

Krogh, Peter F. "The United States, Cuba and Sumner Welles: 1933." Ph.D. dissertation, Fletcher School of Law and Diplomacy, 1966.

Moran, Maria V. "Church and State in Cuba." Master's thesis, Columbia University, 1950.

Schatz, Arthur W. "Cordell Hull and the Struggle for the Reciprocal Trade Agreements Program, 1932–1940." Ph.D. dissertation, University of Oregon, 1965.

White, Byron. "Cuba and Puerto Rico: A Case Study in Comparative Economic Development Policy." Ph.D. dissertation, University of Texas, 1959.

Whitehead, Donald F. "The Making of Foreign Policy during President Roosevelt's First Term, 1933–1937." Ph.D. dissertation, University of Chicago, 1951.

Wolfe, Gregory B. "The Seventh International Conference of American States: A Case Study in Inter-American Relations with Special Attention to Public Opinion." Ph.D. dissertation, Fletcher School of Law and Diplomacy, 1961.

Index